The Philosophy of
Habermas

Continental European Philosophy

This series provides accessible and stimulating introductions to the ideas of continental thinkers who have shaped the fundamentals of European philosophical thought. Powerful and radical, the ideas of these philosophers have often been contested, but they remain key to understanding current philosophical thinking as well as the current direction of disciplines such as political science, literary theory, comparative literature, art history, and cultural studies. Each book seeks to combine clarity with depth, introducing fresh insights and wider perspectives while also providing a comprehensive survey of each thinker's philosophical ideas.

Published titles

The Philosophy of Gadamer
Jean Grondin

The Philosophy of Merleau-Ponty
Eric Matthews

The Philosophy of Habermas
Andrew Edgar

The Philosophy of Nietzsche
Rex Welshon

The Philosophy of Schopenhauer
Dale Jacquette

Forthcoming titles include

The Philosophy of Deleuze
Peter Sedgwick

The Philosophy of Husserl
Burt Hopkins

The Philosophy of Derrida
Mark Dooley and Liam Kavanagh

The Philosophy of Kant
Jim O'Shea

The Philosophy of Foucault
Todd May

The Philosophy of Kierkegaard
George Pattison

The Philosophy of Hegel
Allen Speight

The Philosophy of Marx
Mark Neocleous

The Philosophy of Heidegger
Jeff Malpas

The Philosophy of Rousseau
Patrick Riley, Sr and Patrick Riley, Jr

The Philosophy of Sartre
Anthony Hatzimoysis

The Philosophy of Habermas

Andrew Edgar

McGill-Queen's University Press
Montreal & Kingston • Ithaca

ISBN 0-7735-2782-6 (hardcover)
ISBN 0-7735-2783-4 (paperback)

Legal deposit third quarter 2005
Bibliothèque nationale du Québec

Published simultaneously outside North America
by Acumen Publishing Limited

McGill-Queen's University Press acknowledges the financial support of
the Government of Canada through the Book Publishing Development
Program (BPIDP) for its activities.

Library and Archives Canada Cataloguing in Publication

   Edgar, Andrew
      The philosophy of Habermas / Andrew Edgar.

   (Continental European philosophy)
   Includes bibliographical references and index.
   ISBN 0-7735-2782-6 (bound).—ISBN 0-7735-2783-4 (pbk.)

      1. Habermas, Jürgen. I. Title. II. Series.

   B3258.H324E33 2005   193   C2005-900996-9

Designed and typeset by Kate Williams, Swansea.
Printed and bound by Biddles Ltd., King's Lynn.

Contents

For Grace and Antonia

Preface

The primary objective of this book is to make the reader ready to take on Habermas's own works. Habermas's writings are, if we are honest, complex and on first reading obscure. To read them requires patience, and the ability to recognize the multiple themes that often run in parallel through extended arguments. It also requires a familiarity with the history of German philosophy and the history of sociology and social theory, as well as with contemporary debates in both continental and analytic philosophy, not to mention a fair grasp of cognitive psychology and some psychoanalysis. To meet these demands I am offering a substantial introduction. It is not enough just to offer an introduction, in the sense of a schematic run through Habermas's big ideas. Rather, I have attempted to sketch in something of the detail of his argument, and to convey the manner in which he weaves together multiple strands of thought.

The structure of the book is a more or less chronological account of Habermas's career. Such an account has an intrinsic interest, in so far as it allows us to see the developments, shifts and turns in Habermas's thinking as he strives to refine basic insights, and to incorporate new sources and ideas. It also allows chapters and their subsections to focus largely on specific texts. I am well aware that many readers will approach this text for guidance on reading specific books or essays by Habermas. I have therefore attempted, as far as possible, to achieve a certain self-sufficiency in each chapter. Chapters should make some sense on their own. In this attempt I have almost certainly failed, so I have included cross-references between sections, and would advise any reader to look to the index for further cross-referencing. For the reader who is going to follow the whole book, cover to cover, I apologise in advance for a certain degree of repetition. My only excuse is that Habermas himself returns to themes repeatedly throughout his career. My gloss merely echoes Habermas's own habit of creatively revisiting problems.

The book is not a "critical" introduction. It is, if anything, a case for the defence. This does not mean that I do not have my own reservations about Habermas's project and the particular arguments that he develops; it is just that I did not judge this to be the place to air those doubts. There are a number of reasons for this. First, if this is a preparation for reading Habermas himself, then it is important to get him right (in so far as that term makes any sense at all). As with any complex and demanding thinker, a certain amount of the criticism laid against Habermas either comes from misunderstandings, or from the simple assertion of positions that are dogmatically opposed to his. Such criticisms have no place in an introduction. Secondly, Habermas frequently develops his own arguments by commenting on the work of others. Thus, for example, *Knowledge and Human Interests*, *The Theory of Communicative Action* and *The Philosophical Discourse of Modernity* are constructed as critical engagements with the history of philosophy and social theory. Therefore, any adequate introduction will find much of its space taken up in at least outlining the positions of others, before it clarifies the (still complex and daunting) position of Habermas himself. There is a case here for questioning the accuracy of Habermas's interpretations of others, but again, the proper development of such criticism is best left to other publications. My accounts of those who have influenced Habermas is thus shaped by Habermas's own interpretations, and may at times seem distorted or crude to the specialist; they must be taken as aids to the understanding of Habermas himself, and not exhaustive or definitive accounts of his influences.

Thirdly, and perhaps most importantly, Habermas does a lot of the work of criticism for his reader. What is so distinctive about his thought as a whole is that it has been shaped by his willingness, or indeed eagerness, to engage critically and openly with his critics. This is not in order to refute them, but rather to establish whether they have a valid point against him. If he recognizes such a point, he will modify his arguments. At a number of key moments in his career this consideration of criticism has led to significant reformulations of his basic theory. Thus, to review Habermas is also to review the critical material of which he has taken note. Having said this, the bibliographical material in each chapter includes references to the major sources of criticism, to which the reader is, of course, encouraged to refer.

The title of this book is *The Philosophy of Habermas*. Some readers may suspect that there is too little philosophy in this introduction, and too much sociology and social theory. While many of Habermas's texts can be treated as purely philosophical works, even these are developed in the context of an overarching concern with social theory. Habermas typically raises philosophical questions within the context of broader concerns about the understanding of social and political life. To extract the philosophy from those concerns would not merely rob it of its context, but would, I suspect, also leave its purpose and importance unclear. I have therefore taken Habermas's work as a whole, and not troubled overly in separating philosophy from sociology.

One last introductory question must be addressed, albeit briefly. If Habermas is so difficult to read, is it worth it? First, we should not get carried away. In an age that, more often than is healthy, seems to champion almost wilful obscurity in philosophical debate as a virtue in its own right, Habermas, we can be sure, is always trying to express himself as precisely and as rigorously as possible. In his theoretical works this can lead to the problem of a certain overkill, and that can give them a rather heavy-handed and (dare I say) turgid feel. His more direct engagements in the problems of contemporary politics are generally much more approachable, and for the initiate to Habermas's thought, he is typically an eloquent and precise interviewee (see AS). Yet even with the major theoretical works, once the reader gets inside them, and gets over the superficial difficulties of language and structure, they will encounter a rigorous, creative and often elegant thought process. But above all, they will encounter a thought process that matters, and it matters in a world that struggles under the burdens of environmental crises, major injustices in the global economic order, a "war" against terror of dubious legitimacy, as well as a world populated by ordinary people who struggle on in the face of seemingly obscurant bureaucracies and legal systems, democratically inept governments and ever more threatening and incomprehensible new technologies. At its core, Habermas's work offers a model (albeit of course not the only model) of how anyone who has a privileged and influential place in the Western academic system should handle that responsibility. His work is that of a committed, public intellectual, and especially one who is willing to put aside the lure of modish intellectual fireworks, in favour of the hard work of thinking through the mundane but pressing concerns of ordinary people.

Acknowledgements

My thanks to Steven Gerrard of Acumen for his patience and encouragement; to Kate Williams for exemplary copy-editing; to my colleagues at Cardiff, and in particular to Robin Wackabarth and Tara Yate for enormous help with bibliographies and references, and to Peter Sedgwick for his continual support and for providing a sympathetic ear in the discussion of political philosophy; and above all to my family, for putting up with me over the past few years, and providing far more love and support than I could ever deserve.

Abbreviations

ARC "A Reply to my Critics" (1982).

AS *Autonomy and Solidarity: Interviews with Jürgen Habermas* (1992a).

BFN *Between Facts and Norms: Contributions to a Discourse Theory of Law and Democracy* (1996a).

BR *A Berlin Republic: Writings on Germany* (1997).

CES *Communication and the Evolution of Society* (1979a).

FHN *The Future of Human Nature* (2003b).

FR "Further Reflections on the Public Sphere" (1992c).

G "The Christian Gauss Lectures", in *On the Pragmatics of Social Interaction: Preliminary Studies in the Theory of Communicative Action* (2001c).

G* "Intention, Conventions, and Linguistic Interactions", in *On the Pragmatics of Social Interaction: Preliminary Studies in the Theory of Communicative Action* (2001c).

G** "Reflections on Communicative Pathology", in *On the Pragmatics of Social Interaction: Preliminary Studies in the Theory of Communicative Action* (2001c).

HCU "The Hermeneutic Claim to Universality" (1980).

HE "History and Evolution" (1979b).

IO *The Inclusion of the Other: Studies in Political Theory* (1998a).

JA *Justification and Application: Remarks on Discourse Ethics* (1993a).

KHI *Knowledge and Human Interests* (1971a).

LC *Legitimation Crisis* (1976b).

LSS *On the Logic of the Social Sciences* (1988b).

MCCA *Moral Consciousness and Communicative Action* (1990).

MIP "Modernity – An Incomplete Project" (1983b).

NC *The New Conservatism: Cultural Criticism and the Historians' Debate* (1989b).

OPC   *On the Pragmatics of Communication* (1999a).
OSDC "On Systematically Distorted Communication" (1970a).
OSI   "On Social Identity" (1974a).
PC   *The Postnational Constellation: Political Essays* (2001b).
PD   *The Positivist Dispute in German Sociology* (Adorno *et al.* 1976).
PDM   *The Philosophical Discourse of Modernity* (1988a).
PMT   *Postmetaphysical Thinking: Philosophical Essays* (1992b).
PP   *Philosophical–Political Profiles* (1983a).
PS   "The Public Sphere: An Encyclopaedia Article" (1974b).
PTT   *Philosophy in a Time of Terror: Dialogues with Jürgen Habermas and Jacques Derrida* (Borradori 2003).
R   "A Reply" (1993b).
RJ   "Introduction" (1999b).
RJ*   "A Short Reply" (1999c).
SDUP "Some Distinctions in Universal Pragmatics" (1976e).
SP   *Student und Politik* (1961).
ST   *The Structural Transformation of the Public Sphere: An Inquiry into a Category of Bourgeois Society* (1989a).
TCAI *The Theory of Communicative Action, vol 1: Reason and the Rationalisation of Society* (1984a).
TCAII *The Theory of Communicative Action, vol 2: Lifeworld and System: A Critique of Functionalist Reason* (1987).
TJ   *Truth and Justification* (2003).
TP   *Theory and Practice* (1976a).
TRS   *Toward a Rational Society: Student Protest, Science and Politics* (1971b).

CHAPTER 1

The Marxist heritage

Introduction

Habermas's creativity, alongside the breadth and contemporary relevance of his work, was already evident by the end of the 1960s. Between 1953, when he wrote his first significant academic article (reviewing Heidegger's *Introduction to Metaphysics*), and 1970, when the second edition of *The Logic of the Social Sciences* was published, Habermas matured from a student of what he has himself called a narrowly German philosophy (AS: 80) to the acknowledged inheritor of the Frankfurt tradition of Western Marxism, which is to say, of German critical theory. By 1970 his work was based as profoundly upon an engagement with Anglo-Saxon analytic philosophy, American pragmatism and American and European sociology as it was with the more German traditions of Marxism, psychoanalysis and hermeneutics. Recognizing the strengths of earlier generations of Marxist theorists, while attempting to correct such perceived weaknesses as their understanding of political practice and over-reliance on Hegelian dialectics, Habermas sought to develop a renewed critical theory that would be appropriate to the unique problems and opportunities of late-twentieth-century capitalism. This theory would, in turn, be entwined with his substantive commentaries on the condition of liberal democracy, social policy and the welfare state, on science and technology, and on education. That this period marked no more than the first stage of Habermas's intellectual development, for he was only just beginning to articulate the theory of communicative action that would become the bedrock of his work throughout the next 30 years, is but further testimony to the dynamic and self-critical character of his thought.

Born in 1929, the son of the director of the local Chamber of Commerce, Habermas grew up in Gummersbach (a provincial town some 30 kilometres east of Düsseldorf), during the rise of Nazism. Indeed, he had the unenviable experience of belonging to the Hitler Youth. He has described the events associated with the end of the Second World War as determining his political views (AS: 77). The liberation of Germany, and the subsequent publicity surrounding the Nuremberg trials, brought to consciousness, for the first time, the fact that the Germans "had been living under a politically criminal system ... at the time we had the impression of a normality which afterwards proved to be an illusion. For us to see suddenly that those people were criminals ..." (AS: 78).

He soon began to read the Marxist and Leninist material that was being published in East Germany, and was available in the Communist bookshop in Gummersbach, as well as previously banned material that was being republished by Rowohlt (AS: 45). Yet he admits to his disappointment over the development of Germany, in terms of both the political opportunities that were foregone in the formation of the post-war governments and in the consolidation of the division of East and West Germany, and in the ambiguous relationship that Germany had with its Nazi past.

He says of his own university education (between 1949 and 1954, principally at Gottingham and Bonn) that it was provincial. The approach to teaching resembled that of the 1920s. On one level, this meant that the developments made in philosophy and sociology during the 1930s and 1940s were largely neglected. This weakness only began to be remedied with the return of major figures, such as Max Horkheimer and Helmut Plessner, from exile in the mid-1950s (AS: 45). On another level, significant numbers of university staff in the late 1940s and early 1950s were those who had been in place during the Nazi period, and had more or less actively conformed to the demands of the Nazi regime. It was in this environment that the publication in 1953 of *Introduction to Metaphysics* by Martin Heidegger, who had retained the chair of philosophy at the University of Freiburg throughout the Nazi period, posed a fundamental challenge for Habermas. The *Introduction to Metaphysics* was the text of a lecture given in 1935. That Heidegger could reproduce an original reference to the "inner truth and greatness" of the Nazi movement, and crucially do so without comment or revision, was indicative for Habermas of a continuing reluctance to confront Nazism that was characteristic of post-war Germany. In addition, Habermas judged that Heidegger's political stance was implied by his philosophy and that the uncritical propagation of this philosophy threatened to inculcate the post-war generation of students into the same values that had originally permitted the rise of Nazism (Habermas 1981b: 65–72). Although describing himself as "terribly naive", Habermas was disturbed by the need to recognize the interdependence of one's political and philosophical confessions (AS: 80). In effect, he was beginning to articulate the fundamental seriousness and responsibility of his mature philosophy. It is not sufficient for a philosophy to be good, or even great, merely as philosophy. It must also, in some sense, be politically right. The task of articulating exactly what this sense might be, and thus what the relationship between intellectual effort and political involvement is, has been crucial to Habermas throughout his career.

In 1954 Habermas submitted to the University of Bonn his doctoral dissertation on the early-nineteenth-century German Idealist philosopher Friedrich Schelling. Although Habermas acknowledges that the dissertation was broadly Heideggerian in approach, it did serve to bring him into contact with the work of the young Marx, not least through Karl Löwith's *From Hegel to Nietzsche* (AS: 147).

Around this time, which is to say the mid-1950s, Habermas began to read a number of the core texts in what is typically known as Western Marxism. The term "Western Marxism" was used by the French philosopher Maurice Merleau-Ponty to characterize the broadly humanistic strain of Marxism that has been articulated in western Europe, in contrast to the Leninism and Stalinism of the Soviet Union and the Maoist approach of China. At the root of this tradition stands *History and Class Consciousness*, which the Hungarian philosopher Georg Lukács published in 1923. Habermas first read this in 1953. He described it as a "marvellous book" that excited him, no doubt due to its interpretation of Marx in terms of the heritage of the German Idealist philosophy of Kant, Schelling and Hegel, and its overwhelming commitment to political emancipation from oppression and exploitation (AS: 188). Yet he still felt that it was a largely historical document with its social theory, based on the existence of traditional classes and the possibility of building revolutionary class consciousness, no longer having relevance to the present. It was Max Horkheimer and Theodor Adorno's *Dialectic of Enlightenment* (published in 1944), along with the writings of other Western Marxists such as Ernst Bloch, Walter Benjamin and Herbert Marcuse, that convinced him that Marx could still be utilized in theorizing contemporary society (AS: 98). Whereas Lukács dealt with a capitalism that was in overt crisis, Habermas notes that Horkheimer's approach, especially, appeared to be of more contemporary relevance, precisely because it focused on the problem of the continuing stability of capitalism. Marx could thus be read as a contemporary, rather than as a purely historical figure. This conviction was further reinforced by reading the Marxist economics of Maurice Dobb, Paul Sweezy and Paul Baran (AS: 148). Yet alongside such left-wing theory, Habermas was also reading, and commenting favourably upon, the conservative cultural theories of Arnold Gehlen and Helmut Schelsky. In 1956, thanks in large part to a lecture series co-organized by Horkheimer, he began a serious engagement with Sigmund Freud. Again, the importance of such an engagement lay in reading Freud as a contemporary.

In 1954 Habermas published "The Dialectic of Rationalisation", a substantial essay that already begins to prefigure his later work, and thereby indicates something of the theoretical problems that he would address to the Western Marxists (see Wiggershaus 1994: 540–41). The essay deals with the way in which society and social problems are construed mechanistically, which is to say, as issues that can be resolved through technological reasoning, akin to that used in engineering. This raises a fundamental question as to the nature of social rationality and social progress that Habermas pursues throughout his career. As an issue in sociology this has its roots in Max Weber's account from the first decades of the twentieth century of what has come to be known as the "iron cage of bureaucracy". Weber argues that while impersonal and technocratically conceived bureaucratic administrations are necessary for the effective running of any substantial modern organization, bureaucracy tends to become increasingly anti-democratic and resistant to change, as crucial political decisions are deferred to the expertise of social administrators, and as the resources for public debate and criticism wither. If, on the one hand, Habermas therefore addresses the confrontation of the human subject with constraining bureaucratic structures, on the other he addresses the alienation of the human being as producer – confronted by equally constraining economic processes – but does so in order to explore the role that consumption plays in compensating for the impoverishment of this industrial experience. Here his analysis echoes both that of Horkheimer and Adorno (not least in their analysis of the culture industry (see § "Responding to the First Generation Frankfurt School", p. 238)), and more conservative cultural critics, such as Gehlen and Schelsky. Crucially, Habermas is therefore bringing together orthodox Marxist themes, and here particularly that of alienation, with a recognition of the significant challenge that the increased affluence of the working classes poses to orthodox Marxism.

It was thus as someone who had already begun to school himself in Marxist theory, and who had developed a reputation as a critic of Heidegger and a culture critic, that in 1956 Habermas joined the Frankfurt Institute for Social Research – home of the so-called Frankfurt School of German critical theory – as Adorno's research assistant. Having been founded in 1924 with the purpose of pursuing multi-disciplinary work in Marxist social science, the institute was forced into exile, ultimately in New York, during the Nazi period. The Institute had been re-established in Frankfurt in 1949 with the return of Horkheimer, its director since 1931, and Adorno. During the 1950s Adorno established his reputation as the institute's leading theorist, with a profound influence on philosophy, social and cultural theory, and musicology. Herbert Marcuse, who had been a member of the institute, and whose existentialist Marxism Habermas initially found highly attractive, remained in America (AS: 189–90).

It was in this environment, encouraging work both on Marxist social theory and the multidisciplinary and empirical study of contemporary society, that Habermas would begin his first major works: an empirical study of political consciousness among university students, *Student und Politik*; an historical account of the development of democratic debate in bourgeois society, *The Structural Transformation of the Public Sphere*; and the essays collected in *Theory and Practice*. These works seek to articulate the experience and history of contemporary (or "late") capitalism, and develop an appropriate "theory of society conceived with a practical intention" (TP: 1).[1]

Late capitalism

The capitalist state

Habermas introduces his 1960 essay "Between Philosophy and Science" (1976f) with four characteristics of contemporary society that Marxism must confront (TP: 195–8). First, he suggests that the all-important metaphor of base and superstructure that many Marxists have developed from a chance remark by Marx (Marx 1975a: 425) is thrown into question by the working of the modern state, in so far as it is at once a welfare state, and has the function of managing the economy. For Marx, the economic base is characterized through the relationship of the forces of production (i.e. the technology used in production) and the relations of production (i.e. the traditional, legal and contractual relationships that exist between the producers of goods and the politically dominant owners of the means used in production). The superstructure consists of non-economic social institutions, including law, religion, education, culture and the family. The base–superstructure metaphor suggests that the economy determines the nature and development of the rest of the society in a manner akin to the way in which the size and depth of the foundations of a building determine what may be constructed upon them. Specifically, the level of technological development delimits the degree of sophistication that can be realized in the state, legal system and civil and cultural life. If the state is understood as part of the superstructure, then it functions primarily to promote the economic and political interests of the dominant class. It is, in Marx's phrase, "a committee for managing the common affairs of the whole bourgeoisie" (Marx & Engels 1973: 69).

For Habermas, the modern state has an autonomy unimagined by Marx. Here Weber's account of bureaucracy becomes a necessary complement to Marx's analysis. Modern industrial development requires complex administration, not merely within individual capitalist enterprises, but also in the state's management of the economy as a whole. The state therefore no longer simply reacts to the demands of the economy, setting the fiscal and legal framework within which individual entrepreneurs operate. Nor does it simply pursue the naked interests of the dominant class. Rather, the state actively structures the economy and intervenes as a major producer and consumer of economic goods. The simple causality of base and superstructure is thus thrown into question, as the state exerts its own influence over economic developments. Class tensions are mitigated, not least through the establishing of a welfare state and redistributive taxation. The inherent tendencies of the free-market capitalism that Marx witnessed are forestalled. In effect, as Horkheimer and Adorno recognize, but Lukács does not, capitalism is stabilized, able to manage the crises to which, according to Marx's analysis, it should succumb. It is therefore unrealistic to expect the imminent breakdown of capitalism as it had been predicted by Marx, for example, through the immiseration of the proletariat (TP: 236ff.).

An affluent proletariat

The second characteristic of contemporary society that Habermas suggests Marxism must confront, the increased affluence of the proletariat – where "proletariat" is to be understood not merely in its traditional form as a manual labouring class, but also in the form of the expanding middle class, for both classes survive only by selling their ability to labour – raises again the problem of consumption, and of what Habermas here calls "alienated leisure" (TP: 196). Increased affluence undermines what Marx called the crises of "realisation" (TP: 231–3). According to orthodox Marxist theory, exploitation occurs in capitalism through the appropriation of surplus value. Surplus value may be understood in terms of the costs of production and the revenue received by the capitalist. On the side of costs, the capitalist must pay wages to the labour force, but also cover the costs of replacing the raw materials and machinery used in production. On the other side, revenue is the value of the product when sold, that is, its exchange value. Surplus value is the difference between the costs and revenue, and represents that portion of the working day in which the labourer is effectively working unpaid, in the sense that the value of everything they produce during that period is appropriated by the capitalist. Marx argues that a crisis of realization would occur if the proletariat were to become so poor as to be unable to purchase the products of capitalism. Put simply, with technological advance, capitalist industry substitutes labour power with machinery. In Marx's technical terminology, there will be a rise in the "organic composition" of capital. If capitalist exploitation operates through the accumulation of surplus value, then as the proportion of labour to capital declines, it will be necessary, in order to maintain existing levels of surplus value, for wage levels to be pushed downwards. In effect, with technological advance, the exploitable proportion of the capitalists' total costs declines. The proletariat will thus face immiseration, and the capitalist system will become radically unstable (TP: 222–7). The very fact that the proletariat have not become poorer but, on the contrary, have enjoyed generally greater affluence, especially in the post-war period, suggests that the theory of the crisis of realization is redundant.

If intervention in the economy by an autonomous state mitigates the raw exploitation of nineteenth-century capitalism, it does not wholly remove it. Contemporary society still suffers from forms of exploitation that are characteristic of capitalism, albeit exploitation that is exercised more subtly than it was in the nineteenth century. On the one hand, despite the mitigating effect of state welfare provision the contemporary economic system remains capitalist precisely in so far as it is primarily geared not to meeting the genuine needs of the population, but rather to the realization of surplus value. Marx's distinction between use value and exchange value is therefore still valid (TP: 234). Use value is the genuine utility that a consumer derives from a good. Exchange value is the economic value of the good in comparison to all other goods and services traded on the market. The realization of surplus value requires goods to have an exchange value. Real needs may therefore go unmet, simply because the satisfaction of them would be unprofitable. Indeed, in line with the suggestion of "alienated leisure" made in relation to his first characteristic of contemporary society, Habermas suggests (again following Horkheimer and Adorno's account of the culture industry (see § "Horkheimer and Adorno", p. 215)) that through the growth of the mass media and the advertising industry, the consumer's very perception of need and use value may be subject to manipulation (TP: 234).

On the other hand, technological modes of thought, developed in the domination and manipulation of nature, and which thus contributed to the enormous expansion of industrial technology, are now applied, in the form of large-scale bureaucratic organization, to all aspects of economic, social and cultural life. Crucially, the welfare state itself becomes highly bureaucratic, and thus while ostensibly providing for otherwise unmet needs does so only by subjecting citizens to an exhaustive and at times dehumanizing administrative control. This suggests a nightmare vision, with roots in the novels of Franz Kafka, of a populace that is increasingly powerless in the face of sociotechnical administration and, more disturbingly still, may not even recognize its own subordination. People use their very capacity for free and responsible action to conform to the demands that economic and administrative systems place upon them. In a grim paradox, the style of which frankly owes a good deal to Adorno, Habermas states that those who are well integrated into society are "forced to obey ... are allowed to do, in the consciousness of their freedom, what do they must" (TP: 196).

The third characteristic of contemporary capitalism that Habermas identifies concerns the relevance of the orthodox notion of the proletariat, and of "proletarian consciousness" (TP: 196). Marx had argued that the proletariat would become aware of its position as an oppressed class not least through the immiseration to which it would be inevitably subjected. Late capitalism has avoided any such crisis. Crucially, lack of political or economic power can no longer be associated with material deprivation or insecurity. Put crudely, the working class now has a good deal more to lose than its chains, and so any theory of revolutionary practice must look elsewhere for an agent of social change.

Finally, Habermas points to the challenge that the rise of Soviet Marxism poses. On one level the Soviet political doctrine represents the corruption of Marxism, from a theory of human emancipation to an administrative route to rapid industrialization. On a more profound level, the existence of the Soviet bloc forced the capitalist West to reflect upon its own social organization, leading to the self-regulation and to the more even distribution of affluence and security typical of "new capitalism". Yet, far more ominously, the conflict of the superpowers (in a "global civil war") threatens everyone with nuclear destruction (TP: 197–8).

The positivist dispute

Traditional and critical theory

If these four points sketch the outline of contemporary capitalism (or at least, capitalism at the height of the cold war, and before the economic and political crises of the early 1970s), then it is for this society that Habermas requires a coherent theoretical model, both facilitating further sociological research, and identifying opportunities for social change. Habermas points to the inadequacy of not just orthodox Marxist theory but, equally, of the "traditional theory" of bourgeois sociology. We shall therefore follow Habermas into his first critical engagement with the philosophy of science – what has become known as the "positivist dispute" – in which he explores the complementary strengths and weaknesses of Marxist and "bourgeois" theory. First, however, we may note some of the theoretical resources that Habermas takes into this debate from the Frankfurt School.

In his 1971 "Introduction" to *Theory and Practice*, Habermas presents two conditions that a theory of society conceived with a practical intention must meet (TP: 1). It is a necessary, although not sufficient, condition of such a theory that it addresses the question of the historical possibility of political intervention, and can thus identify those whom it seeks to emancipate. Any theory must provide an account of how society can be changed, and who can change it. Answers will vary from the piecemeal administrative intervention of scientific experts (such as planners, lawyers and economists), who free populations from the blights of chance and inefficiency, to violent revolutionary action by a repressed class that liberates humanity as a whole. Untangling the political implications, and indeed claims to objectivity, of these answers turns upon the further question of the nature and composition of society. Habermas had, early on, recognized the anachronistic nature of Lukács's account of a class-society (and thus class revolution), but he equally questions the coherence and political implications of the social administrator's vision of society as a mechanism that can be subject to technological control.

For Habermas, the problem of justifying one's account of society and social practice evokes the second condition of a practical social theory: social theory must reflect upon its own historical and political origins. This is, in effect, a distinction that Horkheimer introduces as that between traditional theory and critical theory (Horkheimer 1972: 188–243; TP: 211). Traditional theory presupposes that the knowing subject is separated from the object being studied. The world is accepted as a sum of facts (Horkheimer 1972: 200). This approach, characteristic of the natural sciences, takes no account of the formative, historical relations that exist between the subject and object. Critical theory therefore questions that which traditional theory takes for granted as given or even as natural: "tenement houses, factories, cotton, cattle for slaughter, men" (*ibid.*: 201). Cultural processes are evident, both in the object perceived, and in the way in which the subject itself sees and hears, which is to say that human nature, including thoughts and perceptions, may itself be socially constituted (*ibid.*: 200). The question of social practice therefore turns upon a recognition of alienation, such that society does indeed confront the subject as something objective and constraining, and yet also that the human subject is historically active in constructing and maintaining society (*ibid.*: 207–8). For Habermas, any social theory, in its very articulation of what it understands by social science, social practice and society, will imply an account of its own relationship to society, which is to say, an account of its own status as a social activity, and thus of the way in which social and economic forces impinge upon scientific and other intellectual work. Habermas's demand is that this account should be made explicit, so that social theory is self-conscious, not merely of the coherence of its own claims, but also of its stance within an historically and culturally constituted complex of competing interests. Social theory with a practical intent is self-conscious of its place within a scientific and political context, within which it must defend and prove itself.

Positivism

In "The Analytical Theory of Science and Dialectics" (written in 1963), Habermas articulates the distinction between critical and traditional theory by ostensibly arguing for the superiority of a "dialectical" understanding of science over that offered by analytic philosophy, not least as represented by the positivists and Karl Popper. The essay itself is a contribution to what is known as the "positivist dispute", a discussion concerning the nature of the social sciences, initiated in an exchange between Adorno and Popper (Adorno *et al.* 1976). Habermas specifically seeks to defend dialectical social science against the functionalism or systems theory that would then have been dominant in sociology (e.g. through the work of the American Talcott Parsons).

The philosophy that grounds a non-dialectical, positivistic, approach presents the methodology of the social sciences as essentially the same as that of the natural sciences (PD: 133). As with natural science, it is assumed that the scientist is quite distinct from the object of inquiry. If science is to be done well, so that its results describe and explain the world as it is, untainted by the subjectivity of personal preferences or ways of looking at the world, then a rigorous scientific methodology is required. Such a methodology will be valid regardless of the particular inquiry or inquirer. For the natural and social sciences alike, it centres around the articulation of hypotheses about the causal associations that govern the object of inquiry. Hypotheses are verified, or on Popper's more subtle account, corroborated or falsified, by being tested against empirical observations of physical behaviour. Ideally, causal relations can be expressed in mathematical terms. Significantly, this leads to a fundamentally ahistorical way of thinking. Just as the laws of nature are assumed to be valid throughout time and space, so too social science aspires to formulate laws that are similarly universal in scope. The possibility that the "laws" of a society hold only at particular historical moments is marginalized (TP: 207), so placing sociology at odds with more narrative approaches found in the study of history that eschew anything like causal explanation. Social phenomena are therefore presented as being as amenable to explanation and prediction as are natural phenomena. Precisely in so far as they allow for the identification and quantification of uniform and repeatable social processes, the results of a positivistic social science can be utilized in the rational administration of society (TP: 210). A rise in interest rates will reduce inflation, and stricter legal enforcement will reduce rates of drug addiction. Here, then, is the outline of a social theory that presents social practice as administrative intervention by experts.

Ideology critique

Habermas has two lines of response to this analytic, or positivist, philosophy of science, both of which are designed to force it into self-reflection. On the one hand, he rehearses a history of the positivist understanding of science, and on the other complements this with an examination of the internal consistency of analytic philosophy's account of science. In "Dogmatism, Reason and Decision" (1976g), Habermas traces the development of Western thinking about science from the eighteenth century, which is to say, the Enlightenment. Early Enlightenment thinkers (and Habermas's particular example is the Franco-German materialist philosopher Paul Holbach) promote the rational study of nature as a means of combating dogma and prejudice. Crucially, this entails not merely the acquisition of a better understanding of how nature itself works, but also a challenge to the rationally unjustified authority of despotic rulers and the church. Rational and factual errors permit, in Holbach's glorious words, oppression, slavery, "deep rooted enmity ... continual bloodshed and horrifying tragedies" (TP: 257).

Whereas Holbach's commitment to political emancipation is taken further by the German Idealists (writing at the end of the eighteenth and beginning of the nineteenth centuries), the self-understanding of the natural sciences becomes increasingly positivistic, pursuing knowledge of nature, but overtly distancing itself from the pursuit of any political goals. For the positivists, good science will be good science, regardless of the sort of political regime within which it is practised. Yet idealists and positivists alike challenge Holbach's assumption that nature can be a source of moral insight. For both, this entails confusing knowledge of nature – or facts – with knowledge of morality – or values – and as such amounts to a regression back into dogmatism. Whereas both idealism and positivism culminate in what Habermas calls a "critique of ideology", they interpret dogmatism, and thus ideology critique, quite differently.

For the idealist, dogmatism centres upon the uncritical acceptance of the subordination of the human subject to nature. Even if nature exemplifies a harmonious and rational order, as Holbach assumes, he still compromises human freedom, because he has simply accepted nature as a given. Rationality and, crucially, morality become external forces acting upon human beings, and not something that human beings can freely generate or choose.

For the idealists, this entails a failure to recognize that nature may in some sense be the product of human subjectivity (TP: 259). Kant argues that nature is not passively perceived by the human subject; rather, the faculties of the human mind actively appropriate and shape raw sensory experience, in order to constitute the ordered (phenomenal) world that is perceived by human beings. Johann Fichte goes further to offer the image of a subject that does not merely perceive the world but actually creates (or posits) it. Crucially the "dogmatic" subject is unaware of its own creativity, and thus subordinates itself to external forces. In contrast, Fichte's "idealist" subject strives for autonomy from all that is external, as it becomes increasingly conscious of its own productive power (TP: 260–61). Although Fichte's philosophy ultimately fails to offer a coherent account of the idealist subject, for it simply retreats into the arid realm of pure thought, he has nonetheless raised the important possibility that perception and understanding of the world cannot simply be taken for granted. Indeed, in his distinction between two types of human subject, the "idealist" and the "dogmatist", and in his dictum that the sort of philosophy one chooses depends upon what sort of a human being one is (TP: 260), Fichte has opened up the possibility that different categories of people may constitute the world differently. More profoundly still, in his defence of idealism over dogmatism he has suggested that certain positions may be afflicted by what Habermas calls "false consciousness", following orthodox Marxist terminology. For Schelling, there is a "distorted world and a humanity that is concealed from itself". In this situation the external is allowed to dominate the internal, and "the force of dark sediments over purity and clarity" (TP: 235–6). The dogmatist, unwittingly, remains embroiled in error and prejudice, in unwitting submission to the "dark sediments", and unaware of their own human potential. The exposure of false consciousness is therefore one form of ideology critique.

In contrast, for the positivist, good science rests not upon the exposure of false consciousness, and thus upon self-criticism, but more prosaically upon the separation of fact from value. The positivist grounds science in instrumental rationality, and is thus concerned exclusively with the factual issue of the causal associations that exist between phenomena, and with the most effective technological exploitation of those associations. Whether a causal association, or indeed any other fact, is good (say, in the sense of morally or politically desirable, or even aesthetically beautiful), is irrelevant. A commitment to values is simply the result of a personal decision. Although values may still determine the goals to which science (and especially technology) are deployed, a commitment to values, unlike the acceptance of effective causal relationships, cannot be justified through empirical observation, and it is thus seen to be beyond rational debate or determination. The decision to adhere to a given set of values is thus understood, by the positivist, to be little more than an idiosyncratic assertion of will. Such "decisionism", being wholly subjective, is irrational, and fundamentally undesirable. Values should not therefore be allowed to influence the acceptance or rejection of the results of scientific research. Crudely, one cannot accept a scientific hypothesis as true simply because you would like it to be true, or because its truth would serve one's political or moral purposes. But equally this position entails, against Holbach and his moral study of nature, that no empirical facts can determine the values to which a person should be committed. Positivistic ideology critique thereby ceases to be concerned with false consciousness, and becomes rather the exposure of the contamination of scientific research by "the sewage of emotionality" (TP: 265).

Positivist ideology critique is, for Habermas, an important and necessary critical activity. Problems only occur when the critique of values becomes universal, for at that point positivism abandons the possibility of self-reflection, and becomes itself dogmatic. Precisely because it presupposes its own value-neutrality, positivistic science becomes blind to the values that may yet be inherent in its own practice. Habermas argues that because positivistic science is committed to progressive instrumental rationalization, its values are those of efficiency and economy (TP: 269). As such, it suppresses any form of technology, or crucially any social practice, that does not conform to the ideal of instrumental reason, which is to say, any form of reasoning that is not structured in terms of the calculation and assessment of the efficient realization of a given end. This may be welcomed when, for example, traditional or habitual inhibitions to technological progress are removed, and one can find more efficient means to realize one's goals (TP: 263). However, political and moral values that would radically challenge the instrumental or administrative control of society, or indeed values that merely do not make sense within the terms of instrumental reason, are also rendered ineffectual and marginalized. (One might consider, by analogy, the example of computers that have been programmed to play chess. Although they will play effectively, it is not clear that they could meaningfully be said to play recklessly, beautifully or daringly. Values that may be of importance to human beings, and indeed the values by which we might assess the worth of a human agent, may therefore be eroded by an increasingly technocratic, and indeed cybernetically controlled, economy (see TP: 273–4).) More precisely, the increasingly important role that science plays within the forces of production (TP: 254) – so that technological innovation ceases to be haphazard and becomes rather subject to rational planning – and in the relations of production – in the administration of the labour force and the general population – entails that a positivistic, overtly value-neutral science serves the reproduction and stabilization of capitalism. Bluntly, Habermas's claim against the positivist is that science is not an activity that occurs wholly independently of the economic base, and therefore the criteria of good science are not determined purely in terms of the rational consistency of the scientific methodology. Science and the ideals of good science are rather shaped by science's status as a form of social practice. The characteristics of late capitalism that Habermas describes in "Between Philosophy and Science" therefore rest, to a significant degree, upon the expansion of a science grounded in instrumental reason.

Reason

In "The Analytical Theory of Science and Dialectics" (1976c), Habermas begins to expose the limitations of positivism's conception of rationality by examining its internal consistency. His argument centres upon the problem of the empirical testing of scientific hypotheses (PD: 149). A hypothesis is tested by formulating a description of the specific empirical conditions that would falsify or corroborate it. Thus, for example, the Newtonian thesis that the gravitational constant is $6.6742 \times 10^{-11} \mathrm{Nm^2 kg^{-2}}$, allows, in effect, for an infinite series of predictions about how the world will behave. One would be that an object falling towards the earth will accelerate at $980\,\mathrm{cm\,s^{-2}}$ at the earth's surface. If observable conditions conform to this, then, on Popper's account, the hypothesis is corroborated, and if not it is refuted. Habermas notes that a hypothesis is not tested directly by an empirical observation. The relationship described above does not link a hypothesis to an observation, but rather the *statement* of a hypothesis to the *statement* describing empirical conditions. A problem therefore arises in establishing that any given observation is, or is not, an instance of what is referred to in the statement. (This is therefore as much a problem of the philosophy of language as one of epistemology or the philosophy of science.) The classic positivist response is to resolve this through the employment of a purely descriptive language, stripped of the vagaries of ordinary language. Such an approach presupposes that it is possible to establish indubitable foundations upon which the edifice of scientific knowledge can be built in sure deductive steps. Both Habermas and Popper reject this presupposition. Crucially the argument runs that the procedure by which an empirical observation is mapped onto a description or, indeed, by which two separate observations are recognized as two instances of a single description, cannot be formulated in a set of simple, logically consistent and self-contained rules. The recognition that a particular observation is an instance of the statement "An object accelerating towards earth at $980\,\mathrm{cm\,s^{-2}}$" presupposes, not least, an understanding of the theory of gravitation, as well as an awareness of the complex factors that might intervene to disrupt the behaviour of the object. Popper therefore argues that there must be some *discursive* process that allows scientists to determine whether or not the empirical observations reported by a colleague do in fact conform to statements required to test the hypothesis. This process is akin to a trial jury's debate over the relationship between evidence, proffered by both prosecution and defence, and the law (PD: 152).[2]

This seemingly abstruse problem raises fundamental issues, not merely for the understanding of science, but for an understanding of society, and of the very practice of philosophy itself. It may be noted that a parallel problem is raised by the philosopher Ludwig Wittgenstein, from within the analytic tradition, in consideration of the practice of following a rule (Wittgenstein 1958: §201ff.). Again it is argued that it is not possible to formulate exhaustively the procedures that must be obeyed in even the simple operation of successively "adding 2" to generate a series of numbers. Such abilities are always contextual, which is to say that they are learnt and practised in specific practical and cultural contexts. There is no guarantee that such abilities can be transferred unproblematically to another context. The ability cannot therefore be grounded upon any indubitable logical basis, but rests rather on the far more unsettling ground of the complex and typically unarticulated cultural competences of members of a particular community (which Wittgenstein calls a "form of life" (*ibid.*: §19)).

Habermas's point is similar. If there is no logically compelling reason to accept that any given empirical observation is an instance of the statement of the testing conditions of a hypothesis, or equally, that a particular act is an instance of following a given rule, then, on positivism's own account, some decision must be made as to the legitimacy of the observation or act. Yet the positivist has relegated decisions to the realm of non-rational subjective whim (as exemplified in the choice of values). Habermas's point is not that science is itself subjective, and thus ultimately arbitrary. The recognition by Popper of some process akin to the disputation of a jury (or indeed Wittgenstein's form of life), opens up the possibility that there is a rational basis to decision-making, in science and elsewhere, albeit not one that can be understood in terms of pure instrumental rationality. This basis is found in what Habermas initially calls the "re-understanding" that competent scientists have of their activity. In effect, as competent members of a community of scientists, they possess a host of taken-for-granted beliefs and abilities that allow them to act as scientists, and to interact with other scientists. This communal activity is not a bundle of regular and therefore predictable behaviours, but is rather a creative and meaningful activity (just as following a rule is not reducible to an algorithm, but depends rather upon the subtle cultural understanding and creativity of the actors involved). This host of beliefs and competences is, using terminology borrowed from phenomenology, the scientists' "lifeworld". It is drawn upon, usually implicitly, in determining the validity of a hypothesis or the relevance of empirical evidence. Crucially, such beliefs are not merely factual, but are also normative. They are beliefs about the right way to practise science, and indeed, what it means to be a scientist. Typically, if scientists are acting successfully, these beliefs need not be brought into question. The beliefs work in practice, albeit in the particular context of a capitalist society, and can therefore remain implicit.

Habermas is making two points. First, he notes that, while science is ultimately a cultural achievement (and not a mere matter of logic), scientific practice does yet have a high degree of historical stability. The activity of science may thus be grounded in some fundamental aspect of human existence. This he identifies as the human capacity to labour (PD: 154, 156). Yet human beings are not just labourers. The recognition of science itself as a social activity has already served to demonstrate that human beings are also cultural beings. Their lives, importantly, are not simply about technological manipulation of the environment, or indeed each other, but about meaningful communication. Hence decision-making, for example, is not the non-rational act of an isolated human subject, but a meaningful, collective activity. This implies that there must be some form of rationality, beyond instrumental rationality, that can embrace decision-making and the holding of values. The positivist's extension of the methodology of the natural sciences, which emphasizes causal explanation and the observation of purely physical – as opposed to meaningful – behaviour, to the social sciences must, therefore, be in error. Social practice cannot be satisfactorily explained on a model of instrumental manipulation of behaviour alone.

Secondly, a cultural history of science can still be written, and this in effect links Habermas's argument back to the analysis in "Dogmatism, Reason, and Decision". There he identified science as part of the capitalist forces of production. In "The Analytic Theory of Science and Dialectics" he goes further, to suggest that the modern form of science, that emerges, for example, in the work of Galileo in the late sixteenth century, is intimately linked to the contemporary rise of capitalist conceptions of property. As the acquisition of property through labour becomes the norm of the rising bourgeois class, purely theoretical reflection, which was once the privilege of the leisured aristocracy, ceases to be important. For the bourgeoisie, intellectual work comes to be tied to the production process. Legitimate knowledge, which is to say science, now comes to be narrowly focused upon the development and refinement of technological rules (in contrast, say, to the metaphysical speculations of the medieval alchemists) (TP: 156). Habermas is therefore suggesting that the taken-for-granted pre-understanding of science, which all members of the community of scientists share, is a capitalist one. But more ominously, the very success of capitalism and capitalist technology entails that there is no pressing practical reason to bring that cultural pre-understanding into question.

Positivist science, in the very assertion of its own value-neutrality, has become as dogmatic, in its own way, as Holbach's philosophy. The capitalist base, upon which modern science rests, unwittingly comes to appear as if it were part of nature. First, society and its members are treated as causally determined objects. Secondly, and more significantly, by failing to reflect upon the social conditions of its existence, positivist science projects its own, ultimately capitalist, values as being of universal scope and validity. Positivism is no more capable of questioning capitalism than was Holbach of questioning the moral order that he presumed to find in nature. Positivism fails to recognize the possibility that the conditions that make it possible and give it the rigour and success that it has, may be the product of human action, rather than being ultimate givens. Thus, in its advocacy of value-freedom, and in the doctrine of "decisionism", where values are reduced to matters of subjective preference, positivist approaches to philosophy place the ends of capitalism beyond rational reflection, and in the early 1960s such ends may include not merely continued economic exploitation, but also post-colonial warfare (in Algeria and Vietnam, for example), the nuclear arms race and environmental destruction. Habermas's claim is therefore not that positivism is simply in error, but rather that it is false consciousness.[3]

The theory of reification

Commodity fetishism

The next stage of Habermas's argument, and thus the explication of what a "dialectical" science might be, turns upon the concept of "reification". Reification [*Verdinglichung*] literally means turning into a thing, or object. In the context of social theory, the theory of reification is concerned with the way in which social processes, which at root must be the product of human actions, come to confront their human authors as if they were objects, or at least as if they were governed by natural laws. Under conditions of reification, society as a whole thereby appears to be held together not by the free and meaningful actions and interactions of human beings, but by "natural" laws and processes wholly outside the will and control of humanity. More specifically, the Marxist theory of reification is concerned with the way in which economic processes and administrative structures confront human beings as objective, or even as natural constraints upon their actions. Habermas himself presents reification as the tearing asunder of the concrete relationships that human beings have to each other and to objects (PD: 157). In effect, it is the process by which the meaningfulness of social relations, exemplified in the idea of the lifeworld, is undermined by the reduction of social life to its administration and control according to abstract and ahistorical regularities (akin to the laws of nature).

The term "reification" is brought into Marxism by Lukács (1971: 83–222), and substantially developed by Adorno (1973: 189–92). Lukács offers a re-interpretation of Marx's analysis of capitalist commodity exchange – the theory of commodity fetishism – in terms of Weber's analysis of the process of rationalization in Western society. For Marx, the existence of the commodity – which is to say, products traded in the market – is fundamental to the nature of capitalism. In capitalism, the exchange of commodities in the market is the dominant economic relationship. But this process of exchange engenders a peculiar form of false consciousness. Once an object becomes a commodity, it takes on mysterious properties (Marx 1976: 163–77). The exchange of commodities appears, not as a process that is governed by the free activity of human beings, but rather as a process that is governed by the commodities themselves. This is to say that commodities acquire a social life, an intercourse between themselves, that comes to appear quite distinct from, and indeed dominant over, that of their human producers. This social life is the exchange of commodities with each other, and its apparent autonomy from human intervention rests upon the governing role that the value of the commodities plays in determining their exchange. This value is not use value (i.e. the utility derived from using the object), for that is actually determined by a relationship between the object and its human consumer and is thus part of the cultural lifeworld of human creativity and valuation. The value in question is rather exchange value. Exchange value determines the value of one *qualitatively* unique object in comparison to any other, with the value being typically expressed in monetary (and therefore *quantitative*) terms. (For example, one hardback copy of *Theory and Practice* is equivalent to three CDs, is equivalent to €50, and so on.) This value appears to be a property of the object itself, with use value, paradoxically, coming to appear as nothing more than a result of the subjective whim of the consumer. The regularities of the market therefore come to appear as natural laws, derived from the seemingly objective properties of exchange value. This is the process that Marx terms "commodity fetishism".

Habermas's analysis of positivism mirrors this account of commodity fetishism. In extending the methodology of the natural sciences to the social sciences, the positivist can perceive only the reified surface of society: a world of "phantasmagorical" (see Rose 1978: 31) interactions between objects, or Schelling's "distorted world". The lifeworld – which is to say the gamut of competences and beliefs through which human beings constitute, intersubjectively, a meaningful social world – occupies a position parallel to that of use value, precisely in so far as positivism is seen to reduce the lifeworld to the non-rational subjectivity of decisionism. In contrast, by refusing to analyse the historical emergence of social forms, which is a charge that Marx, equally, places against the bourgeois economics of his day, positivism treats social relations as natural laws. Such laws are expressed not in terms of concrete and meaningful relationships between human beings, but only as interconnections between the abstractly quantified, and mathematically formulated properties of a system.

Reification

Yet commodity fetishism is not merely a matter of distorted perception; it is also a distortion of social practice. If market exchange is the dominant social relationship in a capitalist economy, then human beings typically relate to each other as producers, and do so through the market. This entails that they relate not merely through the exchange of the goods that they produce, but by treating their own ability to labour as a commodity which can be sold. In effect, commodity exchange turns the human being into a commodity, their human value being displaced by the exchange value of their labour power. In other words, the abstract values of the market come to displace the concrete and meaningful relationships of the lifeworld. The implications of this are not, however, to be found purely in Marx, but significantly in the work of Weber. Lukács recognizes that there is a fundamental homology between Marx's account of commodity fetishism and Weber's account of rationalization, and he uses this to analyse the way in which fetishism has now entered all aspects of social life (not merely the economic). Weber argues that the technological power of capitalist economies, and thus the global dominance of Western culture, lies in the rigorous deployment of instrumental rationality, which is to say that Western culture, uniquely in Weber's view, can be characterized by the exhaustive manner in which it seeks the most instrumentally efficient means to the achievement of any given goal. Indeed, Weber traces the historical process by which modern conceptions of rationality come to be formulated, so that habit, tradition and emotion cease to be recognized as sound motivations for action or, at least, cease to be accepted in more and more areas of social life. Instrumental rationality thus comes to imbue all forms of social life, from science and technology, through law, accounting and administration to architecture and music (Weber 1976: 13–23; and see § "Horkheimer and Adorno", p. 215). Yet this entails, as has already become clear in Habermas's criticism of positivism, that instrumental rationality displaces the concrete lifeworld in determining social

19

relations. As with commodity exchange, this rationality takes on an autonomy that serves to conceal its cultural origins (see Lukács 1971: 81). Technocratic administration, exemplified in modern bureaucracy, comes to appear to be the only rationally justifiable form of social practice.

This account of reification begins to substantiate the description of late capitalism given in "Between Philosophy and Science". The development of the positivist sciences has served to transform the economy in ways not envisaged by Marx. Not only have the forces of production become more effective, but the very nature of labour has been transformed as skill and training become as significant in determining the productivity of labour as does the level of technology with which labour works (TP: 227ff.). The development of administrative technologies has also given the superstructure greater autonomy over the base. Yet this is not merely a technical issue whereby the welfare state can consciously intervene and disrupt the working of Marx's "laws" of capitalist crisis. The theory of reification suggests that the true significance of administrative expansion lies in its appearance of neutrality and rationality. This fundamentally changes the nature of power relations in late capitalism. There is no longer a clearly delineated subordinate class, for subordination is now subordination to the administrative and economic system, and embraces the administrators as much as the administrated. Traditional ideas of class consciousness become redundant, as increasingly affluent and economically secure workers internalize the positivistic image of themselves as objects. It is thus that human beings come (in the grim paradox noted in § "An affluent proletariat", p. 6) to use their own creative power to do freely what they have no alternative but to do (TP: 196), concealing their humanity from themselves.

Dialectics

Crisis and critique

It has already been noted above that Habermas's criticism of positivism sought to demonstrate not merely that positivism is in error as a philosophy of science, but that it is more significantly a form of false consciousness. Its very advocacy of value-neutrality entails that it is incapable of questioning the values that are inherent to it. In effect, by striving for a formal validity in scientific method, which has universal scope and is justified purely in terms of its logical consistency, it fails to reflect upon the substantial values and interests that must motivate it (TP: 209). At least in part, those values are the values of the dominant capitalist culture. Yet in this criticism

Habermas has still only begun to hint at the dialectics – which is to say the social theory conceived with practical intention – that is to challenge positivism. The central problem that Habermas poses for himself is to demonstrate that dialectics identifies and responds to the objective problems of the age, in a way that positivism does not (PD: 133).

It is already clear, from the criticism of positivism, that dialectics is a form of ideology critique, and as such sets itself against any form of dogmatism. It is through an examination of this concept of "critique" that Habermas defends his conception of a critical social theory (TP: 212–14). "Critique", Habermas notes, is bound up etymologically with the concept of "crisis". In pre-Enlightenment reflection on medicine and spirituality, the origins of "crisis" already indicate the entwining of the crisis with the fate of the human subject. Medical and spiritual crises require decisive action in the face of the imminent threat of death and damnation (TP: 213). In the Enlightenment itself, crisis re-emerges first with a natural disaster (the Lisbon earthquake of 1755). This event challenges humanity's confidence in its ability to control nature. More profoundly, crisis emerges with the experience of industrialization, as technological progress increasingly engenders social oppression and degradation. Crisis is thereby entwined not simply with the fate of the individual, but with the social and historical condition of humanity as such (TP: 214). Critique, or critical judgement, strives to ascertain what is right and just in the face of such a crisis. Crucially, critique is not merely an abstract analysis of a problem, but rather "presses on to a decision" that has practical import (TP: 213). It is therefore suggested that the process of critique rests upon the objectivity of any decision it makes and upon the recognition of the involvement of the subject in the crisis complex. As such it stands in stark contrast to positivism's relegation of decisions to mere subjective whim. Critique and decision-making rest upon the ability not merely to understand a crisis as some objective but external event, but rather, through self-reflection, to recognize the crisis as a crisis of the human subject.

Fichte's response to dogmatism already indicated something of this notion of critique, but it remains hampered by its own idealist sentiments. In effect, Fichte does not press his self-reflection far enough. The relation between the human subject and the object is such that the subject merely perceives the object. Fichte cannot provide a coherent account of the subject acting on the object, to produce or transform it. Thus his recognition that a system of reason is either "a game played in thought" or must have reality "*conferred* upon it" (TP: 260) is at once his strength – for he thereby challenges the universal scope and validity of rationality that the positivist presupposes by asserting that reason must be made to be applicable to reality – and his weakness: the productive act of conferment remains, ultimately, an act of will. It remains, that is to say, a subjective decision, and does so precisely because Fichte has not yet completely worked out the relationship of subject to object. This working out Habermas finds in Marx, as had Lukács and Horkheimer before him. Crucially, Marx recognizes that the human being does not merely conceive the object in consciousness, that is, does not merely perceive and conceptualize the object, but actively transforms it in social labour (TP: 218). The seemingly natural object that confronts humanity, and that constrains and shapes it, is thus revealed as itself the historically achieved product of human agency. Humanity is confronted – in the physical environment that has been transformed by it, as well as in the complex culture that it has created – by the sediment of its own history. The analysis of commodity fetishism and reification rests precisely upon this insight. In addition, because the economy is the determining framework in which the human subject labours to transform the object, a crisis of consciousness presupposes a deeper crisis in the economy. For Marx, the critique of political economy therefore precedes and grounds ideology critique (TP: 222).

Marx's achievement involves a particular understanding of history. It centres, Habermas suggests, on the "myth of an atheistic God" (TP: 218–19). Habermas finds a profound articulation of crisis in certain strands of Jewish and Protestant mysticism. In response to the problem of evil, and thus the problem of how a good and omnipotent God could permit evil, a God is envisaged who goes "into exile within Himself" (TP: 215), which is to say, that God becomes his own other; he becomes the natural world that he has created. He relinquishes his very omnipotence, so that even humanity can defy him. The purpose of such self-abandonment lies in the possibility of salvation, not through God's own action, but through human action. It is this striving for salvation that gives history its shape and meaning. Yet such salvation is achieved only at the risk of irretrievable catastrophe. What if humanity fails to save its god? The crisis of damnation thus remains real and pressing.

A variation on this myth lies at the foundation of Hegel's philosophy. Where Fichte had described a human subject that posits the object, Hegel offers a quasi-divine "spirit" or "mind" [Geist]. The concept of "spirit" is complex and multi-layered, retaining at once theological connotations of the Judaic-Christian God, but also philosophical connotations of pure conceptual and rational thought. It allows Hegel to construct an account of both natural and human history, such that the pure subjectivity of spirit must become objective, manifesting itself in the natural world, but then gradually returning to consciousness of itself through a series of crises in human culture (ultimately articulated in the achievements of art, religion and philosophy). The subject is revealed as identical to the object, for the subject is the rational order that makes the object possible and gives it coherence. The subject, as logical order, is thus the absolute truth to which the partial and provisional truths of history strive.

A demythologized version of such a history lies at the roots of Marxism. The issue is no longer the redemption of a God, but rather the recovery of humanity from the crises that occur through its subordination to the objectified results of its own history. The story of a subject losing itself in its own objective product is thereby the core metaphor of reification. Yet Hegel's metaphysics subtly differs from the myth of the atheist God, and this becomes crucial for Habermas's interpretation of Marxism. Hegel's spirit never completely surrenders itself to the contingencies of the natural and human world (TP: 216). Everything, including salvation, is anticipated and guaranteed from the beginning. Hegel presents, at least in his later and more conservative writings, absolute truth. The idea of crisis in such a history therefore becomes largely vacuous, for there is no real risk of failure. Crises already have their place and resolution determined from the perspective of the absolute. Critique therefore degenerates back into dogma.

Lukács's interpretation of Marx, because it re-emphasizes the Hegelian elements of Marx's thought, runs the risk of similarly side-stepping crisis. Lukács presents the proletariat as the subject–object of history, which is to say that the proletariat takes the place occupied by absolute truth in the Hegelian system. Whereas the individual member of the bourgeoisie may see himself or herself as a historical subject, they do so only as an agent acting upon an external object. In contrast, the proletariat on Lukács's account is uniquely placed, not least in its awareness of itself as a commodity, to understand itself, not merely as the object of historical forces, but also, once it has seen through its false consciousness, as its agent. The proletariat can understand itself as a collective agent of human history, so that its grasp of agency is far more profound than the individualistic conception of the bourgeoisie. Thus, the coming to self-consciousness of the proletariat completes history, redeeming humanity from its subordination to the dead weight of history.

The problem with this account lies, in part, in the failure of history to fulfil Lukács's predictions. The proletariat does not develop class consciousness. Revolution in Germany in 1919 fails. Even the Russian revolution results in a protracted civil war, and dictatorial government. Lukács therefore turns from the empirical class consciousness of the proletariat to the notion of an imputed class consciousness. In effect, Lukács substitutes an empirically informed faith in what will happen, with a theoretic faith in what *ought* to happen. In this, Lukács presumes to find, for the Marxist theorist, a position of absolute and indubitable truth akin to that of Hegel: a true consciousness from which to perceive and act upon the world.

Precisely in so far as the Communist Party assumes that it has the "absolute truth", it can presuppose the legitimacy of its dictatorship over the proletariat. Habermas's argument against Lukács is that, by adopting from Hegel what is in effect a closed account of history, he has reproduced Hegel's idealism and dogmatism. The true nature of the contemporary historical crisis, manifest not least in the failure of the proletariat to come to class consciousness, is lost. The consequence of this is Stalinism (TP: 34).

The failure of dialectics

Lukács's failure is significant as his criticism of "bourgeois thought" anticipates much of Habermas's criticism of positivism. The only alternative that Lukács has to the instrumental reason of bourgeois science is Hegelian reason. Like Habermas, and indeed Horkheimer, Lukács criticizes bourgeois thought for its failure to think historically, and for its associated inability to reflect upon the cultural context within which it develops. Bourgeois science therefore controls the details of existence, without any understanding of society as a whole (Lukács 1971: 121). Habermas expresses this in the distinction between system and totality. A system of explanation in positivist science relates discrete elements according to regularities, which can typically be expressed mathematically. The concepts according to which this system is articulated are developed, in accordance with the philosophy of a general scientific methodology, independently of the specific phenomena under investigation. The system, as an explanatory mechanism, is therefore always external to its social contents (PD: 132, 135). Although Habermas borrows the term "totality" from Lukács and, indeed, Adorno, who both used it in reference to Hegelian logic, his use of the term appeals more readily to phenomenology and hermeneutics. In effect, Habermas is deliberately reworking the term in order to escape the impasse that exists between instrumental and Hegelian reason, into which Lukács and Adorno fall.

For Lukács, Marxism's appeal to totality is the demand that society is understood concretely, in its historical specificity. Yet Lukács's closed understanding of history, dependent as it is on an indisputable assertion of absolute truth, compromises this promise. Lukács's attempt to intervene in society collapses into totalitarianism. Adorno responds by abandoning the possibility of any positive understanding of the totality. Under the catchphrase, "The whole is false" (itself an inversion of Hegel (Adorno 1974: 50)), he generates a fundamental suspicion of any claim to have a definitive grasp of the totality. Yet, in so far as he remains bound by Hegelian reason as the only alternative to instrumental reason, all he can do is offer a thoroughgoing, but ultimately politically impotent, criticism of contemporary society and science. Whereas Lukács offers the promise of a society on the brink of redemptive self-understanding, Adorno proposes a society that is radically incomprehensible in terms of the categories of thought and (typically positivistic) forms of knowledge that it makes possible. It is a society that, he claims, can only be grasped in contradictions. If Lukács overrides crisis in his hubristic anticipation of a perfect society, Adorno is so overwhelmed by the risk of failure in the face of crisis that he dare not act at all. The very possibility of decision, and the distinguishing of true from false consciousness, is thus undermined (TP: 31).

If Lukács and Adorno place Hegelian reason in opposition to bourgeois or positivist thought, then Habermas, perhaps more subtly, places Marxism as critique – and thus dialectics, or social theory with practical intent – between idealist philosophy and positivist science. This space may be articulated through Habermas's appropriation of the concept of "totality". Although for Habermas the term continues to refer to the concrete historical context, as it does for Lukács, it does so by appealing to the lifeworld, rather than to Hegelian reason. The totality is thus an horizon of expectations, through which competent social actors make sense of their environment and the people they encounter within it. For Habermas, dialectical philosophy is therefore concerned with the way in which meaning is constructed and comprehended in contemporary society (PD: 139). Yet crucially, and this is what separates Marxism from idealist philosophy (including its modern forms of phenomenology and hermeneutics; see § "Hermeneutics (Gadamer)", p. 81), is the recognition that meaning attributed to the world is systematically distorted due to reification. The strength of Adorno's work lies, in large part, in his recognition of the infusion of reification into the very ways in which we think and in which we conceive of ourselves. Habermas similarly argues that dialectics proceeds not with the clarity of goals that Lukács ascribes to it, but rather critically, exposing false consciousness (TP: 39). Yet, if the "Nowhere" of Adorno's *Negative Dialectics* (1973) is to be avoided, then reification cannot be as all embracing as he supposes (AS: 93). Habermas makes the following suggestion: just as positivism, in its mechanistic account of social science, presupposes the intersubjective lifeworld, so too Adorno must, in his very criticism of instrumental reason, have "recourse to categories of intersubjectivity from which he abstains philosophically" (AS: 100). For Habermas, intersubjective competences, even in the most reified context, can never be wholly eroded. Society simply could not function if they were. He therefore offers a conception of Marxism as critique that is grounded in a continuing faith in the presence of human agency. Crucially, such agency lies not in the isolated subject of bourgeois thought, nor in Lukács's proletariat as the collective subject of history, but, as has already been indicated in his analysis of science,

25

in intersubjectivity. In contrast to the absolute truth of Lukács's Hegelian reason and the perpetual negativity of Adorno's, Habermas finds in the very falsifiability of scientific hypotheses a key to transcending the impasse of the earlier generations of critical theory. Falsifiability at once mitigates Lukács's totalitarian hubris, but also overrides Adorno's isolated and petrified self, because the pursuit of knowledge, including that of critique, can only proceed through rational dialogue.

These are, at this stage, claims only. They have yet to be worked out in detailed argument. Yet, even at this relatively early stage in his career, Habermas has already marked out theoretical concerns that will occupy him for the next two decades, and will reach their culmination only in the mid-1980s, with the publication of *The Theory of Communicative Action*. At the heart of this exploration lies the problem of avoiding the pitfalls of his Hegelian Marxist heritage, and to do so by articulating an account of reason that avoids the arid dichotomy of instrumentalism on one side and dialectics on the other. This third option will be communicative reason. The first steps that Habermas took to explicating such a notion of reason lay in an exploration of the social history of the social institutions that encouraged and shaped processes of public discussion: the "bourgeois public sphere". That work will be the primary focus of Chapter 2.

CHAPTER 2

The public sphere

Introduction

In the theoretical essays of the late 1950s and early 1960s, Habermas begins to address the problems of developing a Marxism that is relevant to contemporary capitalism: a "theory of society conceived with practical intention" (TP: 1). While critical of the positivism and instrumentalism that dominated both the natural and social sciences at that time, he was equally critical of the alternatives that were offered by Hegelianism, be it that of Lukács or Adorno and Horkheimer: Lukács's dogmatism leading to authoritarianism; Adorno's negativity leading to a politically impotent quietism. Lukács and Adorno, each in his own way, were criticized for denying the potential of rational debate that, paradoxically, the more positivistically minded Popper recognizes in his account of scientific progress in terms of falsificationism.

Two major empirical studies of this period, *Student und Politik* and *The Structural Transformation of the Public Sphere*, begin to substantiate both the critique of contemporary capitalism and an understanding of the potential that it may contain for rational self-criticism and self-transformation. Both studies were initiated within the Frankfurt Institute for Social Research, although neither was published under its auspices. The institute had, throughout its history, produced significant empirical studies including, perhaps most famously, *The Authoritarian Personality*, but also *Studies on Authority and the Family* and a study of political attitudes in West Germany, *Group Experiment* (see Wiggershaus 1994: 149–56, 411–24, 472–8). *Student und Politik*, of which Habermas was the lead author of four, was intended to continue this work, and to be published within the series Frankfurt Contributions to Sociology. Unfortunately, Horkheimer was to express reservations about the work's methodology and, more importantly, he argued that the institute could not afford, politically or financially, to be associated with its overt criticism of bourgeois society (*ibid*.: 554). Similarly,

Horkheimer's antagonism to *The Structural Transformation of the Public Sphere*, which Habermas intended to submit as his *Habilitationsschaft*,[1] led to Habermas's departure from the institute in 1961, in order to seek supervision from the openly radical Professor of Political Science at Marburg, Wolfgang Abendroth (AS: 218–19). Habermas never actually lectured at Marburg. He was offered the post of Extraordinary Professor of Philosophy in Heidelberg in 1962. He stayed in Heidelberg until 1964, before returning to Frankfurt and the university, to succeed Horkheimer as Professor of Philosophy (Wiggershaus 1994: 563).

Students and politics

Student und Politik is a report and analysis of an empirical study of the attitudes to politics of 171 students attending the University of Frankfurt. The interviews, which were structured by guidelines rather than by a formal list of questions – allowing the interviews to proceed like conversations – were conducted in the summer term of 1957. (An appendix, researched and written by Ludwig von Friedeburg, sought to confirm the original study's results using a larger and more representative sample.) The interviewees were told that the research was to do with "study problems". The interview guidelines sought to deflect attention from issues of politics, thus discouraging respondents from trying to give an answer that would please the interviewer (as opposed to giving their actual opinions).

The analysis of the interview data seeks to establish the nature and prevalence of specific types of political attitude. Three levels of analysis are deployed (SP: 58). First, the willingness of the student to become politically engaged (their "political habitus") is identified. Secondly, the student's attitude towards the democratic system ("political tendency") is obtained. Finally, analysis identifies the fund of motives or "images of society" that the respondents may have available to them. The attitudes of the respondents are ultimately determined by establishing the degree of coherence between habitus and tendency, and its ideological confirmation and stabilization by the image of society. The results suggested at the extreme that only 4 per cent of the sample were "stable democrats"; 6 per cent were stubborn authoritarians. The remainder of the sample divided in similar proportions, with the majority tending towards authoritarian attitudes. In addition, the analysis suggested that democrats tended to come from less powerful positions within society, with less opportunity for upward social mobility (SP: 234).

Habermas's introduction seeks to place the interview data – the parochial nature of which is acknowledged – into a broader context by theorizing the political and social conditions of contemporary Germany. This involves, on the one hand, interpreting the phenomenon of political apathy as a response to the distinctive political and economic structures of late capitalist societies. On the other hand, a defence of what he terms "social democracy" is developed, based upon the institutional and intellectual history of the Western liberal ideal of democratic government.

Student und Politik was written in the context of a society within which many citizens, and not least students, felt themselves to be increasingly excluded from the formal processes of political decision-making, a discontent that reached a crisis point in protests over the deployment of nuclear weapons by the West German armed forces in 1958.[2] Habermas's analysis of this disengagement from formal political channels centres upon the increasingly interventionist nature of the modern capitalist state, which is itself entwined with the increased concentration of capital in fewer and larger enterprises, and the emergence of mass-membership labour unions. This leads to what Habermas describes as the "disappearance of the difference between state and society" (SP: 34). The analysis largely mirrors that offered in "Between Philosophy and Science" (see § "The capitalist state", p. 5). The bourgeois liberal state that emerged in Europe at the end of the feudal period could be characterized as a "nightwatchman" state (SP: 18), its powers strictly confined in order to guarantee the autonomy of its citizens. Yet the aspiration to universal freedom guaranteed by such a state comes into contradiction with the restricted scope of bourgeois democracy, precisely because the constitutional basis of that democracy in practice serves the interests of the property-owning bourgeoisie. Democracy, in the sense of direct influence over the government, is a reality for only a small minority of the population. In response to this, state activity expands, with increased intervention into society. The twentieth-century capitalist state does not merely guarantee private freedoms, but comes rather to determine the access that all its citizens have to their means of existence. The state thus comes increasingly to check the operations of the free market by regulating the distribution of goods through, for example, labour laws, business contracts, rent and housing regulations and family law (SP: 21–3). The bureaucracies of modern welfare states, of political parties and trade unions and of oligopolistic enterprises serve to transform all sections of society into areas of political control, precisely in so far as all areas of social life are subjected to administration. Traditional class conflicts are blurred, as members of all classes are "functionalised … to serve various public purposes" (SP: 34). The individual citizen becomes increasingly powerless in the face of these administrations and, indeed, unclear as to the very nature of political power. He or she is either reduced to political apathy or seeks means of political action outside formal state and party channels. This discrepancy between political activity and the actual power of the state and economy culminates in the paradox of "unpolitical citizens within ... a political society" (SP: 24).

An apparent resignation to the impossibility of effective political action is checked by Habermas's interest in the radical implications of the liberal conception of democracy. It is here precisely that Habermas's account of the relationship of critique and crisis from *Theory and Practice* may be seen to bear upon his political work (§ "Crisis and critique", p. 20). The experience of crisis, pressing critical judgement forwards towards a decision (TP: 213), requires that the crisis is recognized as a crisis of the human subject. As such, it cannot ultimately fall outside human control, and thus apathy is an inappropriate response. Although liberal democracies may have been flawed in practice, failing to extend effective political power to all citizens, Habermas still finds within these democracies an ideal of political partici-pation, and thus of action on the part of the collective human subject, that transcends its flawed realization. *Student und Politik* may therefore be understood as offering a defence of political participation in the face of an insensitivity to the urgency of the crisis. On the one hand, certain conserva-tive intellectuals, including Schelsky, justify political apathy and scepticism as a bulwark against the political extremism of Fascism (SP: 14, 49), while on the other radicals fail to theorize democratic participation at all. Within Marxism, Adorno and Horkheimer focus on the overwhelming threat of authoritarianism, and lament the fact that no political action can be guar-anteed not to perpetuate authoritarianism. In contrast, Lukács's idealism too readily assumes an easy and inevitable transition to a "dictatorship of the proletariat", that renders redundant bourgeois conceptions of democratic participation.

Habermas is concerned to explore the nature, conditions and real possi-bility of social democracy, and thus to explore the appropriate means by which one might, as it were, press for a decision. By taking liberal ideas of democracy seriously (if critically) he begins to articulate an ideal of democ-racy in terms of the self-governance of a society of mature human beings (SP: 16). The unavoidable structures of political domination and control are kept in check precisely because they are legitimized through their appeal to a self-determining citizenry. Political apathy – which Habermas sees as a result of the failure of the state to cultivate in its citizens the appropriate attitudes and practices of political participation – therefore does not merely open the way for a return to authoritarianism by leaving the exercise of economic and political power unchecked; rather, it inhibits the realization of the only form of government that is rationally justifiable, which is to say government that is grounded in the active self-determination and self-criticism of the society as a whole or, perhaps more dramatically, as the only form of government that might take crises seriously as crises of the collective human subject.

The public sphere

Definitions and origins

The Structural Transformation of the Public Sphere takes up these themes. Again, Habermas responds to capitalism's current crisis through its history. By placing the category of the "bourgeois public sphere" at the centre of this history, he seeks to draw from political and intellectual history certain core normative ideas about the nature of democracy. The public sphere is that realm of social life within which "something approaching public opinion can be formed" (PS: 49). A public sphere comes into existence when citizens communicate, either face to face or through letters, journals and newspapers and other mass media, in order to express their opinions about matters of general interest, and to subject these opinions to rational discussion (ST: 27). Access to the public sphere should be open to all and within the sphere all are treated as equals. The public sphere thus brings together the interest in democracy of *Student und Politik* with Habermas's commitment to rational discourse as an alternative to instrumental and Hegelian reason.

The category of the "public sphere" is conceived by Habermas "as a category that is typical of an epoch" (ST: xvii), which is to say that it comes to exist, both as an institution and as a politically effective idea, for only a brief period: from the late-seventeenth to the eighteenth century. This very transitoriness dictates the structure of Habermas's study. The first part (Chapters I–III) traces the development of mercantile and early industrial capitalism and thus of the emergence of the bourgeois public sphere itself. The final part (Chapters V–VII) charts the decline of the public sphere in the face of the ascendancy of the interventionist social welfare state. These two parts pivot about a critical account of the development of the idea of publicity and public debate in Western political philosophy (Chapter IV). The methodology of *The Structural Transformation of the Public Sphere* thus divorces itself from the structural functionalism that is characteristic of positivistic sociology (ST: xviii), not merely through its historical approach (and not least through its sensitivity to the historical nuances of ordinary language), but crucially by eschewing value-freedom. The ideology critique at the centre of *The Structural Transformation of the Public Sphere* demands that the historical narrative is interpreted as something that has direct relevance to contemporary politics.

Although the concept of the "public sphere" is formed only in the seventeenth century (and its German equivalent, *Öffentlichkeit*, in the eighteenth), the distinction between the public and private can be traced to ancient Greece, as *polis* and *oikos* (ST: 3). The *polis* is the public realm, where citizens who are free of the constraints of material necessity entered into discussion of internal affairs, which is to say the administration of law, alongside the external affairs of waging war (ST: 52). In addition, as a realm of public competition and display, it is the realm of human existence. Hence virtues are those excellences that are tested and acknowledged in public (ST: 4). Under-pinning membership of the *polis* is the male citizen's private mastery over his household [*oikos*], where the household is the principle unit of economic production, so that the private is the realm of material necessity. Economic activity is not a matter for public regulation and debate.

Although the distinction between public and private survives, through Roman law, into the medieval period, it loses the clarity of its Greco-Roman origins (ST: 6). On the one hand, that which is common to all people is public, and as such is set in opposition to the particularity, and thus privacy, of that which attains to the status of the lord or prince. On the other hand, the lord's power to command, which is already distinct from mastery of a household, is "public" [*publicus*]. "*Publicus*" is set in opposition to the common or private, a sense that Habermas notes continues in the modern notion of the "private" soldier, as one who has no authority to command. Crucially, the medieval commons, unlike the Greek public, is not a sphere of active debate. It is rather an audience before which the lord "displayed himself, presented himself as an embodiment of some sort of 'higher' power" (ST: 7). A concept of "publicness" or "publicity" thus holds, in so far as the lord represents his power before the public.

The distinction between public and private is no less ambiguous in the post-medieval period, although it is significantly transformed. Whereas the feudal period entails the extension of the lord's power into all aspects of social life, early capitalism moving towards the "nightwatchman state" (SP: 144) entails an increasingly radical separation of the state from society. The public status of the court and state comes to be set against both the privacy of the intimate realm of the family, and the private or autonomous activity of the economic agent ("civil society"). Between the public and the private realms lies the town, which displaces the court as the principle context of economic, cultural and political life, and thus becomes the context of the public sphere itself (ST: 30, 31–2).

The early stages of capitalism, which are periods of trade rather than of industrial production, develop within the structures of feudal authority. The town is the initial centre of trade, for example in the form of periodic markets and fairs, but such trade does not threaten the territorial author-ity of the feudal lord. Indeed, markets tend to enforce the town's domina-tion of the surrounding region (ST: 15). Gradually, trade breaks out of parochial confines. Again, in its early stages the feudal aristocracy promote this trade, not least as consumers of luxury goods (ST: 16). Early commer-cial expeditions are sponsored by the feudal state. Yet as this trade expands the town ceases to be a relevant basis for the entrepreneur. Indeed, the entrepreneur ceases to be a "burgher" in the strict sense (the craftworker and shopkeeper based in a particular town). The burgher suffers a loss of economic power and status as a new stratum arises, the "bourgeoisie", formed of merchants, bankers and manufacturers, whose activities and interests transcend the limits of any particular town (ST: 23). The protection of these new markets requires the expanded territory of the nation state as the basis of the entrepreneur's operation. This entails the development of government, in the establishment of a standing army to police and protect the territory, but crucially also of a state administration that is principally orientated to tax collection. A single state guarantees the predictability of legal, financial and tax regulation within the territory, thus allowing the entrepreneur to subject risks and potential profits to rational calculation. Public funds, derived from tax revenue, in contradistinction to the private funds of the lord, therefore come to finance capitalist expansion, with the lord himself becoming one more private economic agent (ST: 17–18). Finally, state activity eventually shifts away from the promotion of trade, to the promotion of production (ST: 19).

At the same time, the economic basis of production is removed from the household. Whereas the members of the household may remain economically significant as consumers and labourers, and indeed take on a new sense of privacy in their apparent autonomy, as economic agents, from political interference (ST: 46), production itself has ceased to be a private concern, as it had been in the Greek *oikos*. Production, and thus economics, is of general interest to the population as a whole, and subject to the promotion and regulation by the state (ST: 19). Economic activity is at once private, in so far as it concerns apparently autonomous producers and consumers, and public, in the sense that it is subject to state regulation, but also, in the rise of the joint stock company, in that it requires collective funding.

The public sphere emerges within the complex interplay of the public realm of the state and the private realm of the economic agent and family member. Whereas in feudalism the common people were simply subject to the power of the state, with little or no recourse against state action, within capitalism a public emerges that has a collective awareness of itself as being opposed to the state. It is composed of citizens who are private, in so far as they are excluded from government, although their everyday life, as well as commercial activity, is regulated by state policy. In contradistinction to the feudal commons, this new public develops the institutional and intellectual resources that allow it to subject state policy to rational debate and criticism (ST: 18, 23–4). This bourgeois public sphere takes two forms: a literary public sphere and a political public sphere.

The literary public sphere

Habermas argues that the foundations for the emergence of the bourgeois public sphere lie in the development not simply of the market economy, but of a market for information. From the mid-seventeenth century, so-called "political journals" are published. Whereas information relevant to select groups of merchants had been circulated in the form of private correspondence or "news letters" in the early capitalist period (ST: 16), the political journals selected from "news letters" information of general commercial interest, "about Imperial Diets, wars, harvests, taxes, transports of precious metals, and ... reports on foreign trade" (ST: 20). "Traditional news" of "miracle cures and thunderstorms, the murders, pestilences, and burnings" could also be included (ST: 21). Precisely in its utility to a certain audience, information thereby comes to have a price. Habermas goes further, however, to suggest that official use of these political journals by state authorities served as the first stage in defining a specific readership: that of the bourgeois public itself. "Political journals" or "advertisers" become sources of information that the court and the government wish to be distributed, and thus become instruments of state administration. Overtly addressed to the whole population, in practice they are read by the "educated classes": government administrators, jurists, "doctors, pastors, officers, professors, and 'scholars'", who would in turn distribute information further down the social hierarchy (ST: 23).

This initial determination of an audience is transformed with the rise of modern literature. Crucially, the press shifts from the role of mere informant to become a medium of critical debate. Although the political public sphere proper will exercise reason against the workings of the state, demanding that law is rationally justified, the ability to reason collectively, as it were, or to subject common issues to rational debate, emerges and is honed first of all with respect to the arts. Similarly, "fiction", as opposed to economic and administrative information, becomes the medium through which the bourgeoisie articulates a distinctive sense of its own subjectivity. The status and interests that make it a distinct class cease to be characteristics that are identified and defined from without, by the state; rather, they are internalized through the ideological negotiation of the contradictions of its economic and social position.

The coffee house and the *salon* in the seventeenth century create a public space for the discussion of commerce and culture. Whereas commercial information could be exchanged in coffee houses, so that even the poorest shopkeeper would visit an appropriate coffee house several times a day, they could also be the context within which new ideas were presented and debated: as Habermas rather elegantly speculates, "in the Rotary Club, presided over by Milton's secretary, Marvell and Pepys met with Harrington who here probably presented the republican ideas of his *Oceana*" (ST: 33). Similarly, while the French *salon* of the eighteenth century may have been primarily a place of "gallant pleasures", it was still the forum within which new intellectual and cultural works would be first presented and subject to criticism (ST: 34).

The institutions of the coffee house and *salon* are complemented by the increasing commercialization of the arts. Whereas under feudalism art is an instrument for the representation of feudal power, in ostentatious display or in the organization of state and church ceremonies, in capitalism it becomes an object of bourgeois consumption. Alluding to Benjamin's concept (Benjamin 1970: 223), Habermas notes that art works lose their "aura of extraordinariness" (ST: 36). Art loses its representational function as an audience is formed that consumes art, literature and music for its own sake (ST: 39). That audience also consumes new works, not simply existing classics (FR: 423). Yet the consumption of art, and especially new art, entails that the audience must hazard an expression of taste, and it is here that public reasoning takes on its distinctive form. The overtly subjective judgement of taste is, on the one hand, subject to potential challenges from others. As such, it cannot be a mere expression of personal preference, but must be amenable to public debate and justification. On the other hand, the art critic comes into existence. In distinction from the connoisseur who might have justified aristocratic consumption to a largely passive and ignorant audience of commoners, the bourgeois art critic both provides his audience with justifications for their taste, so educating them, and must also have those justifications accepted by the audience. The art critic is not above his audience, and his very claim to expertise is validated by them. It is thus that the public comes to exercise the force of argument to legitimate and control an authority (ST: 40–41; see Hume 1996).

At the beginning of the seventeenth century, the "periodical" extends the scope of the circle of people who meet through the coffee house. These weekly publications consolidate further the public sphere as a public of readers and writers. Periodicals such as the *Spectator*, *Tatler*, *Guardian* and Dr Johnson's *Rambler* are journals of art, literature and cultural criticism, but also sources of moral comment and debate, through which the bourgeois audience comes to understand itself. Joseph Addison is thus "a censor of manners and morals; his essays concerned charities and schools for the poor … pleas for civilized conduct, polemics against the vices of gambling, fanaticism, and pedantricities" (ST: 43).

If the coffee house, art criticism and the periodical have allowed the bourgeoisie to hone the skills of rational debate and criticism, then it is in the novel that the substance of bourgeois subjectivity is forged. Habermas argues that the novel emerges out of letter writing, primarily through Richardson's *Pamela* (1740–41), and as such it is acutely sensitive to the complex interplay of privacy and publicity that structures bourgeois family life. It is in this construction of what might be called an ideology of intimacy that the political public sphere itself has its foundation. The intimacy of the private realm has now, in contrast to ancient Greece, come to be seen as the space of authentic human existence. In the mid-eighteenth century the letter is an intimate expression of that which is "purely human" in relationships (ST: 48). In the domestic space of the bourgeois home, each family member has his or her own private room within the family house. Yet, paradoxically, the letter and the bourgeois home alike retain a moment of publicity that mirrors the subjection of personal taste to public scrutiny in art criticism. The private living rooms of the house are complemented by a *salon* or parlour, within which the family can represent itself before a public of neighbours and domestic servants (ST: 45). So, too, letters seek an audience far wider than their addressee. Strangers' letters are circulated and copied, and correspondences are published (ST: 49). Richardson's *Pamela* is originally intended as a series of model letters, and only incidentally does the story that it tells take on greater importance. But again, in telling that story, Richardson is publicly representing the intimacies of the bourgeoisie to itself. Thus, in the fictional intimacy of the novel, the reader could prepare for the intimacy of real life (ST: 50–51).

It is precisely the ideological nature of this intimacy that is at stake in the novel. The bourgeoisie's perception of its own autonomy presupposes that it conceals from itself its dependency upon the economy (not least as property-owners). The articulation of intimacy is thus false, in that it publishes an image of the private that conceals its true relationship to the public realm, and conceals the exclusion of the property-less from the bourgeois public. Yet, it contains a moment of truth in its very humanism. It aspires to a relationship between persons that is determined purely by their common humanity (ST: 48) and, akin to the politics of the Greek *polis*, separate from the realm of necessity and production (ST: 160). Thus, even among those who meet in the coffee houses and *salons*, status is disregarded (ST: 36); and the public nature of periodicals, letters and novels entails that they can exclude anyone who has the means to buy and read them (ST: 37). The significance and indeed fate of the political public sphere lies in its articulation of the ideological tension that exists between understanding its members as bourgeois (and thus property-owners) or as general humanity (*l'homme*).

The political public sphere

Habermas's analysis of the political public sphere falls into two parts, reflecting this tension between the bourgeoisie and *l'homme*. What it is to be human, and thus the truth of the public sphere, is realized in the critical examination to which the public sphere subjects government policy and law. The bourgeoisie, and thus its falsehood, lies in the grounding function that this debate plays in continuing class conflict.

In 1784, Frederick II of Prussia could reject the right of private persons to comment on public – which is to say state and court – affairs on the grounds that "a private person is not at all capable of making such judgements, because he lacks complete knowledge of circumstances and motives" (ST: 25). In contrast, in seventeenth- and eighteenth-century Britain and France politicians and scholars alike were beginning to justify the role of public opinion in government. Although for John Locke "opinion" still referred to a largely unreflective and uneducated habits or prejudices and thus, as it were, merely personal preference, the concept already has some overlap with "conscience", and thus a naive awareness of what is just and right (ST: 91–2). It is precisely this *bon sens* to which Rousseau appeals in the general will, but while Rousseau may refer to this as *opinion publique*, public debate is explicitly rejected (for fear of the effects of political discussion on simple people) (ST: 98–9). In Britain, Edmund Burke, in commenting upon the American Revolution, recognizes that legislative power cannot be exercised justly "without regard to the general opinion of those who are to be governed" (ST: 94). Similarly, the French physiocrats accept absolutist government, but only if the power of governors responds to the rational reflection of scholars (ST: 95).

The bourgeois public sphere was most developed in Britain, as was the capitalist mode of production itself, and the ending of censorship gave new scope to the journals to become involved in political comment. The English government had already abolished the major forms of state censorship with the repeal of the Licensing Act, albeit in the face of periodic royal opposition and concerns about the threat of coffee-house discussions. Writers such as Daniel Defoe, Jonathan Swift, John Gay and Alexander Pope were drawn into political comment, for example by the Whig politician Robert Harley (ST: 59), allowing for a gradual shift from the literary and moral periodicals to overtly political and satirical journals, such as the *Review*, the *Observer* and the *Examiner*. Yet the development of something akin to a modern political press, and thus the fourth estate, required two further steps. First, the exclusive government control of political journals had to be relinquished. Only with the rise of opposition publications, in the form of the Tory *Craftsman* and *Gentleman's Magazine* in the early eighteenth century, did the press engage the public in genuine critical debate (ST: 60). Secondly, the prohibition of the reporting of parliamentary proceedings had to be lifted, and indeed access to parliament by journalists had to be made possible. Only in 1803 was space provided for journalists in the House of

Commons (ST: 62). Jeremy Bentham articulated the link between effective public opinion and the principle of publicity in 1816, arguing that if parliament acted in the name of the public, then the public could superintend its deliberations (ST: 100).

If Frederick II distrusted the public's capacity to understand public policy, British political factions and parties increasingly appealed to "the sense of the people", "the common voice" and the "public spirit", not least in opposition to the formal results of elections and the corruption of the governing majority (ST: 63–4). Although these opposition appeals to public opinion were initially weak, they do represent the first moves by which a parliament becomes genuinely accountable to the people. Thus, in 1792, Charles Fox could oppose William Pitt (the Younger) with the demand not merely that parliament should respect public opinion, but that it should also give the public the means of forming that opinion (ST: 66). The truth of the public sphere may therefore be seen summarily to lie in its subjection of parliamentary activity to publicity, and specifically in the recognition that law should be founded not upon the will of the sovereign, but upon the informed reasoning, not just of scholars, as the physiocrats argued, but of the public (ST: 53, 81).

The activities of the mature political public sphere focus significantly upon the legitimation of law. In effect, law as state domination and control cannot rest upon the subjective will of the sovereign, nor yet upon the overt propagation of the partial interests of one class, but only upon public reason (ST: 83). As Habermas observes, the codification of law is thus paradigmatic of the working of the public sphere, as legal reform occurs through the repeated "public scrutiny of private people come together as a public" (ST: 76). More precisely though, Habermas argues that legal reform focused upon the separation of the private realm of the family and civil society (including economic activity) from state interference. Mercantilist policies gradually withdrew state regulation from economic exchange, leaving the economy and society to develop according to the laws of commodity exchange (ST: 80). Thus, for example, by the early eighteenth century in Britain, state regulation of the transference of property, training and wages has been removed (ST: 77). In the bourgeoisie's self-understanding, the intimate sphere of the family and the free market alike are natural forms that have been freed, under capitalism, from their thrall to feudal intervention. Habermas's contention is, rather, that both are constituted in the capitalist period, not least as functions of class struggles over law, political power and the economy. In effect, the very realm of privacy is an ideological construction, facilitating the bourgeoisie's interests in the exploitation of productive property.

Although the bourgeois public sphere may overtly oppose arbitrary sovereign will with the rational justification of law (ST: 83), Habermas identifies a crucial, and familiar, ambiguity in this notion of rationality. The rationality of critical public scrutiny merges with the instrumental rationality. In practice, Habermas suggests, the bourgeois interest in a rational legal system is a concern with instrumental predictability, and not with the inherent justice of dialogical reason (ST: 80). Bourgeois ideology thus revolves about the conflation of, on the one hand, an economic conception of human being (as an instrumentally calculating owner of productive property) with a conception of humanity as such: that is to say, the conflation of the bourgeoisie with *l'homme*. On the other hand, the order of a free-market capitalist economy is conflated with the natural and just order of society as such. Thus, the rights that bourgeois society grants its citizens are the negative, or libertarian, rights that leave the citizen free from interference by the state or any other agent. Political freedoms of public association and expression of opinion are complemented by the protection of the privacy of the intimate realm and freedom of property-ownership (ST: 83). Similarly, the market can appear just because the economic theory of perfect competition (of many small producers, none of whom can dominate the market or exclude new comers) offers an image of equal opportunity. The bourgeoisie does not appear exclusive; everyone has the opportunity, with skill and fortune, to become a property-owner (ST: 87).

The ideological conceit of the bourgeois public sphere is revealed, most significantly, in the role that it plays in class struggle. Habermas implies that revolutionary action is, at best, a minor component in political change. The exercise of political domination, and thus of sovereign will as opposed to dialogical reason, does not end in practice with the ascendancy of the bourgeoisie. If Habermas's ideal of democracy as the self-governance of a society of mature human beings is recalled from *Student und Politik*, then it may be seen that by excluding both the land-owning aristocracy and the proletariat from political participation – by defeating landed interests within parliament and by denying the franchise to the propertyless – the bourgeoisie fails to institute social democracy. More precisely, it corrupts the ideals of democracy to the narrow class interests of capitalist appropriation.

The philosophy of the public sphere

Kant

The pivotal Chapter 4 of *The Structural Transformation of the Public Sphere* ("The Bourgeois Public Sphere: Idea and Ideology") addresses the philosophical struggle with the idea of the public sphere, from Kant to Hegel and Marx in one direction and to the liberals Mill and Tocqueville in the other.

Crucially, it is the inconsistencies of these philosophies that are significant, not least in so far as they reflect the inconsistencies of the material base of their societies. The tensions between bourgeoisie and *homme*, domination and reason find new expression in each philosopher.

Kant poses the problem of good government in terms of the unity of politics and morality. Such a unity would entail that the compulsion necessary to politics should only be exercised through reason, and not through violence (ST: 103). In effect, this would be a society in which citizens obeyed the law not out of fear of the consequences of disobedience, but because they recognized that the legal constitution expressed what was, in any case, their moral duty. Such a society would fulfil Kant's understanding of enlightenment – which itself profoundly informs Habermas's accounts of social democracy and critical theory – as the freeing of humanity from its self-imposed tutelage (ST: 104; Kant 1983a: 33). Politically, tutelage embraces not merely superstition and prejudice but also domination. It is checked by the public use of critical reason, which is to say, by publicity. Yet this simple outline of a just society hides a deceptive complexity. Its complexity turns upon Kant's distinction between the phenomenal and noumenal. The phenomenal realm is the empirical world as it is actually perceived by human beings. The noumenal realm is the world as it is "in itself", independent of human perception, and indeed such that it cannot be comprehended within the structures of thought that are adequate to the phenomenal realm (see § "Kant and transcendental inquiry", p. 60). As phenomenal beings, human beings are sensual creatures, part of the physical, causally determinate world. As noumenal beings, human beings are autonomous and rational. Here, then, is the tension between domination and reason: domination is construed as phenomenal (and politics as a concern of the *res publica phenomenon*); reason is construed as noumenal (so that the just society is a *res publica noumenon*) (ST: 114). In moral politics, Kant attempts to bridge the phenomenal and the noumenal through publicity.

Kant approaches the problem of unifying morality and politics from two directions. On the one side, he attempts to derive the *res publica noumenon* from the *res publica phenomenon*, by assuming that the juridical conditions necessary for a just or moral society are the product of a natural, historically realized, order. On the other side, these juridical conditions are problematized, such that it is assumed that they must be realized through human action, and crucially through educating the population for moral progress. The *res publica noumenon*, as moral progress, thus gives rise to the *res publica phenomenon*.

To make plausible the realization of free moral agency, and thus a just society, within the empirical conditions of existing societies, Kant posits the historical mechanism of "unsocial sociability" (Kant 1983b: 31–2), which is to say that the inevitable conflicts between individuals and societies has the end result of bringing about peace. Within civil society, this is realized as the process within which empirical individuals, who have become selfish by submitting to their desires and passions rather than to their reason, are forced to check their selfishness by acting in public. Publicity is therefore realized in the workings of the free market. More precisely, the agents involved in this market are property-owners. Kant's point is that wage-labourers, precisely because they have to sell their labour in order to survive, and who are thus subordinated to the realm of material necessity, are not in a condition to exercise freedom. Kant has thus neatly reinterpreted the tension between bourgeoisie and *homme*. The conditions of the free market compel the selfish bourgeoisie to behave morally and rationally. Further, *noumenal* freedom finds its concrete articulation only in the material security of the property-owner. This solution is, however, problematic on two counts. First, while the bourgeoisie may outwardly behave morally, it is not clear that anything more has been achieved than a "pathologically enforced social union" (ST: 109). The just society cannot be based upon compulsion, even if that compulsion is realized through a form of publicity. Secondly, the unity of morality and politics depends upon the realization of a particular form of capitalism: the liberal ideal of perfect competition. This realization is a natural process, so that human freedom is compromised, precisely by placing the conditions of freedom outside human control.

If the natural order of unsocial sociability is rejected, then political intervention is required to bring about the appropriate juridical conditions. Crucially, this requires attention to the problem of welfare. As sensuous beings, human beings seek not to be good but to be happy. If the unity of politics and morality is to be realized through the population's free acceptance of the political order, then it must be happy. It is the task of politics "to make the public satisfied with its condition" (ST: 113). Publicity now becomes the process of educating the public in order to bring about moral progress. Only, Kant suggests, as the population becomes more morally refined, approaching the *res publica noumenon*, does the *res publica phenomenon* become possible.

This solution is equally problematic. The concept of moral progress is ambiguous, not least in terms of its implications for the concept of "publicity". The cultivation of morality suggests that publicity is merely a process of public education, and as such presupposes the leadership of an already enlightened class of scholars. Thus, a division between scholars and the unrefined replaces that between the bourgeoisie and wage-labourers. Further, the basis of the scholars' enlightenment is unclear, for they appear to have a grasp of the noumenal goal of political activity, the *res publica noumenal*, prior to its realization. First, it is unclear how this noumenal

41

condition can be worked out in phenomenal terms, other than through imperfect metaphor, allusion and analogy (Kant 1952: §49). Secondly, if publicity is to bear the true weight of public debate, then the goal of a just society cannot be imposed upon the public, but must rather be worked out within the public. It is perhaps not too fanciful to see in Kant's enlightened scholars an anticipation of Lukács's Party, which can impute the truth to an as yet unselfconscious proletariat.

Hegel and Marx

It is in Hegel that Habermas finds the first articulation of the failure of the bourgeois public sphere. Hegel recognizes the conflict of interests that occurs between property-owners and wage-labourers within civil society, and does not seek to resolve it (for example, by assuming, as Kant does, that there is free mobility into the property-owning class). Hegel asserts rather the "disorganisation of civil society" (ST: 119). If civil society is disorganized, then it cannot be the basis of government, for that would entail merely the projection of the conflicts of civil society into the state. Therefore, Hegel argues that the state must be dominant. The public sphere then assumes a purely educative role, rather than a critical one. Mirroring Kant's distinction between scholars and non-scholars, Hegel places matters of scientific and governmental concern outside the competence of the lay public. Public debate can then serve only to inculcate into that public recognition of their common and objective interest in the state. Only thus are the conflicting subjective interests and opinions of the public brought into coherence (ST: 120).

Marx responds to Hegel by grounding his insight into the disorganization of civil society in a thoroughgoing sociological analysis, while rejecting Hegel's regression to an absolutist state. The false consciousness of bourgeois public opinion, not least in its conflation of bourgeoisie and *homme*, is seen to centre about the pretence that the private sphere is apolitical. In contrast, as Habermas's quasi-Marxist analysis has already indicated, the privacy of the bourgeoisie is constructed through a legal system of negative rights protective of property-ownership (ST: 125). Yet the ideal of the public sphere remains valuable, not least because Marx writes at a time when its bourgeois exclusivity is being eroded by the expansion of a proletarian press. The public sphere can be reformed against its bourgeois founders (ST: 126), not least in so far as supposedly private social relations, including the reified relations of economic exchange, are subject to explicit public reflection. Thus, as the public sphere becomes genuinely inclusive, its fundamental nature changes. Whereas the bourgeois sphere grounds autonomy and reason in an illusory privacy, an inclusive public sphere would shift this grounding to the public.

The autonomous person ceases to be a property-owner, and becomes a citizen. Only thus, Marx implies, can domination be subject to reason, precisely because the abolition of class politics entails that domination becomes public, not political (ST: 128–9).

Whereas on one level Marx sees in the inclusive public sphere a penetration of the quasi-natural or reified appearance of social relations, Habermas suggests that on another level he remains enthralled to a philosophy of history that presents the realization of a just society as part of a natural order. In effect, just as the bourgeoisie assumed that the private realm was natural, and had merely been freed from its suppression by the feudal state, so socialists tended to assume a natural economic order that would be freed from the corruptions of capitalism (ST: 140). This is to suggest that Marx remains indebted to the first of Kant's solutions to the problem of the bourgeois public sphere. Autonomy comes with the realization of the naturally just social order. In contrast, liberals such as Mill and Tocqueville may be seen to follow Kant's alternative solution. Responding, on the one hand, to the accuracy of the socialist diagnosis of the bourgeois ideology of the public sphere, and on the other to the failure of the socialist order to be realized, the liberals recognize the need for active political reform to correct the injustice of bourgeois society (ST: 130–31). Put otherwise, while Marx saw in an inclusive public sphere the solution to the disorganization of civil society, the liberals accept that reform of the public sphere only increases its disorganization.

Mill defends the expansion of the franchise, and approves of movements fighting against the "aristocracy of money, gender, and colour, against the minority democracy of the propertied, and against the plutocracy of the *grande bourgeoisie*" (ST: 132). Yet he interprets the resultant disruption of the bourgeois public sphere, whereby its participants' common interests are exposed to criticism by the propertyless, not as the expansion of rational debate and the subjection of domination to reason, but rather as new forms of conflict and domination (ST: 131). The greater number of interests that are brought into the public sphere leads, at best, to compromise rather than rational agreement. Public opinion thus comes to be seen as an amalgam of subjective opinions, and not the result of rational scrutiny. More ominously, public opinion itself becomes a new form of tyranny, where the weight of a majority opinion demands conformity, and thus an intolerance of the non-conformist and critic. While such public opinion may curb the powers of the state, it cannot, as such, be allowed to direct the state. In a gesture that again echoes Kant, Mill and Tocqueville advocate representative government, where, in Mill's words, "political questions be decided … only by appeal to views, formed after due consideration, of a relatively small number of persons specially educated for this task" (ST: 136). Again, the class division within bourgeois society is incorporated in an exclusive conception of the public sphere.

The structural transformation of the public sphere

Social-welfare mass democracy

In charting the decline of the bourgeois public sphere, the final chapters of *The Structural Transformation of the Public Sphere* offer a detailed analysis of the account of late capitalism as it is sketched in "Between Philosophy and Science" and *Student und Politik*. The Great Depression of 1873 is offered as a significant turning point, not least in so far as a profound international crisis in the capitalist system serves to throw into question not merely the taken-for-granted efficacy of the liberal capitalist economies, but also specific illusions of bourgeois self-understanding (ST: 144). The success of the capitalist economies over the preceding century could no longer be understood as a natural phenomenon – as the equilibrium of a free market – but had rather to be seen as the result of particular historical circumstances. The free market as such begins to lose something of its aura of natural justice. In addition, the increasing concentration of capital in large, oligopolistic enterprises gives the lie to the bourgeois faith in the inevitability of perfect competition between small producers (and thus in the belief that all men can aspire to the state of bourgeois property-owner). These changes in self-understanding are accompanied by parallel changes in state activity. The state comes to realize a newly proactive response to crises (see TP: 236–7). On the one hand, the proletariat is granted greater entitlements to political participation, so that their economic immiseration can be challenged through legitimate claims upon the state; on the other, there is an expansion of state activity that seemingly reverses the classical liberal restriction of the state to a "nightwatchman". The state's functions cease to be merely those of maintaining order, and become increasingly those of regulating the economy and mitigating the material inequalities of the capitalist system. The state thus becomes a major provider of goods and services (ST: 146).

This transformation from a liberal state to a social welfare state, which gathers momentum in the late nineteenth century, is presented by Habermas in terms of a constitutional shift from private to public law. The constitution of the liberal state centres upon the role of private laws that specify the freedoms of the bourgeoisie, and as such appears to leave the organization of civil society to the seemingly just and rational mechanisms of free-market exchange. In jurisprudence, Habermas claims, this liberal constitution is only made explicit in the nineteenth century, precisely as the criticism of negative bourgeois legal rights – that they may appear to be politically neutral, but in fact perpetuate a substantive inequality between the propertied and the propertyless – is consciously articulated (ST: 224). The constitutional shift to a welfare state, in the form of public law, responds to this criticism. Public law offers legal protection to those without property through both the redistribution of income and other material resources (such as housing), and the increased regulation of activity in the private spheres of work and the family (ST: 149). Habermas claims that this does not, as legal theorists argue, represent a radically new attempt by the state to organize civil society. First, the exposure of the substantive inequality that characterized liberal capitalism reveals that the capitalist economy is, far from being the natural condition that occurs independently of the state, an order that is maintained by private law. The capitalist state thus always organized civil society. Secondly, overt intervention became necessary in order to maintain the liberal tradition (ST: 224). In effect, as the hollowness of free-market conceptions of justice is exposed, the reproduction of capitalism requires a state guarantee of substantive justice in order to stave off an otherwise irresolvable political crisis.

Public law is not to be characterized simply in terms of the positive rights of welfare provision, but more significantly in terms of the active promotion of mass participation in the political system. If the state is to determine the organization of society, and particularly if it is to do so by respecting not merely the common interests of the bourgeoisie, but rather the diverse and conflicting interests of society as a whole, then a democratic constitution entails that those who determine social policy should be answerable to all, and not merely to specific economically powerful, interest groups (ST: 229–30). An ideal of an expanded public sphere is thus promised, that embraces not just the bourgeoisie but all society. Habermas is concerned precisely to explain the failure of this ideal.

A consequence of the emergence of the social-welfare mass democracies is a breakdown of the hard-won bourgeois distinctions between state and society, and between public and private. Although on the one hand the state intervenes increasingly in society, acting not least as an economic agent, business enterprises and other private organizations come increasingly into interaction with the state and perform tasks for the state (ST: 197). There is thus an "interweaving of the public and private realm" (PS: 54). Given that the bourgeois public sphere functions precisely as a bridge between state and society, any change in the relationship between state and society must impact upon the public sphere. Crucially, it is in its echo of the Greek *polis* that the bourgeois public sphere is most threatened; the Greek *polis* presupposed that rational debate was conducted on the condition that the participants were free of the economic constraints of material necessity. The bourgeois public sphere was similarly protected from the intrusion of economic interests, but only in so far as the capitalist free market had served as the medium through which conflicts of private material interest could be resolved. The issues that came to the public sphere, and as such were seen as the proper subject matter of rational political debate, were of common concern to all members of the bourgeoisie. The bourgeois public sphere thus presupposed that its members shared common interests, not least in so far as any factional conflicts had already been dealt with in the supposed natural justice of the market. It is precisely this commonality that is lost with the interpenetration of state and society. The individual disputants of the bourgeois public sphere are replaced by special-interest associations, including trade unions, political parties, large joint-stock corporations and latterly pressure groups, which represent collective but factional interests. Economic interests are no longer excluded from political debate. This undermines the possibility of rational agreement on the model of the bourgeois *polis*, so that debate is replaced by state-regulated processes of bargaining and haggling, which themselves echo economic exchange (ST: 198).

Late bourgeois subjectivity

This intrusion of issues of material inequality into the public sphere does not, in itself, appear sufficient to undermine it. Habermas's argument must therefore be seen to rest equally upon an analysis of the fate of the bourgeois subject in late capitalism. In bourgeois society, the private realm embraces both the intimacy of the family and the property-owner's autonomous agency in civil society. In the nineteenth and twentieth centuries, the economic foundations of privacy change. The concentration of capital brings about a fundamental transformation in the experience of work. On the one hand, the small-scale entrepreneur is increasingly displaced by joint-stock companies. Control of businesses therefore shifts away from the autonomous individual, and becomes focused in collective and increasingly bureaucratic structures. With the expansion of modern management, even those who do exercise influence over economic decisions do so as paid administrators, and not as property-owners (ST: 152). On the other hand, large enterprises increasingly seek to integrate the worker into the organization, so that single firms can dominate the life of whole towns, through the provision of housing, social and cultural activities, and pensions (ST: 154). In addition, intrusions from the welfare state serve to erode the traditional functions of the family, including education, health care and care of the elderly. The burden created by the risks of unemployment, accident and illness, and even death, now falls on the welfare state (ST: 157). Ultimately income, be it from work or welfare, replaces property as the basis of family life. The family member in late capitalism therefore exercises his or her autonomy not through the deployment of productive capital, nor even, it might be suggested, in response to crises in the human life cycle, but through commodity consumption based upon regular and relatively high incomes. Here in detail is late capitalism's affluent proletariat as proposed in "Between Philosophy and Science" (see § "The capitalist state", p. 5).

A new form of familial intimacy is constituted. From the perspective of the bourgeois property-owner a loss of privacy has occurred, precisely as the eighteenth-century basis of their autonomy is eroded. The illusion that the bourgeoisie may represent humanity as such is no longer tenable; and yet, Habermas suggests, this amounts to a real loss. The bourgeoisie cultivated an image of humanity as genuinely autonomous, precisely in so far as it appeared to act without being restrained by economic necessity, so that, in Kantian terms, the freedom of rational and noumenal selves depends upon a denial of the demands of the phenomenal and sensual self (ST: 160). In late capitalism, all are subservient to economic and government support and regulation, and one's income acts as a source of autonomy in so far as work functions instrumentally to secure one's ability to exercise subjective preferences in leisure-time consumption. Although from the perspective of the wage-labourer this subservience may yield a new "pseudo-private well-being", with work being both more secure and more fully integrated with all other aspects of one's life (ST: 154), the degree to which freedom is still compromised is revealed in the transformation of the consumption of cultural goods.

The eighteenth-century literary public sphere rested, to no small extent, upon the exploitation of a market for information and culture. Crucially, this market made culture more widely accessible by distributing it at an affordable price. Yet the exchange value of the cultural goods remained distinct from their value as culture, precisely because a bourgeoisie that was able and willing to be educated could respond critically to these goods. This critical response is of a distinctive sort, for it cannot be a mere expression of subjective likes or dislikes, but must rather be an opinion that is rationally defensible. In contrast, as modern forms of consumption displace the critical debate of the literary public sphere, late capitalism realizes a form of commodity fetishism that allows exchange relations to penetrate all aspects of social life (ST: 161). Whereas critical debate within the literary public sphere served to bring the cultural resources of the reader up to the level of the work, modern mass markets dilute the quality of the work to the educational level of the mass, by providing works that are unproblematic (or "pre-digested" (ST: 169)) and thus do not require critical reflection. The modern consumer of culture need only appeal to their subjective taste or preference in judging a work, so that, in a gesture that mirrors the positivist's reduction of judgement to radical subjectivity (see § "Ideology critique", p. 11), rational debate of the cultural goods becomes irrelevant. Autonomy thus ceases to be the Kantian exercise of reason, and becomes mere pursuit of sensuous pleasure; subjectivity ceases to be that cultivated by the bourgeoisie in reading and letter writing, which is to say a subjectivity that was orientated to a rational public (ST: 171), and becomes instead something largely interiorized. What discussion there is of cultural goods is reduced to the mere recirculation of already formulated opinions (ST: 246). Even domestic architecture reflects this privatization, as the public, representational space of the parlour is eliminated (ST: 157).

Habermas is thus suggesting that the erosion of the literary public sphere, not least in the face of the emergence of the mass media in the nineteenth and twentieth centuries, has denied the cultural resources necessary for rational debate and critical reflection to those who are newly granted rights of participation in the welfare state. The possibility of a genuinely inclusive public sphere is further undermined by the emergence of modern advertising techniques, and their exploitation, on the one hand, by commercial enterprises through modern journalism, and on the other, by governments and special-interest associations.

Journalism and advertising

Habermas charts the transformation of journalism from its overtly political form at the end of the eighteenth century to its modern commercial form (ST: 180–89). The formulation of legal constitutions, and thus the moment of transition between liberal and welfare state, is again presented as central. Prior to the establishing of constitutional freedoms, the press either bowed before political censorship, publishing what information it could, or it made freedom of political expression its theme (ST: 184). The latter approach, primarily concerned as it was with political debate within the public sphere, could rarely if ever be commercial. While the removal of censorship is significant to the development of the press, more important is the transformation of all commercial activity under the welfare state. The press is able to exploit not merely the new freedom of expression, but also the newly arising opportunities for advertising. Producers in expanding oligopolistic markets require advertising in order to stabilize markets so that they can absorb the long-term mass production of goods (ST: 189). The readership of a newspaper thus ceases to be of commercial value in itself, for it becomes merely instrumental to selling advertising space within the newspaper, and it is this space that becomes the source of the publisher's profits. The press no longer addresses itself to a bourgeois public who engage in rational and critical debate, but rather to individual consumers, who need only express their subjective preferences for the goods advertised in its pages.

The rise of advertising exemplifies the transformation of the relationship of the private and public realms in late capitalism. Whereas the bourgeois public sphere functioned on the condition that competition between private economic interests was resolved independently of public involvement, advertising makes private economic competition a public event. Advertising presents the private interests of the producer before the public (ST: 192). This occurs more subtly in the form of public relations (or opinion management), which Habermas characterizes as advertising aware of its political character. Thus, while the advertisement addresses the individual consumer, public relations addresses the public as a whole, by seeking to defend the interests of the organization in the face of public criticism. Habermas cites the emergence of public relations in the responses of the Standard Oil Company and the Pennsylvania Railroad to criticisms from social reformers (ST: 193). Advertising and public relations are forms of publicity precisely in that they seek to evoke the approval of a public. Yet, in contrast to the publicity characteristic of the bourgeois public sphere, they neither address the public as a single body – appealing rather to a public that is little more than an aggregate of discrete individuals – nor allow critical reasoning. Critical responses are deflected, in so far as the private interests that motivate the public relations message are typically concealed within a more or less spurious appeal to public welfare and, crucially, the factional values that inform the appeal are concealed behind a presentation of seemingly objective (although in practice highly selective or manipulated) facts (ST: 194). The degree to which advertising takes on a political function and, crucially, the degree to which it becomes the form through which the private interests of all special-interest associations are pursued within a welfare state, is therefore indicative of the corrupting effect that it has on the possibility of realizing rational debate in an expanded public sphere.

Politics

Public relations becomes the dominant instrument of political communication with the rise of the modern political party in the nineteenth century. The eighteenth-century parliamentarian had been primarily answerable to his constituency electorate, which was constituted as a public sphere. As such, the parliamentarian stood as an equal, in rational debate with the electorate (ST: 204). In this context, political parties remain informal alliances, held together through periodic meetings that allowed for rational debate between parliamentarians and constituents (ST: 202). In contrast, the nineteenth century sees the emergence of formally organized parties, initially representing class interests, and then striving for broader appeal to the population as a whole. Such parties develop through increased internal bureaucratic organization, so that the parliamentarian becomes a professional politician, primarily accountable no longer to the electorate, but rather to the party organization. In effect, the politician is now a member of the party before they are a member of the public. Similarly, the party itself breaks its discursive links to local constituencies so that it is no longer led by the constituency. Rather, advertising, public relations and propaganda are drawn upon by the party in order to elicit acclamation for its policies from as large a portion of the electorate as possible (ST: 203, 215). The pressing goal of the political party becomes the securing of power, not the pursuit of the substantive concerns of the electorate.

Habermas's point, crucially, is not that the electorate are the passive dupes of the party systems (no more than consumers are dupes of commercial advertising). Parties, like commercial enterprises, are answerable to the public in so far as their products and their policies can be rejected. Yet advertising techniques have an insidious power, precisely in so far as they short-circuit any appeal to rational reflection, not least by appealing to unconscious inclinations (ST: 217). Habermas suggests that the parties appeal to the "real needs" (ST: 218) of the electorate, which is to say that their messages are sensitive to the discontents and longings of the population. A failure on the part of the party to gauge accurately these discontents, or to offer a suitable response, will meet with rejection. However, to appeal to these felt needs does not entail meeting them. The rational reflection that would allow the felt need to be analysed, so that one may consciously recognize the "objective interests" (ST: 219) of which it is symptomatic, is denied to the public by advertising and public relations. Indeed, the party is similarly denied the possibility of rational reflection if it analyses these discontents through positivistic social surveys, which access only opinions and attitudes (ST: 243), and not the mediation of the individual subject by objective social structures. It is thus being suggested that advertising operates in a form that is analogous to that found in dreams according to psychoanalytic theory: the dream is an illusory solution to a real problem (see § "Critical theory (Freud)", p. 92 on psychoanalytic theory). The task of the analysis is to identify the objective problem, and thus an objective solution. In politics, specifically, it may be suggested that discontents and longings typically have their objective roots in the injustices of the capitalist system. With the rise of a newly affluent proletariat of consumers – making value judgements only in terms of its immediate subjective preferences, and indeed addressing themselves to the state primarily as clients who demand goods and services, and not as citizens (ST: 211) – and the concomitant transformation of class antagonisms, the electorate is unable any longer to recognize any such injustice, and the dominant parties – which are no longer concerned to articulate the grievances of particular social classes, but only to appeal at a necessary superficial level to the electorate as a whole – take no lead in educating the population out of this political immaturity (ST: 203). Elections therefore cease to be genuinely political events during which the direction of society can be subjected to rational scrutiny. Rather, they become plebiscites, through which parties seek nothing more than public acclaim for their policies, in order to secure power.

It is in analysing public relations that Habermas's grim comment from *Theory and Practice*, that in contemporary society the population is "allowed to do, in the consciousness of their freedom, what do they must" (TP: 196; see § "An affluent proletariat", p. 6) has its grounding. He cites Adorno, who sees the ideology of mass culture "as a glorifying reduplication and justification of the state of affairs that exists anyway", encapsulated in the slogan, "Become what you are" (ST: 216). The electorate thus respond actively to the political process, but ultimately do so, not as rational disputants within a public sphere, but as discrete consumers. The objective economic and political structures that underpin their divergent and conflicting interests cannot be debated, because public relations and political propaganda have served to construct an illusory common interest, which offers a distorted mirroring of the common interests of the eighteenth-century bourgeoisie. Public opinion has been replaced by "non-public opinion" (ST: 211), which is to say, a mere aggregate of individual preferences.

Habermas thus offers a bleak picture of contemporary society. The promise of the bourgeois public sphere has been broken, and the intertwining of state and society has lead to a "refeudalisation" (ST: 231), such that the public ceases to be a source of rational criticism of the exercise of power, and becomes rather a group before which special-interest associations display their prestige and reputation (ST: 201).

Yet this is not Habermas's final conclusion. In answer not least to the pessimism and quietism of Adorno, he refuses to condemn political practice as futile. The power of political propaganda and public relations is never, for Habermas, complete or overwhelming. He identifies two competing tendencies in the social-welfare state: the staged publicity of propaganda and public relations and the genuinely critical processes of public communication (ST: 232). Although the latter may be the weaker, Habermas still argues that public spheres may exist within bureaucratic organizations (ST: 248). This is to suggest that while debate between autonomous individual citizens may no longer be politically effective, the individual can still influence organizations, and thus influence the clash between special-interest associations. Crucially, this offers the possibility of state organizations being held in check by equally well-organized political parties and pressure groups (ST: 233), a structure that would mirror the bourgeois public sphere's check on the liberal state. The ideal of a democratically accountable welfare state is thus realizable through "political autonomy" (which is to say, debate and negotiation between associations that are rationally accountable to their members), rather than through the "private autonomy" of the bourgeoisie (ST: 232). Ultimately, Habermas is concerned to defend the continuing relevance of the ideal of objective interests that can be pursued through rational debate (ST: 234). Such a pursuit might, he suggests, be further facilitated by an increase in affluence, which would make struggles over private access to resources irrelevant, or more darkly, by the prospect of nuclear annihilation, relative to which factional private interests pale into insignificance (ST: 234–5).

Further reflections

In 1989, on the occasion of a new German edition of *The Structural Transformation of the Public Sphere* and the publication of an English translation, Habermas offered a series of "Further Reflections on the Public Sphere" that provided a response to the book's critics as well as his own view of its arguments some 30 years after its original publication.[3] Perhaps predictably, given the significant development of his social theory in the intervening years, Habermas expresses his dissatisfaction with what he sees as an overly simplistic account of society. Yet, he confirms much of the general analysis, and not least the importance of democracy and the centrality of rational public debate to a democratic society.

A number of commentators had pointed to an imbalance in tone between the first and last sections of *The Structural Transformation of the Public Sphere*, in so far as the positive account of the ideal of the bourgeois public sphere is met by an unduly negative account of its twentieth-century decline (FR: 430). Habermas acknowledges this, noting that the narrative of a shift from a "culture-debating to a culture-consuming public" was too simplistic and pessimistic (FR: 438). Whereas this pessimism is attributed in part to the political context of Germany in the late 1950s, theoretically Habermas identifies a weakness in the account of human subjectivity, not least in its indebtedness to Adorno. In an argument that mirrors his general criticism of Adorno – to the effect that by overplaying the all-pervasiveness of reification, he at once leaves the human subject in hopeless isolation and fails to recognize its inextinguishable discursive capacity (see § "The failure of dialectics", p. 24) – Habermas criticizes *The Structural Transformation of the*

Public Sphere for failing to take sufficient account of the embeddedness of the human subject in the lifeworld, and thus of the mundane discursive abilities of human beings (FR: 437).

This entails that the remnants of the public sphere need not be confined within narrowly conceived bureaucratic associations, as the most optimistic strands of *The Structural Transformation of the Public Sphere* suggested. On the one hand, the public sphere is realized in the everyday activity of competent social actors. Habermas finds illustrations of this in the part that public discussion continues to play in determining voting behaviour (FR: 438), and in the active and critical responses of which mass media audiences are capable (FR: 439). On the other hand, Habermas identifies a series of "voluntary unions" that lie outside of the state and the economy. These include "churches, cultural associations ... academies ... independent media, sport and leisure clubs, debating societies, groups of concerned citizens and grass-roots petitioning" (ST: 453), which reflect the institutional diversity and complexity that continue to characterize public debate, and that may ground sources of political resistance (as the political changes in central Europe in the late 1980s exemplified) (ST: 454–5). It may, however, be noted that Habermas can still conclude his reflections by noting the pervasiveness of the mass media in contemporary life, such that major political events, including the break up of Soviet communism in the late 1980s, are such that their very "*mode of occurrence*" is televisual (FR: 456).

Beyond the level of the subject, Habermas indicates that the theoretical weakness of *The Structural Transformation of the Public Sphere* lay in an excessively holistic account of society: society is approached as a "totality" (FR: 443). In part, this may be seen in a failure to recognize the degree to which the bourgeois public sphere takes on its particular character by actively excluding certain groups. Although *The Structural Transformation of the Public Sphere* was sensitive to the ideological tensions between the public sphere's overt openness to all and its actual exclusion of the proletariat, Habermas acknowledges that an overwhelming focus upon the bourgeois public sphere underestimates the rational discursive activity that occurs within what he calls the "plebeian" public sphere (ST: xviii; FR: 423) – and which Oskar Negt and Alexander Kluge have subsequently analysed as the proletarian public sphere (1972). Crucially, this is not a mere question of the narrow focus of the account, but rather a neglect of the role that the relationship between the bourgeois and proletarian public spheres played in the constitution of the former.

Habermas acknowledges that *The Structural Transformation of the Public Sphere* treats the proletariat largely as a backdrop to the activities of the bourgeoisie (FR: 427). This issue is equally significant with respect to the role of women within the public sphere. Although the literary public sphere may have included women, the exclusion of women from the political public sphere is significant, again, in so far as the public sphere comes to take its very character from this exclusion. In effect, Habermas raises the possibility that what he had supposed to be the ideal form of the public sphere, and thus a model of rational democratic processes, was an essentially patriarchal structure, predicated upon the exclusion and exploitation of women (FR: 428). The development of Western liberal politics may then be seen to be fundamentally flawed by its inherent blindness to issues of gender.

Yet Habermas counters this criticism by suggesting that the radical discontinuity presented in *The Structural Transformation of the Public Sphere*, between the eighteenth-century public sphere and its late capitalist counterpart, is too stark. He suggests that the eighteenth-century public sphere was presented as too homogeneous an entity. If the bourgeois public sphere is itself seen to be characterized by conflicting interest groups (and thus by "the coexistence of competing public spheres" (FR: 425)), there is scope to see the relationship between early and late as one of self-transformation, rather than as decline (FR: 430). A heterogeneous bourgeois public, which is also actively negotiating its relationship to the plebeian public spheres, has the potential to find space for the voice of marginalized groups (including women, the proletariat and ethnic minorities). The structural transformation is thus not a simple decline into a society of passive culture consumption, but rather an opening of political debate.

Habermas is able to conclude that the analysis and defence of democracy that lay at the heart of *The Structural Transformation of the Public Sphere* may be found wanting. At its heart lay an account of radical democracy that was indebted to Abendroth: the importance of the public sphere lay in its supposed capacity to allow citizens to "generalize their interests and to assert them so effectively that state power is transformed into a fluid medium of society's self-organisation" (FR: 431). It is precisely this image of the self-organization of society that Habermas now questions. First, he suggests that the complexity of contemporary society is such that economic and bureaucratic institutions can no longer be brought under the control of processes of public debate that are rooted in the lifeworld. At best, the purpose of democratic debate shifts to providing a bulwark against the further encroachment of economic and administrative processes into everyday life: in effect, a bulwark against the further transformation of the citizen into a client or consumer (FR: 444).

Secondly, if political debate has limited influence on the economy, then the emphasis that *The Structural Transformation of the Public Sphere* places upon the role of economic conflict in the supposed decline of the public sphere is misplaced. In abandoning the assumption of an original homogeneity in the constitution of the bourgeois public sphere, Habermas opens up the possibility of understanding the public sphere, and thus the process of democratic debate itself, as an inherently pluralistic exercise. Politics ceases to be exclusively, or even primarily, concerned with economic interests. While questions of justice, understood as the equitable distribution of social resources, remain significant, the resolution of these questions will depend upon the achievement of a collective understanding of empirical issues (including the current political and economic conditions and the consequences of policy proposals), but more importantly of "existential issues" (FR: 448). Such existential questions concern the understanding that communities have of their self-identity – of, as it were, what it means to be Welsh, female, a teenager, gay – and of the good life to which they aspire. It is precisely in such issues that a democratic public sphere may be required to give a voice to marginal and deprived groups. Major strands of Habermas's subsequent work may therefore be seen to concern the development, not just of a more sophisticated theory of society, but also of a more sophisticated account of such a democracy, and the open and rational processes of public deliberation that characterize it.

CHAPTER 3

The idea of critical theory

Introduction

After his return to the University of Frankfurt, Habermas published a series of works that brought new focus and coherence to his critique of positivism and his understanding of exactly what is entailed by "a theory of society conceived with a practical intention" (TP: 1). At the core of this work is the attempt to counter "scientism", the tendency of positivism to regard the methods of the natural sciences as the only legitimate form of meaningful inquiry (KHI: 4). *On the Logic of the Social Sciences*, published in 1967, responds to the dominance of scientism in the philosophy of the social sciences by reviewing a "spectrum of nonconventional approaches" to philosophy and social theory, including the philosophy of language, hermeneutics and phenomenology (LSS: xiii), which might facilitate the rethinking of the nature of sociology as a discipline.

In 1968 Habermas published a collection of five essays, *Technik und Wissenschaft als "Ideologie"*. The three central essays, "Technology and Science as 'Ideology'", "Technical Progress and the Social Life-World", and "The Scientization of Politics and Public Opinion" (TRS: 50–122), may be seen to work out the critique of positivism in terms of the social and political relationships that hold between positivism and contemporary capitalism. The first and last essays, which frame the collection as a whole, provide the initial account of a theory – the theory of cognitive interests – that would be articulated in the other major publication of 1968, *Knowledge and Human Interests*.

Knowledge and Human Interests may be regarded as the culmination of this period of Habermas's career. The problem of justifying a critical social science comes into clear focus as a crisis – in the full weight that Habermas attributes to that term – in epistemology (i.e. the theory of knowledge). The dominance that positivism had gained over analytic philosophy is seen to have undermined the tradition of epistemological inquiry that had culminated in Kant's *Critique of Pure Reason* (first published in 1781) (KHI: 3–5). Habermas claims that the core question in Kantian epistemology of how reliable knowledge is possible has been corrupted into "the pseudo-normative regulation" of natural scientific research, that is, a limited concern with the rules and methods that "good" science follows (KHI: 4). As such, Habermas contends, philosophy has ceased to comprehend science. In effect, philosophy has allowed critical reflection on the nature and status of knowledge to wither into little more than quibbling over the efficacy and consistency of experimental method. The crisis of epistemology, which is explicitly presented in terms of Horkheimer's critique of traditional theory (see § "Traditional and critical theory", p. 8), is mirrored in a crisis of science itself, for, in the words of the phenomenologist Edmund Husserl, "in our vital state of need … science has nothing to say to us" (KHI: 302). Habermas therefore sets himself the task of recovering the epistemological ground that has been lost to positivism, for the issue of the "vital state of need" may be handled only by sciences that have gone beyond the subjective and non-rational arbitrariness of decisionism.

In this vein, *Knowledge and Human Interests* reconstructs "the prehistory of modern positivism" (KHI: vii), offering a spectacular review of the development of epistemology and the philosophy of science since the beginning of the nineteenth century. At the core of this account is the struggle between a dominant positivism and the subordinate but more reflective and critical non-positivist understandings of the natural and the social sciences. As such, and again in sharp contrast to scientism, it seeks to differentiate three scientific types: the empirical-analytic or natural sciences; the historical-hermeneutic or social sciences; and the emancipatory science of critical theory. Each of these types generates a different form of knowledge, and each form of knowledge has relevance and validity under quite precise, but quite distinct, conditions.

Knowledge and interests

If a theme is to be sought that unifies Habermas's critique of positivism and his history of the public sphere, then it may be found in the threat that he identifies in the predominance of instrumental reason. The confinement of rationality to instrumental rationality leads to decisionism (and thus the inability to reflect upon and assess values and goals), and to scientism (for in so far as instrumental reason underpins the natural sciences, the natural sciences become the only legitimate model of inquiry). Habermas's frustration at the inability of the earlier generation of Frankfurt School theorists – and indeed other neo-Marxists, including Lukács – to find a workable alternative to instrumental reason has been noted (see § "The failure of dialectics", p. 24). In his contributions to the positivism dispute Habermas had already begun to outline an alternative to both the instrumental reason of the positivists and the dialectical reason of the neo-Marxists, by looking to the interpretative and communicative competences of lay actors in the lifeworld. *The Structural Transformation of the Public Sphere*, in its bleakest moments, charts the erosion and marginalization of these competences, as the bourgeois public sphere collapses into the decisionistic plebicites of modern democracies.

Habermas's early studies have, therefore, been seen to highlight the problem of articulating a form of rationality that could inform the social sciences and political practice (and thus an emancipatory critical theory). Yet this leaves unremarked a further problem: that of the status of the natural sciences. There is a tendency among the first-generation Frankfurt theorists to reject natural science along with instrumental reason. Habermas finds this tendency in the work of Adorno (who alludes vaguely to a science grounded in a mimetic, pre-rational relationship with nature, as opposed to domination over nature) and Marcuse (TRS: 81–5). Marcuse develops Weber's rationalization thesis in order to analyse the loss of revolutionary potential in contemporary capitalism. Weber's instrumental rationality is understood, by Marcuse, to be grounded in the domination of nature and of human beings. For Marcuse, instrumental reason is a rationality of domination. Although any relations of production (such as the bureaucratic administration of late capitalism) that are structured in term of instrumental reason will therefore be repressive, this repression is concealed. The classic contradiction between relations and forces of production that Marx identified is defused as social agents conform to the demands of the relations of production, conformity being the most effective way of realizing for themselves the material affluence that late capitalism has to offer. In effect, while for Marx the productive potential of technology motivated an immiserated proletariat to revolution, today the productive potential of technology is wholly conservative. In addition, any critical stance towards capitalist relations of production is inhibited, precisely because instrumental rationality seemingly serves as the only available ground of legitimate criticism. This much should already be familiar (from § "Late capitalism", p. 5) and as such outlines a thesis to which Habermas is broadly sympathetic.

The problem with Marcuse's argument is revealed when the status of the natural sciences is considered. If natural science is grounded in instrumental reason, and instrumental reason is not, contra positivism, politically neutral, then natural science must be a construct of some kind. It does not represent pure knowledge, but rather knowledge generated in the interests of a dominant class. Yet Marcuse is accused of leaping too readily to the conclusion that the most basic presuppositions of the natural sciences – their "transcendental framework" (TRS: 86) – are exclusively "determined by class interest and historical situation" (TRS: 85), which would be to say that modern science is, in Lukácsian terminology, a "bourgeois science". In contrast, Habermas turns to Gehlen (TRS: 87), who argues that while contemporary technology is necessarily grounded in instrumental reason, it must be understood as an expression of a basic human engagement with the natural world. In order to survive, the human animal must use its body to engage instrumentally with its physical environment. Technology is merely the extension of this bodily engagement, as machines are designed to substitute for and to improve upon the work done by our bodies. Technology grounded in instrumental reason is thus a precondition of human survival. Marcuse's attempt to articulate the idea of a new technology, in which "the viewpoint of possible technical control would be replaced by one of preserving, fostering, and releasing the potentialities of nature" (TRS: 86), is thus rejected as an impossibility. It is inconceivable that even a politically emancipated humanity could develop a distinctive, non-repressive, attitude towards nature, that could still find expression in a reliable technology.

While questioning Marcuse's reduction of contemporary science to class interests, Habermas still accepts that science and technology – and indeed nature, as it is construed as the object of scientific inquiry – must be understood as constructs. The knowledge yielded by natural science and its associated technology is constituted by human beings engaged in a particular type of activity (albeit an activity that is necessary to their survival). Other creatures and, more significantly still, human beings involved in other types of activity will generate other forms of knowledge. Habermas is not therefore rejecting Marcuse's position out of hand. Rather, he is seeking a middle course between the wholesale reduction of science to class interests, and the positivist elevation of science into a pure theory free of any contaminating interests. Habermas accepts something of the positivist notion of ideology critique, whereby the "sewage of emotionality" (TP: 265), or enthralment to particular external interests, is to be rejected. A fascist "national physics" or a "Soviet Marxist genetics" are thus unacceptable (KHI: 315). Yet the implication to be drawn from Gehlen is that certain interests, grounded in the very nature of what it is to be human have a foundational importance that transcends any accusation of particularity. They are universal, in so far as they serve to shape knowledge and the objects of knowledge for all human beings. Gehlen's claim, crucially, is sufficient to begin the reinstatement of the epistemological question of the conditions under which reliable knowledge is possible. Knowledge ceases to be the mere description of "a universe of facts" and their lawlike connections (KHI: 304), as positivism suggests.

Marcuse's appeal, in explicitly Kantian terminology, to the "transcendental framework" of the natural sciences recognizes precisely this point. For Kant, the transcendental framework constitutes the conditions of the possibility of knowledge, which is to say, the conditions that allow the disparate elements of human experience to be brought together (or synthesized) into a coherent understanding of the world. Marcuse's fault, again, lies in too readily reducing this framework to particular political and historical conjunctions, and, ironically mirroring scientism, by assuming that there is but one legitimate form of knowledge, which embraces natural and social sciences alike.

Habermas's claim against Marcuse may therefore be summarized by suggesting that it is not technology or natural sciences as such that are at fault. Within their appropriate range of reference, the natural sciences as currently practised do offer valid knowledge. The problem lies in the positivistic self-understanding of the natural sciences that inhibits philosophical reflection upon their conditions of possibility. This inhibition serves to extend them beyond their legitimate range, and to undermine alternative forms of reliable knowledge. The core issue for *Knowledge and Human Interests*, therefore, is to explicate exactly what the "transcendental framework" of the sciences might be.[1]

Knowledge and Human Interests

Kant and transcendental inquiry

Habermas describes his approach to epistemology as "quasi-transcendental" (TP: 14). Although Kant uses "transcendental" in a number of different ways, according to context (see Caygill 1995: 399–402), its core meaning embraces a distinctive approach to epistemology that synthesizes the two seemingly incompatible approaches that had, to that point, characterized the history of philosophical inquiry: rationalism and empiricism. In broad terms, rationalism takes as its model of knowledge deductive reasoning, as found in mathematics and formal logic. If the premises of a deductive argument are true, then the conclusion that is derived from them must also be true. For the rationalist, knowledge claims therefore aspire to this deductive certainty. On the other hand, empiricism appeals to induction, whereby a set of empirically perceived facts are brought together by being explained in terms of a single general law.

Criticisms of rationalism and empiricism seem to highlight their differences. Rational deduction is held to be unable to generate new knowledge, for deduction can merely make explicit what is already implicit in the premises. Crucially, for the rationalist to say anything at all presupposes the truth of the initial premises. Although empiricism may embrace new and unexpected knowledge claims, precisely because it relies upon potentially novel experiences, as Popper argues (see § "Reason", p. 14) induction can never guarantee the truth of the general laws to which it gives rise. However, further reflection suggests that the rationalist and the empiricist share a basic similarity of approach. First, both presuppose that the knowing subject is fundamentally distinct from the object that is to be known. The problem of epistemology (which is to say, the problem of determining the conditions under which reliable knowledge is to be obtained) is either that of establishing the rational clarity needed to grasp indubitable first premises and to make deductions from them, or that of removing all prejudices that might cloud one's sensory perception. Secondly, as this already suggests, both presuppose some given starting-point. For rationalism this is the intuitive certainty of its initial premises; for empiricism it is the givenness of empirical experience. Both are therefore what are known as "first philosophies" (KHI: 8–10). Kant's transcendentalism begins to challenge both forms of these presuppositions.

A transcendental argument rests on the recognition that the conditions for reliable knowledge must lie in the way in which the subject actively constitutes that object. Thus, as has already been suggested by Horkheimer's account of critical theory, the subject and object are not treated as fundamentally separate. Crucially for Kant, human beings can have knowledge only of the way in which the world appears to them as human beings. Human beings can know only what Kant calls the "phenomenal" world – a world for us – as opposed to the world as it is in itself, or "noumena", which may be considered as the world from a god's eye view or, in the rationalist Leibniz's term, *sub specie aeternitatis* (under the eye of eternity). In part, the world appears as it does to human beings because of the limitations of the human senses; presumably bats, dogs and dolphins, with different or expanded senses, live in a very different world from that of human beings. However, this is perhaps the least important aspect of the phenomenal world. The senses yield, for Kant, only an inchoate "manifold of sensation" (Kant 1933: A20/B34). Kant argues that, while substantial knowledge of a contingent world cannot be acquired through deductive reason alone, equally little of the solidity and regularity that is taken for granted about the phenomenal world can be proved to be derived, as empiricists assume, from sense experience alone. The human mind must therefore actively shape sense experience, constituting, rather than merely encountering, objects of knowledge. The cognitive faculties of the human mind are such that, even prior to any sensuous experience, they are prepared to grasp and understand that experience within a certain framework of structures and conceptual forms (including time and space, and causality). But equally they can experience and comprehend the world *only* within this particular transcendental framework. The objectivity of human knowledge therefore lies, for Kantians, in the necessity of its conforming to the transcendental framework, and in its universality, in so far as every individual human being constitutes his or her phenomenal world in the same way.

We need not worry about the details of this process of constitution here. What is important are the dual claims that the human mind constitutes the phenomenal world and that it can have reliable knowledge only of that phenomenal world. Kant's *Critique of Pure Reason* is, in large part, concerned to demonstrate that knowledge claims about the noumenal world, and thus about many of the traditional areas of metaphysics, are unreliable. If reliable knowledge is confined to a causally determinate realm that exists within time and space, then there is no sense in which human beings can have knowledge of, for example, a divine being that exists outside time or space, or of a human free will that could operate outside the constrictions of causality. This is to say not that such entities may not have some noumenal reality, but merely that human beings cannot prove their existence, nor even properly comprehend them. Human beings simply cannot formulate a consistent idea of God, and however brilliant images of God such as those by Michelangelo or William Blake may be, they are but visual metaphors for something that surpasses human understanding. To summarize, then, by unfolding the structures that the subject deploys to shape the phenomenal world, transcendental analysis has brought to consciousness the conditions of reliable knowledge and, by implication, the abuse of such knowledge in the extension of its cognitive structures beyond the phenomenal world.

By describing his approach as "quasi-*transcendental*", Habermas clearly seeks to reinstate something of this Kantian perspective (not least in the face of the regress of positivism). He echoes Kant in arguing that the conditions of knowledge in which he is interested "cannot be either logically deduced or empirically demonstrated" (KHI: 312). The project of *Knowledge and Human Interests* is, therefore, neither an empirical science, which might reduce knowledge to sociological or biological imperatives, nor yet an exercise in pure reason, seeking a definition of objective knowledge *sub specie aeternitatis*, free of contaminating interests. As with Kant, it seeks the foundation that makes reliable knowledge possible. In effect, it seeks the conditions that make possible the human act of constituting reality as something knowable. Yet, precisely by labelling this a "*quasi*-transcendental" inquiry, Habermas marks his break from Kant.

Habermas offers two broad criticisms of Kant. First, Kant begins his transcendental inquiry already knowing what knowledge is. As such he smuggles into his argument a form of "first philosophy". The prototypes for knowledge are provided by Newtonian physics and Euclidean geometry (KHI: 14). This is problematic in that it tacitly closes off reflection both on the history of the acquisition of knowledge and on the possibility of a diversity of different forms of knowledge. It thus exercises a conservative "pseudonormative force" (KHI: 14) that anticipates positivism. Rather than openly reflecting upon competing claimants to the status of knowledge, Kant legitimizes a single, historically dominant, form. Secondly, Kant fails to reflect adequately upon the knowing subject. Although the transcendental method has opened up the possibility that the object is constituted by the subject, and told us much about the constitutive powers of that subject, it has tacitly silenced further reflection on the constitution of the subject. The history of the subject is lost, and what, in the light of the reflections in *The Structural Transformation of the Public Sphere*, might be considered as the "bourgeois subject" is rendered as a given (KHI: 15–16).

Kant is therefore accused of forestalling the process of critical reflection at crucial points. Genuine critical reflection must therefore, on the one hand, take into account the open-endedness of human knowledge. No particular manifestation of knowledge can stand as the prototype of knowledge per se, for that manifestation is in principle falsifiable (as Popper argues). The theories of neither Newtonian physics nor Euclidean geometry have survived into the twenty-first century as knowledge. On the other hand, the subject cannot be the disembodied transcendental subject of Kantianism but, after Gehlen, must rather be understood as the physical human being as it is manifest as a natural and social being. In effect, Habermas continues to seek transcendental conditions, but searches for them at a deeper level than did Kant: at a level that makes possible both knowledge as a diverse, historically unfolding human achievement, and a humanity that realizes itself, coming to consciousness of itself, in history.

Hegel, labour and interaction

The categories of "labour" and "interaction" serve Habermas in the articulation of this deeper, quasi-transcendental framework within which the human subject and human knowledge unfold. Yet they are also the terms within which Habermas formulates a critical review of post-Kantian philosophy, as Hegel, Marx, the philosophy of science and even the Frankfurt School are assessed in terms of the adequacy with which they make this distinction.

The dichotomy of labour and interaction may be approached, at least initially, as ways of classifying human activity. Labour or purposive-rational action embraces those activities that are structured in terms of the attempt to realize specific goals under given conditions. It is defined as "either instrumental action or rational choice or their conjunction" (TRS: 91), in which the most effective means for controlling and transforming an environment are organized to the achievement of any given end. It is the engagement of the human species, as a tool-using animal, with its physical environment. "Interaction", on the other hand, concerns communicative action or symbolic interaction, which is to say, meaningful exchanges between human beings. It is governed not by instrumental reason, but by binding consensual norms, "which define reciprocal expectations about behaviour and which must be understood and recognized by at least two acting subjects" (TRS: 92).

Habermas finds the first elaboration of the concepts of "labour" and "interaction" in the work of the young Hegel. Hegel's lectures at the University of Jena between 1803 and 1806 – and thus prior to work on *The Phenomenology of Mind* (1807) and substantially before his *Encyclopedia of the Philosophical Sciences* (1817) – presented his then understanding of the relationship between subject and object. While the relationship is, as it is for the mature Hegel, dialectical and thus dynamic, instead of the single all-encompassing *Geist* of the later philosophy, at this stage the relationship is worked out in three heterogeneous and irreducible media: language, labour and interaction. The subject grasps the object by naming it, by manipulating it with tools and, more subtly, in an intersubjective relationship with it (TP: 142). It is in these media that the object is constituted and, crucially, is constituted variously (in contrast to the single, phenomenological realm of Kant). Crudely, the world appears differently to us, depending upon whether we are labelling it, prodding it with a screwdriver or trying to engage it in witty conversation. But perhaps more radically still, Hegel claims that the subject itself is constituted in these media (so that, again in opposition to Kant, the subject is not given, but is undergoing formation as a self or coming to understand itself through its activities).

In language and, more specifically, in the act of naming, the subject fixes and internalizes the external object, giving it a permanence and indeed an independence that it could not have when it existed merely in the fleeting awareness of an animal's perceptions (TP: 153). In addition, the subject begins to see the world in terms of relationships and classifications that are suggested by its language. Language begins to constitute the world as it is inhabited by the subject. Yet, while the language-using subject can thus manipulate the object in thought, language also, crucially, makes the formation of the subject possible. On the one hand, "the symbols of ordinary language penetrate and dominate the perceiving and thinking consciousness" (TP: 155), so that, compared to Kant's transcendental subject, which is structured by immutable categories, the Hegelian subject is a product of the contingency of ordinary languages. On the other hand, language is still something produced by the subject, and in so far as the name is distinguished from the object named, language itself can become an object for reflection. The subject can thus become self-conscious, through reflecting on itself as a language-user (TP: 153).

Language frees the subject from the immediacy of its animal nature, for it allows the subject to manipulate the named object in its memory and imagination. Labour checks this freedom. Labour is the process by which the subject physically manipulates the natural object, ultimately through the use of tools. The production of an instrumentally effective tool demands that the subject submits itself to the external power of nature (TP: 154). Desires that can be freely satisfied in imagination must now be modified or deferred in the face of the irreducible otherness and resistance of nature. The subject can only recover its freedom by outwitting nature in an act of cunning. Submitting itself to the very predictability of nature (and thus recognizing that nature acts in a law-like manner) the subject can use tools instrumentally, predicting nature's responses in order to subvert nature to its own ends (TP: 155). Yet this again entails a contingent unfolding of the subject's self-understanding and realization, as a "cunning consciousness" manifests itself in a developing technological and scientific culture.

With the category of "interaction", Hegel offers a still more subtle dialectic. Here, the subject–object relationship is construed not as the relationship of the human subject to nature, but rather as a relationship between subjects. In love (paradigmatically within the family), this is transparently an intersubjective relationship, for love is the "knowing which recognises itself in the other" (TP: 147). It is mutual recognition. Yet this relationship is fragile. Hegel offers criminality as a typical source of its disruption. By putting their own desires in the place of the community, the criminal refuses to recognize the subjectivity of the other. This act at once fractures the community and the subjectivity of the criminal, as the criminal and the victim alike take rigid positions against each other. Alienated from the community within which it has its true being, the criminal experiences itself in terms of an inchoate loss or deficiency. Equally, the community begins to treat one of its own members as no longer a subject. The power of the lost community is thus transformed into a quasi-natural force: a violence working in the deficiency and alienation of people's lives, as they refuse to recognize their mutual subjectivity. This reification generates a "causality of destiny" (or "fate" [*Schicksal*]) (TP: 147; and see KHI: 56), whereby intersubjective relationships confront their very participants as if they were governed by natural laws (and not by norms chosen by human subjects). "Interaction" therefore begins to articulate the process by which imbalances of power serve to make the subjectivity of the other appear as a mere object.

If, as Hegel argues, language is prior to labour (for the object of labour is identified first in language), then language also precedes interaction. Subjects recognize each other through linguistic communication. The disruption of interaction may thus itself be seen as a disruption of language, as "the dialogic relationship is subject to the causality of split-off symbols and reified logical relations" (TP: 148). In effect, language, which is itself a product of human subjectivity and the basis of human self-reflection and self-consciousness, can equally inhibit self-reflection and understanding. In that language "penetrate[s] and dominate[s] the perceiving and thinking consciousness", a language that mislabels the criminal as object or, consequently, fails to acknowledge that what the criminal says is a meaningful utterance, spoils the self-identity of the language-user. Thus, in contradistinction to Kant, moral relationships, and thus what may be termed the moral consciousness, are again to be understood as products of a contingent process. Kant's moral subject is criticized by Hegel precisely because, in that it is a given, it is not actually required to enter into interaction with others. Kant's moral order is condemned as little more than a pre-established harmony between wholly autonomous beings (TP: 150–51), rather than a condition to be fought for and achieved in real social interaction.

The young Hegel has thus offered three distinct media within which consciousness and the object is formed. Both as "name-giving consciousness" (in the medium of language) and as "cunning consciousness" (in the medium of labour) the subject dominates the object. The object is appropriated for the purpose, ultimately, of the subject's survival. Precisely because the initial act of naming entails that the subject names the object from its own perspective, and that this perspective will determine its instrumental action towards the object, the subject can never be identical to the object. The young Hegel, in contrast to the mature Hegel of the *Encyclopedia of the Philosophical Sciences*, does not therefore understand the subject–object dialectic as straightforwardly culminating in the absolute of subject–object identity. Indeed, the Jena lectures do not seem to presuppose the inevitable and pre-given resolution of the dialectic. The threat of crisis that looms over and inspires atheistic theology is therefore not yet suppressed (see § "Crisis and critique", p. 20). Subject–object identity is only conceivable within the medium of interaction, as the alienation of subject and object (where the object is uniquely conceived as the subject sundered from itself) is reconciled in love. Within the medium of labour (and its associated language use) the object remains external to the subject, and can thus only be appropriated (TP: 164).

The separation of labour and interaction has therefore allowed the young Hegel to make what is, in effect, a distinction between first and second nature – between that which is irrevocably separate from the subject, and that which is reified subjectivity – or the "causality of nature" and the "causality of destiny" (TP: 159). The mature Hegel (like Marcuse) fails to respect this distinction, subsuming the dialectic of labour within the dialectic of interaction, so that first nature comes to be treated as a hidden subject with which one can communicate and be reconciled. It is thus not in Hegel's work that Habermas finds further expression of the categories of labour and interaction, but rather in the work of American philosophers, hermeneutians, Marx and psychoanalysts.

Pragmatism

Habermas looks to Marx and to the nineteenth-century American philosopher and originator of pragmatism, Charles Sanders Peirce, for the further articulation of "labour" as the transcendental condition of a certain form of knowledge. An appeal to Marx might be expected. The importance of the category of labour in Marx's historical materialism is evident from even a superficial acquaintance, although the presentation of historical materialism as a quasi-transcendental philosophy is somewhat more audacious. The ascription of some form of transcendentalism to Peirce is much less problematic; Peirce explicitly situated much of his work as a response to Kant. However, for Habermas to find something of significance in Peirce is an indication of the remarkable breadth of his philosophical interests, not least in comparison with those of his predecessors in the Frankfurt School. Horkheimer, for example, was aware of pragmatism, but had been dismissive in his assessment (Horkheimer 1992: 44–57). In addition, it is worth remarking that, by the 1960s, Peirce's work had fallen into neglect in his native United States, let alone Germany. It was Habermas's friend and colleague Karl-Otto Apel (who was himself developing a version of the theory of cognitive interests (see Apel 1980)) who was among the first to rediscover Peirce (Apel 1981). Just as an interest in pragmatism was to grow, internationally, in the succeeding decades, so Peirce's work and pragmatism as a whole come to play an increasingly important role in Habermas's own thought.[2] This first public engagement with pragmatism is therefore of major significance in terms of the future possibilities that it begins to suggest for Habermas's work.

Marx articulates the category of labour within the context of political and economic theory; Peirce articulates it within the philosophy of science and thereby, Habermas suggests, makes explicit that which Marx had left implicit in his own work (KHI: 36). Yet, although Marx and Peirce develop complementary accounts of labour, Habermas argues that they are both trapped within a positivistic self-misunderstanding, and are consequently unable to work through the implications that their arguments have for the categories of labour and interaction.

In Peirce's pragmatism, Habermas seeks to find a transcendental episte-mology that avoids the pitfalls of a first philosophy, which is to say a transcendentalism that makes no substantial presuppositions as to what should count as knowledge. As such, it would embrace a fallibilism akin to that found in Popper's philosophy of science (see § "Reason", p. 14). Whereas Kant presupposed that Newton had provided a definitive account of the workings of the physical world, Popperianism holds that no scientific theory can have any greater status than that of a provisional truth. Science progresses by proving old theories to be false, and replacing them with better theories. Peirce anticipates such fallibilism but, precisely through his explic-itly transcendental framework, he is able to offer a more subtle account of both the constitution of the object of scientific knowledge and of the inquir-ing subject.

Peirce's pragmatism may be seen to begin from the question of how we deal with doubt or, more graphically, the "irritation of doubt" (Peirce 1960: 5.374[3]). Competent human agents possess a set of beliefs about how the world works. Some such beliefs may be consciously articulated, but the bulk are held implicitly and are expressed simply in our actions (and principally in our habitual actions) (KHI: 120). Peirce follows the nineteenth-century Scottish psychologist Alexander Bain in defining a belief (in opposition to something the possibility of which we merely entertain) as that upon which we are willing to act. Thus, I may not consciously articulate the thought that chairs are substantial and enduring objects, but my habitual willingness to trust chairs to take my weight indicates that I do indeed hold this belief. Problems arise only when such beliefs are thwarted, for example, when a chair gives way under me. Here, in a most mundane form, is the irritation of doubt. Doubt occurs when the world ceases to respond to us in the way in which we expect. From the secure, predictable and even taken-for-granted place it previously was, the world becomes, even in small part, radi-cally unpredictable. This unpredictability can be removed by refining our beliefs. Perhaps the chair was already weakened by earlier use (or misuse), or perhaps it is time for a diet. A practical engagement with the world can be used to test these hypotheses: gingerly try sitting on another chair; examine the old one for signs of damage and so on.

Already, in such a simple example, there are radical implications for philosophical inquiry. First, Peirce is suggesting (not least in opposition to Cartesian rationalism) that what counts as knowledge need not be defined with the certainty of mathematical deduction. Knowledge is simply what works now. As technology advances, or as we become more adventurous in our activities, then current beliefs may well be revealed to be inadequate, but until that time, there is simply no point in questioning them. This entails that knowledge advances not simply by rational reflection, but through practical engagement in the world. Yet, secondly, if rationalism is inadequate as an epistemology, so too is a naive empiricism that presupposes that knowledge is grounded in an immediate and intuitive contact with the world. All knowledge must be generated in the context of a challenge to prior beliefs. Knowledge, and crucially contact with the world, is therefore always already mediated by prior beliefs (and thus practical expectations of how the world works) (KHI: 97).

The recognition of the inadequacy of both rationalism and empiricism therefore leads Peirce to look (much as Kant had done before him) for a transcendental grounding to knowledge, and according to Habermas's interpretation this grounding for Peirce lies in labour understood as a behavioural circuit of feedback-controlled action (KHI: 120–26). In effect, instrumental action makes possible a certain form of knowledge of the world. Peirce presents this graphically in the following example: "There is absolutely no difference between a hard thing and a soft thing so long as they are not brought to the test" (1960: 5.403). This is not to argue that hardness only comes into existence when human beings are able to test for it. Peirce, as a realist, explicitly states that the hardness of a diamond pre-exists any test. Rather, it is to argue that it is not meaningful to attribute "hardness" to an object, if it is not possible to subject that property to some form of practical test (KHI: 130) and, equally, if human beings are unable to test for a property, that property is irrelevant to their understanding (and thus the constitution) of the object. The paradoxical nature of Peirce's claim lies, in no small part, in the fact that the very survival of most creatures presupposes that they have a great facility in distinguishing between hard and soft things (frequently by sight, let alone touch). That such a facility exists early in both the evolutionary development of a species and in the growth of an individual creature does not entail that it is due to any immediate intuition of the world; it is acquired (and often painfully). Labour makes possible that acquisition, and the consequent synthesis of the subject's experience of the world in terms of specific, contingently acquired, concepts. (One might consider how the world is constituted for a human culture that lacks any conception of, say, magnetism, and that lacks any technology to discover the magnetic properties of metals or even the earth itself. Navigation at sea, for example, would be a wholly different concern than it is in, say, modern Western culture, although the desire to travel and explore may stimulate a far more profound knowledge of the night sky.)

The fixing of belief in response to the irritation of doubt occurs at an everyday level, and here Peirce may be seen to be anticipating something of Husserl's and later Alfred Schutz's understanding of the lifeworld. However,

69

the transition between mundane doubt and the disciplined structure of science is more complex. Again it may be understood in terms of contingent historical factors (so that the subject of scientific inquiry acquires, under Peirce's analysis, and once again in contrast to Kant's, a constitutive history). Peirce (1960: 5.377ff.) recognizes four methods of responding to doubt: tenacity, authority, the *a priori* and science. A tenacious approach refuses to acknowledge a problem; the appeal to authority allows another party to resolve the problem on your behalf; and the *a priori* method (which is itself typical of rationalism) resolves the problem through rational reflection, rather than practical engagement with the world. Of the four methods, science alone, Peirce claims, will be effective in the long run (KHI: 119). What precisely is meant by science in this context is slightly ambiguous. If, in mundane life, a doubt is taken seriously as a practical problem, then something of the scientific method is employed. The science of, say, the modern physics or chemistry laboratory merely systematizes that lay competence, and through reflection makes explicit what is always already implicit to labour. As Habermas summarizes this, formal science is a process of inquiry that isolates the process of discovery and learning from mundane life processes, so that (for example in the controlled experiment) feedback can be reduced to a few significant forms. Results are presented in precise, intersubjectively accessible and typically quantified forms. Finally, the progress of science (and thus the acquisition of reliable knowledge) is made systematic in so far as research programmes are increasingly planned in advance, rather than being allowed to occur on an ad hoc basis, in response to contingent problems and opportunities (KHI: 124).

Science is distinguished from other forms of learning by two qualities: its logic of inquiry and its assumption of the "hypothesis of reality". For Peirce, the logic of scientific inquiry is based in neither rationalist deduction nor yet empiricist induction. Deduction can reveal nothing that is not already implicit to its premises (albeit that it is important in drawing out the implications of a scientific hypothesis); induction can be used only to test the factual validity of scientific hypotheses (for example, by experimentally confirming a prediction derived from a scientific hypothesis). Peirce therefore turns to what he calls (after medieval Scholastic logic) "abduction", as the form of inference that generates new hypotheses (KHI: 114). Yet Peirce must still justify this logic, and here Habermas begins to untangle the major ambiguities and problems of Peirce's epistemology. On the one hand, the logic of scientific inquiry cannot be justified purely in terms of its logical coherence. At the very least, this would suggest a paradoxical reversion to the *a priori* method, and the ultimate divorce of science from reality. Yet, on the other hand, the logic of inquiry cannot be justified by a simple appeal to the real. If all experience of reality is mediated by prior belief (as Peirce argues), then the accuracy of a scientific hypothesis (let alone the abductive method that generated it) cannot be tested by an appeal to any immediate knowledge of the real. Indeed, if such a naive empiricism were possible, there would be no need for abduction in the first place (for the nature of reality would be self-evident). Thus, for science to assume that there is a reality, and crucially a reality that is primarily experienced as the irritation of doubt – that which intrudes to destabilize an inadequate belief – entails that reality itself has a transcendental status. Reality is constituted in the process of inquiry (KHI: 95).

The explication of this claim is complex. On one level its meaning has already been encountered in the example of hardness given above. The real at once exists prior to inquiry and yet is only recognized and constituted through inquiry. This entails, in effect, an ambiguity in the concept of the real, or, as Habermas subsequently argues, the need to distinguish the issue of the constitution of reality from that of the truth of scientific propositions about that reality (KHI: 360). On the one hand the real is relative to the current state of science or, more precisely, to the current capacity to engage instrumentally with nature. On the other hand, reality is "the totality of true propositions" (KHI: 107). This is to argue that science progresses towards a definitive account of the nature of reality (and specifically, an articulation of the universal laws of nature), and that any present knowledge claim (and thus constitution of the real), is but a step on that journey. For Peirce, "[t]he rational meaning of every proposition lies in the future" (1960: 5.427). The crucial term here is "meaning". Peirce recognizes that beliefs are formulated in language. This is perhaps most clearly expressed in one of his most fundamental formulations of pragmatism: "Consider what effects, that might conceivably have practical bearings, we conceive the object of our conception to have. Then, our conception of these effects is the whole of our conception of the object" (ibid.: 5.2). Thus, the meaning of the word "chair", to return to an earlier example, is something upon which we can sit, which is to say, do something with. Similarly, for Peirce, our conception of "oxygen" is the empirical tests that need to be done to establish that this substance is oxygen. In effect, this is to return to the issue noted in Chapter 1 (§ "Reason", p. 14), with respect to Popper. There it was argued that a scientific hypothesis, that is itself a proposition, cannot be contradicted by an observation, but only by a proposition that expresses that observation. The process of refuting hypotheses therefore revolves about the process by which an observation is recognized as being an instance of the statement of the refuting conditions. Peirce allows this problem to be taken further.

If beliefs are necessarily linguistic, then to assert that an experience is always mediated by prior beliefs is also to assert that experience is always mediated by language. Reality is therefore constituted in language. (Again,

71

it is the "totality of true propositions".) This leaves a major problem for Peirce's understanding of reality. If the real is constituted in language and all experience is mediated by language, then there can be no immediate non-linguistic experience that can disrupt belief. Although this reasserts Peirce's objection to naive empiricism, it is counter-intuitive on a number of levels. First, it would again appear to reduce the logic of inquiry to something akin to the *a priori* method, in so far as inquiry now appears as a process that is wholly internal to language (with language simply taking the place of reason within the method). There appears to be no resistance from anything external to the process of inquiry itself (see KHI: 99). Secondly, it renders highly problematic Peirce's claim that science is progressing. This is a problem Peirce appears to share with Popper. Even if it is possible to recognize that a given hypothesis is false, then it is still not possible to guarantee that any substituted hypothesis is any closer to being one of the totality of true propositions that will be achieved at the end of scientific inquiry. This is due to the fact that if there is no access to reality independent of language and belief, then there are no independent criteria by which to assess the progress of science.[4]

At this point, Habermas makes a bold move. He confronts Peirce with his German near contemporary Nietzsche and the idea of "perspectivism" (see also § "Nietzsche", p. 200). The Nietzschean claim is that language does not serve to constitute a single reality, but rather "a plurality of fictions relative to multiple standpoints" (KHI: 118). (Again, we might consider the different worlds inhabited by those sailors with compasses, and thus the concept of magnetism, and those without. The perspectivist point is that these are merely different worlds, with there being no way to establish that the former is epistemologically superior to the latter.) The suggestion is that reality can be constructed in numerous *equally valid* ways. Habermas wants to side with Peirce, and above all his commitment to the transcendental implications of the "hypothesis of reality". Such a disciplining "reality", articulated through labour, would serve to ground our intuitive notion that science does progress rather than merely change. Nietzschean perspectivism is disturbing for Habermas because Nietzsche comes to his conclusion by linking knowledge to interests, and thereby seems to anticipate the concept of knowledge-constitutive interests. Yet Nietzsche does this naturalistically, and not transcendentally (KHI: 297). Nietzschean perspectivism reduces pragmatism to the empirical claim that the categorical framework of science has been produced for the purpose of mastering nature, and thereby facilitating human survival. At worst, this is a biological claim: in effect, that what passes for knowledge is wholly relative to the biological needs of the human species. At best, it is a sociological thesis: what a community recognizes as knowledge is shaped by the particular survival needs of that community (KHI: 297–8).

Hence, on either interpretation, any constitution of reality is valid, if it will serve the survival of some group (KHI: 295). Such perspectivism ultimately collapses into decisionism, for one "fiction" is no more or no less correct than any other "fiction", not least because criteria of correctness or, more properly, truth are always intrinsic to these fictions, and thus can never adjudicate between them. The problem for Peirce, and indeed for Habermas's interpretation of Peirce, is therefore to justify the claim that the constitutive role of labour, and thus the interest in mastery over nature, is a genuinely transcendental claim, and not a merely empirical one. For, on Habermas's account, only if the relationship between interests and knowledge is transcendental can perspectivism be avoided. In effect, this is then to ask anew what "transcendentalism" means. The remainder of *Knowledge and Human Interests* is devoted to precisely this problem.

It is Habermas's contention that Peirce ultimately fails to justify his own transcendental realism, or at least that his transcendentalism is left incomplete. He is therefore unable to justify his faith in scientific progress. This failure is due to Peirce's inability to work out the implications that the category of interaction has for his philosophy. (This, in turn, is due to the influence that a tacit positivism has on his thought. Positivism renders relevant insights from the likes of the young Hegel inaccessible, for they are dogmatically condemned as metaphysical nonsense (KHI: 197).) A mere appeal to the universality of labour as constitutive of knowledge is insufficient. The Nietzschean challenge, precisely in so far as it draws attention to the role of historically contingent beliefs and language in the constitution of the "real", makes the reliability of any knowledge claim problematic. Bluntly, an appeal to labour alone is not enough to make Peirce's case. He is, however, vaguely aware of this. In articulating labour as the transcendental condition of science, Peirce has necessarily complemented his account of the logic of inquiry by a philosophy of language (and has thus unwittingly invoked the second of Hegel's categories). The problem lies in Peirce's failure to explicate either language or inquiry as properly intersubjective. Inquiry understood as a relationship of deduction, induction and abduction remains monological, which is to say, a process that could occur in the head of a lone inquirer. More precisely, the transcendental question as to the constitution of that inquiring subject is thereby lost. The subject comes to be identified, ahistorically, with the logic of inquiry itself. Similarly, the understanding of language seemingly loses sight of the problem raised in relation to Popper: that of acknowledging that a particular observation is an instance of a given proposition. Popper compared this process to that of legal debate, and here is the clue to a consistent interpretation of Peirce.

Unmediated experience of the "real" may be allowed to occur within a private stream of consciousness. However, the real, and significantly true propositions about the real, are public (KHI: 100). It is through experience, and not least experience that is literally incomprehensible – that cannot be meaningfully articulated – that the "immediate quality of reality" asserts itself. As such it is the source of challenges to the publicly accepted interpretation of reality (KHI: 101). Knowledge may thus be constituted intersubjectively in processes akin to that of legal interpretation, whereby problematic experiences are either interpreted within existing frameworks, or serve to bring about the reinterpretation of these frameworks. Knowledge would not then be constituted monologically (by either the mere recognition that a linguistic sign corresponds to a pre-linguistic experience, or by the mechanical working out of the logic of inquiry). It is precisely this that Peirce recognizes when he reflects upon the inquiring subject. A key insight offered by Peirce, and one that will play a major part in Habermas's own later work, is the recognition that science is carried out not by isolated thinkers and experimenters, but by a community of scientists (see PMT: 88–112). Indeed, Peirce lauds good scientific practice because it takes account of what he calls humanity's "social impulse": in effect, individuals' unavoidable tendency to influence and take account of each others' opinions (Peirce 1960: 5.378). The real, in the sense of true facts, is therefore the totality of true interpretations that a "community of all intelligible beings" achieves in the long run (KHI: 108). A point is again being made against Kant's epistemology. Just as, according to Hegel, Kant's moral philosophy is to be criticized for ultimately eliminating real moral practice (for it asserts a pre-existing harmony of moral agents that is to be revealed through reason alone), so, too, an interpretation of phenomenal reality as that which all human beings construct independently, and yet identically, for themselves is to be rejected. Human beings come to share an understanding of reality only in so far as their engagement with reality is mediated by concrete intersubjective relationships to each other. An understanding and justification of scientific progress lies, therefore, in the explication not of an ahistorical logic, but rather of the forms of open and critical debate that allow knowledge claims to acquire genuine, universal acceptability. Peirce recognizes that universal agreement can be – and frequently is – brought about, not by open and rational consideration of evidence, but through violence: "a general massacre of all who have not thought in a certain way" (Peirce 1960: 5.378). Reality and the collective subject that constitutes it may thus be allowed to have complex and contingent histories. However, within that flawed history there may be glimpsed in the discursive practices of that community an ideal against which history can be judged. In sum, in the notion of the community of scientists, Peirce has begun to recognize that labour alone cannot be the only transcendental condition of (even natural scientific) knowledge. If it were, Nietzsche would be right. Labour would entail nothing more than the empirical grounding of scientific knowledge in the capacities of the human species. Labour must be complemented by interaction as at least a first step in justifying transcendentalism (KHI: 138).

Hermeneutics (Dilthey)

In defending the transcendental status of interaction, Habermas makes what in certain respects is as surprising a move as was his earlier appeal to American pragmatism. He turns to a tradition that was either ignored or treated with hostility by the first generation of Frankfurt thinkers: that of hermeneutics. Habermas defines "hermeneutics" as "the art of understanding linguistically communicable meaning" (HCU: 181). As a discipline, philosophical hermeneutics – which is to say, conscious reflection upon agents' everyday competence in interpretation – emerges as an approach to the problems of interpretation and authentication of scriptures after the Reformation. In nineteenth-century Germany, this was further developed by the theologian Friedrich Schleiermacher as an exploration and clarification of the skills used in the interpretation of any text. Wilhelm Dilthey subsequently finds in hermeneutics the methodology that makes the historical and cultural sciences (or *Geisteswissenschaften*) distinct from the natural sciences (KHI: 141). Philosophical hermeneutics thereby becomes an approach to understanding human behaviour and its products, be these written texts and utterances, art works, laws, value systems or even the objects of material culture such as tools and buildings. In the twentieth century, the hermeneutic tradition is carried forward by Heidegger and pre-eminently by his pupil Hans-Georg Gadamer. Although it is Dilthey who is the principle concern of *Knowledge and Human Interests* – for Dilthey represents that pre-history of positivism that is the book's main theme – the debate with Gadamer that was initiated by the latter's *Truth and Method* (LSS: Ch. 8) is equally relevant.

Dilthey's hermeneutics rests upon the distinction he draws between the methodologies of the natural and cultural sciences, and the consequent epistemological superiority of the latter. Natural scientists explain; cultural scientists understand. The methodology of the natural sciences presupposes that its subject matter has been brought into existence independently of human will. It is alien and, contra the idealism of Hegel (or Marcuse), can never be unified with the knowing subject. In contrast, the subject matter of the cultural sciences is approached as a product of intentional human action. Thus, while explanation is the imposition of provisional hypotheses upon alien material, understanding grasps the cultural events "from within" (KHI: 145), precisely because of the commonality between the subject matter and the scientist; the historian is, after all, an historical being (KHI: 149). In the cultural sciences, humanity comes to understand its own creation (and thereby understands culture as only a creator God could understand nature).

One may usefully approach hermeneutics, albeit at something of a tangent, by suggesting that its core problem is the clarification of whatever it is that links the cultural scientist with their subject matter. In his early works, Dilthey treats this as a problem of empathy. The task of the historian is to bridge the gap between their own psychic states, or "experience" [*Erlebnis*], and those of the historical agent. The German neologism "*Erlebnis*" is crucial. Experience is not merely composed of sense data (as it might be for the positivists (see Gadamer 1975: 59)), but is rather a meaningful whole: it is the sense that the agent makes of the world in which they live and their actions in that world. Empathy links the historian and their subject in so far as the historian strives to re-live or re-experience [*zu nacherleben*] that experience in their own consciousness. This might seem to be intuitively plausible – consider, for example, how one might try to imagine Julius Caesar's state of mind as he uttered the words, "*Veni, vidi, vici*" – until Dilthey's justification of empathy is revealed to rest upon a highly problematic metaphysics. Empathy is held to be possible in so far as the experiences of both historical agent and historian are manifestations (or objectifications) of an "omnipresent stream of life" (KHI: 183). The link between *Erlebnis* and this metaphysics of vitalism allows the process of historical understanding to be construed as a psychological and, paradoxically, ultimately monological achievement (KHI: 148, 180).

Dilthey brings about a partial break from this monological approach by beginning to work through the implications of articulating *Erlebnis* as meaningful experience. If "experience" is not raw sense data, this is because it is structured symbolically. The objectifications of the supposed stream of life, such as "states, churches, institutions, mores, books, art works" (KHI: 146) through which the experience of the historian is made possible, are symbolic structures. The historian does not attempt to jump, immediately, into the mind of Caesar. Rather, they will read documents (including his own, propagandizing memoirs and Plutarch's commentaries), and examine material objects (such as triumphal arches, with their inscriptions and images of battle), in an attempt to reconstruct them as bearers of meaning. The monological process of empathy can therefore be discarded, in order to be substituted by intersubjective understanding [*Verstehen*], grounded in a recognition that what is constitutive of meaningful experience is the human capacity to generate and comprehend symbols: in other words, to use language.

The contrast between the methodologies of the natural and the cultural sciences can now be redrawn, specifically in terms of the way in which they deal with the tension between particular experiences and the generality of language. The tension between immediate experience and scientific hypothesis was seen, in the previous section, to pose a core problem for Peirce. Ultimately, this was the problem of how experience is expressed in a proposition. Peirce's transcendental concept of reality entails a reality that pre-exists, and is referred to by, any propositional formulation of it. Whereas reality may be the totality of true propositions, science is still about a reality that is independent of, and resistant to, the provisional formulations of scientific laws that precede the utopian perfection of the community of scientists. Language is thus distinguishable from the facts expressed in it. The experience of the individual scientist is dealt with by formulating it in a statement that allows it to be subsumed under a universal law (be it corroborating or refuting that law). The individuality of the experience is thus lost. The scientific method proceeds precisely by abstracting from the richness of personal experience, leaving only that which is experimentally reproducible (KHI: 162). In addition, the very language within which this experience is expressed strives to be a "pure" or theoretical language, such as that of mathematics. Unlike ordinary languages, the symbols and rules of pure language aspire to be unambiguous. The reference of the symbols to an extra-linguistic world and the combination and manipulation of those symbols are determined by a precisely delimited set of rules. Crudely, what is meant by $2 + 2 = 4$, or even $E = mc^2$, should be the same for all who understand the languages within which elementary mathematics or Einsteinian physics are expressed. Who makes the statement and in which context are irrelevant to its interpretation (KHI: 163). Understanding here is thus a monological process, for there is no need to negotiate, inter-subjectively, nuances or ambiguities of meaning (KHI: 161). Not so in the historical sciences, where it matters that it was Caesar, and not someone else, who said "*Veni, vidi, vici*".

The natural sciences subsume the particularity of experience within the universality of natural law (and within pure languages that allow only a certain type of experience to be expressed). Hermeneutics, conversely, recognizes that mundane communication presupposes the possibility of invoking the particularity of experience. The very need to bridge between the experience of the historical actor and that of the historian entails that these experiences are different (and thus particulars). The cultural sciences proceed not by subsuming strange experience under general meanings, but rather by finding a way to articulate that strange experience so that it becomes comprehensible, in its particularity and difference, to the historians and their contemporaries. The problem of the cultural sciences therefore becomes that of articulating the particular within the generality of a shared language. The model of pure language, which is appropriate to the natural sciences, is as irrelevant to this project as is the model of natural scientific experience. In contrast to Peirce's immediate experience, Dilthey's *Erlebnis* is always already linguistically mediated. The sharp distinction that natural science makes between language and reality is lost in hermeneutics. The reality with which hermeneutics deals is constituted in language, for it is a reality of "meanings". Crucially, this constitution occurs in ordinary language. If a pure language eliminates particularity, then it can communicate only that which is already shared. In contrast, ordinary language must be such as to allow the expression of unique and novel experience, albeit in the shared (and thus general) structures of that language. Ordinary language must therefore be such that it at once makes possible a community and the reciprocal identification of its members, and yet also preserves the non-identity (or particularity) of those members from each other (KHI: 157).

Dilthey identifies three elements to ordinary language: linguistic expressions, actions and experiential expressions (KHI: 163). Pure languages consist of nothing but linguistic expressions. As such, the context within which they are uttered is irrelevant to their interpretation (or, more precisely, the context of scientific experiment and theory formation is taken for granted). In contrast, ordinary language is "polluted" by the intrusion of heterogeneous material (KHI: 164): the interpretation of the ordinary language utterance presupposes an awareness of the context within which it is uttered, and the person who utters it. Crucially, much of this context is alien even to the speaker. It is a raft of taken-for-granted assumptions (and Gadamer will use the term "prejudices" or "pre-judgements" [*Vorurteile*] (LSS: 152), although it may be noted that this does not have quite the pejorative tone of the English "prejudice") about the social, physical and mental environment that shapes the speaker's responses and actions (KHI: 164). So, consider again "*Veni, vidi, veci*": one's presuppositions about Roman life and Imperial conquest, about Caesar's political ambitions, and even the worth of Plutarch's writings (and so on) will shape how one makes sense of that utterance.

However, the linguistic utterance itself does not explicitly or unambiguously refer to its particular context, which is to say that a given word or phrase can be used in many different contexts, and will mean something different in each. The explicating of this context constitutes the core problem of hermeneutic interpretation. The reconstruction of what a speaker intends by their utterance will depend in large part upon reconstructing the way in which they interpret and respond to their cultural and physical context. An example from English law illustrates this rather graphically. In 1952, the instruction "Let him have it, Chris" was given by Derek Bentley to Christopher Craig, in the context of an attempted robbery, with Craig aiming a gun at a policeman, Sidney Miles. The utterance can be interpreted as an order either to shoot or to hand over the gun. Craig interpreted it as the former and, crucially, a jury convicted Bentley of murder on the grounds that this is what he intended by the utterance. (Craig was a juvenile, and thus presumed incapable of being responsible for murder.) The hermeneutic problem therefore becomes that of reconstructing the symbolically mediated context, as well as the relations of that context to the utterance, as it was understood by the speaker.

In part, this weakness is compensated by the human capacity for intentional, rule-governed and thus meaningful action. Crucially, language does not do the work of interpretation. It merely provides the resources through which competent human agents interpret and re-interpret each other's meaningful utterances, writings and actions. This is to recognize an intimate link between linguistic expression and action. Again, outside of pure language, an utterance may be linked to an infinite variety of actions. The interpretation of an utterance therefore requires that the linguistic expression and the action are grasped as reciprocally interpreting each other (KHI: 168). Thus, for example, an utterance may be interpreted with reference to a long sequence of the speaker's actions, and these actions carry with them certain indications as to what further actions might be expected, and what these actions mean. (That "Let him have it" is uttered by a man with a history of aggression suggests one interpretation; uttered by a man with a history of capitulation or even flight suggests altogether different interpretations. That Bentley's psychological and intellectual development was possibly inferior to that of the chronologically younger Craig was an important issue in the trial and subsequent attempts to gain a pardon for Bentley.)

Habermas appeals to Wittgenstein, and his concept of "language-games" to explicate this point (see also § "Wittgenstein and language-games", p. 140).[5] A "language-game" is a way of using language, and within any given natural language (e.g. English, Welsh, German) there will be infinite possibilities for language-games, as language is used in different contexts and bound up with different actions and social roles (LSS: 117ff.). Again, precisely because of this potential diversity of language-games, the interpretation of action is no more definitive than the interpretation of linguistic expression (KHI: 165–6). A word will change its meaning according to the context within which it is used. Thus, the term "exists" may mean something different when used by the astronomer confirming an empirical discovery (e.g. "Planets exist outside our solar system"), and when used by the religious believer affirming their faith ("God exists"). Unless one understands the nature of the language-game within which the utterance is made, one cannot understand the utterance itself (and thus might an atheist astronomer dismiss the believer's words as confused nonsense.) Finally, Dilthey sees in physical gestures a final level, and not least one where physiological expressions such as blushing might betray lies and deceptions. More mundanely, the tone of voice can modify the meaning of a statement. Tone of voice can do little to change the meaning of "$E = mc^2$", but can infinitely nuance "Let him have it".

Dilthey's account of language begins to indicate the lay competences that language-users have in repairing disruptions to communication. Hermeneutics makes explicit this lay competence. In learning a language, a speaker does not merely learn the meaning of words, nor even the grammatical rules that determine their combination and manipulation; rather, the speaker becomes sensitive to the reflexivity of ordinary language (KHI: 168). That is, they become aware of the intimate interrelationship between linguistic expression and the context of the utterance, and are thus able to exploit that interrelationship. Ordinary language can be used to comment upon itself. It is its own "meta-language" (HCU: 182). Actions can be interpreted in linguistic utterances; utterances can allude to action and context; and further actions can comment upon those utterances. Again, consider the Bentley example. An eyewitness might interpret the events in the following utterance: "Bentley told Craig to shoot Miles". Bentley's own utterance presupposes his interpretation of the situation that he and Craig had found themselves in and, presumably, his anticipation of how Craig would understand him. Finally, Craig responds to Bentley's utterance with an action, thereby expressing his own interpretation. The competent speaker plays with this potential, and draws upon it in maintaining an intersubjectivity that is continually under threat of breaking. The Bentley case is a tragic example of such broken intersubjectivity.

Habermas is critical of Dilthey for failing to work through the implications of his own insight into the nature of language. At the crucial moment when he could break through to perceive the transcendental foundations of the cultural sciences, he turns back towards positivism. It is as if he takes fright at the fluidity and fragility of interpretation, and so seeks to ground hermeneutics in the possibility of objectively correct interpretations. Hermeneutic interpretations are seen to be defensible according to the criteria that are more appropriate to natural scientific methodology, and not least in the aspiration to objective knowledge. In doing this, he sunders a supposedly scientific hermeneutics from its ground in the everyday interpretative competence of ordinary social agents. The model of empathic re-experience thus comes to dominate even Dilthey's later writings. This blurs the implications of this account of language – which recognized that the immediate psychic state of the other can only be expressed in so far as it can be mediated by language – which rendered the monological process of empathy inadequate, for the experience of the other can only be approached, gradually and hesitantly, through dialogue (KHI: 179–80). In contrast, Dilthey seeks to free the process of interpretation, as a science, from the corrupting influence of mundane life and, not least, from the particularity of one's own linguistically constituted cultural perspective (KHI: 182). In so doing, he again fails to recognize that his own account of language entails that language is not something that hinders or distorts understanding, but is the very resource that makes understanding possible.

Only if one can speak a language – if one is already a competent member of a linguistic culture – can one understand the language of another. The implication of this is that a scientistic conception of truth, such that propositions are true according to their correspondence to reality, becomes inappropriate for hermeneutics, and this on two counts (KHI: 182). First, understanding cannot aspire to be definitive. Understanding is always from the linguistic and cultural position of the interpreters. As this context changes, so too will the interpretation. Secondly, understanding cannot be merely descriptive, as Dilthey suggests. In separating hermeneutics as a science from its life context, Dilthey has concealed hermeneutics' grounding in the interest in communication. Against Dilthey, Habermas is therefore arguing that hermeneutics is grounded in the practical interest in communicating with others, and that such an interest entails not re-experiencing the psychic state of the other, but rather the initiation of a dialogue with them. Such a dialogue will have consequences for one's practical relationship to the other, and for one's self-understanding.

Hermeneutics (Gadamer)

Dilthey's defence of the cultural sciences asserted, as a precondition of historical understanding, that the historian is a historical being. Dilthey ultimately misconstrued the nature of the commonality that must exist between the historian and their subject matter. Gadamer's hermeneutics makes this commonality clear: both are competent language-users. This does not necessarily entail that they are both competent in the same natural language. Gadamer's hermeneutics, indeed, takes the problem of translation between natural languages as a paradigm of the hermeneutic task. Gadamer's claim is, however, that in having learnt one language we have acquired the capacity to learn languages in general. In effect, this is to reassert the problem of the particular and general at a new level. The generality of language as such is manifest in each particular language. There is no universal, pure language, which might ground all natural languages, and there is no need for such a language, for each particular natural language equips its speakers with the capacity to transcend it.

Translation does not, however, merely proceed by expressing the meanings of the other in one's own language. In that hermeneutics collapses the distinction between statement and fact that natural science presupposes, it recognizes the close correlation of language and the way in which we percieve and make sense of our environment: language is entwined with our worldviews (LSS: 143). As Gadamer expresses this, "the subject matter can scarcely be separated from the language" (Gadamer 1975: 349; LSS: 147) or, still more dramatically, in acquiring language one acquires a "world", which is to say, an interpretation of reality (Gadamer 1975: 401). There is no reality outside a language. Precisely in being symbolically interpreted, the subject matter of an utterance is constituted by the language in which it is uttered. In this context, Gadamer offers the powerful image of an hermeneutic horizon, as the framework that at once makes possible and confines interpretation. The allusion here might be to Plato's analogy of the cave (*Republic*, Book 7). Plato asks us to image that human beings are confined to a cave and, having no knowledge of the world outside the cave, they assume that the shadows cast upon the walls of the cave are real. This initiates a debate about whether or not the task of the philosopher is to step outside the cave, in order to view that "absolute" or "noumenal" reality. Dilthey sought in vain to step outside the cave. Gadamer's position (and it is one with which Habermas is cautiously sympathetic) accepts that human beings are within a metaphorical cave or the "horizon" that is shaped out of their language and its traditions. The linguistic cave is the source of the prejudices through which one constitutes and interprets one's world. Although one can step outside this particular cave, for one can experience the products of other cultures (and hence, again, the centrality of translation to Gadamer's project), one can never step outside linguistic caves as such, or even step into a pure, universal, language-cave that constructs the world as it is. Rather, one steps partially outside one's language, as one continues to use its resources to engage with the dwellers in the neighbouring cave.

In sum, living within a language carries with it possibilities of expression, as well as expectations and prejudices about the world, and these shape what the speaker can mean (LSS: 151). The problem of translation, and indeed of interpretation in general is, then, not that of finding an equivalent in one's own language for the meanings of the speaker, for an exact equivalence is unlikely to exist. It is rather that of finding a way of extending one's own language to encompass the alien meaning of the other language (LSS: 147). In Gadamer's imagery, there is a fusion of horizons (LSS: 151). In translating a text, one strives for a more or less adequate reconstruction of how the writer lives their life and constitutes their world, albeit that one's approximation is grounded in the resources offered by one's own language. Here one might usefully consider, if only for the sake of a little variety, the way in which the post-Impressionist painters, such as Van Gogh, creatively incorporated their experience of Japanese prints into their own works.

The image of the fusion of horizons begins to articulate the final decisive elements of hermeneutics. In failures to communicate with or understand each other – that is, broken intersubjectivity – the interpreter encounters the other as a strange particular. The generality of a shared language is not immediately present. In order to invoke this language, a prior "anticipation" of the stranger's meaning is required (LSS: 152). This is to suggest that some guess must be made, at least as to the sort of meaning the stranger intends. In effect, a dialogue is being opened up. One's anticipation is a question addressed to the stranger – or at least to the text or behaviour – asking, is this what it means? This anticipation will be justified – the question affirmatively answered – only if the meaning of the particular text is clarified; in so far as the particular continues to resist interpretation, the anticipation must be revised. This is called the "hermeneutic circle": an interpretative movement between general and particular, wherein each side may challenge and correct the other (KHI: 169ff.). Precisely in that hermeneutics is the explication and systematization of lay competences, it is already present in mundane interpretations. Hence, the particular "Let him have it" is initially approached in terms of strong presuppositions of the sort of utterance it is, and the sort of context within which it occurs or the sort of intentions that gun-wielding robbers have, just as, when one first opens a book, one has certain expectations of the sort of book it is (novel, philosophical monograph, film script or whatever). But consideration of further particulars may lead to this initial anticipation being changed or refined (so that one appeals to Bentley's tone of voice or past conduct; one finds that the supposed "novel" is written in verse). The particulars are now reinterpreted in the light of this revised context (and so on). Intersubjective agreement, and indeed the commonality of language, is restored only as revisions to this anticipation bring about a consistency between the general context and the particular utterance, each illuminating the meaning of the other (e.g. "It was a dark and stormy night …" as the beginning of a novel; when I ask you to give me the gun, you do it). Again, against Dilthey, the ultimate achievement of hermeneutics is not the reproduction of the other's psychic state. The emphasis is rather upon the context (of prejudices that have now come to be shared) that makes this meaning possible. In so far as this context occurs behind the back of the competent social agent, for it is taken for granted by them, the hermeneutician can be seen to understand the other's meaning better than the other understands him or herself.

The hermeneutic circle may be approached also through the idea of anticipation. The interpreter tries to anticipate what their interlocutor will do (say or write) next. Anticipation is grounded in the horizon of the interpreter. As such, as Gadamer observes, anticipation is not a subjective act, but rather one grounded in the interpreter's participation in a wider culture, with the preoccupations of that culture (Gadamer 1975: 261; LSS: 152). To revise the anticipation is therefore to revise the horizon, extending it to encompass the stranger's meaning, and thereby challenging the relevance of one's own prejudices and preoccupations. In extending the horizon the interpreter thereby also revises their own self-understanding. In order to explain this, Habermas presents the problem of broken intersubjectivity as occurring along two dimensions: the horizontal dimension is a break between contemporaries (e.g. between two different languages or language-games, as addressed above); the vertical dimension is historical (KHI: 158). Dilthey's concern with the vertical dimension had focused – again somewhat monologically – upon the problem of autobiography, which is to say, how the individual human being maintains his or her own ego identity (as distinct from the biological identity of the physical body) (KHI: 153). For the ego to have an identity, such that it is unified as the same entity throughout its life, its diverse experiences must be capable of being brought together into a coherent whole, with present events being linked, at once to a remembered past and to an anticipated future (KHI: 152). My response to an experience now therefore depends both upon how I narrate the course of my life up to this point, and how I anticipate or wish it to continue. At the level of a culture, which is Gadamer's primary concern, one looks not simply at one's own past, but at the past of the tradition of the community to which one belongs and within which one is constituted as a subject. Tradition is the "effective historical consciousness" of that language community (Gadamer 1975: 267). It is, again, the generality from within which this particular must be interpreted, and yet by which the particular will be challenged. To interpret or reinterpret the particular events of the past is, therefore, contra Dilthey, not merely to describe an objectified past, but rather to engage critically with one's own cultural identity, and the anticipation of the future of one's culture. This process of interpretation – the movement of the hermeneutic circle – never comes to a definitive close. Ultimately, the horizontal and vertical may be seen to fuse. To engage with a stranger is always to engage critically with one's own self-understanding, and thus with one's own tradition (LSS: 152). In sum, Gadamer's philosophical hermeneutics recognizes that language is a restriction on the interpreter, placing him or her within a horizon of expectations and prejudices that constitute his or her world. Yet, against Dilthey, this is not a failing, for competence in a natural language also provides the resources necessary to transcend its own limitations – to fuse horizons and engage in self-criticism – albeit never to the achievement of an objective, god's eye view.

Although Habermas accepts much of Gadamer's account of hermeneutics, he remains critical of its implicit relativism. Akin to the spectre of perspectivism with which Habermas confronted Peirce, with its attendant danger of a regression into decisionism, so the grounding of interpretation in tradition implies that there are no criteria of criticism that can transcend any particular tradition. Dilthey had responded to this problem by turning to an unsustainable objectivism; Gadamer appeals rather to Heidegger's notion of the ontological. This entails that hermeneutics is understood not as an interpretative method, but more problematically as an account of the constitutive role that language plays in human life: "not what we do or what we ought to do, but what happens to us over and above our wanting and doing" (Gadamer 1975: xvi; LSS: 167). In part this reproduces, but inverts, Dilthey's misguided separation of life and science. Whereas Dilthey falsely reduces hermeneutics to a naturalistic science, Gadamer denies hermeneutics any scientific status, but thereby equally inhibits its intervention in practical life (LSS: 167). According to the ontological account, the relativism of any particular tradition is overcome, precisely in so far as competence in one language gives the speaker access to language as such (and thus, Gadamer claims, to the constitutive ground of human being). Language, as the ground of human understanding and sustained intersubjectivity, is thus posited as an initial position of consensus from which the misunderstandings of broken intersubjectivity can be addressed. In effect, human beings begin as competent language-users embedded within a tradition. While a strange text or action may temporarily disrupt that understanding, the basic competence in language per se provides the resources to recover a new consensus (HCU: 203–4). Habermas's objection to this revolves about the status of consensus, and thus the authoritative status that tradition holds for its participants.

Bluntly the problem is this. Whereas a particular tradition, and its inherent structure of prejudices, provides the grounds upon which the interpreter engages with the stranger, it is unclear that there is any guarantee that these prejudices do not distort or corrupt the stranger's position, rather than illuminating it. Put slightly differently, there are no clear criteria by which one can judge whether a particular consensus has been realized through free and open dialogue, or through the overt or covert exercise of power. For Gadamer, this is not obviously problematic, in so far as the ontological status of language as such facilitates self-critical reflection within *any* particular tradition. The fusion of horizons, along with its resultant self-criticism, gives authority to the particular tradition, precisely in so far as it demands that the interpreter reflects upon their tradition and thus brings their prejudices to consciousness. The tradition is authorized through its "dogmatic recognition" (HCU: 207). In effect, the tacit acceptance of a particular tradition that comes through socialization is replaced by a conscious acknowledgement of it, not least through the developed awareness of its particularity in relation to the university of language. For Habermas, however, this still entails a conflation of authority and reason that at once defies the Enlightenment's commitment to reason, and ignores the account of reflection developed by Kant, Fichte and Hegel (HCU: 207; LSS: 170).

Habermas confronts Gadamer's hermeneutics with the possibility that the very linguistic and discursive resources that are made available within a tradition are themselves corrupted by unequal power relations. To recognize that language can be a medium of power and domination, as well as understanding (LSS: 172) is, in effect, to reject Gadamer's ontology as a mere mystification. There is no guarantee of unconstrained, and thus rational, consensus in language as such, let alone a particular language or language-game. Ironically, Dilthey hints at this, for he recognizes the need to distinguish between historical and systematic cultural sciences (KHI: 183). Economics is taken as the model of the latter. Such systematic cultural sciences deal with social phenomena that relate to each other, not meaningfully, but rather causally as law-governed empirical variables (KHI: 185). They are reified. In effect, this is to suggest that the breakdown of intersubjectivity can occur, not merely through a lack of a shared language or language-game, but through a disruption in one's very competence to use language. Socialization into a distorted language of what Habermas calls "split-off symbols" will systematically inhibit communication and the possibility of any appeal to an unconstrained consensual intersubjectivity. Habermas thereby concludes that hermeneutics alone is inadequate for the understanding of social life. The naive presupposition of consensus as the starting-point of the hermeneutic process fails to distinguish between consensus grounded in the exercise of power and a rationally achieved consensus. Here, then, is the difference between Habermas's and Gadamer's understanding of consensus: both ground their inquiry in a form of consensus, yet if for Gadamer this is at the beginning of the process, for Habermas, deliberately echoing the consensus of Peirce's community of scientists, it is at the end of the process.[6]

Critical theory (Marx)

In the final sections of *Knowledge and Human Interests*, Habermas strives to bring together the theory of cognitive interests. In his accounts of Peirce and Dilthey, he has defended the thesis that reality can be constituted in accord with either an interest in its instrumental manipulation, or an interest in communicating with and about reality. Crucially, this is an epistemological thesis. It is not a matter of recognizing two different forms of reality, but rather of knowing reality in different ways, for different purposes (KHI: 141). Consider my thought "The lawn needs mowing". The lawn is constituted as the object of potential instrumental action. Yet, if I ask my partner, "Do you have time to mow the lawn today?", that same lawn is drawn into the intersubjective negotiation of who actually gets behind the mower.

The problem with this thesis, as it stands, has been indicated by the threat of perspectivism or relativism that hangs over both Peirce and Dilthey (KHI: 198, 209). In effect, it is not clear that Habermas has done anything different, at least in form, to Lukács's appeal to class interest in explaining the constitution of ideology. At best, Habermas has merely dug deeper, in order to uncover interests that are grounded in the survival of the human species, rather than any particular class. If Habermas's claim that the interests are transcendental is to be born out, then the simple reduction of the transcendental interests to empirical features of human being must be forestalled. This is done if the interests can be understood as not merely empirical, but also rational. The appeal to reason is crucial, not least because it entails asking exactly what is meant by "rationality". In effect, it is to raise again Habermas's dissatisfaction with the previous generation of the Frankfurt School, and to find an alternative to the sterile opposition of instrumental and dialectical reason. The first two cognitive interests give rise to two forms of reason: instrumental reason and communicative reason. Although communicative reason does indeed offer a third alternative, the criticism of Gadamer suggests that it is not alone sufficient to stave off decisionism. It cuts short the very process of self-reflection and self-criticism that it has initiated against the objectivism of positivism. It cannot therefore claim a position of universality from which the relation of knowledge and interests as a whole could be grasped. Only the acknowledgement of the third cognitive interest will achieve that. This final interest is the interest in emancipation from domination and, as such, it at once offers a third constitution of reality and a notion of reason that allows for a genuine self-reflection.

The interest in emancipation constitutes reality in terms of second nature (or reification). As is hinted at in Dilthey's notion of the systematic cultural sciences, it accepts the possibility that the causally determinate object that confronts the subject is a product of the subject's own agency. As such, neither Peirce's natural science, which recognizes only first nature, nor yet hermeneutics, which presupposes that all products of human subjectivity are ultimately accessible to natural language, are adequate. Rather, a form of self-reflection akin to Fichte's idealism (precisely in that it is set against dogmatism) or Hegel's phenomenology is required (KHI: 210). Reason thereby comes to be understood in a sense that is fundamental to the Enlightenment. That which is rational is that which frees humanity from, in Kant's words, its self-imposed tutelage (Kant 1983a: 41). It is that which brings about human autonomy or maturity [*Mundigkeit*] (KHI: 197–8). Reason is, therefore, itself interested (precisely in so far as reason is exercised in the interest of achieving autonomy) (KHI: 212). This rational interest is achieved through uninhibited self-reflection. In effect, this is to ground the first two cognitive interests, for making the interests in instrumental manipulation and communication explicit brings them to human consciousness, and thereby reshapes human understanding and practice. In the context of an interest in emancipation, the history of instrumental reason (as one of cumulative learning processes) and of communicative reason (as the stability of tradition) (KHI: 211), provides the material conditions that make politically effective self-reflection possible (for reflection alone will not bring about political change (KHI: 210)). The first two cognitive interests therefore have a justification beyond the mere survival of the human species: looking rather to the political maturation of that species.

Yet, if the cognitive interests make political emancipation possible, they also make it necessary, for the history of science, technology and communication is also the history of political domination and ideological distortion. The writing of such a history is most explicit in Marx and, in broad terms, Habermas presents Marx as mirroring Peirce's concern with labour, albeit infused by the emancipatory interest. Yet critical theory, as knowledge grounded in the emancipatory interest, also finds a powerful model in Freud's psychoanalysis, not least as an emancipatory version of hermeneutics.

Marx defines "labour" as "a process between man and nature, a process in which man through his own action mediates, regulates and controls his material exchange with nature" (KHI: 27; Marx 1976: 283). His position is coherent with that of Peirce, in so far as both offer a transcendentalism that invokes labour as the condition of possible knowledge. The difference between them lies in their approach to epistemology. Peirce treats epistemological issues as matters of logic (as did Kant and Hegel before him). Marx treats them as matters of economics (KHI: 31). This is to say that in a materialist epistemology the Kantian problem of synthesis is construed as a problem that is solved in the practical contingencies of economic production, rather than in thought. The object of knowledge is constituted, for Marx, in a technological engagement with nature (KHI: 35).

On one level, labour merely serves to bring about the survival of the individual human being and of the species. As such, it is grounded in the natural evolution of humanity as a species. On a deeper level, Marx's claim is that labour does not merely make nature useful for human beings, by allowing the appropriation of isolated natural objects; rather, it constitutes a "world" (KHI: 28). That is to say, first, that nature is not immediately given to human beings, but rather is understood and processed in terms of the possibilities that are opened up by technology. Tools and technology therefore take the place in Marx's materialism that beliefs and habits held in Peirce's logic of inquiry. They mediate human experience of nature, and thus constitute the object as a possible object of experience. Secondly, the constitution of a world entails that labour does not merely constitute nature, but also constitutes the human subject. Again, the subject does not engage with discrete elements of nature, but with a more or less integrated structure of resources and tools, which allows it to respond creatively to nature, and thereby to understand itself, forming an identity in terms of its ability to transform its environment (KHI: 36). In addition, in constituting a world, labour acquires a history. Species other than human beings are able to transform nature, but do so within the instinctively given limits of their biological natures. In contrast, the very form in which human labour is manifest changes, and does so through the conscious decisions of human beings. As Marx remarks, the worse of architects is better than the best of bees, for however elegant and efficient the bees' honeycomb cells, the architect builds their structure in the imagination before they built it in stone (Marx 1976: 284). A human history can be constructed in terms of the consequent development of forces of production, while at best the history of the bee is the natural history of the blind force of natural evolution. For Habermas, Marx's materialism is to be understood and assessed precisely in terms of how it interprets this history.

Habermas suggests that there is a fundamental tension running through Marx's work, and one that raises basic questions about the interpretation of Marxism as a politically engaged social theory. On the one hand, Marx's self-understanding of what he is doing as a social theorist overly privileges the constitutive role of labour, not least in so far as the goal of political emancipation is wholly interpreted in terms of the human subject as labourer. On the other hand, in his more substantive analyses, Marx has to appeal to the category of interaction, and thus sees political emancipation not as an outcome of labour processes, but rather as a response to social interaction that has been systematically distorted by imbalances of power. In effect, this tension revolves around the question of how social science is to be understood.

On the first interpretation, the development of the forces of production serve gradually to reduce the amount of time that human beings need to spend in activities necessary to the reproduction of their lives. Functions previously carried out by humans are increasingly transferred to machines. Ultimately, they may be relieved altogether of the burden of necessary labour. An emancipated social subject would thereby come to take its place alongside, but separate from, the production process (KHI: 48). The problems with such a superficially attractive vision are multiple. First, the only criterion of progress available to this history is one defined in terms of instrumental efficacy. It presupposes that material affluence can be equated with political emancipation. The model that Habermas has already given of late capitalism serves to challenge any such assumption. More precisely, it may be suggested that the privileging of instrumental efficiency in fact entails a perspectivism (somewhat akin to that which haunts Peirce) as to the assessment of genuinely political progress. As has already been suggested by Habermas's response to positivism, the apparent value-neutrality of instrumental reason only serves to conceal the actual goals and values of the dominant class, and so exclude them from rational scrutiny. Progress thereby becomes whatever is in that class's interests (KHI: 60). Secondly, if emancipation is only to be understood in terms of the development of the forces of production, then the conception of human self-understanding and reflection themselves are radically impoverished. The self-understanding of humanity is realized merely in the sedimentation of human labour in technological culture. Crucially, self-understanding is not articulated in language; more precisely, the linguistic narration of the development of humanity by, for example, the historian or social scientist is fundamentally separate from the process of development itself. Development takes place regardless of any discursive understanding that human subjects may have of it. At best self-consciousness becomes a steering mechanism for what Marx himself terms the "animated monster" of fixed capital (KHI: 51) and, at worst, human subjectivity is no more than historically sedimented labour. Human history has, under the exclusive framework of labour, taken on the aspect of a natural law (KHI: 45).

Marx's alternative model of emancipation centres upon class conflict. The basic concerns, however, remain those of an epistemology. Marx complements an understanding of synthesis in terms of labour with synthesis through political action (KHI: 56). The fundamental difference is that the knowing subject is no longer taken to be unified, but rather is recognized as being divided against itself (KHI: 54), and thus akin to the young Hegel's model of criminality. The recognition of class conflict allows Marx to open up possibilities of systematic analysis that were only obscurely recognized by Peirce. Peirce's community of scientists is a unified subject, although his throwaway remark on the use of violence in bringing about consensus hints at a politically divided subject. Once this division is explicitly recognized, the transcendental conditions for the constitution of the possible object of knowledge cannot be understood exclusively in terms of labour. Not only must intersubjective relationships be recognised but, more significantly, interaction must itself be understood in terms of Hegel's causality of fate.

The recognition of class conflict allows the complementing of a human history written in terms of the development of the forces of production – and thus labour – with one grounded in the relations of production – and thus interaction. It is the interdependence of the forces and relations that is crucial. The gradual freeing of humanity from the constraint of necessary labour remains fundamental. However, from the perspective of the relations of production and class conflict, historical transitions from one mode of production to the next occur, not through the blind mechanical necessity of increased material productivity, but through the reflection of the politically active classes upon their own identity. This is to say that the understanding of human self-consciousness as the mechanical sedimentation of the human subject in labour is replaced by a discursive (and thus necessarily linguistic) process, through which classes come to understand themselves as beings engaged in political (as well as merely economic) practice. At the core of this process is the recognition that the constraints upon the satisfaction of needs and wishes that are imposed by the institutions of the old mode of production – and which within that mode appeared to be natural – are no longer justifiable. It is precisely here that the Hegelian concept of the causality of fate is re-encountered, in the form of a seemingly natural causality that is, in fact, generated by the internal fracturing and conflict of the social subject. The institutional constraints are typically internalized, as social norms, by competent members of society. It is these constraints that are ultimately "constitutive of a world" – which is to say, a lifeworld – and this world will be manifest in ordinary language as much as in habits and norms of behaviour. The breaking of such constraints requires a fundamental reinterpretation of that world, and thus of oneself as a moral and political agent (KHI: 55–8). Hence, in contrast to a history of the development of the forces of production, which remains external to that development, the written history of class struggle is integral to political struggle. Precisely in writing history – and, more broadly, in practising social science – the subject becomes aware of its political constitution as a subject, and thus of the political practice that is available to it.

A critical social science cannot then be grounded in labour alone. Marx's tendency to conflate natural and social science led to the misunderstanding of economic history in terms of natural laws. A critical social science, which recognizes the transcendental condition of interaction alongside that of labour, avoids this conflation, not least by distinguishing between first and second nature. Here, in sum, is perhaps the principle distinction between Marx and Peirce. It was noted that, for Peirce, the immediate experience of the real was problematic. In contrast, Marx's parallel recognition of the immediacy (or "immovable facticity" (KHI: 34)) of nature begins to clarify these problems. In materialist epistemology, nature marks a crucial element of contingency. On the one hand, humanity is itself a product of nature. Thus, human knowledge is shaped by the contingencies of human biology (KHI: 41). On the other hand, however extensive human technology, nature will never be wholly revealed to humanity (KHI: 33). Nature always resists humanity, and thus can never be a subject with which humanity can identify (in contradiction to the presuppositions of the mature Hegel, or even Marcuse). From these two premises it follows that human knowledge is always contingent and incomplete, which suggests a fallibilism, somewhat akin to Peirce's. The acquisition of knowledge, and thus the very process of synthesis, necessarily occurs within human history. There is no position, *sub specie aeternitatis* from which progress can be judged. However, the perspectivism that threatened Peirce, and which is implicit to a purely economic interpretation of history, is avoided, precisely through Marx's entwining of technological and political perspectives. Even progress in the natural sciences is not to be assessed in terms of an ever closer approximation to some pre-existing and immediate reality. Rather, the task of assessing progress requires a turn towards the political imbalances that inhibit the process of rational inquiry (within Peirce's community of scientists, as much as in society as a whole). Crucially, this entails that truth is not conceived primarily as an ever closer approximation to first nature, but rather as the gradual exposure of the objective illusions of second nature. Put more precisely, the task of a critical social science is to expose the repressions that are constituted and reproduced through the mundane use of the "split-off symbols and reified grammatical relations" of a language and set of beliefs that have been systematically distorted by imbalances of power (KHI: 59).

Critical theory (Freud)

While Freud was still a student of Joseph Breuer, he encountered Breuer's patient "Anna O". Freud himself acknowledged Breuer's work with Anna O as the origin of psychoanalysis (Freud 1962: 31). The 21-year-old Anna O presented herself as suffering from a series of physical and psychological impairments, including paralysis on her right side, disturbed vision and hydrophobia. In addition, she suffered occasional "*absences*", or periods of aberrant behaviour and delirium, followed by deep sleep. Physical examination found the patient to be in good health, thereby implying that the illness was "hysterical" in origin. According to Freud, and untypically when compared to other medical doctors, Breuer took this hysteria seriously. "Hysterical" symptoms were frequently dismissed as little more than a sign of the natural weakness (and inferiority) of women (with "hysteria" being etymologically derived from the Greek for "womb"). Crucially, however, the very nature of Anna O's illness allowed Breuer insight into a cure. During periods of *absence*, the patient would utter words and, in response to questions, would develop the fantasies or daydreams of which these words were but fragments. After this, the patient was temporarily relieved of certain symptoms. Under hypnosis, this exploration of her mental life was taken further. The patient was gradually brought to the point of recalling the first occasion upon which a particular symptom occurred. The hydrophobia, for example, originated in an incident concerning the dog belonging to her lady companion. She disliked the companion, but had once discovered the dog drinking from a glass. Although she found this disgusting, out of politeness she said nothing. Once the patient had "energetically" expressed this disgust, under hypnosis, the hydrophobia was permanently cured (*ibid.*: 36).

A second case is equally telling. Elisabeth von R's symptoms included difficulty in walking and pains in her legs. Freud assumed that there was some original, psychically traumatic event behind the hysterical symptoms, but the patient would not succumb to hypnosis, Breuer's chosen method. Freud turned instead to word association. The method was partially successful, but at key points the patient remained silent. That Freud persisted at these points is crucial. Gradually a series of events was revealed that the patient had seemingly forgotten, concerning the attraction that she felt towards her brother-in-law, and her immediate thought, upon learning of her sister's early death: "Now he is free and can marry me" (*ibid.*: 49). Once this event was consciously recalled by the patient, the hysterical symptoms were cured.

These two short cases are significant in that they indicate much of how the psychoanalyst approaches the patient, and thus how the object of knowledge is constituted. First, the patient's symptoms may be understood as a form of second nature (KHI: 256); that is to say, that which initially appears to be a physical symptom is revealed to be an intentional product of human agency, albeit of an agency that is unrecognized as such by the agent. This insight entails the second crucial point. The agent is, in some sense, divided against themselves. Freud initially formulated this, in what is known as the topological model, as the distinction between the conscious and the unconscious. The agent has certain traumatic memories that they are unable to bear. Unwittingly, the patient deals with this burden through repression. Memories, such as those of Elisabeth von R about her reaction to her sister's death, are confined to the unconscious. Whereas the trauma associated with the memory finds expression in hysterical and neurotic symptoms, the processes of resistance continue to inhibit the memory's return to consciousness. Elisabeth von R's silences, during therapy, marked moments of resistance. This leads to a third point. The patient is cured not by physical intervention, but by a "talking cure". The dialogue with the analyst strives to make traumatic memories conscious, and thus to bring them under the autonomous control of the patient. The objective of psychoanalysis is thus one of personal enlightenment, which corresponds closely to Kant's sense of an alleviation from self-imposed tutelage.

This brief summary may already indicate why psychoanalysis plays a crucial role in concluding the argument of *Knowledge and Human Interests*. The first generation of Frankfurt School thinkers had devoted a great deal of attention to Freud, and indeed to the synthesis of psychoanalysis and Marxism. Habermas's interest in Freud is thereby very much in line with his Frankfurt inheritance. What makes Habermas's interpretation of psychoanalysis distinctive is his treatment of it as a "depth hermeneutics" (KHI: 218, 256–7). This is to suggest that psychoanalysis is to be understood primarily as a process of interpretation, akin to philosophical hermeneutics, albeit one that engages with superficially meaningless phenomena. As such, psychoanalysis presupposes a theory of language, although this is only obscurely recognized by Freud himself (KHI: 238).

In developing this notion of "depth hermeneutics", Habermas compares Freud to Dilthey. Both are concerned with the autobiography of their subjects. For Dilthey, autobiography is paradigmatic of the hermeneutic process as such, in so far as the individual agent in recounting their life history recounts from within a sequence of events and intentional actions that is transparent to them (KHI: 215). This grounds Dilthey's distinction between understanding and explanation. The difference between Freud and Dilthey lies in the fact that Dilthey sees flaws in memory as purely accidental. In contrast, Freud suggests that omissions and distortions are systematic (KHI: 217). This is to suggest that what initially may appear as purely natural phenomena, such as memory loss or neurotic behaviour, and thus as deserving of only explanation, are actually meaningful. Put in terms of a theory of language: "The essentially *grammatical* connection between linguistic symbols appears as a *causal* connection between empirical events and rigidified personality traits" (KHI: 257, original emphasis).

The task of a depth hermeneutics is to find meaning in that which superficially appears to be mere nature. This process may clearly be seen in Freud's interpretation of dreams. A dream may be treated as a text, and as such as the intentional creation of the dreamer, even if it is largely meaningless to them upon waking. Freud thus distinguishes between the manifest and latent content of the dream. The manifest content is the incoherent jumble recalled upon waking. Its raw material consists of fragmentary memories from the previous day. Interpretation will reveal a meaning – a latent content – concealed within this jumble, but in so doing will also explain the significance of the distortion itself (KHI: 220). Distortion is not accidental, but is the systematic product of the very trauma that ails the dreamer.

As has already been indicated with the hysteria and amnesia of Elisabeth von R, the phenomenon of resistance is a key to the relationship between manifest and latent content. The manifest content of the dream is a result of a process of censorship (KHI: 221). The dreamer entertains certain wishes, that Freud argues typically have their origin in childhood experiences, that the agent cannot consciously acknowledge or act upon in the waking world. In sleep, the control that governs this conscious self is weakened. The dreamer thus has scope to express their wish, but not in the way they want (KHI: 223). As Freud describes this, the manifest dream is "a *disguised* fulfilment of *repressed* wishes" (Freud 1962: 63, original emphasis). The wish is fulfilled in a form that is meaningless to the conscious self, and thus safely discharged. Yet the latent meaning can be recovered, for the process of distortion by which latent content is transformed into manifest content is rule-governed, albeit that the actual deployment and combination of rules employed in any particular dream will be largely unique to that dream. There is no simple dream dictionary, or even dream grammar, for the decoding of manifest content. The rules, or "dream work", include condensation – whereby an idea is elided, or two or more ideas are expressed by a single element of the dream – and displacement – where ideas are alluded to by related ideas, or where the emphasis of the dream is shifted from what should be its real focus. The more complex the dream work, the greater the degree of resistance. The analyst thus seeks to reconstruct the process of dream work, reversing the work of censorship, so that the patient can come to a conscious awareness of the wishes and childhood traumas that trouble them (KHI: 221).

Dreams are paradigms of hysterical and neurotic symptoms. Precisely in that Freud treats them as meaningful, Habermas can use them to develop a general reading of psychoanalysis in terms of a theory of language. At its most basic, Habermas suggests that hysterical and neurotic symptoms, along with the manifest content of dreams, are in a private language (KHI: 228) (and here Habermas may be seen to be invoking Wittgenstein's famous argument against private languages (Wittgenstein 1958: §269)). The division between the conscious and the unconscious is, starkly, that between public and private language. The trauma or wish that the conscious self cannot handle is made unproblematic by placing it outside public language. It is made incomprehensible. A symptom can then be defined as "a mutilation and distortion of the text of everyday habitual language games" (KHI: 238), or as "a substitute for a symbol whose function has been altered" (KHI: 257).

In explicating this, Habermas draws on the early Hegel. Symptoms are forms of the "split-off symbols": that is to say, elements of language split-off from public communication. The term "excommunication" is among the host of metaphors that Freud uses to describe repression. Habermas links this to "a specific category of punishment, whose efficacy was striking especially in archaic times: the expulsion, ostracism, and isolation of the criminal from the social group whose language he shares" (KHI: 241). Here, then, is Hegel's criminal (KHI: 236), expelled from their moral community. Yet, this expulsion is significant precisely in that it invokes the causality of fate. As language ceases to be a resource for giving meaning to the situation of the criminal – so that the possibility of grasping the sundering of the moral community is lost – this social process of exclusion begins to take on an illusory causal aspect. This mirrors the process of repression, in that the trauma returns in such seemingly causal phenomena as hysterical or neurotic symptoms. This is to begin to suggest that repression is thus a model of the process of reification already encountered in Marx's analysis of commodity fetishism. Again, Freud and Marx are both identifying processes through which what ought to be the meaningful actions of human subjects come instead to confront their authors as objectified, causal determinate events and relationships. Hermeneutic inquiry alone is incapable of penetrating this objectivity.

Habermas argues that Freud himself reveals a continual tendency to succumb to this very illusion. Freud, like Peirce, Dilthey and Marx, is the victim of positivism. This is most graphically manifest in his aspiration to turn psychoanalysis into a natural science of psychopharmacology (whereby neuroses would be cured through the causal intervention of drugs) (KHI: 246–50). More subtly, this same tendency is seen in Freud's tendency to take the meaninglessness of the unconscious realm literally. He tends to present the relationship between the conscious and the unconscious in terms that echo Peirce: that is to say, as the problem of the relationship between language and a pre-linguistic reality. Freud poses the question, "How does a thing become conscious?" His solution, to ask how a thing becomes preconscious, misses the point (KHI: 241). In so far as the "thing" is the unconscious, Habermas's contention is that it must be understood as, to coin a phrase, "post-linguistic" rather than pre-linguistic. It is a second nature, and as such the problem is not one of attaching language to it, but rather that of restoring it to language.

The role that language must play in Freud's analysis may be explored through his development of the concepts of the "ego" [das Ich], "id" [das Es] and "super-ego" [das Über-Ich]. The human being, in contrast to non-human animals, does not merely act upon its instincts. The motivations for human actions are not the mere givens of first nature, but are rather linguistically interpreted (KHI: 255). The role of the ego is to test wishes and desires against reality. This entails both a linguistically mediated interpretation of reality (which is to say, a lifeworld (KHI: 256)), which makes possible a range of realizable projects and an assessment of their advantages and risks, and an assessment of the motives for action themselves. Freud here again echoes Hegel, in recognizing the role that language plays in the realization of instrumental action (KHI: 239). Crucially, linguistic media-tion is not merely a classification or description of reality, but also an evalu-ation of it. Here is the root of repression. If there is a conflict between reality and the wish, typically the ego will either seek to transform reality or, if this is not possible, flee from reality. Should this conflict become habitual, Freud argues that the ego will turn from reality to the instinctual demands themselves. Unable to transform or flee from reality, the ego flees from its own wishes (KHI: 239–40). Subjective and meaningful wishes are thereby excommunicated, so as to confront the ego as mere things. They become "it" ("*id*" in Latin, "*es*" in German). The id is therefore properly understood as a post-linguistic unconscious, and not, as Freud sometimes positivistically reduces it to, a source of natural instincts and drives.

The "super-ego" is introduced into the structural model (as Freud calls it), to explain the interpretation of reality and wish. The super-ego represents that part of the ego that actually carries out the task of repression. It is formed through the social existence of the ego. In effect, it is the internalization of the expectations placed upon the developing ego by society (KHI: 243). The evaluation of reality and wish is thus achieved by the super-ego. The case of Elisabeth von R illustrates this neatly. The sexual desire for her brother-in-law is condemned by the super-ego. The desire can neither be realized nor con-sciously abandoned. The super-ego therefore forces it into the unconscious. Sundered from language, Elisabeth von R cannot remember it, and therefore confronts it, in the causality of fate, only in hysterical symptoms.

If the psychoanalytic account of repression is understood in terms of a theory of language, then the "talking-cure" becomes the only possible form of therapy, contra Freud's positivistic leanings. The patient is cured through a process of self-reflection that reverses resistance (KHI: 231). Yet, this reversal is possible only if a dialogue can be initiated between the two, sundered parts of the subject: ego and id (KHI: 257). A link must be established between the public language of the ego, and the private language of the id, so that the patient can come to recognize the id, and thus the trauma or repressed wishes objectified in it, as their own (and indeed as a meaningful part of their life history). This dialogue is realized through the therapeutic dialogue between the patient and analyst. The phenomenon of "transference" is crucial here. Within the "sheltered communication" (KHI: 252) of the analytic dialogue, the patient comes to direct towards the ana-lyst "a degree of affectionate feeling … which … can only be traced back to old wishful phantasies of the patient's which have become unconscious" (Freud 1962: 82). That is to say, that in relieving the patient of the pressures of normal life (KHI: 232), the patient comes to experience, in their relation-ship to the analyst, "that part of [their] emotional life which [they] can no longer recall to memory" (Freud 1962: 82). The analyst's interpretations of the patient's symptoms are thus crucial in stimulating the patient's own self-reflection. The analyst offers "interpretative suggestions for a story that the patient cannot tell" (KHI: 260).

The therapeutic dialogue is not, however, important merely for the cure of the patient. It is, more emphatically, the condition of possibility of emancipatory analytic knowledge as such. In Freud's phrase, "research and treatment coincide" (KHI: 252). In invoking this claim, Habermas is staking out the transcendental conditions of emancipatory knowledge. The conditions of natural scientific knowledge are those of controlled feedback (and thus, paradigmatically, the experimental conditions of the modern laboratory). The conditions of hermeneutic knowledge are the particular histories of the particular person or community that is author of a text. As an example of emancipatory knowledge, psychoanalysis presupposes a synthesis of the generality of natural scientific explanation with the particularity of hermeneutic understanding. Freud is not himself necessarily aware of this and, in appealing to a theory of instincts or drives, tends to offer a quasi-natural scientific account of human psychology and ego development. Such a positivistic account once again ignores the role of language, and thus that instincts, as the needs of the individual human being, must be linguistically interpreted and, further, that such interpretation depends wholly upon the unique life history of that particular person.

The analyst comes to a therapeutic dialogue armed with certain general theories of ego development. These may be understood as general narrative schemas, which indicate the stages of self-formation through which the individual must pass. Each stage is a problem, which the child must solve for itself. Thus, for example, the Oedipal conflict is one such stage. In theory it is articulated in a neutral language stripped of all contextual references (KHI: 264). As such, it is a hypothesis, and it may be corroborated or refuted in terms of the predictions that may be drawn from it (KHI: 258). However, the theory cannot then be employed in the instrumental manipulation of the patient. Within the therapeutic dialogue, general theory offers a framework within which the fragmentary evidence presented by the patient may be approached. It assists the analyst in offering suggested interpretations. The interpretation cannot be validated, however, unless it is accepted by the patient. The patient must remember their own life history, and this remembrance must be manifest in their action. Newly emancipated from the burden of reified wishes and memories, their autonomy will be restored. In effect, this is to demand that the context-neutral language of the general theory is reinterpreted, as appropriate, into the context-rich language of the patient's autobiography (KHI: 264).

The truth of emancipatory science lies, therefore, not in theories that allow effective instrumental engagement with the physical world, nor yet in interpretations of alien texts. Psychoanalytic interpretation is unlike hermeneutic interpretation, precisely in that its model cannot be, as it is for Gadamer, translation between languages (KHI: 227). Paradoxically, the text that is being interpreted by the analyst is a text in the language of the patient, albeit a language that the patient no longer recognizes. Again, psychoanalysis deals with systematic, rather than contingent, disruptions of communication. The truth of an emancipatory science therefore lies in the subject of inquiry freely remembering a reified and split-off portion of their life as their own, as was seen in the cases of Anna O and Elisabeth von R.

One problem remains with this account. The phenomenon of resistance, which is so fundamental to the whole development of Freud's theory, destabilizes this process of validation. A true interpretation may be rejected by the patient if their resistance is sufficiently strong. Indeed, an emancipatory interpretation may be rejected, precisely on the grounds that it will bring the trauma to consciousness. The emancipatory sciences, not least in their rejection of first philosophy and dogmatism, are thus left radically ambiguous in their results (KHI: 266–9). In part, this merely emphasizes that even emancipatory science cannot, and should not, seek to remove the threat of crisis. Perhaps more fundamentally it is to argue both for the importance and insufficiency of theory. The theorist is required to have a humble and yet obstinate faith in the worth of their interpretation (as manifest, for example, in Freud's persistence with Elizabeth von R). Yet, ultimately, theory can only be tested in the practice of the subject to whom it is applied. The radical uncertainty of emancipatory theory and practice ultimately demands the continued and open dialogue between theorist and patient.

The implications of this can be seen in Freud's writings on culture and history. Habermas treats these late writings (not least *Civilisation and its Discontents* and *The Future of an Illusion* (both in Freud 1985)) as complementary to Marx's historical materialism. Both recognize the role that technological development and struggles over the distribution of economic resources play in human history (KHI: 275–6). Yet, for Habermas, Freud's account of culture is better developed than Marx's, not least in that Freud's account rests upon an explicit understanding of the role of language and interaction (in contrast to Marx's tendency to reduce history to the movement of labour). If Freud's account of hysteria and neurosis, as a conflict between wishes and reality, is understood sociologically, then reality and, crucially, the wishes that it can allow to be realized, are dependent upon the development of the forces of production. The social institutions that constrain social members, and that they internalize as the super-ego, may thus be understood as a collective neurosis. They emerge as attempts to resolve the tension between the surplus wishes of agents, and the constraints of a technologically and politically structured reality. Individual needs are sanctioned, redirected, transformed and suppressed (KHI: 279).

The reality that is a given for the individual can, Freud recognizes, be changed by the society or the species (KHI: 280). The motivation for such changes has its roots in the very process of constraint. If civilization demands renunciation of wishes, then it also provides compensations. The "mental assets of civilisation" (KHI: 279) include religious worldviews, ideals and value systems, and art. As legitimations of the existing social order, they are split off from critical reflection. But, as dreams stand in a determinate relationship to the neuroses of the dreamer, so these collective "illusions" stand in a determinate relationship to social repression. Social institutions, as much as dreams and neuroses, express and satisfy the wishes of the neurotic, albeit not in the manner they want. Freud is at pains to explain that illusions are therefore not delusions. Illusions may have a utopian content that can be realized, if not in this reality, then in one that is technologically or politically transformed. In effect, Freud's analysis mirrors Marx, when he refers to religion as the "opium of the masses" (Marx 1975b: 244). It is not the numbing effect of opium that is at stake here, but rather the opium dream. Religions contain, in Freud's term, "phantasies", which while in their original form may deflect the adherent from the real political problems of this world, but may nonetheless contain a utopian seed – a yearning for a better life – that can motivate the demand for change. For Freud, an interest in the overcoming of a pathological compulsion will be present, and felt more or less obscurely, at the social as much as the individual level (KHI: 288). Repression thus provides the conditions under which a question formulated by Kant can be appropriated: "For what may we hope?" (KHI: 285).

Freud grasps history as a series of attempts to realize illusions. Reality is reshaped and reinterpreted in order to make previously suppressed wishes both practicable and acceptable. Crucially, in the context of the radical lack of certainty of psychoanalysis as an emancipatory science, this process is one of trial and error. Any realization of an illusion is tentative (KHI: 288), and may thus fail at great human cost. The truth of the illusion is tested only in practice and even then only provisionally. Freud himself refers to the "great experiment in civilisation" then being conducted in the Soviet Union (KHI: 284).

In sum, the illusions and opium dreams that are contained within even repressive ideologies are the substantive form that interests in the abolition of repression take. They are affirmative images of where emancipation is moving. Yet underpinning these particular images is a more general expression of the interest in emancipation. In Freud's words, this is the "provision of a rational basis for the precepts of civilisation". Habermas glosses "rationality" here as "an organisation of social relations according to the principles that the validity of every norm of political consequence be made dependent on a consensus arrived at in communication free from domination" (KHI: 284). Thus, even if emancipatory science can give no guarantee as to the worth of the substantive direction of political and therapeutic change, it still invokes a crucial critical ideal. This ideal is, for Habermas, the rational core that grounds all human activity. Free and open dialogue is present in Peirce's ideal community of scientists as much as in the hermeneutic dialogue between text and interpreter. In revealing the interest in communicative reason, the emancipatory sciences thereby unify and justify the transcendental status of the three knowledge-constitutive interests.

In *Knowledge and Human Interests*, Habermas argues against pure theory. Knowledge is necessarily bound to interests, and these interests are themselves grounded in the biological and social imperatives of human survival. The recognition of an interest in communication free from domination (which is to say, an interest in communicative reason) entails that an appeal to knowledge-constitutive interests can never be mere biological or even sociological reductionism. The interests are not mere facts of human nature, but necessarily entail procedures for the rational assessment of claims of both fact and value. Perspectivism and decisionism are thereby equally irrational, in so far as neither recognizes the transcendental status of communicative reason. It is precisely this theme of communicative reason, which is only obscurely articulated in *Knowledge and Human Interests*, that will become Habermas's abiding concern for the rest of his career.[7]

CHAPTER 4

Legitimation crisis

Criticisms of *Knowledge and Human Interests*

In 1973 Habermas left Frankfurt in order to become Director of Research at the Max Plank Institute for Research into the Living Conditions of the Scientific–Technical World in Starnberg. An initial product of this new working environment was *Legitimation Crisis*, published some five years after the completion of *Knowledge and Human Interests*. *Legitimation Crisis* (the direct translation of its German title is *Legitimation Problems in Late Capitalism*) is concerned with the nature of contemporary capitalism. Habermas formulates a series of immensely rich and subtle conjectures about the potential for fundamental structural and political change in capitalism, grounded in an analysis of the various forms of crisis that are understood to assail it, and which are managed with greater or lesser effectiveness.

To read *Legitimation Crisis* after *Knowledge and Human Interests* is to encounter a new, and at times bewilderingly unfamiliar, Habermas. This is not due to a change in subject matter – from philosophy to social theory – for the substantive concerns of *Legitimation Crisis* are those of the essays collected in *Towards a Rational Society* and *Theory and Practice*, albeit that Habermas does acknowledge that certain themes of his earlier work, and not least the argument against scientism, are rendered less pressing as they have been taken up by others (KHI: 354). The unfamiliarity lies rather in what is, superficially at least, a staggering shift in grounding theory. In part, this is due to Habermas's seemingly insatiable appetite for engaging with new theoretical frameworks. Systems theory and the cognitive psychology of Jean Piaget play a new and major role in shaping Habermas's thinking about society, and with them comes a plethora of new concepts (such as "steering mechanism" and "learning capacity"). But perhaps even more fundamentally, Habermas has responded to the intense discussion that was stimulated by *Knowledge and Human Interests*.[1] The failures and ambiguities that he acknowledges in *Knowledge and Human Interest* leads to a gradual abandonment of transcendental analysis in favour of an attempt to formulate a "language-theoretic foundation" to social theory (TCAI: xxxix). In effect, the concern with communicative reason, which had run as an important undercurrent of Habermas's thought since at least *Structural Transformation of the Public Sphere*, has now been brought to the fore. In *Legitimation Crisis*, Habermas approaches the problem of contemporary crisis through the fundamental part played by communication and language use in the reproduction of society.

The development of Habermas's thought may be approached by rehearsing his own criticisms of *Knowledge and Human Interests*. At the core of these criticisms lies a perceived failure to articulate adequately a theory of truth. At one level, Habermas sees himself as having conflated questions of truth with questions of object constitution (KHI: 360–61). That is to say that, in focusing on the role of the cognitive interests in constituting variously the objects of the natural, social and emancipatory sciences, Habermas lost sight of the problem of how truth claims within any science are justified. It is one thing to establish that the object of natural science is constituted through instrumental action; it is another to establish that a particular proposition within the natural sciences is true or false. On the first level, objects are experienced in so far as they are capable of being manipulated (in contrast to the objects constituted according to interaction, such as persons and utterances, which must be understood). On the second level, one asks if the propositions formulated about these objects are true or false. Although the same object may be experienced by all, not everyone will formulate their experience in the same way, and some of those formulations may be wrong. An apple's fall to earth is experienced, but to describe this event in terms of the apple's movement to its Aristotelian state of rest is false; to describe it in terms of the attraction of the earth's gravitational field is true. The truth of a proposition cannot merely be established through the instrumental feedback made possible by labour, although that may play a dominant role in simple observational propositions (KHI: 364). As Habermas has already suggested in his discussion of Peirce's community of scientists (see § "Pragmatism", p. 67) – and indeed before that, in his appeal to Popper's legal metaphor for the process of establishing the relevance of an observation statement to the refutation or corroboration of a hypothesis (see § "Reason", p. 14) – to establish truth requires discussion within the community.

In effect, Habermas's later work brings the phenomenon of communal debate to the foreground of his analyses. The question of truth is not thereby simply separated from that of object constitution, but is also reconfigured as a problem of communicative reason. The problem of finding a third way between the instrumental reason (and its attendant decisionism) and dialectics (and its decay into either Adorno's quietism or Lukács's authoritarianism) is resolved by explicating the rational processes that competent agents must follow in order to challenge or defend the truth of propositions. The problems of object constitution, and thus transcendental analysis, retreat into the background.

Knowledge and Human Interests did offer a theory of truth. However, it did so through the analysis of the emancipatory interest. Truth lay in the subject's recognition and acceptance of its own unconscious or reified actions, and thus in the restoration of autonomy. The particular subject therefore engages in a process of reflection, giving rise to a personal narrative of repressed memories that serves to restore autonomous agency. Habermas criticizes this position as "reconstruction" for failing to articulate a second sense of reflection (KHI: 377; TP: 22–3). Reconstruction similarly brings to consciousness something that is otherwise "unconscious". Yet, the unconscious processes considered in reconstruction do not spoil autonomous action. The issue here is not one of false consciousness; rather, reconstruction brings to light the rule systems that are followed by competent agents and that make possible their very competence. (Consider, for example, the grammatical rules of ordinary languages. Competent speakers must have mastered these rules, but few will be able to articulate in any detail the rules that they follow with such fluency.) Reconstructions do not change the behaviour of the subject (so that one does not typically communicate any better having studied grammar), and nor, indeed, are they tied to particular subjects, as is the therapeutic narrative of the psychoanalytic patient. Reconstructions are of "anonymous" systems of rules, intuitively followed by all competent agents.

Something akin to reconstruction has already been encountered in psychoanalysis and historical materialism. The narrative of an individual patient is constructed against the background of a general theory of ego development. Similarly, general accounts of the development and succession of modes of production frame the historical narratives of particular societies. As such, Habermas can suggest that the "theoretical development of self-reflection" is dependent on reconstruction (TP: 24). However, once one acknowledges both the distinction between reflection and reconstruction, and that reconstructions are legitimate forms of inquiry independently of their role in the emancipatory sciences, then the theory of cognitive interests becomes problematic. This is because the reconstructive sciences then appear to lie outside the scope of any of the three interests, "untouched by the technical as well as the practical interest" (TP: 24). Rational reconstruction may thereby be seen as coming to displace transcendental inquiry at the heart of Habermas's later work, not least in the centrality of the rational reconstruction of the rules followed in communication (which he terms "universal pragmatics" (see p. 138)).

This shift from reflection to reconstruction also has implications for Habermas's understanding of power, and thus for the political and normative implications of the work. In *Knowledge and Human Interests* power is primarily understood in terms of unconscious or reified structures inhibiting autonomous action (and thus, again, questions of truth are inextricably entwined with the problem of dissolving such inhibitions). A model for the resolution of power relations is provided by the dialogue between the psychoanalyst and the patient. Yet, as Habermas notes, this dialogue itself entails an imbalance of power, given the doctor's greater theoretical expertise and authority (TP: 15). This raises doubts about its appropriateness as a model for political action (not least in so far as it invites abuses similar to those suffered by Lukács's model of the party and "imputed class consciousness"). In response to the first problem, Habermas reasserts the importance of historical materialism, albeit now in a rational reconstruction as a theory of social evolution. He responds to the second problem of power differentials by, effectively, replacing Freud's psychoanalytic dialogue with Peirce's community of scientists as the key to unlocking the problem of power. Peirce's dialogue is open to all competent participants, and crucially is held between equals. The relationship between truth and power is fundamentally refigured, as something akin to the Peircean community is recognized as the context within which the truth of any given proposition is discursively and rationally defended. The rules of such discursive processes are, at least in part, the subject matter of a reconstructive inquiry. Power now lies not simply in the split-off symbols that spoil the potential for self-understanding and autonomy, but rather in processes that serve to exclude agents from full participation in the discursive community, and thus inhibit the exercise of communicative competence, leading to what Habermas will term "systematically distorted communication" (KHI: 371). At this level, the reconstructive science responds to something akin to the emancipatory interest, for the reconstruction of the rule system followed by the discursive community does not merely offer an account of how discussion does proceed, but, as will be seen, also explicates the implicit norms (the aspiration to open, consensual agreement, and the counterfactual presupposition of this ideal in all mundane discussion (TP: 17)), which competent communicants intuitively acknowledge.

The work that comes after *Knowledge and Human Interests* may, in summary, be seen to pursue familiar goals, but to do so with radically new means. Clarifying the ambiguities that existed between issues of truth and object constitution, and between reflection and reconstruction threw into question the primacy of transcendentalism in *Knowledge and Human*

Interests. Yet, this clarification also opened up the space within which a universal pragmatics, which is to say the reconstruction of the communicative competence of lay social agents, could be worked out. This provides Habermas with a complex theory of truth and rationality that retains the practical and emancipatory aspirations of the theory of cognitive interests. Crucially, by making explicit the centrality of language and communication in his social theory, Habermas is able to revitalize basic issues in social and political theory, not least those concerning the reproduction and transformation of society. The substantiation of these general remarks may thus be attempted, by examining the issues at the core of *Legitimation Crisis*, and rehearsing in details the theoretical resources that Habermas develops to deal with them.

Systems theory

The concept of "crisis" is already familiar from Habermas's early work, not least in the link made between "crisis" and "critique" in "Between Philosophy and Science" (see § "Crisis and critique", p. 20). "Crisis" was there seen to be intimately related to the experience of the subject, and the critical need to press for a decision (TP: 213). The initial remarks in *Legitimation Crisis* suggest a similar trajectory through reference to the ideas of medical and spiritual crisis, and in addition that of dramatic or tragic crisis (LC: 1–2). As such, crisis is situated in relation to reflection, and emancipation through self-knowledge. By immediately refiguring crisis in the language of social systems theory, Habermas challenges this presupposition, precisely because systems theory appears to do away with the notion of the subject.

A systems theory of society had been developed in the mid-twentieth century by the American sociologist Talcott Parsons as a refinement of functionalism, and Habermas comments upon this body of theory in *On the Logic of the Social Sciences* (LSS: 74–88). However, systems theory was revitalized in Germany in the early 1970s by Niklas Luhmann (1982, 1987), and it is principally Luhmann's work that now concerns Habermas. Initially the approach of treating society as a system entailed drawing an analogy between society and a biological organism (as had been done by American functionalism), and thus drawing upon the development of a systems theory approach to biology. More sophisticated versions draw upon cybernetics. The crucial relationship for both models is that between the system and its environment. An environment is highly complex, and a system must maintain its existence by bringing "its own complexity into an appropriate relationship to that of the environment" (Luhmann 1987: 176). This is to suggest that the system is more ordered than its environment and, indeed, that the death or destruction of the system occurs with the loss of that particular form of organization. The system survives by appropriating resources from its environment, and using those resources to reduce its internal complexity and contingency relative to that of the environment. This may entail the complex differentiation of the system into subsystems (such as, for society, the economy, the family, the state and so on). Steering mechanisms are the means by which this internal organization, or "system integration" (LC: 2), is maintained.

On Habermas's account, a social system must respond, not merely to the external physical environment, but also to the internal environment of human subjectivity. The economic system of production appropriates the external environment, and processes of socialization appropriate the inner environment, moulding individuals to the needs of the social system, and crucially, providing them with the normative resources that allow their actions to be coordinated and thus the internal structure of the system to be maintained (LC: 8). Almost in passing he notes two sources of tension within contemporary capitalism (over and above his principal concern with legitimation crises, which are themselves grounded in socialization). These are the ecological problems that result from the relationship between the economic system and the physical environment, and the threat of nuclear war that emerges from the relationship between nations as social systems (LC: 41–4).

Paradoxically, the weaknesses and strengths of systems theory alike lie in its neglect of the creativity and autonomy of the human subject. Both Parsons and Luhmann acknowledge that a purely cybernetic description of society cannot be sufficient. However, Habermas finds neither Parsons's appropriation of action theory, nor Luhmann's attempt to theorize meaning in terms of a system (whereby society is understood as a "meaning-using system" (Luhmann 1987: 177)) adequate. Systems theory reduces meaning to behaviour (LC: 6) or, more dramatically, draws "too hastily a continuity [of human action] with the intelligent performance of animals" (LC: 9). That is to say that the problem of the subject's understanding of society (and thus most fundamentally, the intersubjective participation of individuals in the creation and maintenance of social relationships) is marginalized, and at worst it is reduced to a mere inflection of the imperatives of the system. Yet, this theoretical impasse is a strength, if only because it highlights the insufficiency of emancipatory reflection. *Knowledge and Human Interests*, drawing its inspiration from Marx, suggested that reification can be dissolved – akin to an individual's neurosis in psychoanalysis – so that the social world becomes wholly transparent or meaningful to its members. Habermas is now becoming increasingly suspicious of this optimism. He is beginning to entertain the idea that some degree of reification or objectification is necessary in the organization of complex modern societies. (At the very least, this requires a refinement in the definition of "reification", which in practice waits until *The Theory of Communicative Action*.) A complex society is typically experienced by its own members as a constraining and objective entity. Systems theory does not merely acknowledge and indeed focus upon that aspect of society, but in addition draws attention to it as a material substrate that provides the conditions that make social change possible. The problem for Habermas is to demonstrate the interconnection between society as a (reified) system and society as something understood and maintained by autonomous and competent social actors (LC: 4).

In *Knowledge and Human Interests* this is the problem of how the revolutionary potential of the material contradiction between the forces of production and the relations of production is taken up and realized as a political problem in the consciousness of social actors (see § "Critical theory (Marx)", p. 86). It is here that the notion of crisis is situated. A social crisis occurs when a society, considered as a system, has insufficient resources to solve problems that threaten its continued existence (LC: 2). Hence, unable to resolve the contradiction between the potential of its forces of production and the unjustifiable distribution of income and wealth of its relations of production, the feudal system disintegrates. Yet a pure systems theory approach to crisis is inadequate, precisely because it cannot explain how a crisis in the material substrate of society is realized as a crisis in the consciousness of its members. If society is ultimately composed of conscious human beings, then there can be a response to crises only if those human beings are, in some sense, aware of a problem to be solved.

Habermas approaches this issue by setting the concept of "system integration" against that of "social integration", or "system" against the familiar, but now enriched, concept of "lifeworld" (LC: 3–4). The lifeworld encompasses the normative structures, worldviews and shared meanings (LC: 10) through which members of society make sense of themselves and their social and physical environments. At one level, such normative structures are instilled into human beings through the process of socialization, as systems theory suggests. However, at another level, Habermas is at pains to avoid the classic reduction of human beings to what Irving Garfinkel called "judgmental dopes" (1967: 68). This is to say that, for Habermas, human beings can never be reduced to the merely passive recipients of social imperatives, as earlier forms of functionalism suggested. For Habermas, a crucial paradox that systems theory must confront therefore lies in the fact that the human being – the inner environment that the system must appropriate – is both system environment and system element (LC: 14). This is to say that the process of socialization does not reduce the human being to the

judgemental dope who merely functions as the system demands. Socialization equips individuals with competences that simultaneously allow them to
perform as the system requires, but also to question or challenge those
requirements.

It is here that Habermas begins to account for the relationship between
system and lifeworld and, indeed, between the Marxist material base and class
consciousness. From a systems theory perspective, the outer environment is
appropriated through production and the inner environment through
socialization. From the perspective of the lifeworld, and thus from the perspective of meaningful human action as opposed to mere behaviour, production takes place "through the medium of utterances that admit of truth", and
socialization through "norms that have need of justification" (LC: 8).

Habermas is thus reasserting the importance of labour and interaction. Yet,
this point also depends upon his break from their transcendental interpretation in *Knowledge and Human Interests*. In criticism of *Knowledge and
Human Interests*, Habermas now distinguishes between objects of experience
and facts (KHI: 365). The mere event of production must therefore be
distinguished from the way in which that event is interpreted and, crucially,
the way in which the knowledge claims upon which social production rests
are evaluated (or, in Habermas's terminology, "redeemed"). Similarly,
socialization is not to be understood as a monological process (metaphorically
imprinting a normative structure upon the developing individual). Socialization is a dialogical process, whereby norms and their attendant worldviews
must be explained and justified. Social integration (as opposed to system
integration) is therefore understood by Habermas to be a fundamentally
linguistic process. This is to say that social integration does not rest upon the
conformity of individual social agents (as elements of the system) to predetermined places in the structure, but rather upon an active negotiation and
reproduction of that structure.

Habermas can now respond to the problem of how a social system
handles a crisis by treating the system's adaptive steering mechanisms
(production and socialization) as learning processes. That is to say, that a
society responds to crises through the capacity that its members have for
learning and problem solving. In broad outline, Habermas will argue that
threats from the external environment are dealt with through developments
in science and technology, and threats to social stability – from tensions
within the society – are dealt with through the development of moral, legal
and cultural resources. Thus, he is asserting that human beings are inherently creative beings. As he expresses this, human beings have "an automatic
inability not to learn. Not *learning*, but *not-learning* is the phenomenon that
calls for explanation" (LC: 15). Yet, these learning capacities do not merely
respond to system imperatives. The ability of the system to respond to a

crisis, and the nature of that response, will be determined by a complex of contingent social and historical factors. These will include, on the one hand, the technological and cultural resources that are available to social actors. On the other hand, it will depend upon the degree of the sophistication that their learning capacities have reached (LC: 11). This is to suggest that learning capacity is to be grasped as a formal condition that facilitates the agent's response to a concrete situation; but that it is not a mere given, being rather something that will unfold over the course of history.[2]

The reconstruction of historical materialism

Explaining social change

A theory of social crisis inevitably entails a theory of social change, and it is precisely in such a theory that the above suggestions, concerning the place of the learning capacity of societies, can be developed and defended. Habermas looks towards Marx's historical materialism for a tentative first model for this theory; and yet he offers a series of what seem to be damning criticisms of historical materialism and, indeed, his "reconstruction" of it has little obviously in common with its predecessor.[3]

Habermas's theory of social change may be explicated by rehearsing his four principle criticisms of historical materialism. His first criticism concerns precisely the expectation that the conflict of the forces and relations of production provides an explanation of social change. Habermas's point is that this conflict may provide an example of a system crisis, not least in so far as that conflict threatens the destruction of the current mode of production, and as such triggers social change. However, it cannot explain the mechanism of change and, crucially, it cannot account for the construction of a new mode of production (CES: 146). This failing is not, however, exclusive to historical materialism. In reviewing a series of theories that attempt to explain the transition to early class society, Habermas notes that they typically fail to distinguish between the systems problems that overload the adaptive capacity of earlier forms of society, and the learning capacity that must exist in order to create a new form of social organization (CES: 160). The theoretical distinction between these two levels is necessary if the theory is to recognize that change does not occur according to quasi-natural iron laws (as positivistic theories from Henri de Saint-Simon and Auguste Comte onwards suggested), but is rather an open-ended process. The mere occurrence of system crisis does not allow one to predict the nature of the change, but merely to assert that change will indeed occur. As noted above, the nature and direction of change will depend upon other factors, such as the material and cultural resources available to the society's members.

The second criticism can be seen as a further elaboration of the first. Marx appears to offer an explanation for change in the autonomous development of the forces of production. This is seen to be problematic on a number of fronts. The first front is that even if the thesis of autonomous development of the forces of production was empirically corroborated, it is not clear from empirical evidence that the mere development of technological resources is a common source of system crises (CES: 146). An appeal to the transformative power of the forces of production is plausible only within the context of the primacy that Marx gives to the economic base as the source of social change (and indeed of the shaping of the whole social superstructure). Hence, the second front lies precisely in this economic determinism. Habermas does not reject the metaphor of base and superstructure. However, he does question whether the economy can always be identified with the base (LC: 17). The base may be understood as the crucial social subsystem in so far as a crisis within this system will lead to a crisis in the society as a whole. However, only in capitalism does the economy emerge as the base subsystem. In early societies, Habermas suggests, it is the family that is basic, and in pre-capitalist civilizations (which is to say, pre-industrial societies with government through a state) it is the political subsystem that forms the base (CES: 144).

The problem of economic determinism may be taken one step further, once it is recognized that even if the development of the forces of production were to bring about crisis, theoretically, the fact of the autonomous development of productive technology is insufficient to account for social change, for such change requires not just a renewal of the economic and technical subsystems of the society, but also of its moral, legal and cultural subsystems (CES: 146). This is, in effect, to repeat the criticism that is already familiar from *Knowledge and Human Interests*, that Marx gives a spurious primacy to labour over interaction. Habermas now develops this criticism by approaching historical materialism as a theory of the development of the human species. As such, it should contain within itself the criteria to distinguish the development of animals from that of human beings – which is to say, natural evolution from social evolution.

Marx aspires to do this by seeing social labour as the distinctive capacity of human beings (CES: 131, 138). This, Habermas argues, is empirically incorrect. Social labour may be understood as the capacity to transform the environment freely, and as such entails not merely the individual creature's ability to labour and to use tools, but also the cultural embodiment of technological knowledge, and the ability to organize producers together. By appealing to recent anthropological speculation, Habermas suggests that this capacity is enjoyed, not only by human beings (which is to say, *Homo sapiens*), but also by the hominids that were their immediate evolutionary ancestors. This leads to a subtle point, for social labour serves to stave off the immediate pressures of the environment that bring about natural evolution. In effect, rather than the species evolving in response to environmental pressure, the species can remain unchanged while it changes the environment. However, hominids did evolve naturally. Habermas points, for example, to the development of the size of the brain and changes in anatomy (CES: 133). Thus, the hominids must have been subject to both natural and social evolution.

Homo sapiens are not subject to natural evolution. Therefore a second factor must be in place to explain their difference from hominids. Habermas suggests that this is the development of language, which in turn makes possible a radically different form of social organization. He speculates that hominids would have achieved a division of labour, based for example on a gender distinction between male hunters and female gatherers. The power hierarchy in such a society would however be akin to that found in other primate societies, which is to say a one-dimensional structure, based upon the physical prowess of the individuals concerned. In contrast, the development of a distinctively human language (as opposed to the system of "signal calls" attributed to hominids (CES: 134)) allows the one-dimensional hierarchy to be replaced by a hierarchy of linguistically and thus morally interpreted social roles (principally those centring upon the family). Roles acquire an intersubjective validity, in so far as they rest upon a set of reciprocal expectations as to how the role occupant would behave. "Alter can count on ego fulfilling [alter's] expectations because ego is counting on alter fulfilling [ego's] expectations" (CES: 136). This allows the human agent to perceive a social situation from the perspective of a role they do not currently occupy. Habermas can thus conclude: "Labour and language are older than man and society" (CES: 137).[4]

Social evolution and history

A third criticism of historical materialism is that it invalidly presupposes what Habermas calls a "macrosubject" (CES: 140). That is to say, historical materialism presents history as if it were the story of the development of a specifiable actor, albeit that this actor is the human species. This may be understood as a residue of Marx's Hegelianism. The logical and cultural development that is charted by Hegel's *Encyclopedia of the Philosophical Sciences* may be read as a narrative, the hero of which, Spirit [*Geist*], is coming to a mature self-understanding. It is a story of growth and maturation

(HE: 30). So, too, Marx may be read as providing a narrative of the coming to self-consciousness of the human species. In particular, this may be seen in Lukács's account of the proletariat as the bearers of human emancipation. The fallacy here for Habermas lies in the fact that the processes traced in historical materialism are in fact borne by societies, not by the human species as such. There is therefore no single protagonist in social evolution, for particular societies cease to exist and are replaced by others. Again, this is to distinguish between natural evolution (which concerns the development of species) and social evolution (where the species remains unchanged, while its culture, politics and technology are transformed). In effect, as reconstructive sciences, both theories of natural and social evolution establish the rules that make possible not just processes of change, but also the existence of subjects (be these species or societies). However, such rules outline the mechanisms by which either natural species or societies are transformed. As such, neither theory requires a guiding intelligence. Just as natural evolution does not require a watchmaking macro-subject (as favoured by natural theology) to direct it, so social evolution does not need a Hegelian macro-subject becoming self-consciousness within its machinations.

Perhaps more profoundly, the fallacy also lies in a conflation of social evolution with historical narrative. In broad terms, historical materialism has presented the contingent history of Western societies as a necessary and universal development. The reconstruction of historical materialism therefore rests precisely on a strong distinction between the writing of historical narratives (which trace contingent events, recognizable to social actors) and social evolution (which is an account of the emergence of the highly abstract and general structures that underpin and make possible the changes that are recorded at the level of narrative).

Habermas's understanding of historical science is still broadly that articulated in *Knowledge and Human Interest*. History is grounded in the practical cognitive interest. As such, the historian draws upon their everyday communicative skills, and thus upon the resources that are embedded in the lifeworld, and does so in order to engage in a dialogue with the past. In this dialogue, the self-understanding of the historian's own community is at stake (either by reinforcing and amplifying the existing tradition of interpretation or, more radically, by questioning and subverting that tradition) (HE: 40–41). In contrast, social evolution is presented as a rational reconstruction, and as such is a scientific inquiry that is divorced from the cognitive interests. This entails that while the historian draws upon concrete competences of the lifeworld that are available alike to both scientists and to their subjects, the theory of social evolution looks to the otherwise hidden (or "unconscious") structures that make possible the competences of the lifeworld. Precisely what these structures are will gradually become clear.

Historical science, as it is presented in *Knowledge and Human Interests*, is concerned to produce narratives of particular communities. As such, it is always haunted by the threat of relativism. History is necessarily written from a particular historical perspective, and thus potentially distorted by the ideological blind-spots and ignorances that characterize that historical moment. In *Knowledge and Human Interests*, Habermas was concerned to remedy that relativism through emancipatory science. At this later stage, putting to one side the reshaping of the emancipatory sciences that will occur in the development of universal pragmatics, Habermas seeks rather to complement the relativism of history with the universalism of social evolution. Put otherwise, the historian writes of the contingent events of history – and does so necessarily in ignorance of later historical developments – while the social evolutionist examines the universal structures that underpin the movement of history as such. Yet, as has already been noted, Habermas is at pains to avoid the reduction of social evolution to quasi-natural laws of historical development (not least because such a reduction would misconceive the historical sciences in terms of the technological cognitive interest, and thus capitulate to a form of positivism). Social evolution is concerned rather with what Habermas calls universal learning capacities, which is to say, general competences that are deeply embedded in the very nature of human beings, and which as such make possible the human ability to respond to environmental challenges. Put in broad terms, as these competences develop, so too does the sophistication of a given society's capacity to solve problems. Although the presence of such capacities may thus serve to explain the ability of a society to respond to crises and thus change, they do not describe inevitable changes. The potential that learning capacities make available at any given moment in history may or may not be realized. Much will depend on the concrete circumstances of the system crisis. In effect, universal competences may be seen as purely formal, defining the "logical space in which more comprehensive structural formations can take shape" (CES: 140). It may also be noted that Habermas acknowledges that the human potential to know that these universal capacities exist is itself dependent upon concrete historical circumstances. The capacities must have been sufficiently manifest in human society for the social evolutionist to be aware of them. He thus notes that one cannot logically rule out the possibility of the emergence of further previously unrecognized universal capacities in the future (HE: 43). This is a problem that nags Habermas's project, and it is not clear that his appeals to pragmatism and the place of fallibilism in science wholly resolves it.

Habermas identifies a number of precursors of social evolutionary theory other than historical materialism. An examination of these will help to clarify the scope and nature of social evolution, and so begin to explain exactly what universal capacities may be, and how they come to replace the problematic macro-subject of Marx's historical materialism. Hegel's history of philosophy provides an initial example. Following a style of argument that runs back to Aristotle, Hegel presents the history of philosophy as a series of problems, with each stage in the development of philosophy being understood as a solution to the problems left by its predecessor. As such he begins to outline not a narrative that is tied to particular historical figures, but rather a reconstruction that explores the logic of the development of a profound philosophical competence (HE: 16–17). The problem with such an approach is that it typically reconstructs only one specific learning capacity. Hegel is ultimately concerned with only one style of philosophy. Despite Hegel's aspirations, philosophy was not completed in his *Encyclopedia of the Philosophical Sciences*. Similar reconstructions could therefore be provided for other schools of philosophy, and Habermas suggests that they have indeed been written for other intellectual developments, including the history of geographical discoveries, and technological and scientific innovation (HE: 17; CES: 146). Such accounts remain histories, for two reasons.

First, while the achievements with which they are concerned may have very general significance, they remain particular competences. (The Europeans' discovery and colonization of America may well represent the overcoming of a series of technical and even social problems. It remains, nonetheless, a particular achievement. The development of navigational technologies and modern understandings of geographical space are fundamentally more general in their scope and application.) The histories of such particular achievements are written from a contingent perspective. As with all historical narratives, their importance is vulnerable to the continuing march of events, and thus to the possibility of the identification of ever new problems and solutions (so that, for example, the colonization of America shifts in significance as American political influence wanes and waxes, and it is a different history from the perspective of the European settler in comparison to that of the Native American; the achievements of Hegelian philosophy are rewritten in the light of their subsumption into Marxism and critical theory, or their rejection by Anglo-Saxon analytic philosophy). Here Habermas gives what seems to be a profound, yet puzzling example. Werner Heisenberg's unified field theory in physics "closes off a series of 'completed theories'" (HE: 18). As such it rules out further development along certain paths, and as soon as that openness to the future is lost, history may become reconstruction.

Secondly, as histories these putative reconstructions chart the success and failure of attempts to realize the given competence. Habermas thus distinguishes between the history of a particular technology, and that of, say, "bronze metallurgy" or "the rational history of technology or of modern science" (HE: 17). The latter two would be such that they could not be satisfactorily shaped as histories. In effect – and this seems to be the point of the Heisenberg example – once the competence reaches a certain level and a certain degree of generality (i.e. once it can genuinely be called universal) one need no longer be interested solely in the contingent historical narrative of its development, but rather in the very nature of the competence itself. A logical development that defines and explains the competence may then come to replace the historical narrative. The shift is from an interest in the historical actors who gradually acquire this competence to an interest in the emergence or manifestation of this competence in history, precisely in so far as this allows an understanding of exactly what the competence is and to the way in which it makes a given stage of history possible (HE: 18). (Hence, for example, an understanding of exactly what bronze metallurgy entails – not least in terms of the sophistication of the problem-solving skills that it demands – clarifies the meaning of the "bronze age" as a general stage in human development.)

A second example may further clarify this. Habermas turns to the work of the sociologist Max Weber. Weber's rationalization thesis traces the process of rationalization as it is manifest in various different social institutions and cultural activities, including science and technology, law, bookkeeping, and even architecture and music (Weber 1976: 13–23). The process of rationalization, precisely in so far as it is seen to facilitate the transformation of diverse social institutions (and indeed Western society as a whole) therefore has the form of the development of a universal competence. The reservations that Habermas nonetheless retains about the rationalization thesis are linked to the fact that Weber understands rationality in terms of instrumental reason, and as such it can only be a partial explanation of human evolutionary capacities, accounting for technological and economic change, but not interaction. More significantly, however, Weber is criticized for failing to reflect upon rationalization as a structure of universal competence. Rationalization is understood as a contingent achievement of Western societies. Weber presents his sociology as a Western understanding of history. It claims superiority over other accounts, not on the grounds of any objectivity or universality, but simply on the basis of the global dominance (and thus instrumental efficacy) that Western culture has achieved in comparison to any rival. Weber's thesis thus falls short of a rational reconstruction precisely because of its overt perspectivism (HE: 35–6).

The Weberian scholar Benjamin Nelson takes this problematic further by reflecting upon the emergence of modern consciousness from the twelfth and thirteenth centuries. Crucially, at the core of Nelson's argument lies the recognition that the development of modern philosophical, theological and legal competence lay in the shift to "universally oriented thinking based only on argument" (HE: 36). As such, the Weberian account of instrumental rationality is complemented by a developing awareness of the importance of communicative rationality. Habermas thus sees in Weber and Nelson's work the first indications of the level of generality at which the social evolutionary reconstruction of competences must work. Social evolution is not interested in the reconstruction of theology, philosophy or law, let alone science or technology, but rather in the structures of thought that underpin and make any institutional development possible. Nelson's fault, Habermas suggests, like Weber's, lies in failing to recognize the true nature of such competences. Nelson traces them back, historically, to contingent features of the early medieval European worldview. Habermas responds by taking this historical trace further, noting that similar, universalistic, worldviews arise between 800 and 300 BCE in China, India, Greece and Israel (HE: 37). However, the reliance upon contingent historical developments is broken altogether if it is accepted, as Habermas suggests, that these competences are "anthropologically deep-lying" (HE: 42). This evokes once more Habermas's speculative appeal to the natural evolution of the hominid. It is to suggest that social evolution is concerned with the reconstruction of the logical development of those competences, the combination of which distinguished *Homo sapiens* from the other hominids: these competences are therefore grounded in labour and interaction.

In sum, Habermas is arguing that the availability of given levels of theoretical and practical competence (or, in other words, cognitive–instrumental and moral–practical consciousness structures) at a moment of system crisis is the key factor in explaining the possibility of its resolution, in so far as the system can bring about the evolution of a new and higher social formation. Whereas historians narrate the contingent changes that do occur, social evolutionists, divorcing themselves entirely from the concrete historical narrative, concern themselves with the unfolding of universal and highly abstract structures of labour and interaction that make possible the response of a society of *Homo sapiens* to a systems crisis (HE: 43).

After this rather long excursus on the relation of history and evolution, Habermas's fourth criticism of historical materialism may be dealt with briefly, not least because it follows inevitably from the preceding criticisms. The sequence of modes of production that Marx identifies is rejected on the grounds that it is under-theorized, and thus that the key distinctions made between modes of production are arbitrary. Six modes of production are generally accepted: primitive communism; ancient civilizations based upon slavery; feudalism; capitalism; socialism; and the Asiatic mode of production encompassing ancient civilizations in the Orient and the Americas (CES: 139). Habermas identifies a series of ambiguities in the definition of these modes (CES: 150–52). The theorization of contemporary capitalism remains problematic, being disputed in terms of competing theories of "post-industrial society" and "organized capitalism", while its evolutionary relation to the bureaucratic socialism of twentieth-century eastern Europe and contemporary China remains undecided. The statuses of both the feudal mode (which may or may not be uniquely European) and the Asiatic mode (which seems divorced from the evolutionary movement of the other modes) are ambiguous. Perhaps most crucially there is no distinction between what Habermas terms archaic and more developed civilizations. That is to say that the orthodox concept of the ancient mode fails to recognize precisely that moment, between the eighth and third centuries BCE, when a change of worldviews in China, India, Israel and Greece marked a significant development in universal learning capacities. Orthodox historical materialism is thus indifferent to what Habermas, after Karl Jaspers, calls "axial periods" in history (CES: 228; HE: 38).

A pause for breath

Habermas's response to the problems of orthodox historical materialism may now be seen as the extraordinarily ambitious programme it is. In so radically separating social evolution from the writing of history Habermas is, on the one hand, ensuring that he does not offer a contingent history as a necessary and universal movement. (Orthodox historical materialism, after all, does tend to present the contingency of western European history as if it were a necessary development, hence, not least, the embarrassing question of the Asiatic mode of production.) On the other hand, he is eschewing all perspectivism. The theory of social evolution aspires to the same definitiveness as did Hegel's *Encyclopedia of the Philosophical Sciences* and, indeed, Marx's own theory. Habermas is not put off by the failure of his predecessors. He relinquishes even the comparative modesty of Weberian theory. Like the Weberian analysis of rationalization, social evolution looks beneath the surface of history and lifeworld, and in looking to a deep-seated developmental logic does away with any superficial classification of more or less advanced social formations. Unlike Weber, however, Habermas does not ascribe this developmental logic to an accident of Western culture. It lies, rather, in the very nature of what it is to be human, and thus in labour and interaction. Habermas's only concession to the possibility that the theory may be in need of future revision lies in the probability of new universal competences being brought to consciousness by future social crises. Such revision would, however, merely add to the theory, and not demand the revision of what was already in place. Social evolution may therefore be seen to be tracing the development of the rules that make possible emancipated societies. The claim is indeed this strong. Habermas is not simply interested in the evolution to contemporary capitalist society. This, after all, would return the whole theory to the level of Weberian perspectivism. The theory of social evolution is intended to allow a projection beyond contemporary society in order to explicate the standards of justice and truth that will make possible objective criticism of contemporary society, thereby restoring the intentions of critical theory. (It is here that the theory of social evolution meets that of universal pragmatics (see p. 138).)

Ontogenesis and phylogenesis

As has been suggested in criticism of historical materialism and other accounts of social change, a social evolutionary explanation requires two key elements (CES: 122, 160). First, it must be able to identify the source of challenge to the continuing existence of the social system. This challenge may be external (from the physical environment or other societies), but more significantly comes from the internal incoherence of the system itself. Secondly, it must identify the capacity that the society has to respond to this crisis, and thereby to generate a solution in terms of a new form of society. Here Habermas makes what is in many respects his boldest move in reconstructing historical materialism. Social evolution has been construed as a process of social learning. Habermas therefore suggests that a model for a reconstructed historical materialism already exists in studies of the learning capacities of individual human beings. Developmental cognitive psychology, understood as a reconstructive science, traces the logical unfolding of the rules that make possible the skills that mature and competent human beings exercise in the lifeworld. Habermas therefore appeals to such arguments to provide an explanatory framework for social evolution. Bluntly put, ontogenesis (the development of the individual) becomes the model for phylogenesis (the development of the species).

Habermas suggests that there is an intuitive plausibility about this homology, and indeed that it is therefore more than a matter of simply modelling one inquiry upon another. On the one hand, the very development of individuals presupposes that they are social beings (CES: 98–9). The development of the individual is not an autonomous process, but rather one stimulated through interaction with others, and is dependent upon the sophistication of the linguistic structures that mediate this interaction (CES: 154). It may then be suggested that if cognitive psychologists are correct, and the learning processes that they have traced are not simply culturally specific, but are general to all cultures, then these may be tied to equally universal structures of social evolution. On the other hand, the capacity of a society to evolve rests, ultimately, upon the learning capacities of its individual members (CES: 154). Individual human beings, not societies, solve problems. Only if certain forms of problem-solving have been mastered by its members, can the society as a whole respond to specific structural crises. The problem-solving capacity of the society will therefore be directly related to the problem-solving capacities of its members. However, the problems with the conflation of ontogenesis and phylogensis are manifold, and Habermas is well aware of them (CES: 102–3, 110–11). He notes, not least, the danger of suggesting that the developmental stage of society so limits the development of its members that, for example, the members of archaic societies are held in a perpetual childhood. Just as complex modern and post-industrial societies may be populated by the morally and cognitively naive, so archaic societies will be populated by mature and competent agents (CES: 102). Indeed, if social and systems crises are to be solved by individuals, then there must be people in any viable society who can see beyond the existing (and inadequate) ways of dealing with technological and moral problems (CES: 121).

Brief consideration of Piaget's account of ego development and Lawrence Kohlberg's account of moral development (both of whom are major stimuli to Habermas) may help bring the model of social evolution into focus. From Piaget's work on cognition and ego identity, Habermas derives four stages through which the development of the ego occurs. The first of these is the symbiotic stage, where the child has not yet differentiated itself from that environment. The second is the egocentric stage. Here subject–object differentiation has taken place, but there is no differentiation of the environment into the physical and the social (which is to say, people are not clearly distinguished from anything else). In addition, the child cannot yet view the world from any perspective but its own. In the third stage, the sociocentric-objectivistic stage, the child comes to master not merely the differentiation of the environment into physical and social beings, but also an ability to imagine that environment from the perspective of others. It can thus recognize and respond to generalized expectations. It also gains a fuller mastery of language, being able to distinguish linguistic signs from their referents and can use its command of language deliberately to make things happen in the world (e.g. by giving orders or making requests). Finally, in the universalistic stage, the adolescent develops the ability to think hypothetically, and thus to question the norms and rules that govern its behaviour. It is capable of seeking rational justification for normative and cognitive assertions (CES: 100–101). Kohlberg's work on moral competence offers three broad stages of moral understanding: the pre-conventional, the conventional and the post-conventional (CES: 156). At the pre-conventional stage, actions are assessed only in terms of their concrete consequences. The child obeys because it fears punishment or desires a reward. At the conventional stage, the assessment of the action is made in terms of the particular norms and rules that govern social roles, so that the child seeks approval or recognizes the authority of others. Finally, post-conventional stage assessment entails the justification of actions from a universal viewpoint. Here the child obeys because it has been given good reason to (CES: 77). Both developmental structures therefore chart a gradual progression from particularism to universalism; from a satisfaction with the given to an increasingly sophisticated questioning of it.

Such cognitive and moral developments do not mechanically map onto social processes. Rather, the ideas of Piaget and Kohlberg offer a guide to a series of highly tentative, and indeed not obviously consistent, accounts of social progression (see OSI; CES: 69–129), albeit a progression that, as for Piaget and Kohlberg, moves from the particularistic to the universal. Social evolution is articulated through four stages: archaic societies, early civilizations, developed civilizations and capitalism. Each stage represents a distinct "principle of organization", and this term comes to replace Marx's concept of "mode of production". Habermas defines "principle of organization", coherently with what has already been noted about the subject matter of social evolutionary theory, as a highly abstract set of regulations that determine the society's capacity to learn (LC: 16–17; CES: 153). The concept is introduced, however, by suggesting an institution (or "institutional core") that is responsible for social integration at each stage. In effect, it is the subsystem that defines the base of society, and as such it gives unity to the lifeworld. That is to say that lay actors have a more or less coherent and meaningful view of the world, thanks to specific norms and values into which they are socialized, and these norms and values emerge from the social base (CES: 144). As such, the institutional core is also the source of systems crises, for it is precisely the failure of this subsystem to secure unity that threatens social continuity. Three institutional cores are identified: the kinship system (in archaic societies); the state (in archaic and developed civilizations) and the economy (in capitalism) (CES: 154).

Within each stage, Habermas suggests three domains through which normal interaction is regulated and conflicts are resolved (CES: 99, 156): worldviews, social identity and, finally, legal and moral institutions. Piaget's account of ego development guides the analysis of the first two; Kohlberg's arguments guide the analysis of the third. Although analytically distinct, in practice the three domains are closely entwined, with the worldview typically providing resources for the articulation of social identity and the legitimation of power structures. The following broad sketch may indicate something of Habermas's intentions.

From archaic society to capitalism

Social integration within archaic societies occurs through the totemic interpretation of family structures. This entails that the worldview of such societies does not yet adequately distinguish between the social and the natural worlds (CES: 111–12). Human families are understood to be continuous with their totemic natural species. Further, totemism is seen to be articulated in a series of loosely related narratives. There is no systematic cosmology (CES: 103). This in turn entails a weak understanding of the workings of nature, and indeed a blurring of hermeneutics and explanation, such that the cognitive interests of interaction and labour are not yet adequately differentiated. The unexpected and contingent is "interpreted away", rather than treated as an event in need of purposive-rational explanation (OSI: 91). Habermas therefore suggests that such worldviews are akin to the "natural identity of the child" (OSI: 92) or, more precisely, to the stage of egocentricism (CES: 104). Although the everyday interactions within such a society will be governed by a conventional respect for rules, Habermas suggests that conflict will be addressed at a pre-conventional level. This entails that legal action is typically understood only in terms of retribution and feuding. The particularity of the criminal and the crime matters, not the consistent application of a legal system (CES: 157).

An explanation of the evolution from archaic societies to early civilization is offered by seeing archaic society threatened, typically, by extrinsic factors (including attacks from other societies, or environmental crises) or by inequalities in the distribution of wealth, which in turn lead to conflicts that cannot be satisfactorily resolved within pre-conventional legal thinking (CES: 162). What Habermas calls "evolutionary promising" societies will have the potential within them to conceive of and test new forms of social organization. Archaic worldviews may already sustain more generalized forms of thought and analysis, possibly in groups marginal to the core of the society. This allows a shift from short-term and particularistic responses to increasingly long-term and generalizable responses. Temporary solutions to crises, whereby, for example, one clan leader takes charge of the whole society, may then have the potential for becoming permanent. Crucially, such experiments are not guaranteed to succeed. Just as natural evolution tests mutations against the environment and finds many wanting, so social innovations are similarly tested. Many will fail, and the society dissolves rather than mutates (CES: 162). Successful innovations will, however, be institutionalized. The evolution out of archaic society takes the form of the institutionalization of permanent political leadership, so that power is uncoupled from kinship. The very notion of "uncoupling" (which Habermas uses frequently) suggests a process of increasing sophistication, akin to Piaget's account of the ego's demarcation of itself from its environment. This new formation creates the space within which the potential of the old society, not least to greater generalization of worldviews and the application of technology, can be realized.

Social integration in early civilizations focuses around the problem of legitimizing the state and its associated class divisions. This legitimation is grounded in the development of a polytheistic religion. The particularistic narratives of totemic mythology are increasingly systematized into a more or less coherent set. This entails a new awareness of the differentiation of the human and the divine. Interaction with the gods is thus established through prayer, sacrifice and worship, allowing for the emergence of a priesthood (OSI: 92). The dominant class legitimates its position through this religion. Crucially, this presupposes a more sophisticated conception of time than that available in archaic worldviews. An emerging notion of an historical past allows the dominant class to legitimate its power through appeal to foundational, historical events (CES: 104). In addition, the increasing rationalization of religion and the differentiation of power from particular families, allows legal conflict resolution to itself become conventional. The ruler administers justice in terms of an increasingly disinterested punishment, not retaliation (CES: 156).

Although the human subject is now clearly differentiated from the natural world, its self-understanding remains bound up with that of its particular community (OSI: 95). The polytheistic gods serve to articulate the fragmentation of society into separate communities, localities and class strata. Crises thus occur within these archaic empires through their very expansion. Legitimation of state authority requires that conflicts of interest within the society are suppressed, so that claims cannot be publicly raised against the ruling elite. This becomes more problematic as the empire expands (CES: 112). The identity of the empire is placed at risk by its very diversity. This problem is solved, in part, by the evolutionary transition to monotheism. On the one hand, this encourages the development of a theology, whereby rational explanation replaces narrative (CES: 104–5). On the other hand, this transforms the self-understanding of the members of society. They are no longer defined in terms of local deities, but rather in terms of a universal god. Thus, for example, St Paul asserts that in Christianity there is no longer Jew nor Gentile, freeman nor slave (Colossians 3.11). The self is thereby differentiated from society (OSI: 95). The very universality that is inherent in this self-understanding begins to promise rights that human beings have, merely on the grounds of their humanity, and not because of their birth or place within the social structure. Legal systems are thereby detached from the person of the ruler, and become increasingly systematic and historically stable codes, albeit that these codes remain conventional, not least in their reliance upon traditional notions of justice (CES: 157).

The very solution that allowed for the expansion of the empire is at once the source of a new crisis in legitimacy. The universal claims of the members of the empire must be more violently repressed in the face of continuing inequality. The legal system thereby becomes increasingly unable to resolve conflict, for example as a rising bourgeoisie perceives itself to be excluded from power. It is at this point that Habermas returns to one of the historical issues of *The Structural Transformation of the Public Sphere*: the transition to capitalism. However, precisely because *The Structural Transformation of the Public Sphere* was an historical narrative, albeit one articulated through ideology critique, the events described in it now take on a new evolutionary depth. The uncoupling of political power from the economy, so that, as Habermas presents it, the ruling class convinces itself that it no longer rules (LC: 22), may be understood as the resolution of the systems crisis of a developed civilization. Public questioning of overt material and political inequality is rendered ineffectual (rather than having to be actively repressed) by presenting that inequality as a consequence of the fair operations of the quasi-natural exchanges of the market. In Habermas's technical terminology, social integration is therefore no longer achieved through an overt system of norms and values, but, ironically, through system integration grounded in the economy (LC: 24).

It is the crisis tendencies within this very solution that explain the subsequent development from a free-market to a welfare-state capitalism (and, indeed, *Legitimation Crisis* is concerned precisely with this development and the subsequent crisis tendencies within welfare-state capitalism (see § "Legitimation Crisis, p. 125). At the level of worldviews, religion has given way to morality and philosophy (and that in turn to science). Both moral practice and technology therefore come to be understood within a universalistic perspective that requires rational justification of the rules that govern them. Practice within modern societies thereby comes to be governed by post-conventional requirements for justification (CES: 157). Thus, while crises tendencies in the economic subsystem (not least in terms of the limitations of capital accumulation) may be the fundamental cause of the destabilization of modern societies, they are not necessarily experienced as such. At the level of the lifeworld, this tendency to systems crisis will be experienced as a series of tensions between the particular and the universal. At the core of this is the double identity, central to the argument of *The Structural Transformation of the Public Sphere*, of citizen and *homme* (CES: 115). A universal aspiration to justice is checked by political structures that privilege the bourgeoisie. The expansion of the franchise in the nineteenth century, which passed in *The Structural Transformation of the Public Sphere* as little more than a contingent event of European history, may now be understood as the exploitation of precisely the potential to universalization that is inherit in the modern, post-conventional worldview. This serves to defer a deeper systems crisis. Habermas now suggests that this tension is reproduced as the citizen is reinterpreted, not as a bourgeois, but as a member of a particular nation state. Nationalism thereby becomes a potential source of crisis within capitalism (OSI: 95).

One final point may be made about the relationship of the reconstruction of historical materialism to *The Structural Transformation of the Public Sphere*. The public sphere has found a new and deeper justification through the theory of social evolution. If *The Structural Transformation of the Public Sphere* is read as a narrative, then at best Habermas may be seen to have offered a contingent defence of the superiority of Western forms of government and public involvement over any alternative forms of government, and to have defended communicative reason against the dialectical reason of either Lukács or Adorno. From the perspective of social evolution, the public sphere is a manifestation not of a contingent quirk of European history – which is to say, it is not being assessed from a Weberian perspective – but rather of the realization of the anthropologically deep-seated potential that lies in interaction. It is precisely in this respect that the implications of public debate will be explicated in universal pragmatics.

Legitimation Crisis

Marxism and late capitalism

At the core of *Legitimation Crisis* lies Habermas's tentative analysis of contemporary (or late) capitalism. *Legitimation Crisis* presupposes the evolutionary framework of a reconstructed historical materialism, precisely in that it is concerned with the potential for change that lies within contemporary capitalism. The basic account of late capitalism, as a social welfare mass democracy, is reminiscent of that given in "Between Philosophy and Science" (in 1960) and, indeed, in the later parts of *Structural Transformation of the Public Sphere*. Similarly, there is a common theoretical problem: how is this new form of capitalism to be explained within the theoretical resources of Marxism (or, more precisely, how do Marxist theories have to be revised, in order to account for late capitalism)?

Habermas begins with the recognition that the interventionist role of the state has changed, in both degree and kind, in comparison to that of the liberal capitalist state, and additionally that capitalist production itself has changed through the growing concentration of capital in a diminishing number of multinational corporations (LC: 33–4). The expansion of state intervention may be seen as a response to the conflicts of liberal capitalism. The state seeks to mitigate the dysfunctional side-effects of capitalism, for at least certain groups and individuals, through a series of strategies: the stabilization of the business cycle and the consequent sustaining of steady economic growth; the regulation of production to meet collective needs and to handle the external costs of production (such as environmental damage); and the reduction of extremes of social inequality through redistributive taxation and the provision of social welfare and education (CES: 194). These changes in the economic role of the state are complemented by political changes, as the franchise is expanded and the state becomes democratically accountable for its actions.

To describe late capitalism so is to raise two fundamental and interrelated questions for Marxism. It is to ask, first, in what sense is late capitalism still capitalism? That is to say, are the structural features that identified liberal capitalism as capitalism still present, most fundamentally the organizational role of the free market and, tied to this, a class structure characterized in terms of the appropriation of surplus value? Secondly, it is to ask how a Marxist theory that was forged in relation to liberal capitalism works as an explanation of late capitalism. How must core notions, such as the labour theory of value and class conflict, be refigured?

Habermas notes that there are responses from within Marxism to this problem, and in particular the "orthodox" approach, which holds that the late capitalist state does not interfere in the anarchy of commodity production (LC: 51), and the "revisionist" approach, which holds that the anarchy of commodity production has been replaced through the state operating as the planning agent of a monopolistic capitalism (LC: 59). The former position falls foul of the fact that surplus value and labour value cannot be determined in late capitalism as they were in liberal capitalism. First, state intervention has served to increase the productivity of labour, through the improvement of the material infrastructure of society, the education of the workforce, and the institution and application of scientific research and technical innovation. In sum, this amounts to an increase in the contribution of "reflexive" labour (LC: 56). The reflexive labour of scientists, engineers and teachers does not directly contribute to productivity, and so is discounted in orthodox Marxist theories as unproductive. Habermas observes, rather, that along with the other changes stimulated and supported by the state, reflexive labour serves to increase "relative surplus value". That is to say, as the extraction of absolute surplus value reaches its natural limit, by extending the working day or through the employment of women and children at low wages, capitalism can continue to maintain the rate of surplus value only by making the workforce more productive. Reflexive labour increases the productivity of direct labour (LC: 55–7). This already begins to suggest that the law of surplus value is no longer intimately linked to the immiseration of the proletariat (and, indeed, that the conception of the proletariat as a homogeneous class entity is not viable in the light of a fundamental distinction between manual and non-manual, or reflexive, labour).

Further, fundamental changes in the labour market in late capitalism also throw into question the orthodox account of the labour theory of value. A structure of "quasi-political" wages now replaces the determination of wage by the free market. In part, this is due to stronger unionization. Yet Habermas also suggests that at crucial points within the economy, including strategic industries and industries such as agriculture and mining that, under free-market conditions, would be in decline, wages will be determined by, or at least negotiated with, the government (LC: 38, 57). In such a context, the determination of the value of labour (or at least the reduction of the value of labour down to what is required for its reproduction) is highly problematic. Finally, use value takes on new significance in late capitalism, precisely in so far as the allocation of use values (such as education, health care and housing) within a welfare state becomes the focus of political struggles, and crucially means by which the state can appease the interests either of capital or enfranchised labour (LC: 58). In effect, the orthodox model too readily reduces democracy to a mere epiphenomenon of the class structure. The concession of democracy does not merely appease labour. Even in an imperfect form, it provides citizens with a resource by which pressure can be exerted upon the government.

Although a revisionist Marxism may be able to acknowledge this "recoupling" (LC: 36) of political and economic activity, Habermas suggests that it is naive in its expectations of the powers of the state to plan the framework of economic development. Planning is typically a form of crisis management. In effect, by stressing that late capitalism is characterized by both increased state intervention and the concentration of capital, Habermas is suggesting that the state cannot wholly manage economic contradiction. Something of the anarchy of commodity production remains (LC: 60).

Both the orthodox and the revisionist Marxist models may be accused of oversimplifying the relationship between the economy and the state. The orthodox model focuses on their separation, the revisionist model on their convergence. Habermas implies a more complex and elusive relationship between the two. Although the state may intervene in the economy, it also maintains a distance. That is to say that while the state intervenes, it must also appear to leave the economy free (CES: 195). A fundamental tension thus exists between the maintenance of private appropriation and the use of surplus value on the one hand, and the administration of socialized production (which is to say, the administration of the economic and social processes in the collective interest) on the other (LC: 36). The latter demand emerges from the need for the state to secure legitimacy from its citizens. The former emerges from the economy, and the interests of capital. Thus there continues to be something distinctively capitalistic about that economy. The class structure is still in place, even if consciousness of it is manifest differently.

Systems theory and late capitalism

Habermas seeks to respond to the weaknesses of both orthodox and revisionist Marxism by following the lead of Claus Offe, and appealing to a form of systems theory. Capitalist society is analysed in terms of three core subsystems: the economic, the political and the sociocultural. Whereas the economy may be understood in terms of its role in appropriating outer nature, and thus in securing the "requisite quantity of consumable values" (LC: 49), within the context of a Marxist interpretation of systems theory, a system imperative of the capitalist economy must be that of securing surplus value. The sociocultural system serves to appropriate inner nature, and thus to secure social integration through appropriate normative structures and worldviews. Intermediate between these two systems lies a complex polity that Habermas, following Offe (1992; and see Offe 1984, 1985), subdivides into the administrative system and the legitimation system. The administrative system is complemented by processes of "conflict resolution and consensus formation, of decision and implementation" (LC: 60).

The relationship between subsystems is theorized in terms of inputs and outputs. Thus, the output of the economy is consumable values. The output of the political system is administrative decisions, and the output of the sociocultural system is constituted by the network of norms, meanings and worldviews that secure social integration. The inputs into the economic system will include land, capital and labour, but also the improvement to labour that is brought about by education and other state-sponsored programmes, along with the other administrative decisions of the state (including legal and regulative frameworks), and finally the motivations of the sociocultural system. The inputs into the political system include the consumable values produced by the economy, but also mass loyalty (or broad popular support from its citizens). The inputs into the sociocultural system are the consumable values of the economy, and the administrative decisions of the polity. This interlocking of the three subsystems entails that crisis tendencies within capitalism cannot be understood (as in orthodox Marxism) as being reducible to political crises. The crisis within one system places strains upon the other two, either in terms of an input crisis (where vital resources are denied the system) or in terms of an output crisis (where it is unable to provide the output demanded by another subsystem).

Habermas identifies four forms of crisis within late capitalism. Economic crises emerge in the economic system, typically as the problem of production and allocation of consumable values, in a manner that is coherent with the values of the system as a whole, and thus, fundamentally, in a manner that manages the tension between economic interests in the appropriation of surplus value, on the one hand, and a polity and culture that is orientated to the satisfaction of collective needs and the egalitarian distribution of use values, on the other. The political system falls into crisis either through the inability to manage the economy – a rationality crisis – or through the inability to acquire mass loyalty (e.g. through formal democratic procedures) – a legitimation crisis. Finally, the sociocultural system comes into crisis when the inherent development of worldviews and normative structures (expressed in the interpreted needs and expectations of citizens) comes into conflict with the distribution of consumable values and administrative decisions: a motivation crisis.

Whereas economic and rationality crises occur at the level of the system, legitimation and motivation crises occur at the level of the society or lifeworld, which is to say that they are manifest as problems in the social agent's ability to make sense of their world. The question of the fate of capitalism (LC: 31) – of the long-term sustainability of late capitalism, and thus of the potential for change – therefore comes to rest on the analysis of these crises and the system's ability to resolve them (LC: 39–40).

Rationality crisis

The output of the political system (which is to say legal regulation of the economy and society, the support of the material infrastructure, provision of education and other cultural improvements of labour, as well as compensation for the dysfunctional side-effects of capitalism) must be paid for through taxation. The raising and use of tax must be justified in terms of instrumental rationality, which is to say, as the most effective means to the end of system integration (LC: 62). A rationality crisis occurs if insufficient rationally justifiable decisions are made. Or, again, rationality crises occur if the state fails in its maintenance and stabilization of the economy and society. Failure is made likely, once again, because of the conflicting goals of the economy (and the individual capitalists' interest in the accumulation of surplus value) and society.

Habermas rehearses two analyses of rationality crises (LC: 47). The first, from Joachim Hirsch, may be seen to pick up from the orthodox Marxist

defence of the continuing anarchy of late capitalism. In contrast to revisionist Marxism, this position recognizes the limitations of state planning, but
suggests that this imperfection lies in the fact that the anarchy of the liberal
capitalist economy has been transferred to the state. The weakness of this
argument lies, for Habermas, in its inability to understand that planning
failures on the part of the state, in contrast to failures in the economy, are
not clear-cut. Economic failure is marked by bankruptcy and unemployment. In contrast, the failure of the state can be negotiated. It will ultimately
depend upon culturally specific expectations and tolerances of failure (LC:
63–4). In addition, the presence of unintended consequences or unantici-
pated problems resulting from state planning – which is to say, the very
imperfection of the planning process – can be beneficial to the state,
precisely in so far as they allow the state to reduce its responsibility for its
actions. Imperfections become a façade behind which the state can shelter,
and thus minimize the claims that the victims of capitalism can make upon
it (LC: 65). Habermas's comments thus begin to indicate that, although
rationality crises may be analysed as system crises, which is to say problems
occurring through the conflicting imperatives within systems or between
subsystems, they are also raising questions of meaning. That is to say that
crises of rationalization occur within given worldviews or normative
structures.

This theme becomes explicit in the second interpretation of rationality
crisis that Habermas considers: that offered by Offe. Offe argues that rationality crises occur because the mechanisms that the state has available to control and manipulate the economy and society are becoming increasingly
ineffective. Mechanisms such as interest rates, taxation, subsidies, business
concessions and the redistribution of income (LC: 67) all presuppose that
the behaviour of social agents can be manipulated through the influence of
monetary values. Offe, however, argues that at crucial points within the
economy monetary values are no longer relevant in motivating action. Most
obviously this relates to the increasing number of people who stand outside
the labour market (such as children and students, the retired, the chronically
sick and the criminal). In addition, certain occupations are characterized as
"concrete labour" (as opposed to "abstract labour"). Such labour, typified
by work within the public services (such as health care, social work and
teaching), is motivated by the inherent goals of the occupation, and not by
the extrinsic goals of wages or salaries. Finally, the complexity of the economic system also entails that corporations are increasingly unable to secure
sufficient economic data upon which to base planning and investment decisions. These decisions must then become explicitly political in so far as the
goals and values motivating the decision – as opposed to the simple means
to their realization – are brought into the decision-making process (LC:

66–7). In broad terms, the instrumental reason that allows the analysis and resolution of systems problems is increasingly complemented or displaced by an appeal to communicative reason (within which not merely the means, but also the goals and orientating values of the decision can be subject to criticism and justification). Offe's point, then, is that crises that originate at the level of the system come to be handled at the level of the lifeworld. Rationality crises shift, becoming legitimation crises (which is to say, problems grounded in the interpretative and discursive capacities of social agents).

Legitimation crisis

As the scope of the administrative system expands, so that it comes to cover not merely the economy, but also substantial areas of social life, such as education, health care, and the family, its requirement for legitimation increases (LC: 71). Habermas explores two theorems that may account for the problematic nature of this increase. First, there is what he terms a "structural dissimilarity" between the administrative system and the areas of culture that are the source of meanings, normative structures and worldviews that may secure legitimacy. The dissimilarity inhibits the capacity of the administrative system to generate legitimacy. Secondly, even if the expansion of legitimacy is successful it may have unintended side-effects, not least in enabling the population critically to scrutinize political processes (LC: 50). These two theorems may be considered in turn.

The structural dissimilarity of administration and culture (and, indeed, its relevance to the question of legitimation) may be understood in terms of the tension between instrumental and communicative rationality. Precisely because the administrative system works at the level of instrumental reason, and as such is concerned with system integration, questions of meaning are largely anathema to it. This may be understood at a number of levels. It has already been noted above that it may be in the interest of the administrative system to utilize the unpredictability and imperfection of planning processes in order to stave of rationality crises. This may be taken further, if it is recognized that the areas into which the administration intervenes typically have the appearance of quasi-natural processes, and do so in part because of their intimate link to the class structure. This observation applies most obviously to the economy, where the market mechanisms and economic cycles of liberal capitalism appeared (in their reified form) as akin to natural laws. Yet the observation may also be applied to cultural traditions, and thus to the sources of meaning that are drawn on in legitimation. Traditional worldviews and normative structures, precisely because they are not subject to critical reflection and evaluation, have a nature-like structure (LC: 70).

Legitimation crises are threatened because, on the one hand, as the administration intervenes into these quasi-natural areas, their very naturalness is thrown into question. More and more they become overtly subject to human will, and thus human beings must take responsibility for the decisions applied in these areas. Yet, on the other hand, if the administration system works through instrumental and not communicative reason, then it cannot, of its own resources, generate meaningful explanations and justifications for its actions. There can be, as Habermas puts it, "no administrative production of meaning" (LC: 70).

More precisely, as soon as the administration is seen to manipulate symbolic expressions for the purposes of securing mass loyalty, the process becomes self-defeating (LC: 71). At best the administrative system can exploit existing prejudices and expectations, and not least those of "civic" and "familial–vocational privatism", where "civic privatism" is understood as an attitude to life that is interested in accumulating the material goods produced and distributed by the state and the economy but is not interested in participating in the political process. Similarly, "familial–vocational privatism" marks a retreat into the family, an interest in consumption and leisure and thus the material rewards of individual competition in the labour market (LC: 75). So the state can rely on the fact that access to a sufficient supply of material goods will be enough to distract many from political action. Yet, beyond relying on privatism, the administration can still seek to define problems as issues of subjective judgement rather than collective and rational debate; or attempt to direct public concern away from core problems (LC: 70). The limited scope that the administrative system consequently has to control meanings is not a problem while the administrative system is distributing consumable values in accordance with the population's (privatized) expectations. However, the underlying tension of attempting to serve the interests of capital and the collective interests of the population (which is to say, the underlying class structure of capitalism) makes this unviable in the long term (LC: 73). Collective expectations of the use values that the state and economy should supply come to outstrip what is possible if surplus value is still to be appropriated.

The analysis of the problems inherent in the dissimilarity of the administrative and cultural systems leads to the second theorem. The expansion of administrative planning into previously traditional areas of the lifeworld renders what were otherwise stable norms and meanings problematic. Taken-for-granted ways of dealing with the world will no longer work. The most probable lay response to this problem, for Habermas, will not be a retreat into confusion or fatalism, but rather the stimulation of learning capacities. Administrative intervention encourages renewed critical and interpretative discussion of those norms and meanings. This tendency is manifest in the continuing vitality of communal activities (such as those centred on schools and universities, churches, publishing enterprises and arts centres) that strive to question and renew moral, cultural and spiritual traditions. All of these may be seen to mitigate against a growing privatism. The government is itself recognized as responding to this tendency by encouraging citizen participation in certain planning decisions, thereby co-opting community or citizens groups into the process of legitimizing administrative decisions (LC: 72). Yet the unintended side-effect of administrative expansion is the development of the population's ability to criticize the actions of the state (LC: 73). This is crucial in the context of the underlying class structures of late capitalism, precisely in so far as it makes the exposure of those class structures all the more likely.

Motivation crisis

The above analysis suggests that a legitimation crisis emerges due to the failure of the polity to secure mass loyalty. This failure occurs in part due to the restrictions on the polity's capacity to control and manipulate meanings, but also, by implication, due to the recalcitrance of the sociocultural system. A legitimation crisis may occur in the polity precisely because it is receiving insufficient inputs from the sociocultural system. This failure of output is a motivational crisis. Such a crisis will be stimulated by the failure of the other systems to provide sufficient inputs (in terms of consumable values and administrative decisions) into the lives of lay members of society (LC: 48), although the form that it takes will depend upon the inherent logic and tensions of the system. However, what is crucial is that it is at this level that the crisis tendencies within the social system confront those lay members as problems that demand action (which is to say, that the problems are problems of interpretation, criticism and human practice, and not of the instrumental and largely meaningless movements of the economic or administrative systems). It is, therefore, at the level of motivation that systems crises are fully manifest as social crises.

Habermas approaches the problem of the motivational crisis, as he has the other crises, in terms of two theorems. The first suggests that late capitalism is vulnerable to motivation crises because the familial–vocational and civic privatism upon which the polity depends is under threat. This involves a two-part thesis: first, that the traditions that support privatism are under threat and, secondly, that no functional equivalent for them is likely to emerge. The second complementary theorem develops precisely this point, to argue that the sociocultural system does not merely culminate in irresolvable crises, but rather that it "overloads" capitalism, due to the inherent development within the sociocultural system of a newly universal morality and politics, which will be critical of the class structure (LC: 50).

With respect to the first theorem, Habermas suggests that privatism may be understood as a combination of specifically bourgeois ideology and pre-bourgeois tradition. Civic privatism draws on bourgeois formal law, which is to say, the notion that the citizen is defined primarily as a rights holder, where rights serve to define personal freedoms that the state will protect, rather than as an active participant in political debate and public life (see § "Human rights and popular sovereignty", p. 253). But still more paradoxically, from the perspective of a traditional civic ethic, the state requires political participation at certain levels or in response to certain issues, while allowing a pre-bourgeois paternalism to hold with respect to other areas (so that the good citizen trusts the state on certain core issues) (LC: 76). Similarly, familial–vocational privatism has its roots in possessive individualism and utilitarianism (not least in so far as utilitarianism tends to reduce all forms of valuation down to matters of subjective judgements of pleasure), but also in religious traditions (including the Protestant work ethic for the dominant classes, and a more fatalistic work ethic amongst the subordinate classes) that will ensure commitment to capitalist values (LC: 77). Beyond its detail, Habermas's key point is that the capitalist system was never able to generate a comprehensive ideology of its own (nor thus, again, its own legitimacy), but was always parasitic upon earlier traditions.

In late capitalism, both the traditional and the ideological aspects of this culture are under threat. Traditions are being eroded at a number of points (LC: 79–80). Most significantly, not least in reflecting Habermas's earlier concerns, there is the scientization of politics (see § "Introduction", p. 56). The expansion in the scope of instrumental and technocratic reasoning, in both the economy and the polity, serves to render tradition, and thus the communicative reason that draws upon the tradition of the lifeworld, increasingly ineffectual. Secondly, an increasing cultural pluralism serves to undermine the potential of personal belief systems to form coherent worldviews. One's personal values are always challenged by other sets of values current in one's culture. A worldview becomes merely a matter of personal commitment, and cannot be discussed in terms of its truth or inherent justice. It entails, as it were, a reversion to the polytheism that characterized early civilization (Weber 1946c: 149; and see § "Horkheimer and Adorno", p. 215). Finally the ideological components of privatism – and crucially the expected link between labour and material reward – that superficially might be thought to be most resistant to erosion, are thrown into question due to changes in practices within late capitalism. The emergence of "concrete" labour has already been noted (LC: 83–4). In addition, higher levels of general affluence may disrupt the expression of need by consumers (and the motivation to participate in the economy) (LC: 83). Perhaps most fundamentally, the belief that sees reward as being linked to personal achievement has become more sophisticated, not least in recognizing that the market is not necessarily a fair mechanism. In this more sophisticated form, reward is linked to fair opportunity, not least through access to education. Habermas suggests that even this expectation is increasingly frustrated, for example as access to higher education is expanded without a corresponding expansion in occupational rewards (LC: 81–2).

The critical potential of late capitalist culture

The undermining of privatism is not a merely negative phenomenon. Habermas identifies within the inherent developmental logic of science, art and ethics a new potential for self-reflection that, if it were to be embedded in the socialization process, would not merely inhibit the possibility of a new (late capitalist) ideology developing, but would do so precisely because of its critical and universalistic character. In effect, Habermas is suggesting that late capitalist culture has the potential to develop the intellectual resources that aspire to genuinely universal scope, and thus undermine the threats of subjectivism and perspectivism that, for Habermas at least, blight contemporary intellectual inquiry.

This potential is perhaps most ambiguous in science. Scientism has already been noted for its inhibiting of rational reflection on values. However, science also develops standards that allow it to be criticized for its own residual dogmatism (LC: 84). More significant is the development of the arts during the twentieth century. Habermas distinguishes between the bourgeois art of the nineteenth century and what he calls "post-auratic" art. The former is characterized by the continuation of largely naturalistic representation and the pursuit of beauty. It thereby provided for its bourgeois audience a fictive or illusory image of bourgeois ideals. The term "post-auratic", in contrast, alludes to the work of Benjamin and Adorno. For Benjamin (1970), the expansion of mechanical reproduction (e.g. in photography and cinema) destroys the aura of uniqueness that clung to bourgeois art. Art thereby breaks out of its narrow class appeal. For Adorno (1984: Ch. 6), more fundamentally, avant-garde art in the twentieth century (beginning for example with expressionism) is characterized by its disturbance of the illusion of naturalness of bourgeois art. Such art eschews beauty, but more profoundly still it begins a process of radical reflection on the very nature of art and the process of artistic production. Art ceases to be a product, and becomes rather a process. The audience cannot avoid the fact that they are in the presence of art, and that art is conventional rather than natural. (One might consider, as an obvious example, Brecht's alienation techniques.) Post-auratic art therefore does not confirm the bourgeois ideal, but rather expresses "the irretrievable sacrifice of bourgeois rationalism" (LC: 85). The problem that remains with post-auratic art lies in its limited potential for communicating this self-reflective capacity to a mass audience; which is to say, empirically, that Adorno's pessimism about the confinement of criticism to an elite art tends to be preferred to Benjamin's optimism about the mass consumption of politically revolutionary art (LC: 86).[5]

If science and art remain problematic, then the development of law and morality suggests, for Habermas, an unambiguous unfolding of critical potential. Habermas provides a brief historical overview of this develop-ment (LC: 86–9). Its crucial stage lies in the emergence of the bourgeois doctrine of natural law and natural rights. This doctrine entails a complex relationship between law and morality but, crucially, one that has already been sketched in consideration of the social evolution of law from pre-conventional to post-conventional thinking. On the one hand, the concept of natural rights serves fundamentally to separate modern law from the particularistic or subjectivist claims of personal (pre-conventional) morality. As such, a law articulated in terms of natural rights aspires to a universal-ism, precisely in so far as it was grounded not in cultural traditions (as had been the case in pre-bourgeois society), but in abstract principles. This formal law strives to logical consistency, and the citizen's obedience to the law is motivated not through pure force, but through an argument that demonstrates this very consistency. It is precisely here that it begins to suggest the post-conventional. However, on the other hand, this aspiration is frustrated, for legal systems remain specific to particular societies. As such, law governs the citizen, and not *l'homme*. But if law remains compro-mised, it may yet be outstripped by morality. That morality should appeal to conscience, and thus to something that potentially transcends particular legal systems, gives it a parallel claim to universality. This claim, crucially, is now seen to be worked out in the history of European philosophical eth-ics. Utilitarianism offers a form of universal justification – in its principle of adjudicating moral decisions in terms of the securing of the greatest happi-ness for the greatness numbers of people (to follow Bentham's interpreta-tion (1843: 142)) – but thereby leaves the adjudication of "happiness" to individual preference, and as such leaves a core aspect of motivation beyond rational argument. Kantian ethics is more promising. Here an action is motivated explicitly by the rational justification that the general principle that governs the action can be universalized to apply to all human actors (Kant 1983c: 15). Yet the formalism of Kantian ethics remains problematic, for it inhibits reflection on the cultural formation and inter-pretation of needs (and thus upon the way in which motivations to moral action are embedded in historically and politically unfolding moral communities). This broaches a new and difficult subtlety for working out the tensions between the universal and particular, not least because it throws into question the impression of a relentless march to universality that was left by the theory of social evolution. Habermas's response to this problem marks perhaps the most radical move in the whole project of universal pragmatics. He suggests that a genuinely universal ethics can be achieved only if moral norms acquire universality through the fact that all those affected by them agree, without constraint, upon their adoption, and that this is achieved through a discursive process of collective will-formation. This is to say that motivation to action lies in the intersubjective offering and acceptance of good reasons for action. This he terms communicative (or discourse) ethics (LC: 89). The implication is that communicative ethics possesses the resources necessary to redeem not merely moral but also legal norms from their embedding in the particularism of unequal and unjust political structures, but without neglecting the important role that particularism plays in constituting our individual and collective identities (see § "Discourse ethics", p. 157).

Habermas's analysis of science, art and morality turns on the suggestion that the critical resources that are being developed within these fields are becoming routine elements in the socialization of members of late capitalism. Competent members of contemporary society do not merely accept norms and ideologies. They accept only that which can be rationally justified to them (LC: 91). The issue of legitimation therefore may be seen to have its overriding importance in the fact that the legitimacy of any belief or belief system cannot be decided on purely factual grounds. That is to say that the mere fact that a belief is accepted in society is not sufficient to say that the belief is legitimate. Systems theory, Habermas argues, treats legitimation as just such an empirical matter, asking only if the mechanisms exist within a social system that would serve to secure legitimacy for the system (CES: 199). Legitimacy would be wholly defined in terms of the mundane expectations of people within that particular society (CES: 202). The question as to whether the power structures within that system are *just* or *unjust* cannot then be asked, and so systems theory collapses into perspectivism. The forms of inquiry that are beginning to be tested in the reconstruction of historical materialism, as well as in *Legitimation Crisis*, suggest the potential to inquire into the sources of legitimacy (and thus, for example, to distinguish a post-conventional legitimacy that is grounded in "good" reasons from the mere threat of violence that grounds pre-conventional and even conventional law). The next stage in explicating these forms of inquiry lies in Habermas's reconstructive analysis of the preconditions of communicative action, which is to say, in universal pragmatics.[6]

CHAPTER 5

The theory of communicative action

Universal pragmatics

Introduction

Habermas's work between 1973 and 1983 may be seen to be primarily concerned to work out the implications of *Legitimation Crisis*. This entails the development of a theoretical reconstruction of the competences that people use in everyday communication: universal pragmatics. This takes its final form in the magisterial *The Theory of Communicative Action*. At the same time he is working out the ethical theory that is outlined in the final part of *Legitimation Crisis*. (A collection of essays on this theme was published in 1983.) As is perhaps unsurprising given the direct link between universal pragmatics and *The Theory of Communicative Action*, characterized as it is with a synoptic engagement with the grand traditions of sociology, Habermas approaches universal pragmatics as a comprehensive social theory. At one level this is a continuation of his exploration of the tensions between instrumental and hermeneutic practice that had concerned him in the 1960s. While he makes a distinction between non-social instrumental action (which is to say, instrumental work on the natural world) and "social action", he further divides social action into "strategic action" and "communicative action". Strategic action is orientated to success, which is to say that the agent takes an objectifying attitude to the social world, and thus seeks to manipulate social "objects". In constrast, communicative action is orientated to mutual understanding. The agent treats others as subjects with whom one establishes meaningful intersubjective relations (ARC: 263; CES: 209). Although universal pragmatics is concerned, on the one hand, to provide a rational reconstruction of the competences that allow human beings to act communicatively, on the other hand, it seeks in this competence the capacity of social actors to produce and sustain everyday social life as stable, ordered and meaningful. Habermas's contention is that social life can, at root, be explained in terms of the ability of actors to communicate and use what he, after the philosophers J. L. Austin and John Searle, calls "speech acts" (G: 85). In Austin's glorious phrase, speakers "do things with words" (1975), which is to say that speech is approached as a form of social practice, realizing social relationships between actors. Universal pragmatics, precisely in so far as it explores communication and communicative competence, may thus be understood as the reconstructive science that explains the generation of society as such.

Habermas presents universal pragmatics as the culmination of a history of attempts to explain the generation of society as a meaningfully structured reality. The details of this pre-history need not be rehearsed at length. However, Habermas's assessment of the failings of previous attempts at a generative theory of society does indicate what he expects from universal pragmatics. He identifies first a bundle of "constitutive theories" (G: 18–22). These are characterized by an appeal to a transcendental subject. This is to say that such theories follow Kant, and where Kant looked to ground the possibility of our experience of nature (and thus the possibility of nature itself – see § "Kant and transcendental inquiry", p. 60) in the constitutive powers of the subject, so constitutive social theory sees society as being made possible by the constitutive capacities of the social agent. Different theorists characterized these constitutive powers differently, and we have already encountered, for example in *Knowledge and Human Interests*, Marx's appeal to labour and Dilthey and Gadamer's appeal to hermeneutic inter- pretation. To these Habermas adds Husserl's and Schutz's theorization of the lifeworld (G: 24–5). As social theories, these accounts break from their Kantian model precisely in so far as they recognize that the constitution of society (unlike the constitution of nature) cannot be a matter of mere cognition. Society is not constituted in being known or recognized; rather, it is constituted through mundane practice. Constitutive theories of society therefore serve to call attention to the taken-for-granted practical abilities that competent social agents have in producing and sustaining society. The weakness of these theories, for Habermas, lies in their monological form. We are already familiar with this criticism, and we shall see it play a major part in his subsequent theorizing (as a criticism of what he calls the "philoso- phy of consciousness"). Habermas argues that constitutive theories have neglected the dimension of interaction. They attribute constitutive powers either to discrete members of society (Husserl) or to a holistic social subject (Marx, Lukács). As such, they are incapable of explicating constitution as something that is realized only intersubjectively.

Systems theory, be it the ahistorical version offered by structuralism (and in particular Claude Lévi-Strauss's structural anthropology) or Luhmann's version of social evolution, does away with the concept of a subject altogether, and refers only to subjectless rule systems (G: 16). Again, we are already familiar with Habermas's criticisms of systems theory: crucially it is incapable of distinguishing between system and lifeworld, and so ultimately reduces the social actor to a "judgemental dope" (see § "Systems theory", p. 106). However, systems theory does highlight the importance of deep-seated rules that generate the society. Habermas refers approvingly to Noam Chomsky's structuralist linguistics as a model for universal pragmatics (G: 68). Chomsky is concerned with reconstructing the tacit knowledge that competent speakers of any language must have in order to be able to generate sentences that are syntactically, semantically and phonetically well formed, and also to be able intuitively to recognize a malformed sentence. The "deep grammar" to which Chomsky refers may therefore be understood as a set of rules that competent speakers are able to follow, albeit without the capacity to bring to consciousness what those rules are. It is precisely this notion of a competence to follow rules that Habermas finds developed in Wittgenstein's philosophy of language, and in particular in the notion of a language-game.

Wittgenstein and language-games

For Wittgenstein language is like a game (G: 52). Games, such as noughts and crosses, chess or football, are rule-governed activities. Indeed, rules are constitutive of a game, in the sense that they define what it means to play a particular game. A games player expresses their basic competence precisely in so far as they are able to abide by those rules. However, an important and superficially paradoxical point follows from this: it is not necessary for the competent player to be able to describe those rules in detail. The player's competence primarily lies in "know-how", rather than in "know that" (Ryle 1963: 28–32). This is to say, that knowledge is bound up with the practical ability to play the game, rather than in a theoretical or dispassionate ability to articulate the rules. More precisely, the competent player knows how to go on in novel situations; that is to say, they can spontaneously continue to play, in full obedience to the rules, despite the fact that the state of play is one that has never been encountered before (G: 54). Here, then, is Wittgenstein's first important parallel between language use and games playing. Two consequences follow from the fact that language, like a game, is rule-governed. First, it requires the philosophy of language to relinquish monological explanations. The phenomenon of following a rule cannot be explained monologically. Wittgenstein expresses this point most vividly in his argument against the possibility of a private language (see § "Hermeneutics

(Dilthey)", p. 75). Consider a Robinson Crusoe figure walking about his lonely island, pointing at different plants and uttering noises. He may be attempting to develop a private language. This plant he will call "Y", that plant "X" and so on. Such a language is rule-governed (e.g. when I wish to record that this plant is flowering I should write "Y" in my diary). The problem for Wittgenstein lies in the fact that there is no external check on the consistency with which Robinson uses these signs. If his memory fails him, how can he know if "Y" should be used for this or that plant? More poignantly, how can he even tell that his memory has failed him? Wittgenstein therefore argues that the notion of a private language is inherently incoherent, precisely because a language, like any rule-governed activity, presupposes a community to check that the individual agent is following the rules.

Secondly, the nature of the rules with which Wittgenstein is concerned leads to a fundamental reassessment of our understanding of the nature of language and meaning in comparison to those entertained by early philosophies of language (and not least that found in Wittgenstein's own early *Tractatus*). Correspondence theories, as we have already noted, entail that the meaning and truth of a proposition are largely dependent upon the reference of the proposition to objects in the non-linguistic world. Such a theory emphasizes what Habermas calls the cognitive role of language, which is to say, language as a means to communicate facts about the non-linguistic world (e.g. "It is raining", "The cat is sitting on the mat"). Correspondence theories, as much as Wittgensteinian arguments, entail that language is rule-governed. However, the nature of the rules is subtly different. Rules of correspondence (such that the sentence "It is raining" is true if indeed it is raining) are replaced by Wittgenstein by rules concerning the way in which speakers use the language. What matters to Wittgenstein is less the truth of "It is raining", and more the appropriateness of using that sentence in that particular social context. This leads to something quite radical. Wittgenstein's point is not merely that language is like a game, but rather that it is composed of an ad hoc series of games, and here it is more important to consider not simple acts like questioning, but rather the more complex contexts within which one speaks. Thus, the rules that govern the use of language in the expression of religious belief differ from those governing scientific experiments, and those governing poetry differ from those governing journalism. In each case, what is entailed in making a true or even meaningful statement is distinctive to that particular language-game. A different set of rules will govern the use of language in different situations, in so far as each situation amounts to a different and possibly incommensurable language-game.

These ideas may be explicated as follows. If the competent speaker's competence lies in "know-how" as opposed to "know-that", then they demonstrate their competence (which is to say, their knowledge of the meaning of words) not by reciting dictionary definitions, but by using words in the appropriate places in utterances. Again, like the games player, they know how to go on, following the rules that are appropriate to novel situations. Yet, crucially, these rules are more than the rules of grammar and syntax (or even of Chomsky's "deep grammar"). Consider the statement "The author of *Knowledge and Human Interests* is Jürgen Habermas". This is seemingly well formed and meaningful (and indeed, as a straightforward cognitive proposition, true). However, as a reply to the question "What is the capital of France?" it is meaningless gibberish (and it is meaningless for much the same reasons as moving the rook diagonally in chess is meaningless: it is not part of the way the game is played). "The author of *Knowledge and Human Interests* is Jürgen Habermas" can only be meaningful in a given context (as, indeed, can the question "What is the capital of France?"). This entails that the competence of a speaker rests not just in the (tacit) understanding of the rules that govern the parts of a sentence, but rather in the ability to engage with other speakers in concrete situations. It entails the ability to recognize that the game that we are now playing demands certain forms of question and answer, for example, and that only certain types of statement can be appropriate (and therefore meaningful) responses to certain types of question. Indeed, one may go further, and note that the context is not strictly independent of the use of certain rules. In playing the language-game that involves questioning (which is to say, in formulating a question according to appropriate rules), we mutually create the context for a certain form of questioning, and so establish the conditions in which the respondent can meaningfully reply (G: 73).

Here, then, is the point at which Wittgenstein's philosophy of language flips over into social theory. Where pre-Wittgensteinian philosophy of language (like linguistics) is concerned with sentences, Wittgenstein and, more significantly, universal pragmatics, are concerned with utterances or "speech acts" (CES: 31–2). Examples of speech acts might include questions, promises, orders, requests and baptisms. Consider a promise. I say to you, "I promise that I shall meet you at the library at six o'clock". By this utterance I have not merely imparted information (that I shall be there at six o'clock), but added to it a normative commitment on my part. If I am not there, then I have wronged you, however mildly, and you are due an explanation and in all likelihood an apology. Similarly, if a priest says, "I baptise you in the name of the Father …" then, by little other than making the utterance itself, the person spoken to is brought into the religious community. Their social identity is changed. Speech acts thus establish specific social and moral relationships between speaker and hearer. My utterances and your responses to them (e.g. accepting the promise, demanding an apology if it is broken and so on) are thus constitutive of the social fabric of everyday life. Speech acts may be distinguished from language-games precisely in so far as they are the irreducible communicative units that occur within the broader context of a language-game. Questioning is a speech act, but what is entailed in questioning will vary between, say, the language-game of religious belief and that of scientific inquiry.

If Wittgenstein's arguments suggest the beginning of a social theory, they do not as yet, for Habermas, constitute it as a whole. Habermas characterizes Wittgenstein's approach as one of therapy, as opposed to theory (G: 53). This is to suggest that, precisely in so far as he conceived of ordinary language as an ad hoc series of games, the rules of which might shift relative to context and culture, Wittgenstein attributed to language no systematic or universal core. The task of Wittgenstein's philosophy was no more than that of clarifying any confusion that might exist over the rules used in particular language-games. In contrast, universal pragmatics seeks to reconstruct a communicative competence that is common to all language-users and, indeed, all competent members of society, independently of the particular language-games in which they are involved, or the culture in which they live. The fundamental problem that Habermas finds in Wittgenstein is that he still allows room for – and indeed embraces – perspectivism. Put more precisely, the problem is that while Wittgenstein begins to demonstrate how social life presupposes the intersubjective acknowledgement and acceptance of rules, his account does not explain the processes by which the legitimacy and acceptability of rules might be established. In effect, Wittgenstein embeds the speaker so deeply within the particular language-game that they are allowed no critical purchase upon it. Habermas develops this criticism by identifying two fundamental weaknesses in Wittgenstein's game analogy: first that it fails adequately to grasp the relationship that exists between competent communicators; and, secondly, that Wittgenstein places too little emphasis on the role of cognitive language use. Together, these points amount to the concern that the game analogy conceals what Habermas calls the "double structure" of ordinary language, which is to say that in using language the competent speaker must at once relate to another social subject, and to the matters about which they are communicating (G: 62; SDUP: 156–7). The explication of these weaknesses will be seen to have important implications for Habermas's understanding of language and communicative competence as such.

In playing chess, for example, I relate to my opponent merely as another chess player. The humanity of my opponent and their competence as a social subject may indeed be wholly irrelevant to my satisfaction in playing them, as perhaps is indicated by the development of chess computer programs. The simulacra of a human being, providing that it has the appropriate competence in chess, is sufficient for a good and meaningful game. Communication is thus unlike games playing precisely in so far as the inherent telos of communication is mutual understanding between subjects (G: 101–2). Habermas defends this claim by suggesting that communication is characterized by the participants' mutual anticipation of each other's intentions (G: 59). In contrast, a game proceeds strategically. Each player attempts to predict the causal consequences that their action will have upon their opponent. A game can therefore carry on successfully despite the fact that the players have failed to understand each other's intentions. Indeed, a good player of a strategic game such as chess is frequently good precisely because they are able to conceal their intentions from their opponent. The players do not therefore communicate; they merely follow the same set of conventional rules.

Conversely, in communication, if I do not understand my interlocutor's intentions – which is to say, if I do not understand what the other person means, what they are trying to do with their words, or what they are trying to get me to do – then communication is breaking down. Games break down only if the two sides fail to acknowledge the same set of rules. To remedy this breakdown, the game may be suspended and the rules discussed. For example, an experienced chess player might explain to their novice opponent how a pawn can take *en passant*, and may equally well agree to suspend that rule for this particular game. If linguistic communication breaks down, all one can do is to resort to yet more linguistic communication. One asks, "What do you mean?", "How dare you say that?" or "How can you promise me that?" or some such, and the other may repeat, rephrase or justify what they have said. This is to observe (as Habermas has frequently done beforehand) that natural languages, unlike games, are reflexive: they are their own metalanguages (G: 57–8, 73). The competence of a language-user, unlike that of a games player, must therefore encompass both this complex ability to relate to the other as a subject and to use language's own metalinguistic capacity to sustain communication.

This point may be taken further. If the game analogy distorts the relationship between communicators, it also distorts the relationship between the speaker and language. Habermas acknowledges that Wittgenstein himself recognizes this problem in so far as he recognizes the intimacy of our relationship with language. The way we use language "meshes with our life" (G: 57). Habermas's point is that we develop as human beings precisely in so far as we are intersubjective language-using creatures. This may be illustrated in terms of the early stages of human development. Habermas suggests that a key stage in the development of the child occurs when it can use the word "no". Its very subjectivity is being articulated in this language use. For example, to say "no" to its mother's order to go to bed entails that the child has recognized that both it and its mother are social agents. It has recognized that the mother's prohibition is, unlike a law of nature, something that could be otherwise. Bedtime is not like the painful heat of fire. Fire always hurts, but bedtime could be later if mother willed differently. In addition, the child can meaningfully (and sometimes fruitfully) protest against the imposition of bedtime. In saying "no" it has recognized its mother's intentions, but also expressed its own intention to refuse to comply with them. This nay-saying is, therefore, the primitive mode of the breakdown of communication noted above. It is akin to asking "How dare you say that?" ("What right have you to send me to bed?"). Genuine communication, therefore, may be seen to entail not merely the possibility that participants misunderstand each other's intentions but, more profoundly, that they may negate each other's intentions (G*: 140). It is precisely at this point that Habermas's analysis goes beyond Wittgenstein's. Wittgenstein's games players merely accept the legitimacy of the rules of their game, at least while playing it. Habermas's communicators are capable of assessing the legitimacy of social conventions as part of the very process of using them. They can, however, only do this, in so far as they acknowledge each other as competent subjects (G: 60).

Propositional content and illocutionary force

The above points address the intersubjectivity of language. As such they address speech acts, for they begin to explore the role that language and communicative competence play in establishing and sustaining relationships between social subjects. Yet, to focus exclusively upon this aspect of language, as Wittgenstein tends to do, is to focus upon only one side of language's double structure. It fails to explicate the cognitive role of language, and as such suggests that language-games float free of non-linguistic reality. Indeed, certain interpretations of Wittgenstein might suggest that "reality" is wholly constituted within language-games (just as the reality or the meaning of moves within a game is wholly constituted by its rules). Habermas's contention is, rather, that language (or more precisely the universals of communicative competence) constitutes not reality as such, but rather the possibility of our experience of reality (G: 58). This deliberately Kantian formulation, in stressing the transcendental role of communicative competence, suggests that communicative competence structures the way in which human beings engage with reality (and, as such occupies the place similar to that held by labour and interaction in his earlier works (CES: 41)).

An initial attempt to articulate the double structure of language can be found in Austin's speech act theory. Austin drew a radical separation between speech acts and cognitive utterances. In the technical terminology of the theory, speech acts had "illocutionary" content while cognitive utterances had "propositional" content (CES: 36, 41; SDUP: 157). In effect, one either did things with words, or one made statements about the world. Habermas's contention is that these two sides are necessarily present in all utterances. In cognitive utterances one *asserts* the propositional content (so that subsequent discussion will be expected to focus upon the truth or falsehood of this proposition), while in non-cognitive utterances one merely *mentions* it (focusing the communicants' attention on the intersubjective or performative aspects of the utterance) (CES: 36, 50; SDUP: 157). Here we may recall that we have established that when I ask you what the capital of France is, I am performing a speech act and thereby establishing a social relationship between us. However, I also imply that France has a capital, and I thus make a statement about the world. My speech act therefore has cognitive content. Similarly, if I promise to meet you at six o'clock, I make a statement about the practical feasibility of that meeting, and you might reply, "But it is already ten past six", or "The library will be closed by then". Conversely, in a purely cognitive statement, such as "Habermas is the author of *Knowledge and Human Interests*", not only am I making a statement about the non-linguistic world, but I shall also be performing a speech act. I might be teaching you, or answering a question.

Habermas's point, then, is that when I try to do something with words (such as promising) I may be challenged, not as might usually be expected about this putative intersubjective relationship between speaker and hearer, but rather about the facts mentioned in the utterance; so, too, when I assert a fact in a cognitive utterance, the conversation may continue by focusing on the relationship that has been established between the speaker and the listener (rather than upon that fact). You might, for example, challenge my right to be teaching on Habermas. What is happening, in either case, is that a potential breakdown in communication is being avoided by the speaker's resort to the reflexivity of language. The conversation carries on by using language to talk about the conversation itself (G: 74). Habermas thus re-establishes the telos of communication, mutual understanding, and sees this to be encapsulated in the concept of "illocutionary force". The illocutionary component of an utterance does not merely concern the relatively trivial point that speech acts occur between at least two subjects, but rather the more profound point that speech acts can be adjudged successful if and only if they have the force to generate an interpersonal relationship between two or more subjects that is freely entered into by all parties. Put otherwise, a successful speech act generates the context within which questions, agreements, objections, denials, confessions, betrayals, promises and apologies (e.g. G: 82–3)) can make sense and be binding on all involved. (It may be noted that Habermas is primarily concerned with those speech acts that generate a context, as opposed to those, such as baptising, marrying and voting, that presuppose some already existing social institution (G: 84; CES: 38).) The success of a speech act therefore centres upon participants *understanding* and *accepting* each other's intentions (CES: 35; G*: 144).[1] Acceptance may well require that the participants resort to the reflexivity of language in order to clarify not merely what their intentions are, but also whether or not these intentions are legitimate. ("You intend to teach me about Habermas, but are you qualified to do so?"; "You promise to meet me at the library, but is that practically feasible?") To explicate this force is not merely to explicate the mechanism through which competent agents establish interpersonal relationships, but rather to begin to explicate the role that was promised for universal pragmatics in the final section of *Legitimation Crisis*, which is to say, to provide a form of ideology critique. The illocutionary force of speech acts has, for Habermas, a rational foundation. The point at stake is not that of how interpersonal relationships are established, but rather how they ought to the established.

In suggesting that illocutionary force has a rationality, Habermas is responding to the problem posed by Wittgenstein's game analogy. Habermas is suggesting that we do not merely accept language-games and their rules. We are not passively thrown into them. Rather, we can be given good reasons for accepting them (and, indeed, if these reasons cannot be given, then we have every right to abandon them). But, in addition and more importantly, Habermas is renewing the challenge to instrumental (and indeed dialectical) reason that has been a continuing theme of his work. To explicate the rationality of illocutionary force is to explicate the nature of communicative reason, and thereby establish a viable alternative to instrumental and dialectical reason.

Validity claims

It is at this point that one of Habermas's most fundamental technical terms may be introduced: that of "validity claims". Whenever I make an utterance I can, in principle, be challenged by my listeners, and such challenges amount to the demand to demonstrate that what is claimed, implicitly or explicitly, in my utterance is valid or acceptable. Here, then, lies the core of the rationality of illocutionary force: not merely that my listeners are free to challenge me, but that once challenged I am expected to provide them with satisfactory answers (which is to say, answers that are characterized by the "unforced force of better argument" (G: 95)) before the conversation can continue. This may be unfolded by examining the four kinds of validity claim that Habermas suggests to be entailed in any utterance: truth, rightness, intelligibility and truthfulness or sincerity. The first two have already been encountered in the examples above. We have seen that all utterances contain cognitive content. It is this content that is challenged in truth claims. Similarly, it was suggested that a speaker may be challenged in terms of their right to initiate, through a certain speech act, a specific social relationship (e.g. to teach on a certain topic, but equally one might consider the right to give an order or disclose a secret). Thus, the roles of the speaker and hearer are normatively prescribed, and the validity claim to rightness will demand that the speakers focus upon the legitimacy of the relevant norms and their relationships to them. Intelligibility refers to the basic sense that the utterance makes, and the listener may ask for a gloss or an interpretation of the utterance. Finally, sincerity refers to the degree to which the utterance accurately expresses the speaker's intentions ("Do you really mean to keep that promise?"). These four validity claims may further be mapped onto what Habermas calls four domains of reality: "the" world of external nature; "our" world of society; language itself; and "my" world of internal nature (CES: 68). In raising a truth claim, I am asking about the relationship of the utterance to the objective world; in raising a claim to rightness I am asking about the relationship of the speaker to the social, cultural and moral world; intelligibility inquires into the linguistic coherence of the utterance; and, finally, sincerity asks about the relationship between the utterance and the speaker himself or herself.

The redemption of a truth claim occurs at two possible levels (CES: 63–4). Superficially, empirical evidence or experiences may be provided that will satisfy the challenger. (Consider even our trivial example of "Habermas is the author of *Knowledge and Human Interests*". If this is challenged, I simply produce a copy of the book and point to the author's name.) However, at a deeper level, evidence is more significant in so far as it is disruptive rather than supportive of language-games. A language-game will continue unproblematically until an unexpected piece of evidence – an unexpected encounter with the real – runs against routine expectations. (Consider the other trivial example of promising to meet at the library. One source of disruption of this language-game was the ignorance of the time on the part of the one making the promise. The experience of time halts the routine course of the promise.) To treat evidence in this way is to return to Habermas's engagement with Peirce's pragmatism. As was seen above (§ "Pragmatism", p. 67), reality works in the Peircean model of scientific inquiry as that which disrupts those taken-for-granted expectations and beliefs upon which, otherwise, we would base our actions (G: 88). This entails that, if experience is typically disruptive, then as an unexpected intrusion of reality into the language-game it is also typically incomprehensible in the existing terms of that game. A naive appeal to further experience is therefore only going to redeem the truth claim in the most humdrum cases, where all participants can immediately agree upon its interpretation and relevance to the language-game (as is the case with the Habermas-author example). If the language-game has been disrupted by experience, then it is more likely that a process of argumentation will be required in order to establish its relevance to the contested truth claim. (Again, consider the other problem with the library promise: that the library closes before six o'clock. "But", comes the response, "today is Thursday and the library stays open late on Thursdays". Here, in a most rudimentary form, is an argued justification.) This is to return once more, in effect, to the legal analogy for scientific argumentation offered by Popper (§ "Reason", p. 14).

Habermas has rejected a correspondence theory of truth (whether the correspondence be to reality or to a naively experienced evidence (G: 86–8)). In rejecting the correspondence theory, he is not arguing that the truth or falsehood of a proposition is independent of the proposition's relationship to reality (G*: 148). "Habermas is the author of *Knowledge and Human Interests*" is true because Habermas did indeed write that book. However, correspondence theory fails to grasp that any such proposition is asserted within a speech act (G: 86). The key problem of truth is, then, not the correspondence to reality, but rather the process by which truth comes to be ascribed to a proposition. To explicate this process Habermas has turned to a consensus theory, whereby a proposition is true if and only if "everyone else who could enter into discourse with me" would freely accept it as true (G: 89). Crucially, Habermas's formulation entails that his theory does not degenerate into a simple relativism, such that "truth" is relative to this particular community (or these particular participants in this language-game). We cannot, for example, simply agree among ourselves that actually Horkheimer wrote *Knowledge and Human Interests* and so construct truth independently of reality. Rather, Habermas's argument is again grounded in Peirce's pragmatism. Peirce defined truth as that which will be accepted by the community of scientists in the long run (or at the end of scientific inquiry). This idea is now placed much more centrally to Habermas's argument than it was in *Knowledge and Human Interests*, and it is thus that he seeks to resolve the problems he identified in its emancipatory account of truth (see § "Criticisms of *Knowledge and Human Interests*", p. 102). Truth is determined by the agreement not of those present, but of all those who could be present (including, in principle, those who are not yet born). A proposition that is held true now, is, as Peirce's pragmatism suggests, held true only provisionally, awaiting further disruptive evidence or argumentation.

Yet Habermas's theory focuses not merely upon the participants in discussion, but also upon the nature of that discussion. Truth is redeemed through "discourse" (and discourse is contrasted to the more mundane process of "communication"). Discourse is characterized as that form of argument that is pursued once the assertive force of the propositional content has been suspended (SDUP: 164; G: 100). In communication one asserts, for example, that "Habermas is the author of *Knowledge and Human Interests*", or that "The structure of DNA is a double helix". In discourse, such claims are entertained merely hypothetically. Put otherwise, one acknowledges the possibility that the proposition may express a merely subjective appearance, rather than the reality of "being" (SDUP: 165–6). However, discourse continues to be disciplined by certain normative requirements. First, the very definition of truth in terms of those propositions that would be accepted by all participants entails that no competent speaker can be excluded from the discussion. Habermas acknowledges that there is an unavoidable circularity in this formulation, for the very competence of participants is something that cannot necessarily be established independently of communication and discourse itself (G: 96). This is not necessarily problematic, precisely because it coheres with the idea that truth claims made now are only held provisionally. Even in discourse, discussion proceeds against a background of taken-for-granted assumptions about how the natural and social worlds work, and indeed what might count as evidence (ARC: 273). It is therefore possible that problems with evidence and discursive competence are simply unrecognizable at a given moment within a given language-game. The subsequent evidence that may lead to a revision of a truth claim may therefore include a reassessment of the competence of earlier disputants. Indeed, the whole tenor of Habermas's argument is to instil a humility into all our judgements, be they of the natural world, or the human. Secondly, given that all may participate in discourse, then all must have equal opportunities to participate. Crucially, discourse cannot be distorted by imbalances of power. All participants have equal opportunities to initiate and continue arguments, for example, by posing questions and answers, and by interpreting, explaining or justifying statements (G: 98). Only under these admittedly highly rarefied conditions can problematic truth claims be redeemed in such a manner as to restore free consensus and mutual understanding.

Normative claims, or claims to rightness, are redeemed through a similar process. If one's right to initiate a certain social relationship is challenged, then one can superficially draw attention to the social norm that gives one that right (e.g. I can give you orders because I am of higher rank than you, or I am older than you) or, if this is unsatisfactory, one can revert to practical discourse that is akin to the theoretical discourse through which truth claims are redeemed. Here it is the legitimacy of the norm that is at stake and, again, during discourse itself the norm's binding power is suspended, and its legitimacy is treated hypothetically (CES: 64) (so that, for example, the participants might debate the relevance of age in justifying a social hierarchy). Put otherwise, one entertains the possibility that the norm expresses not a binding "ought" (i.e. a rule that one ought to obey because it is morally legitimate) but a mere "is" (i.e. a rule that is merely part of a reified social reality) (SDUP: 166).

Claims to intelligibility and truthfulness stand outside this model. In the case of intelligibility, if simple processes of glossing or rephrasing fail to resolve the disruption, then redemption must be achieved through what Habermas terms "hermeneutic" discourse. This is to suggest that participants must appeal to the hermeneutic techniques (and not least interpretation through a hermeneutic circle of provisional "pre-judgements" and their revision in the light of particular elements of the utterance) as outlined in *Knowledge and Human Interests* (G: 94; G*: 148) Truthfulness is redeemed not through discourse, but rather through an examination of the consistency that exists between the linguistically expressed intentions of the agent and their behaviour. Thus, a response to my promise to meet may be to observe that I have rarely if ever kept my promises in the past. I reply by offering my assurance that I mean it this time, but ultimately it is only observation of my subsequent behaviour that will redeem this validity claim (CES: 64; G: 90).

This review of validity claims and their redemption, and thus of what Habermas sees as the most universal properties of speech (SDUP: 161), begins to consolidate a notion of communicative competence as the ground of agents' ability to act as competent social beings, and thereby to constitute and maintain social relations. Perhaps more importantly it also begins to outline an inherent communicative rationality in the illocutionary force of speech acts (precisely in so far as all speech acts allow, at least in principle, for their being challenged and redeemed through discourse).[2]

The development of communicative competence

Before looking in more detail at the implications and applications of communicative rationality in the next sections, a brief note may be added concerning the development of communicative competence. As might be expected, Habermas is concerned to present communicative competence not as a mere given, but rather as a phenomenon with an identifiable ontogenesis. During the 1970s and early 1980s, he thus struggles to refine a reconstruction of three stages of development, broadly akin to Kohlberg's pre-conventional, conventional and post-conventional levels (SDUP: 162–6; G*: 137–46; CES: 69ff.; MCCA: 116ff.). However, while Kohlberg is primarily concerned with the development of a moral competence, Habermas is concerned with a broader conception of communicative competence, of which moral awareness is but one component. Kohlberg's three levels thereby become the framework within which a complex series of interrelated and mutually supportive developments occur, as the child's sense of identity and ability to handle ever more complex forms of social interaction mature. In so far as social interaction is understood in terms of the child's ability to maintain and to repair communicative relationships to other social agents, then that ability will be dependent upon a complex of capacities, including the child's understanding of the reciprocal nature of relationships, of the nature and source of motivations to act (and thus the recognition of relevant sources of authority), and its ability to understand the world, not just from its own subjective or first-person viewpoint, but also from the viewpoint of its interlocutors (second person) and that of a neutral observer (third person) (MCCA: 138). Above all, this complex is tied to a process of "decentring", as the child overcomes the purely subjective perspective of pre-conventional natural identity and learns to differentiate not merely the subjectivity of its own perspective from that of an external world, but more significantly the "world perspectives" of its inner psychological world from both the natural world and the social world. This process of differentiation and decentring is bound up with the capacity not simply to use language, but to differentiate between cognitive, normative and expressive speech acts (MCCA: 137–8).

In brief, the three levels may be understood as follows. At the first, pre-conventional, level, the young child is developing a capacity to use language, so that their interactions are symbolically mediated (SDUP: 162). However, precisely in so far as their sense of self-identity remains "natural", their relationships to others are largely immediate and particularistic. They are motivated and recognize authority primarily in terms of the provision of rewards and punishments. Yet, as the discussion of nay-saying above indicated, the child is developing an awareness of itself as an object of reflection, and thus of the distinction between first- and second-person perspectives. At the second, conventional, level the child develops from a recognition that others use different types of speech acts (and that it should respond differently to those different acts) to an ability to use them itself (so that the child can distinguish between the propositional and illocutionary components of an utterance as a social actor). Here the child comes to distinguish fully the four domains (the objectified external world, the moral or social world, the inner psychological world and the intersubjectivity of language), and thus master, not merely the perspectives of speaker and hearer, but also that of the observer (third-person) so that it can begin to understand the world from someone else's viewpoint. Obedience to norms is now secured through an awareness of the binding nature of the norm itself (rather than the consequences of trespassing that norm). The child thus orientates itself to social roles (that norms define and justify), so that a role identity replaces the earlier natural identity. Finally, only in the post-conventional level associated with adolescence does the agent become capable of discourse. Each level may be seen to surpass its predecessor in terms of the developing reflective capacity of the agent. That which is taken for granted at one level becomes the object of critical reflection at the next. Having acquired full command of the distinction between apparent truth claims and those grounded in the way the world is (i.e. in being), and between norms that merely obtain, and those that ought to obtain (ARC: 272), the adolescent thus acquires the ability to challenge the legitimacy of norms and demand their rational redemption (cf. LC: 89ff.). Being now motivated by the strength of better argument, and not the mere presence of a norm, the adolescent acquires full communicative competence (in the ability to challenge and redeem validity claims). Role identity is replaced by an ego identity, through the capacity to recognize oneself and others as agents independently of any particular situation or social role, and thus as beings whose reasoning and motivation should aspire to a generality that transcends any particular situation or activity.

Habermas sums up this development as the "differentiation between the lifeworld and the world" (MCCA: 138). This is merely to suggest that maturity, as a cognitive and moral being, lies in the ability to question the taken-for-granted and secure assumptions of the lifeworld. It is the ability to treat one's own treasured assumptions and values as hypothetical: to suspend the binding force that they exert upon one's beliefs and actions. The next three sections of this chapter will deal, within the fields of the theory of ideology, ethical theory and social theory, with Habermas's fundamental concern with this process of differentiation and critical reflection.

The account of systematically distorted communication

The ideal speech situation

The intention behind universal pragmatics, as we have already noted, is not merely explanatory. While it does indeed offer an explanation of the constitution of social relations through communicative competence, it also provides a critical resource through which illegitimate forms of social organization may be recognized. In effect, it substantiates a theme that runs throughout *Legitimation Crisis*: that legitimacy is not, as Luhmann suggests, merely a matter of the current acceptability of norms, but rather of the way in which that acceptance has been achieved (LC: 98–9; CES: 188). The ideas of a freely achieved consensus and the rationality that underpins illocutionary force, both of which lie at the core of Habermas's notions of communicative action and discourse, already contain in substantial part the germs of such a critical resource. They may be further explicated through two key terms: the "ideal speech situation" and "systematically distorted communication".

Habermas's approach, as ever, may be seen as an attempt to steer a course between the paralysing suspicion of Adorno's negative dialectics and the dogmatism of Lukács's historical materialism, and once again pragmatism provides him with a theoretical guide. An Adorno-like sensitivity to the fact that imbalances of political power can invade, covertly, the very nature of our language and thought is tempered by a pragmatic acceptance of a taken-for-granted and largely unproblematic world. In effect, everything can, as Adorno suggests, be questioned, but such blanket suspicion is as counter-productive as is Cartesian scepticism in epistemology. Habermas therefore suggests that in entering communicative interaction with others, competent social agents assume, albeit with a certain studied naivety, that the subsequent communication will not be distorted by imbalances of power. In effect, they assume that all participants are equally able and willing to redeem the validity claims implicit in their utterances (which is to say that they can give evidence for their assertions, or refer to the norms that legitimate their interactions and, if necessary, resort to discourse to redeem these claims). All are equally free to contribute to the discussion and to challenge each other. If a claim cannot be redeemed by persuasive argument then it will be abandoned. Put otherwise, all the participants consider themselves and their interlocutors to be accountable (G*: 147). They are all seeking mutual understanding, which is to say a consensus freely entered into by all (G*: 148; cf. LC: 110). They relate to each other as subjects and not, as in a strategic game, as opponents.

In practice, real communication is, of course, not like this. However, Habermas's point is that social agents, as a fundamental part of their communicative competence, must make the counterfactual assumption of the "fiction" (G: 102) of this, the ideal speech situation. Put bluntly, I do not have to have the sincerity of my interlocutors demonstrated to me before I start talking to them. I assume that they are sincere, open and accountable unless I encounter evidence to the contrary. If I did not make this assumption then the reproduction of a meaningful lifeworld, which universal pragmatics analyses, would be impossible. Adorno's radically suspicious agents would simply be incapable of entering into meaningful relationships with others, not least because there could then be no possibility of reaching mutual understanding. At best they might achieve the coordination of games players, each in isolation acknowledging the same set of rules. The unavoidable presupposition of the ideal speech situation further entails that there is a critical standard (G: 97) inherent in mundane communicative (and thus social) competence. Put otherwise, Lukács's dogmatic assertion of an image of a perfect society has been replaced by an image that all competent agents intuit. Only thus, Habermas suggests, could we intuitively recognize deviations from this ideal, and recognize them as morally problematic (G: 97).

As with Peirce's pragmatist theory of truth, the naive assumption of the ideal speech situation is disturbed by evidence, which is to say that there needs to be good reason to abandon a taken-for-granted belief in such a useful fiction. Certain disruptions will be obvious, and Habermas sums them up neatly as one party making use of "privileged access to weapons, wealth or standing, in order to *wring* agreement from another party" (ARC: 272). Thus consensus brought about by overt threats of violence, by bribery or by the undefended resort to political or status hierarchies is not communicative action; it is, rather, strategic action, whereby one party treats the others as objects that can be manipulated, rather than as subjects with whom one communicates. Similarly, the use of rhetoric, precisely in so far as the rhetorician attempts to persuade an audience by means other than evidence and rational argument (and, indeed, thereby seeks to forestall the raising of problematic validity claims) is an example of strategic action (R: 266-7).

Systematically distorted communication

Habermas seeks to distinguish such overt deviations from the more subtle and problematic phenomenon of systematically distorted communication. This form of disruption is characterized by its covert character, precisely in that it is grounded in the self-deception of one or more of the participants. It is here that Habermas comes closest to making use of something akin to Adorno's suspicion about the impossibility of communication in contemporary society, for – precisely because of its covert nature – systematically distorted communication may not strike the participants as being problematic (OSDC: 206). Habermas's early presentation of systematically distorted communication draws heavily upon the account of psychoanalysis given in *Knowledge and Human Interests*. The psychoanalytic model suggests that defence mechanisms may inhibit the public articulation of neuroses. Neuroses are expressed in the split-off symbols of a private language.[3] The neurotic thereby deceives themselves, in so far as they are unable to recognize themselves as the authors of, for example, hysterical symptoms, parapraxis and dreams. Habermas thus offers the example of a speaker who regards their utterances as meaningful, while these very utterances are unintelligible to others. This will be an example of systematically distorted communication only if the unintelligibility cannot be resolved through hermeneutic discourse, which is to say that it is due to neither the speaker's nor the hearer's incompetence in a particular natural language. Rather, the unintelligibility is due to intrusion of neurotic split-off symbols (G*: 150). Still more poignantly, Habermas offers the example of a married couple who, unable to acknowledge and face the decay of their relationship, deceive themselves about their continuing mutual love (G*: 152). From the perspective of universal pragmatics, as opposed to psychoanalysis, these two cases may be understood as the inability to raise validity claims to intelligibility and to truthfulness respectively. As Habermas presents this, an overburdening of the external organization of speech has shifted into the internal organization of speech (G*: 147). Put simply, an inability to deal with conflict (akin to the neurotic's inability to deal with the original trauma) manifests itself in a disruption of communicative competence (and, specifically, an inhibition on raising the very validity claims that might make public that conflict).

The notion of overburdening may be represented in terms of the language of systems theory: systematically distorted communication occurs when social systems are unable to satisfy their imperatives, due to power imbalances. Put otherwise, systems crises lead to problems at the level of meaning in the lifeworld. Habermas illustrates this by considering the family as a social system (G*: 159–64). He suggests that there is empirical evidence that a family's capacity to solve systems problems, and indeed to fulfil its functions as a social system, is inversely proportional to its internal potential for conflict. Conflict arises from an unequal distribution of power among the adult family members. While the members of such hierarchical families may manifest a mutual consensus, this consensus is maintained, paradoxically, only by repressing the full potential of communicative action. The conflicts that are inherent in the family structure are systematically excluded from communication and discourse. Such conflict could be resolved through resort to something akin to an ideal speech situation, whereby all members of the family have an equal opportunity to challenge the norms upon which the current organization of family life rests. However, this would destroy the consensus, and thus the family, as it currently exists. The possibility of a discursive challenge to the family's organizational structure is thereby rendered unthinkable to its members. The very nature and problem of the rigid hierarchy cannot be recognized or acknowledged. The cost of this to the members is that the fluid communicative relations that should ensure that the family fulfils its core functions – of meeting its members' needs, and of securing and allowing for the development of their personal identities – are replaced by more rigid and stereotypical strategic relations. Precisely in that human beings develop, through the intersubjective use of language (as, for example, the "nay-saying" child suggested above), systematically distorted communication does not merely inhibit communication between competent subjects; rather, it reaches into the very possibility of the subject's development as a competent human being.

Habermas's analysis of the family is, at a micro-level, the root argument of *Legitimation Crisis*. Differentials of power and wealth that could not be justified in an ideal speech situation lie at the core of contemporary society. The crises that arise from this overburdening of the economic, administrative and legitimation systems culminate in a crisis of meaning. As Habermas puts this, meaning is now a "scarce resource", because a coherent justification of the norms that underpin current economic and social organization cannot be given (LC: 77). Late capitalism retains its stability only in so far as it can repress the possibility of the discursive articulation of its own legitimacy (and does this, for example, by substituting supplies of values, including consumer goods, for meaning). Thus, in evoking the notion of "systematically distorted communication" alongside that of the "ideal speech situation", Habermas is not simply claiming that certain forms of political and economic organisation cannot be given rational legitimation; rather, he has begun to trace the mechanisms that repress the very demand for legitimacy. In effect, he is offering something akin to Adorno's notion of reification, precisely in so far as Adorno saw reification, not simply as a problem of the social structure, but rather as a problem of thought (see § "Reification", p. 19). In a line of argument that has its origins in the positivism dispute, Habermas is, like Adorno, suggesting that dominant forms of thought may be incapable of grasping society as it really is, and that a contradictory social base will inhibit the possibility of meaningful thought and communication within the superstructure. The self-deceptions of systematically distorted communication thus take the place of what Adorno termed "identity thinking" (the dogmatic assumption that the human cognitive subject is capable of reconstructing in thought an objective and exhaustive model of reality), but in doing so works through more rigorously the social and psychological mechanisms that link the base subsystem to culture and language, and thus to personality and agency. From this analysis, Adorno's radical suspicion and quietism may be avoided precisely in so far as the very possibility of society presupposes the communicative competence that is reconstructed in universal pragmatics, and thus the intuition of a critical standard in the ideal speech situation.

Discourse ethics

In *Legitimation Crisis*, universal pragmatics is presented as the foundation of a theory of "communicative" ethics (LC: 89, 102–10).[4] The outlines of this theory are already familiar to us, for it focuses upon the moral competence or know-how that social actors develop as part of their communicative competence (JA: 34). This competence is the ability to challenge and redeem normative validity claims through practical discourse. However, over the decade or more that followed the publication of *Legitimation Crisis*, Habermas, along with Apel (1980: 225–300), refined this theory as one of "discourse ethics". This refinement may be seen to mark a subtle shift in the nature of Habermas's theorizing. Communicative ethics was, from the first, concerned not merely with the moral domain (of interpersonal relations) but also with broader political issues (and not least the legitimacy of the normative structure governing any particular society). This political concern is carried through into discourse ethics. However, while *Legitimation Crisis*, as a political theory, articulates itself in broadly Marxist terms (and the notion of "systematically distorted communication", for example, serves to place the Marxist concern with ideology at the centre of the argument), discourse ethics turns to engage with the more overtly liberal discussions of justice.

This argumentative shift is marked, in part, by a shift of emphasis away from the concept of "ideal speech situation". Something of its content is retained in Apel's Peircean concept of an "unrestricted communication community" (MCCA: 88). But, more importantly, the work of explicating what is necessarily presupposed by all competent participants in argumentation (and thus the redemption of validity claims) is deferred to an explicit set of "rules of discourse". These include:

1. Every subject with the competence to speak and act is allowed to take part in a discourse.
2a. Everyone is allowed to question any assertion whatever.
2b. Everyone is allowed to introduce any assertion whatever into the discourse.
2c. Everyone is allowed to express his attitudes, desires, and needs.
3. No speaker may be prevented, by internal or external coercion, from exercising his rights as laid down in (1) and (2).   (MCCA: 89)

These rules refine what has already been offered in the earlier analyses of discourse, and again Habermas emphasizes the normative character of these rules. Thus, in entering into communicative action, the competent speaker is committing himself or herself (wittingly or otherwise) to a set of rules that define the force of better argument. They govern not merely the logical structure of discourse (e.g. "No speaker may contradict themselves" (MCCA: 87)), but also the moral relationship that is established between the participants. This formulation now allows Habermas (along with Apel) to argue that a failure to recognize this normative relationship embroils the speaker in a "performative contradiction" (MCCA: 80). For example, if a consensus is secured only by excluding certain parties from the dialogue, then the very principles that make communicative action – and thus the achievement of even this spurious consensus – possible in the first place (i.e. rules 1 and 3) are being undermined. In practice, performative contradiction has long been a powerful tool in philosophical argument. Habermas and Apel note, for example, that it underpins Decartes's *"cogito ergo sum"* argument. If I doubt my own existence then I contradict myself, for I must exist in order to doubt (MCCA: 80). Similarly, one may suggest that Habermas's objection to Adorno's negative dialectics runs along the same lines: the very exercise of such rigorous doubt actually presupposes the very standards that allow one to overcome the quietism into which Adorno falls.

One might criticize the above analysis of a spurious consensus by suggesting that those who attempt to bring about forced consensuses explicitly reject any interest in the rules of discourse. Their actions are intentionally strategic, not communicative, and therefore the rules of discourse do not apply to them. If so, then the principles that make communicative action possible are irrelevant, and no contradiction occurs. It may be suggested that this criticism is avoided once it is recognized that "performative contradiction" bears some of the burden within discourse ethics that systematically distorted communication bore within *Legitimation Crisis*. Although the failure to approximate ideal or unrestricted communication is now primarily approached as a problem of argumentation, rather than one of ideology, there remains a common theme. Just as the participants to communication are unaware of systematic distortion, so a performative contradiction occurs when the participants assume that the consensus achieved is genuine. The argument may, however, be taken further in order to ask whether it is coherent to take a rigorously strategic approach to social action: could one consistently deny one's moral involvement with other human beings? The position of the pure strategist might be defended as one of moral scepticism or nihilism (and thus the denial of the existence of any binding norms or moral arguments). However, as soon as the strategist seeks to defend their scepticism, they once more fall into a performative contradiction. This is because to enter into any argument (and not merely the practical discourse of morality) presupposes the normative rules of discourse (as well as the more purely logical ones) (MCCA: 80–81). In effect, the attempt to defend moral scepticism in rational argument is seen, by Habermas and Apel, to be as inconsistent as attempting to doubt one's own existence. Further, just as a thoroughgoing doubt about one's own existence cannot be realized in the practice of everyday life – it is, after all, difficult to conceive what it would mean in practical terms to doubt one's own existence – so even a mute retreat of the strategist into a solipsistic isolation, refusing to defend or articulate their position and refusing to engage communicatively with any other human being, is impossible. Simply as a competently socialized living being, the strategist is constituted by the very rules that their scepticism strives to deny (MCCA: 100). To attempt to live outside this constitution is not a defence or realization of moral scepticism; it is the manifestation of a profound social immaturity, incompetence or insanity.

Habermas argues that a principle of universalization is at least implicitly recognized by all social actors who are capable of discursive argumentation. This principle of universalization asserts that every valid norm fulfils the following condition:

> *All* affected can accept the consequences and the side effects its *general* observance can be anticipated to have for the satisfaction of *everyone's* interests (and these consequences are preferred to those of known alternative possibilities for regulation).
> (MCCA: 65; and see MCCA: 93, 120)

In short, a norm is valid if all relevant parties agree to accept it, and do so in the light of all the information that is available. The principle of universalization has a strongly Kantian flavour, not least in echoing Kant's demand that all genuinely moral principles must be universifiable (i.e. any moral principle that I am myself happy to abide by should also be one that I am happy for everyone else to abide by; so, crudely, "Do not steal" is fine but "Tell lies"' is not, even if it might get me out of trouble in the short term). However, the principle of universalization says nothing of how this acceptance by all affected is to be achieved. That is specified by the principle of discourse ethics itself, and it is precisely this that makes discourse ethics distinctive, and in addition makes its strong claim against moral scepticism (and by default, decisionism) plausible. The principle of discourse ethics runs:

> Only those norms can claim to be valid that meet (or could meet) with the approval of all affected in their capacity *as participants in a practical discourse.* (MCCA: 66; and see MCCA: 93, 121)

Again, in short, Habermas is arguing that norms can only be validated through open and intersubjective argumentation.

From this outline, Habermas draws out three characteristics of discourse ethics that serve not merely to clarify the scope of discourse ethics, but also to distinguish it from other competing ethical theories. Discourse ethics is cognitive, universal and formal (MCCA: 120–21). A cognitive ethical theory entails that moral judgements are justifiable through argumentation, and as such is set against moral scepticism, decisionism and emotivism. If Habermas's characterization of practical discourse is accepted, not least in so far as it defends communicative reason as an alternative to the instrumental or purely deductive reason presupposed by decisionism, then ethics can be cognitive (see LC: 105–6). Cognitivism entails that moral judgements cannot be reduced to subjective preferences, and similarly universalism entails that the validity of moral judgements cannot be reduced to cultural circumstances, as moral relativists (or perspectivists) claim. The validity of a norm depends not upon the cultural presuppositions that social agents bring to moral practice, but upon the weight of better argument. Ironically, universal ethics is, even so, recognized by Habermas to be a historical achievement. Only in post-conventional societies do norms routinely require rational justification and only in such societies do the procedures of justification come to be articulated (LC: 90; MCCA: 107).

The assertions of ethical cognitivism and universalism are bold and controversial. Superficially they together suggest a dangerous arrogance: that of a self-proclaimed moral expert dictating objective moral principles. This, crucially, is not Habermas's intention, and it is the third characteristic of formalism that saves Habermas from such hubris. A discourse ethics is not primarily concerned with the content of valid norms. It is not an algorithm through which a set of definitive moral principles could be generated. As such, Habermas is at pains to distinguish his position from that of the liberal political theorist John Rawls (MCCA: 198). Rawls similarly aspires to a cognitivist and universalist ethical theory, and does so by proposing a thought experiment, grounded in the tradition of liberal social contract theory (Rawls 1972: 17). Rawls asks his readers to imagine a conference (or "original position") at which the principles that will govern a society are developed. To ensure the justice or fairness of those principles, he argues that all delegates to that conference must be ignorant of the place they will occupy in that society, or the intellectual, physical and other advantages that might determine their place and the rewards society would yield to them. This "veil of ignorance" should guarantee that, in deriving the basic principles of a just society, the delegates consider the effect that those principles might have upon everyone, regardless of their abilities, talents, gender, skin colour or whatever. Put most vividly, Rawls asks the delegates to design a society in which their place will be determined by their worst enemy (Rawls 1972: 152). In a society designed under those conditions, Rawls claims, the rewards and treatment of every individual will be rationally justifiable.

Rawls's argument seems to be very much in the spirit of Habermas's. Not least, they equally recognize the importance of the pragmatist George Herbert Mead's notion of "ideal role taking", which is to say that moral relations presuppose ego's ability to recognize and take on alter's position (MCCA: 121, 154). However, the differences are fundamental. First, Rawls proceeds to derive two substantial principles of justice (and indeed a series of refinements and applications of these principles).[5] Secondly, the Rawlsian procedure for deriving these principles contradicts the principle of discourse ethics. The thought experiment of the original position suggests an appeal to practical discourse in order to debate the merits and implications of the principles. If conference delegates are rendered ignorant of their individual abilities and experiences within the social world through the veil of ignorance, then they all become identical. Dialogue degenerates into monologue, for no delegate can bring anything distinctive to the discussion. It may be suggested that it is precisely this concealed monological character of the argument that allows a (pseudo-)consensus over the substantive principles of justice. Habermas seeks to check this through the strict formalism of discourse ethics. Discourse ethics is concerned only with the procedures through which competent social agents resolve, for themselves, real and pressing moral problems, and not with the substantial solutions upon which they agree. In his later dialogue with Rawls, Habermas also makes clear that he is concerned with the procedure by which a political constitution (such as is expressed in Rawls's two principles) is achieved, and not with the substance of the constitution itself (IO: 49–73).

Put otherwise, discourse ethics works by establishing a subtle relationship between the everyday lifeworld and the abstraction of practical discourse (MCCA: 177–8). At the level of the lifeworld, it may be accepted that the identities of societies and their members is largely secured through cultural values that are embodied in everyday practices and self-understandings. The undermining of these values would lead to the sort of crisis in collective or individual identity that is the concern of *Legitimation Crisis*. The lifeworld is thus a source of solidarity, and as such cultural values cannot be questioned as a totality. Such questioning would be akin to Cartesian doubt, in attempting to strip away all dubious elements of beliefs, before rebuilding on a bedrock of certainty. This is the conceit of first philosophy (and there is indeed something of this in Rawls's conception of the original position). The values of any given lifeworld make possible the agency of its members (including their capacity to recognize moral problems). Yet, that lifeworld is also potentially oppressive if the individual member has no recourse to moral standards independently of the concrete values of the particular lifeworld. One need only consider the manner in which patriarchal cultural values serve to constitute a second nature within which women's supposed inferiority and resultant subordination become taken for granted. This is the problem faced by the moral relativist and certain forms of contemporary communitarian political philosophy. While the community may indeed provide constitutive solidarity and support, it may also be a source of exploitation and repression by denying the realization of real human needs or through the marginalization of the interests of certain groups. Discourse ethics avoids this problem, initially, by recognizing that social actors have the capacity and the right to challenge not cultural values as a totality, but problematic individual norms. The possibility of thus challenging norms is, for Habermas, the moment of justice, grounded in communicative competence, and thus in the conditions of possibility of society (and thus the lifeworld) per se (as opposed to the concrete values that are constitutive of particular social and individual identities). In principle, the vulnerable individual is protected from the potential threat of the collective through the right to say "no" to any norm, and thus to demand its rational redemption (MCCA: 200).

Habermas describes discourse ethics as a minimal ethics (alluding to Adorno's *Minima Moralia* (1974)). It cannot provide any substantive moral insight that does not have its origins in a concrete lifeworld (MCCA: 86, 121). Put simply, in moral crises norms become problematic and social actors cannot proceed with their everyday activities, or at least cannot proceed in unanimity. Discourse ethics is concerned only with how social agents restore sufficient consensus in order to allow them to proceed. If we recall Peirce's pragmatist image of the irritation of doubt (see § "Pragmatism", p. 67), Habermas is asking how the irritation of moral doubt *ought* to be overcome (just as Peirce himself evaluated different methods for resolving epistemological doubt). Yet, precisely because the discursive redemption of norms remains reliant upon participation in a concrete lifeworld, it may seem to fall back into the very problems of moral relativism that discourse ethics seeks so vigorously to avoid. It appears to be vulnerable to cultural values that may be constitutive of repressive social identities, precisely in so far as systematically distorted communication serves to blind the participants of those societies to their involvement in repression. To a certain extent this may be true. Discourse ethics is historically situated by Habermas as a product of post-conventional society, and if historically situated it may remain vulnerable to future developments (much in the way that Habermas acknowledged that the reconstruction of social evolution could be vulnerable to the future emergence of previously unrecognized universal human capacities (HE: 43; see § "Social evolution and history", p. 112)). Yet the notion of a minimal ethics attempts to avoid this problem, and again does so in a form that owes much to Adorno.

A substantive (and thus "maximal") ethics, at least within the Aristotelian tradition, articulates the constitutive role of cultural values in terms of the notion of a good life. This is to suggest that an individual's evaluative statements are grounded in an anticipatory image of what a good society would be like (and this in turn is dependent upon the cultural values of the society). The task of a maximal ethical theory would be to articulate this good life (and something of this approach can be seen in contemporary communitarian political theory (Mulhall & Swift 1992)). Again, the problem here is that such an approach has no defence against systematically distorted communication, and indeed its own inevitable historical short-sightedness, with Hegel's promotion of the early-nineteenth-century Prussian state as the approximation to absolute political organization being a case in point. Habermas responds to the dependence of discourse ethics upon cultural values, and thus indirectly upon notions of the good life, for the generation of moral problems by invoking the second Judeo-Christian commandment: the taboo on graven images (MCCA: 205). A discourse ethics appeals not to positive depictions of the good life, but rather to a sensitivity to the discrepancy, registered in human suffering, between actual existence and any possible image of the good life. It thus responds to what Adorno, in the subtitle of *Minima Moralia*, had referred to as the "damaged life" (1974). Discourse ethics thereby limits its dependency upon any particular social or historical moment by refusing to affirm any given set of cultural values. Just as pragmatist epistemology accepts statements to be true provisionally until there is a real need to question them, so discourse ethics tentatively accepts the validity of cultural values until historical circumstances demand their testing. One important consequence of this is that, even in *Legitimation Crisis*, the early articulation of the ideal speech situation was not to be understood as a model of a utopian social order (and the appeal to rules of discourse is important, not least, in avoiding this ambiguity) (ARC: 261ff.).

In conclusion, discourse ethics may be summarized in Paul Ricoeur's phrase as an "hermeneutics of suspicion" (1970: 32–5). That is to say that, as a formal and minimal ethics, its role is to expose false consensus, rather than to affirm or anticipate any true consensus. It is suspicious of any existing consensus. This point is important, not least insofar as certain critics (and most notably Jean-François Lyotard (1984: 60–67, 1985: 19–43)) have seen Habermas's emphasis upon consensus as stifling debate and mitigating against the pluralism of contemporary society.[6] A plurality of values in a society is, for Habermas, fruitful, precisely in so far as it stimulates practical discourse (and thus rational reflection on the sources of those values and the implications that holding them has for others). In contrast, what Weber described as a "polytheism of values" (1946c: 149), whereby a plurality of value orientations exist in society and are assumed to be incommensurable (precisely because instrumental reason allows of no means by which values may be examined and evaluated), is unacceptable. It relinquishes the resources of communicative reason, and abandons moral theory to decisionism (and see also "Richard Rorty's Pragmatic Turn" (OPC: 343–82), for Habermas's criticism of Rorty for precisely this failing).

Lifeworld and system

Introduction

The various problems that had concerned Habermas throughout the 1970s – the articulation of a universal pragmatics and the development of the account of late capitalism that was offered in *Legitimation Crisis* – are brought together in 1981 with the publication of *The Theory of Communicative Action*.[7] This is a massive (thousand-page) and complex essay, with its complexity lying not merely in the range of its subject matter, but also in its organization and style of argument. Habermas himself identifies three inter-related themes in *The Theory of Communicative Action*: the concept of communicative rationality; a conceptualization of society in terms of the two levels of "system" and "lifeworld"; and, finally, a theory of modernity (TCAI: xl). Yet these themes are not presented systematically, but in large part through an engagement with the history of sociological thought (from the "founders", Marx, Weber and Durkheim, through Mead's pragmatism, the critical theory of Horkheimer and Adorno, and Parsons's structural functionalism, to social constructionists, neo-Wittgensteinians, ethnomethologists and contemporary system theorists). These "historical reconstructions" are complemented by more systematic excursuses on the theory of communicative action. Such a style of presentation should not, perhaps, be that surprising. Habermas has always grounded himself in traditions of thought, and developed his own ideas out of that grounding (with *Knowledge and Human Interests* being exemplary in this respect). However, it can leave the exact lines of Habermas's argument obscure, and what turn out to be key concepts may, at least at first reading, become lost in the detail of historical exposition and criticism.

Of the three themes, much of the weight of the first has already been addressed in the exposition of universal pragmatics. It is, however, an over-simplification to simply see *The Theory of Communicative Action* as a con-solidation of all Habermas's previous writing. On the one hand, the account of communicative action renews his criticism of contemporary social and philosophical theory, enriching the arguments against positivism and instru-mental reason that had occupied him since the early 1960s. *The Theory of Communicative Action* begins to ground a more thoroughgoing criticism of what Habermas terms the "theory of consciousness". His point, and this will be developed more fully in Chapter 6 in reference to *The Philosophical Discourse of Modernity*, is that philosophical and sociological thought has been hampered by a failure to recognize the importance and nature of both lan-guage and intersubjectivity. Thus, at one level, the theory of communicative action is an account of the fundamentally linguistic and intersubjective nature of human existence. On the other hand, Habermas is concerned that

165

his own earlier exposition of universal pragmatics had been flawed precisely in so far as it drew him away from the substantive sociological issues that should have been the primary concern of the theory, in favour of philosophical issues. *The Theory of Communicative Action* therefore attempts to address this, not least by binding universal (or, as it is now termed, formal) pragmatics closely to social theory. In effect, this is to satisfy the assertion, made since the closing chapter of *Legitmation Crisis*, that universal pragmatics and a critical (and indeed evolutionary) sociology are necessarily complementary.

The second theme will be of most concern to us in this section. It emerges from Habermas's self-criticism of *Legitimation Crisis*. Although that book outlined in some detail a theory of society, not least through the tension established between theories of the lifeworld and system theories, Habermas held that the relationship between lifeworld and system was inadequately worked out. In part, this weakness lies in a failure to develop the concept of "lifeworld" much beyond its origins in Husserl's and Schutz's phenomenology. As such, it remains embedded in a philosophy of consciousness, which is to say that it remains concerned with the experience of the individual. At the core of *The Theory of Communicative Action*, therefore, lies a new exposition of the concept of "lifeworld" and, crucially, one that takes full account of its linguistic and intersubjective nature. In turn this paves the way for the third theme. The critical account of modernity is a return to the question upon which *Knowledge and Human Interest* concluded: the nature of a contemporary critical theory. This third theme will be largely left for Chapter 6.

Lifeworld

The social theory at the core of *The Theory of Communicative Action* revolves around the familiar question of the constitution and reproduction of society. This is the question that Habermas had attempted to resolve in the Gauss lectures through universal pragmatics. In effect, the social world was seen to be a product of human beings either striving for mutual understanding or strategically manipulating each other. While this analysis explicated the formal competences required of mature members of a society, it failed to explicate adequately those competences that would be relevant to particular cultures or social situations. In part, this is the tension that has already been noted in Habermas's account of discourse ethics, between the formalism of the principles of universalization and discourse ethics and the constitution of the moral agent within a particular and concrete culture. Here it may be understood as the problem of moving from the universal knowledge or know-how that human beings have, such as the ability to form grammatical sentences, to recognize and challenge validity claims, and to distinguish between the subjective, social and objective worlds (OPC: 238) – which constitutes linguistic and communicative competence – to the knowledge that agents require in order to act within particular and meaningful social situations. As the repository of such knowledge, the lifeworld is the necessary complement to communicative competence, being the resource upon which it feeds (TCAI: 70–71; TCAII: 130).

Habermas illustrates this move with the example of a building site (TCAII: 121ff.). A new and youthful recruit is asked by one of the older workers to get beer for the morning break. As an example of the raising of validity claims, this utterance can be readily analysed. The youth might question the meaning of the language used, the right of the older worker to issue such instructions, the utterance's factual presuppositions (such as a supply of beer being available nearby), or the sincerity of the older worker. Yet this analysis can be taken further. The youth's refusal raises not simply questions about the validity of the utterance, but more profoundly the way in which the whole situation within which it is made is understood by the youth and his elder. In effect, the youth's challenge throws into question a naive presumption on the older worker's part that they understand the physical and cultural surroundings in a similar way. If the youth says that the break cannot be due yet, then he presupposes a rhythm of work quite different to that presupposed by his elder; if he challenges the right of the older worker to issue orders, he fails to recognize the informal hierarchy that exists on this particular building site. Such knowledge is not included in the general communicative competence.

Repairing such breakdowns in social interaction and mutual understanding entails that the participants draw, not merely on their general communicative competence, but also upon the particular cultural presuppositions and competences that constitute their lifeworlds. The older worker presupposes an informal hierarchy and a work rhythm that are quite foreign to the new recruit. They are elements of the taken-for-granted knowledge that he draws upon to make sense of, and crucially to act in, the social world around him. In line with the pragmatist thinking that Habermas has drawn from Peirce it may be noted that the beliefs and competences of the lifeworld typically remain implicit and beyond doubt until a crisis forces the agents to confront them (OPC: 243). Indeed, Habermas characterizes the lifeworld as a "naïve familiarity with an unproblematically given background" (TCAII: 130). Any utterance potentially tests the lifeworld. An utterance is made at the risk that the taken-for-granted assumption of shared definitions will be proved false, and thus the social link between speaker and hearer will become temporarily or permanently unstable.

A disagreement makes problematic certain beliefs. The disagreement cannot make problematic the agent's lifeworld as a whole (TCAII: 132). Such radical Cartesian doubt would lead to the complete collapse of the agent's world, and his or her ability to act. The question of which particular beliefs will be rendered problematic will depend upon the actions that agents are engaged in at the moment of the utterance. In the above example, the actions concern a plan to get beer for a break. The dispute highlights what Habermas calls "topic-dependent contextual knowledge" (OPC: 241), such as the timing of breaks and the informal hierarchy. Repairing of the breakdown in intersubjectivity requires that the two actors bring their interpretations of the relevant parts of the lifeworlds into agreement. In part, this entails that they draw upon that upon which they do agree: both accept that there are mid-morning breaks, so the only question is whether they are at nine o'clock or ten o'clock, and so on. The youth is thus taught the traditions of this particular building site, or perhaps the older worker modifies his presuppositions about the site's hierarchy, and agrees that it is unfair to ask someone who does not yet know the area to get the beer on his first day.

In any dispute much will still be agreed upon, and much will not even be drawn into discussion (for example, that this is a building site, and there are regular breaks; that they are building a new housing estate; that certain short-cuts are being taken with respect to building regulations). As actions change, so different elements of the lifeworld may become relevant. The young worker falls from scaffolding, and the fact that he is a foreign worker employed illegally suddenly becomes relevant. The taken-for-granted practice of ignoring certain safety regulations and employment laws becomes a real moral and legal problem; the worker's ignorance of local law and custom ceases to be a matter for mild teasing, and becomes perhaps a problem of the continued existence of the building site, the company and thus the employment of all the workers. What is at issue here is the way in which the immediate activity or "situation" is defined by those participating in it. Habermas defines a "situation" as "a segment of lifeworld contexts of relevance" (TCAII: 122). That is to say that a situation is understood in terms of the nature and purposes (or "theme") of the activities in which everyone is involved. This theme determines what beliefs and competences from all those constitutive of the lifeworld are relevant *now*, hence the term a "segment" of the lifeworld. This segment is of immediate relevance to making sense of one's current practices (and of thus being able, in the Wittgensteinian sense, to go on). Disagreements over who gets the beer invoke a quite restricted segment, and raise no questions about the legal regulations recognized on the building site. An accident does, and thus the framework within which one's activities and interactions are understood shifts. As Habermas notes, a lifeworld is at once determinate (in that it shapes one's understanding and interpretation of the situation) and yet porous, for it shifts and is redefined with each new experience (TCAII: 130). In effect, this is to think of the segment of the lifeworld as a "horizon" (in Gadamer's sense of the term; see § "Hermeneutics (Gadamer)", p. 81).

Crucially, the beliefs and competences constitutive of the lifeworld are articulated, challenged and defended through language. In contrast to Husserl's conception of "lifeworld", which largely concerned the structuring of an individual's perceptual experience of the world, Habermas's "lifeworld" is a linguistically mediated resource. It does not shape experience per se, but rather the meaning of the situation one is in. A crisis, such as a refusal to obey an instruction to get the beer, or the collapse of scaffolding, is initially meaningless, at the very least in the sense of there being no shared understanding of the event. The experience as crisis, much in the sense of Peirce's "reality", intrudes into one's taken-for-granted but meaningful world. Agents must strive mutually to draw the experience back into the meaningful world, albeit at the cost of some redefinition of that world. The world suddenly contains young workers who defy their seniors, or working conditions that place one's life in danger. In summary, Habermas's point is that a breakdown in communication or the disruptive effect of experience is a breakdown in the shared definition and interpretation of the situation. As such, it can only be repaired through the substantive resources that are inherent in the agents' lifeworlds (as well as in their general communicative competence). It is thus that Habermas begins to give a new substance to the concept of "mutual understanding", in comparison to the formalism of the early expositions of universal pragmatics.

If the foregoing analysis has begun to develop the concept of the "lifeworld", it has done so only to a limited degree. In terms of the problem of the reproduction of society, it has shown only how participants reproduce and repair situations, which is to say, segments of the lifeworld, and not the lifeworld as a whole (TCAII: 137). For Habermas, the danger of leaving the analysis here is that the lifeworld as a whole will come to be understood as a macro-subject directing social agents, rather than being an interactive achievement of those agents. In effect, this would be a reversion back into the philosophy of consciousness (PDM: 342). This problem is avoided if it is accepted that what Habermas has analysed to this point is the lifeworld from the perspective of the participant in society. As such, the general competences analysed in formal pragmatics have been complemented by competences that are particular to given cultures. However, a more adequate account of the lifeworld must turn to the perspective of one who observes rather than directly participates in social action. Concretely, and still within a particular culture, social agents can step back from their participation and offer narratives of the actions of others (or even of their own past actions). In doing this, be they ordinary storytellers or professional historians, they intuitively draw upon a broader conception of the lifeworld as constituted in historical time and social space. Put more precisely, Habermas suggests that the narrator is drawing upon rich cultural traditions, upon the sense of belonging to certain social groups, as well as an awareness of themselves as narrator and of the personhood and agency of those involved in the events they narrate (TCAII: 137). The next step in an explanation of the reproduction of the lifeworld (and indeed society) as a whole is to formalize this intuitive knowledge. In effect, just as the first move of linking formal pragmatics to the lifeworld was one of increased particularity, this second move restores generality, now by identifying the general structural components in lifeworlds. As Habermas presents this, it is a shift from a formal–pragmatic category of lifeworld to a sociological one (ARC: 247).

Three structural components of the lifeworld are identified: culture, society and personality (TCAII: 138). These terms are defined initially as follows: culture is the "store of knowledge from which those engaged in communicative action draw interpretations susceptible of consensus as they come to an understanding about something in the world"; society is "the legitimate order from which those engaged in communicative action gather solidarity, based on belonging to groups, as they enter into interpersonal relationships with one another"; and personality is composed of the "acquired competences that render a subject capable of speech and action and hence able to participate in processes of mutual understanding in a given context and to maintain his own identity in the shifting contexts of interaction" (PDM: 343). What lies behind these definitions, and what begins to give them some substance and sense, is a move of extraordinary theoretical neatness on Habermas's part. He effectively takes three technical terms already current in sociology (from the work of Parsons), and maps them onto the three domains that are necessarily associated with any understandable utterance. Thus, culture is linked to the objective world (and may therefore be grasped as the general resources that agents require in order to challenge and redeem validity claims to truth); society is linked to the intersubjective world (and is composed of the resources necessary to redeem normative claims); and personality is linked to the subjective world (and claims to truthfulness). This move is intuitively sensible. Habermas has established that we live in a linguistically mediated world. Human beings must acquire the competence to distinguish the three worlds. The structural components of the lifeworld are therefore the resources necessary to make and sustain that distinction (TCAII: 137). What is perhaps less intuitively acceptable is the manner in which Habermas must, then, spell out what is entailed by each term.

If culture is entwined with claims about truth, then it is not to be understood in the sense of an artistic culture. This should be unsurprising, given that the focus to this point has been upon the phenomenological or cultural anthropological approaches to culture (although Habermas acknowledges that his initial analyses pay too little attention to the "world-disclosing" role of art, and thus to the complex position that art occupies in articulating and developing our inner experiences of objects, and in thus modifying our perception, attitudes and behaviour (OPC: 245–6)). What is superficially more surprising is the link between culture and science. In part, Habermas's inspiration here comes from the later Husserl, and his original analysis of the lifeworld as the presuppositions that underpinned scientific practice (and thus Husserl's arguments against the positivistic assumption that natural sciences immediately reproduce the objective world as it is) (OPC: 239-40). In line with his own arguments against positivism, Habermas is arguing that science and scientific knowledge are necessarily cultural achievements. While his Peircean pragmatism prevents him from construing scientific knowledge as a pure cultural construction, for knowledge is necessarily checked by a resisting reality, understood within the framework of the theory of communicative action, he is still arguing that scientific knowledge (and indeed other factual knowledge) is generated by agents interacting within a shared cultural tradition. Culture is the resource that allows agents to come to a mutual understanding or shared interpretation of the objective world, and it may be accepted that different societies will provide radically different resources for interpretation (and here one need only contrast the early modern thought of Galileo with the neo-Aristotelian culture that preceded it). Interpretations are judged in terms of their rationality, which here entails that they are sufficiently coherent with the stocks of knowledge, belief and competence that agents hold, in order for those agents to continue in their mundane social practices (TCAII: 137). Put slightly differently, culture is a rational resource in so far as it allows the agent to establish a continuity between a particular situation and their lifeworld as a whole (PDM: 344). If these are interpretative resources, Habermas concludes, culture is then to do with meaning. It allows the building-site workers to make sense of the accident, in terms, say, of its cause and consequences. In effect, culture is the source of a meaningful world, and a failure to reproduce the lifeworld results in meaning becoming a scare resource (TCAII: 140).

As the resources that facilitate the coordination of action, society may be understood in terms of the norms that govern the appropriateness of relationships between individuals, most particularly in terms of the individuals' awareness of their membership of a common society. If the success of culture is determined by its rationality, then the success of society is measured in terms of solidarity. The failure to reproduce the lifeworld leads to anomie (a loss of normative motivation) (ARC: 280). Again, if successful, society serves to bring a new situation into coherence with the existing understanding of one's social identity, allowing one to go on in mundane practice. Society therefore serves to define the meaningful and normative social space within which practice continues. In effect, it allows the building-site workers to answer the question of how people *like us* respond in this situation (and thus how norms such as compassion for a fellow worker, ties to a trade union or legal responsibility are applied and negotiated).

In contrast, personality concerns historical time. The individual must be socialized into a set of competences that allow them to speak and act responsibly. Habermas's model for such processes of socialization is borrowed from Mead (and thus points to the process by which a member of society gradually attains individuality through internalizing the anticipated views and judgements of others, initially of particular members of the family, and subsequently through the developing ability to perform the social roles of generalized members of society (PMT: 149–204)). The success of such processes is measured in terms of the harmony that is established between the identity of the individual and that of the wider society (and their failure is marked by mental illness or psychopathology). In effect, as with culture and society, continuity is established between the particular and the general. In this case, the continuity runs between one's experience as an individual and as a member of society (and thus as an inheritor of an historical tradition) (TCAII: 140–41). As Habermas notes, the individual can then only be understood to be a *member* of society metaphorically (PDM: 343). On the one hand society does not exist independently of the individual, at least in the sense that Bayern Munich football club existed before Franz Beckenbauer joined it. On the other hand, society neither generates individuality (so that the individual is a simple product of a social process), nor is society an aggregate of individuals (as some forms of liberal social contract theory suggest). Rather, the processes of symbolic reproduction that are Habermas's concern are circular, moving between the resources embedded in the lifeworld and the competences of social agents. The building-site workers' social response is therefore not determinate. They do not simply fill a pre-existing role. An individual may still question both the scientific explanation of the accident and the moral and legal responses of his workmates.

Reproduction may therefore be understood in terms of the interrelationship between the three structural components. Whereas the socialization of the individual may serve to establish the individual's personal identity, in so far as it also entails the internalization of values it motivates the individual's action in relation to the normative structures of society. In addition, the fully socialized individual has acquired the interpretative skills necessary to constitute and discuss an objective world. Similarly, whereas a successful society entails the legitimate ordering of interpersonal relations and thus a coordinated lifeworld, it also provides the individual with a sense of membership of an identifiable and integrated group, and makes culture possible by being the source of the articulation of the normative obligations that are inherent in discourse and the achievement of mutual understanding. Finally, culture at once secures and transmits rational knowledge, and provides a source of legitimation for social institutions and the knowledge that will be relevant to the rearing and education of children (TCAII: 141–4).

Rationalization of the lifeworld

This account is still incomplete; it neglects the social evolutionary dimension that was fundamental to *Legitimation Crisis*. That is to say, the lifeworld is treated as a given, rather than something that will itself develop historically. A related problem lies in its excessively conservative aspect. By stressing the continuity that is established between the general and the particular, it seemingly gives little scope for social change or innovation. Put otherwise, it fails to account for the inherent potential of lifeworlds to become increasingly rational. Habermas finds tentative solutions to these problems throughout classical social theory, and not least in the work of Weber (on disenchantment) and Durkheim (on the move from the "mechanical" solidarity of small-scale societies with a minimal division of labour, to the "organic" solidarity of complex industrial societies). A thought experiment, based upon Durkheim's notion of mechanical solidarity, is proposed: imagine a totally integrated society (TCAII: 87ff.). Such a society would be held together through religious ritual to such a degree that a fundamental uniformity is achieved in the cultural beliefs, social practices and personalities of all social agents. Crucially, such a society would repress potential conflict because all disputes would have been resolved in advance by the dominant religious beliefs. Habermas presents this as a society in which language has gone on holiday (TCAII: 87). The phrase alludes to Wittgenstein, and refers to those situations where we are in thrall to the ambiguities and vaguenesses of ordinary language, so that our ability to understand a situation is inhibited. Habermas develops this in terms of the inhibition or under-development of communicative competence. While language is on holiday, social agents are unable to raise and challenge validity claims. In our imagined society, precisely because there is no alternative to the dominant religious beliefs, and because all social agents perceive the world in the same way, there exist no resources for challenge or debate. Put otherwise, it is a "sociocentric" society. Social agents have not yet achieved what Piaget calls "decentring" (TCAI: 69). They are not yet able to distinguish between their own perspective on the world and the perspective of others (precisely because, at this imaginary point, no difference exists). Only once one can recognize the difference between one's own perspective and that of another may one need to enter discussion about which beliefs or perspectives are valid (and indeed, begin to generate criteria of validity). Again, once this distinction is recognized, agreement ceases to be guaranteed in advance by the substance of one's cultural tradition. Rather, agreement must be achieved, either through force or through linguistic communication.

Putting aside for one moment the problem of force (and strategic action), social evolution as the rationalization of the lifeworld may then be understood as the gradual emergence out of this imaginary condition of total solidarity. Initially this occurs through what Habermas calls a "linguistification of the sacred" (TCAII: 77ff.): that is, the development of a communicative competence on the part of social agents that allows them to subject existing beliefs to some form of rational scrutiny. Language is recalled from its holiday. The cost of such evolution is that the maintenance of social integration becomes all the more risky (PDM: 345). Attempts to bind together society and to overcome conflict may fail. Put otherwise, the problem is not just that of binding society together, but also of binding the particular experience of the present to that of the past. In more traditional and conservative societies, the substance of the tradition will have greater weight in predetermining the meaning of a novel experience, so that it has less potential to disrupt the lifeworld. Social evolution therefore entails the potential for increased abstraction (in the sense that responses to conflict and crisis are less and less confined by the particular cultural, social or personal beliefs that characterize a given lifeworld). Form and content are separated (TCAII: 146). Increasingly abstract and universal forms of justification are required for the validation of the contents of culture (for example, in the development of scientific method) and society (in the development of universal morality and law), while the socialization of the person is increasingly orientated to the development of abstract competences that will allow the individual to deal with an unpredictable diversity of problems (rather than to respond dogmatically to known ones). The distinction between culture and society is thus more clearly articulated as the content of the cultural worldview comes to be increasingly separated from the social institutions through which it is realized. Put otherwise, questions of truth (at the level of culture) are distinguished from questions of justice (at the level of society). The legitimacy of government is thus increasingly differentiated from issues of factual inquiry, and thus the mere fact that the government is in power. Society and personality are differentiated as greater scope is allowed for the diversity of interpersonal relationships into which agents may enter. The person cannot simply be identified with the finite number of social roles that they may occupy. (The building-site worker may thus have a personal conscience that obligates him to actions at odds with those of his role as a union member.) Finally, culture and personality are differentiated through the increasing need for culture to be renewed in the critical and innovative work of individuals (as opposed to the dogmatic imposition of culture on the individual) (TCAII: 148). In sum, continuity is established not by the dogmatic and conservative imposition of the past, but through a potentially disruptive critical attitude to the past. Rational critique replaces dogmatism.

If an imaginary world of total social integration is the beginning of this journey, then a wholly rationalized lifeworld is its "vanishing point" (TCAII: 146). In such a condition, cultural traditions are subject to continuous rational revision; the legitimacy of norms is determined by formally rational and democratic procedures; and ego-identities acquire increasingly abstract autonomy. All three dimensions rely on the continual refinement of communicative rationality, as received wisdom is increasingly subject to cooperative processes of discursive will formation, where all participants have an effective right to challenge any decisions made, and agreement is realized solely through the force of better argument.

System

Habermas is aware that this account of the lifeworld, and of the processes of social evolution that are extrapolated from it, is one-sided. It is idealistic, both in the sense of the utopian happy ending that it finds, in effect, in the institutionalization of the grounding of all social interaction in discourse, and in the fact that it ignores the processes of material reproduction upon which the cultural reproduction of the lifeworld must depend. He therefore turns, as he did in *Legitimation Crisis*, to systems theory.

The discussion of the lifeworld has focused on the problem of cultural reproduction. As such, it has tacitly assumed that the problem of the reproduction of society as a whole can be resolved through reference to the competences of social actors, and to the resources that they derive from the lifeworld. The integrity of the social world is understood in terms of the skills and processes through which competent actors bring about their mutual understanding of a situation. Such an approach to sociology reproduces what, in the early 1970s, Habermas had attacked as the "hermeneutic claim to universality" (see HCU). This is the assumption of hermeneutic-based sociologies that sociological inquiry is exhausted by reproducing the self-understanding that lay actors have of their culture (TCAII: 148). The debate with Gadamer, stemming from the role that psychoanalysis played as a model of critical inquiry in *Knowledge and Human Interests*, served to establish Habermas's position against a pure hermeneutics (see § "Hermeneutics (Gadamer)", p. 81). Crucially, precisely because such an approach presupposed, not merely that the lifeworld provided the competent agent with the resources necessary to proceed autonomously in society, but more problematically that those resources were sufficient to make sense of society, it could not acknowledge the possibility of systematically distorted communication (be this as a result of individual neurosis or social reification) (TCAII: 149–50).

The problem may be illustrated by noting a second interpretation that Habermas offers of Durkheimian mechanical solidarity. Whereas the first interpretation, noted above, stresses the undifferentiated nature of the early lifeworld, and so opens up the possibility of a history of rational progress (as humanity grows out of a naive innocence), the second interpretation stresses the hermeneutic transparency of the early lifeworld. The lack of differentiation of the lifeworld, along with the resultant homogeneity of the members of that society, entails that all social interactions that are possible are in principle comprehensible to all adult members of the society. The simplicity of the possibilities that exist for social interaction entails that the culture of the society, into which all members are socialized equally, is sufficient to give those interactions appropriate shared meanings (TCAII: 156–7). From this interpretation of archaic society, Habermas can project a quite different vanishing point to that of a rationalized lifeworld. As society grows more complex, so it becomes less transparent. This culminates in the vision of a society held together, not through mutual understanding, but through forms of coordination that defy meaningful interpretation, precisely in so far as they fall outside the scope of the lifeworld, and thus cannot be challenged through raising and defending validity claims. Ironically, such a society returns to the naive inhibition of validity claims found in mechanical solidarity. It is a pure system, reminiscent of Adorno's vision of total administration, or a society where the lifeworld has atrophied (as Luhmann's systems theory suggests is the truth of contemporary existence) (PDM: 353).

The task that Habermas sets himself is to explain this more negative side of the process of social evolution in terms of a growth in system complexity that is necessarily complementary to the rational differentiation of the lifeworld. Such an explanation must turn to the resources provided by systems theory, albeit that the extremes of Luhmann's approach are to be checked by recognizing the continuing (and indispensable) resource of the lifeworld. The framework is, of course, familiar from *Legitimation Crisis*, and in particular the relationship of social integration and system integration. Already social integration has been rethought in terms of the structural differentiation of the lifeworld (so that, given the differentiation of culture, society and personality, social integration refers specifically to the part that society in a "narrow" sense plays, through moral and legal institutions, in coordinating the actions of socialized agents). Yet the conception of social integration still entails that it is approached and indeed constituted through a methodology that focuses upon the hermeneutic and communicative achievement of the lifeworld. In a lifeworld, action is coordinated by competent agents either striving to reach mutual understanding or through strategic action.

The understanding of system integration undergoes a subtle change from *Legitimation Crisis*. A system is still analysed in terms of its ability to maintain a boundary between itself and a more complex environment (TCAII: 151), and the problem of system integration is constituted through the methodology of systems theory. Habermas's point is here that social phenomena can be analysed through either a methodology orientated to the lifeworld or through one orientated to systems. Thus, for example, culture can be understood as a structural component of the lifeworld, or as a subsystem within an environment that includes society and personality as subsystems alongside nature and the physical body of the agent (so that the relationships between culture, society and personality can be analysed in terms of the inputs they each require and the outputs they generate). The difference is not an ontological one, or at least not at this stage in the argument. It is an analytic distinction (R: 252), and each methodology offers an approximate account of society, differing in what Habermas calls their "depth of field" (R: 253).

More precisely, this difference can be seen in two respects. First, a lifeworld approach works within the participants' understanding of their society. Successful sociological explanations will make sense to those to whom they apply, even if they make explicit what was otherwise tacit knowledge. Thus, for example, even the account of the differentiation of the lifeworld into culture, society and personality, while not obvious to lay members of society, will make sense to them in terms of their tacitly accepted orientations to a cosmological realm of facts and myths, a realm of morality and law, and a subjective realm of personal experience. It is bound up with their communicative competence. In contrast, systems theory takes an observer's perspective on society, and as such generates what Habermas calls "counter-intuitive" explanations (R: 252). This is to suggest that not just the terminology of the social scientist, but also the way in which they see the social world being organized and sustained, will have little obvious purchase in terms of the cultural and linguistic resources of the lay member. Not least, it will seem to play down human agency, and leave the agent as a mere dupe to overarching social mechanisms.

The second sense in which this difference can be understood is in terms of what each must leave unexplained, and thus abandon as contingent raw material. A lifeworld approach, precisely in so far as it privileges human agency and the comprehensibility of the social world, must accept that the unintended consequences of human action must go unexplained. In being unintended, they become contingent and meaningless. It is here that systems theory has its purchase. Whereas social integration can be understood through the ability of competent agents to coordinate their actions in terms of mutual understanding, system integration realizes a coordination through the consequences of those actions (TCAII: 202). At the level of the system, the agent is orientated, sometimes unwittingly, not to what another agent's actions mean, but rather to the instrumental consequences of those actions.

Consider the example of a simple market. The buyer and seller do not orientate to each other in terms of meaning. The substantial use to which the buyer might put the desired commodity is irrelevant. The seller typically need take, for example, no moral responsibility for the uses to which the buyer might put their purchase, whether it be the music they might play on a CD player, or what they might kill with a pesticide. Buyers' and sellers' actions are orientated wholly in terms of the price (or exchange value) of the commodity. Price serves to coordinate the actions of buyers and sellers in terms of their consequences. If more buyers come on to the market, this has the (unintended) consequence of bidding up the price, and thereby attracting more sellers. If more sellers come on to the market, this has the (unintended) consequence of bidding down the price, but attracting more buyers. Money thereby becomes an example of what Habermas calls a steering media. Crucially, money coordinates action, without having any qualitative meaning. It bears a minimal quantitative value, which can coordinate action in simple, schematic forms (but not with the infinite subtlety of language).

If the lifeworld approach cannot deal with the unintended consequences of action, in contrast systems theory cannot incorporate the understandings that lay actors have of society. As such, the limitations that are placed upon system integration by the very inability of agents to understand economic and administrative processes – and thus the impact that experiences of alienation, anomie and disenchantment have upon social reproduction – cannot be explained (R: 253; TCAII: 151). Thus, while each approach may have its weaknesses – or at least areas of shallowness – at least Habermas strives to make them complementary rather than inimical.

The complementary nature of the two methodologies may be illustrated by the way in which Habermas takes up the problem of social evolution. *The Theory of Communicative Action* tends to presuppose much of his work on the reconstruction of historical materialism, and in particular the under-standing of evolution as a process by which societies respond to crises through the institutionalization of learning potentials (TCAII: 153–4). Similarly, it is taken as read that such change will occur only in response to challenges posed by the internal and external environment (and indeed, that the direction of change is reversible (TCAII: 162–3)). The emphasis therefore falls on the resultant stages of social evolution, which are now presented as: egalitarian tribal societies (corresponding to the tribal or archaic societies of the earlier account of social evolution (see § "From archaic society to capitalism", p. 122)); hierarchical tribal societies (corresponding to early civilizations); politically stratified class societies (corresponding to developed civilizations); and economically constituted class societies (capitalism) (TCAII: 167). These four stages are explained in terms of a simple but bold account of the mechanisms available for system differentiation. Returning to tribal society, Habermas suggests that there are only two dimensions along which the complexity of a social system might increase: horizontal stratification, in terms of age, gender and kinship; and vertical stratification in terms of political hierarchies (TCAII: 159, 161–2). Horizontal stratification works through exchange relations being established between the strata, and vertical stratification works through power relations. Habermas's bold stroke is to suggest that egalitarian tribal society and capitalism are systematically integrated through horizontal exchange relations, while hierarchical tribal society and politically stratified class society are integrated through vertical power, and from these two forms of system integration he extrapolates two steering media: power and money.

Because early tribal society is organized around family groups, vertical stratification in terms of kinship lineages offers an immediately available resource for increased complexity. Largely homogeneous small family groups can become more complex and differentiated either through a growth in internal complexity or through combining with other similar groups. Internal complexity can be developed through a division of labour, typically organized in terms of gender and age (TCAII: 159). This serves to establish elementary exchange relationships between members within the group. Combining with other groups is more problematic, as Durkheim recognized in his original formulation of the idea of mechanical solidarity (Durkheim 1984). Family-based tribal groups will be largely self-sufficient, and each group will be producing similar products. There is, then, little or no incentive for economic trade between them. Durkheim looked at the problem in terms of the question of what prevented a society already composed of family groups from fragmenting into its separate component parts, and resolved it in terms of an overarching collective conscience that imposed a taken-for-granted unity within the society. This is, in effect, to point to the homogeneity of the lifeworld. Habermas, approaching the problem from the opposite direction, and thus in terms of the development of a coordinated differentiation, draws on the early work of Lévi-Strauss (1969) on kinship structures and the incest taboo. The moral taboo on incest forces each group to look outside itself for marriage partners. Crucially, it is not, then, the economic exchange that results from a division of labour that matters, but rather a morally and ritually imbued exchange of women between lineages. This exchange is further compounded with ritual (again, rather than economic) exchanges of goods (in what Marcel Mauss (1966) initially analysed as the gift relationship). In all such cases, the exchange establishes a morally binding relationship of mutual obligations between the two sides (TCAII: 161).

From the perspective of systems theory, ritual exchanges may be understood as the mechanisms by which the internal coherence of the society is maintained. However, as Habermas notes, at this stage in social evolution, system integration and social integration are interwoven (TCAII: 163). What this means is that there is, as yet, very little difference between a lifeworld account and a systems account. Although lay members of the society will interpret exchanges in terms of the obligations placed upon them through ritual and morality, their function in binding society together remains relatively transparent to them. Yet, perhaps more importantly, tribal society also makes explicit the entwining of system and lifeworld that must occur at the level of social integration throughout evolution. System integration hooks on to the lifeworld, and thus on to the mundane experience and competences of social agents, through being institutionalized within society (with society being understood here in its "narrow" sense, as a structural component of the lifeworld). A pre-conventional morality grounded in ritual practices inhibits any violation of the incest taboo and the gift relationship and so makes exchange obligatory (TCAII: 174). In effect, this is to renew the role that the concept of "institutional core" played in *Legitimation Crisis*. Kinship relations form the institutional core or base (TCAII: 173) of egalitarian tribal societies.

The analysis of hierarchical tribal societies requires that Habermas turns from vertical stratification (and exchange relations) to the potential for horizontal stratification (and power relations). The transition is to a more complex form of society, and thus to a society that is able to exploit the learning potential inherent in the gradual rationalization of the lifeworld in increased material productivity. As Habermas expresses this, the practical "know-how" of earlier societies is opened up to some degree of rational reflection and revision (TCAII: 194). Power becomes central as the means of organizing increasingly disparate individuals together, in order to achieve collective goals. Although the institutional base remains tied to kinship structures and pre-conventional morality, different families now have different degrees of status and power. Older lineages will have greater prestige, giving them the power to coordinate the actions of others (TCAII: 162). From a lifeworld perspective, social integration becomes more problematic as the homogeneity of the lifeworld becomes more fragile. Habermas suggests that at this stage the potential for conflict is controlled through a split between the sacred and profane. The sacred provides ritual and mythical accounts that legitimate the power structures in society. Mythical narratives account for the position of dominant families. These accounts cannot yet be subject to critical reflection and challenge because mythical thought remains so intimately tied up with ritual practices. Myth and ritual provide the participant with no critical resources through which they could challenge either the efficacy of the practice or the truth of the myth. The mythical story thus carries an unchallengable normative weight. The collective goals proposed by the dominant families, by being bound into the mythology, are therefore accepted as being legitimate. In contrast, in the secular world a distinction between communicative action and purposive action is possible, so that the participant has the capacity, in this tightly defined secular sphere alone, to question the instrumentally effective ways of achieving a given goal (TCAII: 193–4).

From a systems perspective, the very prestige of the dominant families provides the medium that facilitates the organization of society in order to exploit the physical environment (through economic production), to defend itself against a hostile social environment (in warfare), and to resolve conflicts within the system. Crucially, Habermas suggests, prestige rests not upon the rational redemption of the family's right to wield power, but rather upon subjects' empirical orientation to the effects that obeying or defying that prestige will have. The mere fact that the family can mobilize punishments or rewards is sufficient to motivate the subject's actions. The subject thus acts instrumentally with respect to the predictable consequences of the family's actions (TCAII: 181). However, precisely because this form of integration is again institutionalized in terms of kinship structures (albeit now reinterpreted in terms of ranks or status groups), system integration remains relatively transparent, and bound up with the lay members' understanding of social integration (although the observer's functional interpretation of mythology in terms of the need to stabilize a political hierarchy may well be incomprehensible to the participant). It is only with the next stage in social evolution, the transition to states, that the significance of systems integration for increasing the society's scope for complex organization becomes clear.

Hierarchical tribal societies attach power or prestige to an existing social structure (of kinship relationships). In contrast, in politically stratified societies the social structure is defined in terms of the possession of power. Power now rests in formally defined offices (which is to say that the powers of the office exist independently of any particular office holder) (TCAII: 177). From a lifeworld perspective, political offices are the primary principle of social integration, and the participant's self-understanding is that of a citizen (as opposed to a family member), who has an obligation to obey the law. The law itself is conventional, which is to say that criminal acts are no longer seen as violations either against another individual or against society as a whole (as they were in pre-conventional tribal society), but as intentional violations against communally accepted norms. What is significant here is the fact that obedience to the law and recognition of the power of office-holders facilitates the organization of much more complex social structures. The complexity is grounded in the developing rationalization of the lifeworld, not least in that the step up to conventional thought about law and morality entails what Habermas describes as an expanded "scope for generalised value orientations" (TCAII: 179). This is to say that, increasingly, participants orientate themselves, not to the particular qualities or values of a situation, but to general features that will recur, largely unchanged, in all relevant situations. Thus, an office is an office regardless of the post-holder and, in confrontation with a post-holder, that is the only relevant feature of the situation that need be recognized; so, too, the law is to be obeyed regardless of the particular features of the situation one is in. Crucially, this entails that interaction can proceed without the participants having to come to a full mutual understanding of the situation in which they find themselves.

The point of this lies in the contrast between tribal and more complex societies, and the different nature of social interaction in each. In a tribal society, the scope for novel interaction is limited. The typical participant is going to encounter the same people every day. As society gets larger and more complex, then the scope for citizens coming into contact with each other in a greater variety of novel situations widens. The potential of the lifeworld, as a resource for maintaining interaction through mutual understanding, is thereby overburdened (PDM: 350). In complex societies it would both cost too much in effort and generate too much risk of conflict and the breakdown of interaction were all participants to come to a mutual understanding of the situation in which they meet. Without the familiarity of situations, or the homogeneity of participants, the struggle to overcome competing perspectives and opinions would be wearing and possibly futile. The burden of reaching understanding is therefore short-circuited, by exploiting the distinction between action orientated to understanding and action orientated to success (or purposive-rational action) that has been achieved in the secular lifeworld of hierarchical tribal societies. What Habermas calls "relief mechanisms" are developed, which serve to organize individuals together through purposive, rather than communicative, action (TCAII: 181).

Power is one such relief mechanism. In complex societies it generalizes the potential of prestige in tribal society. From the systems perspective, power becomes a steering medium that makes possible system integration. Power is presented as a code that transmits information from receiver to recipient. However, unlike ordinary language, as a steering medium it does not tolerate rational challenges. It is an *"impoverished* and *standardised* language"* (PDM: 350, original emphasis), which simplifies the definition of the situation and polarizes the recipient's choices of action. It is backed by the appeal to force (through the imposition of either negative sanctions or rewards). As a means to the end of effectively realizing collective goals, power therefore lays before the recipient the simple choice of complying or disobeying. The recipient's decision is not then based upon the reasonableness of the command, but upon the predictable consequences of their actions (TCAII: 268). Although Habermas describes this as a form of strategic action, it is perhaps worth clarifying the exact meaning of the term here. Strategic action does occur in lifeworlds (and Habermas is at pains to avoid a simple dichotomy between the lifeworld and action orientated to understanding, and systems and action orientated to success). However, within the lifeworld, strategic action appears to take a subtly different form. We have already had the example of the exchange of women in tribal societies. Here the women are reduced to mere objects, and their autonomy is denied. This is one form of strategic action, and it occurs within the lifeworld. With power as a steering medium (and, as we shall see, so too with money), the subject's autonomous agency is not wholly undermined, but rather channelled in the direction of a purposive response to the situation. Ironically, the powerful exercise their power by forcing the powerless to treat power-holders as if they were natural objects (so that they will be as wholly predictable in the way in which they will respond to an action – and not least a violation of the law or infringement of one's place in the hierarchy – as might be a storm on a poorly constructed house).

System integration in politically stratified societies consists in the organization of society through the establishment of offices and the power relationships between them. Crucially, system integration is now becoming "uncoupled" from the lifeworld, precisely in that social organization can seemingly be explained without reference to the lifeworld competences of participants. This is what Habermas, following Luhmann, terms a "technicising of the lifeworld" (TCAII: 183, 281), such that the existence of steering media makes possible a growth in the complexity of society through the differentiation of further subsystems (and thus the allocation of specific functions to specialist subsystems). Within the subsystem, the participant is motivated not by a rational understanding of their task, but by the pursuit of empirical rewards.

Yet the lifeworld cannot be abandoned completely. It is Habermas's contention (very much against Luhmann) that the purely purposive-rational motivations of steering media are insufficient. Offices are defined in law, and it was noted above that in politically stratified societies law is conventionally understood as norms accepted by the community. This raises the problem of identifying from where that acceptability might come. (Crucially, Habermas is refusing to rest with the mere fact of the system, and insists upon the ineradicability of the question of its legitimacy, for both the participant and the social scientist.) The inquiry is thereby thrown back to the lifeworld, as the potential source, not merely of the legitimacy of law, but also of power itself. The problem of the legitimacy of law in politically stratified society is that it has to be maintained against extreme inequality and repression (TCAII: 188–9, 270). Habermas's suggested solution appeals again to the distinction between the sacred and the profane.

The profane realm has grown in rationality with the transition to political society. The three validity claims of truth, right and truthfulness are now clearly differentiated, not least in so far as the role of the citizen presupposes that the agent is competent in distinguishing between the natural order, the legal order of the polity and their private experience. This entails, most crucially, that their identity and position in society is not exhausted by the particularity of their position in a family lineage. Rather, the organizational capacity of the society is increased through the ability to move individuals into purposive activities that are understood independently of the particularities of the kinship structure (TCAII: 194–5). Hence, for example, tasks such as potter, labourer, scribe or whatever are not tied to particular families (and for this reason, perhaps, Habermas stresses that he is discussing class-based societies, presumably as opposed to castes). Thus, as has been noted, there is a greater competence in thinking and acting in terms of generalities. In contrast to the profane, the sacred has not achieved the same level of rationalization. It has developed from the stage of mythology to that of religion. This entails that a distinction is now recognized between questions of meaning (articulated at the level of theology) and issues of practice (expressed no longer in ritual, but now in prayer, where a relationship is established between the believer and an external deity). The three validity claims, nonetheless, remain undifferentiated. Although there may be a theology that explicates the meaning of sacred texts and doctrines, utterances within that theology tend still to be simultaneously expressions of personal belief, normative assertions and statements about the objective world (TCAII: 189). In illustration one might consider the writings of a prophet such as Ezekiel. The report of a personal vision is at once conflated with a statement about the external world (so leaving ambiguous the question of the vision's reality), and is taken as an endorsement of the prophet's right to speak in God's name. Paradoxically, precisely because of this comparative irrationality, the sacred can continue to perform an ideological role, and assume dominance over the profane. The impaired rationality of religious thought serves to inhibit the possibility of raising rational criticisms against the legal norms, the legitimacy of which it grounds.

Such ideological strategies are vulnerable to the growing rationalization of the lifeworld. In modern society, the sacred realm begins to lose its hold over society (TCAII: 196). Positive law becomes a profane phenomenon, and as such subject to the demands of the post-conventional morality that is characteristic of modern society. That is to say that in politically stratified societies, questions of the legitimacy of the law could be confined to the rationality of the procedures applied in the interpretation and enactment of the law. The substance of the law is left unconsidered. In modern society, increasingly, it is the substance of the law, which was previously grounded by a sacred tradition, that comes under rational scrutiny (TCAII: 178). Crucially, it is no longer enough to appeal to the traditional grounding of accepted norms. The procedures that lead to the development and acceptance of law are now as important as the rationality of the process of interpreting and applying law. In *Legitimation Crisis* it was this recognition of a crisis in legitimacy, yielding to the potential of discursive criticism, that grounded the optimistic tone of its conclusion; similarly, it is the optimism of the first interpretation of Durkheim's account of mechanical solidarity – which culminated in a vision of a wholly rationalized lifeworld – rehearsed at the end of the previous section. *The Theory of Communicative Action* takes up the more pessimistic second interpretation, to suggest that system integration has further resources by which the enlightened transparency of the lifeworld may be thwarted. The system does not merely uncouple itself from the lifeworld, but in capitalism returns to colonize the lifeworld.

Colonization of the lifeworld

The uncoupling of system and lifeworld entails that what was initially a distinction constituted in the methodologies of the social sciences now, in modern capitalist societies, becomes a real distinction (R: 255). The state in a politically stratified civilization has been seen to be still grounded in the social institutions of the lifeworld, not least through its need for legitimation. The law can thus be characterized as a "shell" within which social interaction takes place (TCAII: 178). That is to say that while the state may organize the framework of society, interactions need not themselves be directly constituted through legally sanctioned power relations (and in practice, they more readily rely on traditional mores). In contrast, in capitalism, as money becomes the principle steering medium, the system intrudes into all areas of social life, threatening the very coherence and viability of the lifeworld itself.

We have already encountered money as an example of a steering medium, in the example of a simple market. There money allowed two strangers to relate to each other, in terms of a schematically defined situation, through instrumental orientations to the consequences of each other's actions. Money is indeed the purest example of a steering medium. Like power it can be conceptualized as a code for transmitting highly simplified and schematic messages, and it thereby facilitates the free actions of its holder and recipient, albeit along instrumental lines. It surpasses power, however, on a number of levels (TCAII: 265–6): it is more precisely quantifiable; it can be accumulated and stored; and it can be circulated about a system more readily. Most importantly, while money needs to be backed, it does not require legitimation. This is to say that, while the users of money may require some factual evidence as to its worth and stability (such as a gold standard or a reliable central bank), the user needs no normative justification for using money. Because "money is as money does", providing it works as money (be it dollar bills, gold bars or cigarettes) it is money, and no one need ask in addition whether or not it ought to be money. Finally, the circulatory nature of money entails that its use does not overtly put the recipient of its "message" at a disadvantage, unlike power.

Simple markets of the kind encountered above obviously existed in political and even tribal societies. It is thus not the existence of the market as such that leads to the colonization of the lifeworld, but rather the extension of the principles of market exchange to all aspects of social life. In effect, in capitalism, it is precisely the principle of exchange that becomes the core social institution. In early modern societies, the market is institutionalized through bourgeois law, specifically in the forms of property law and contractual law. At one level, bourgeois law thereby serves as a framework (or meta-institution) within which conflicts between self-interested competitors in the market can be resolved, should the market itself fail (TCAII: 178). Yet the efficacy of money as a steering medium entails that it does not act merely within the subsystem of the economy, but rather develops to regulate the relationships that exist between the subsystem and its social environment (including the polity and legal system), and thereby becomes the steering medium of other, non-economic subsystems. This may be seen to develop in the polity in the reliance of the state upon taxation, and in the rest of society in the institutionalization of wage labour. The state thereby becomes increasingly dependent upon the economy, which entails that power as a steering medium is increasingly assimilated to money. Similarly, the rise of wage labour undermines traditional forms of work, and in particular shifts the labourer's orientation away from their product and its use value, and towards the monetary reward for labouring. The very nature of labour, but also everyday life, is therefore changed (and is manifest, first of all, in increased industrialization and urbanization) (PDM: 351).

Here, then, in essence, is the colonization of the lifeworld. The steering media of money and power increasingly intrude into lifeworld institutions. The initial institutionalization of economic exchange in property and contract law is itself transformed, as the state comes to be organized in terms of the economy. The economy therefore appears to sunder itself from the lifeworld, developing a new degree of autonomy and threatening to transform all other social interactions into mere subsystems. Most significantly, the lifeworld itself is threatened with becoming a subsystem. As such, action orientated to mutual understanding would be undermined, as social life would be coordinated only in terms of purposive-rational action orientated to consequences. The loss of the ideological purpose of the sacred sphere is therefore made up for, precisely because exchange, as the core institution of society, inhibits critical discourse. Requiring no normative justification, the economy, and the principle of exchange that runs throughout society, continues seemingly immune from critical purchase. The actions of the economy and the state merely fulfil the unavoidable imperatives of the system (PDM: 355).

Habermas's key critical move at this point is to argue that such colonization can only come at a major cost. A system, precisely because it lacks the resources of linguistic meaning (and inhibits the communicative competence of its participants), is insufficient for the requirements of cultural reproduction (which is to say, sustaining all that has been rehearsed above under the rubric of the lifeworld). The colonization of the lifeworld leads to a series of pathologies or crises in reproduction, including a loss of meaning, anomie and psychological pathology (TCAII: 145). To fill out these broad claims is to substantiate the criticism of contemporary society that was, from the first, one of the three purposes of *The Theory of Communicative Action*. It is to this project that we shall turn in Chapter 6 (with § "The tasks of a critical theory of society", p. 233 finally substantiating our understanding of the colonization of the lifeworld).

CHAPTER 6

Modernity

Introduction

In the early 1980s Habermas gave a short address entitled "Modernity – An Incomplete Project", first in German in Frankfurt and then in English in New York. This address clearly summarized the change that Habermas's thought had undergone since the late 1960s. In part this change was due to the "linguistic turn" that had seen him shift the very foundation of philosophical inquiry away from the subjectivity of consciousness to the intersubjectivity of communication. Yet perhaps more fundamentally, "Modernity – An Incomplete Project" marked a recognition of the change that European intellectual culture had undergone since the 1960s. In the 1960s Habermas was primarily concerned with the problems posed by positivism and scientism. At stake was the self-understanding of the social sciences, and the impact that a positivistic social administration would have upon the democratic constitution of society. Habermas was, at that time, predominantly in debate with fellow Germans. His contribution to the positivism dispute, and his exchanges with Gadamer are typical of this period (see § "Late capitalism", p. 5 and § "Hermeneutics (Gadamer), p. 81). By the 1980s, Habermas's concerns had shifted from the threat of a misplaced positivism to the dangers of grounding social and philosophical inquiry in the philosophy of consciousness; which is to say, the sociological and philosophical traditions had failed to recognize, with sufficient rigour, the intersubjective and communicative nature of human existence.[1]

Two other factors are also significant. First, the political climate in many first-world nations has changed from a broad commitment to an interventionist (Keynesian) state, which would maintain an extensive welfare state and full employment, to New Right thinking, which was deeply suspicious of state intervention, seeing it as a threat to the liberty of the individual citizen (see PDM: 356). Secondly, and perhaps more significantly, German

188

thinkers could no longer ignore the philosophical innovations that were coming from France. The intellectual avant-garde was now made up of a conglomeration of poststructuralists, deconstructionists and postmodernists. They were reshaping thought, not just in European philosophy, but also in social theory in both Europe and the English-speaking countries. In contrast to them, Habermas can appear rather staid and dull. He offers none of the verbal wizardry of Derrida, nor even Foucault's heady retelling of the histories of insanity, punishment and sexuality. At its heart the intellectual avant-garde challenged the fundamental values and presuppositions of the European Enlightenment, specifically in so far as these values were seen to be definitive of modernity. Enlightenment thinkers, such as Locke and Descartes in the seventeenth century, or Popper and the positivists in the twentieth, appealed to empirical evidence and the application of universal reason in the cause of undermining prejudice, superstition and the blind reliance on traditional forms of authority. Humanity may thereby be placed upon a path of scientific and social progress that will culminate in its perfection. Contemporary achievements can be assessed in terms of rationally articulated criteria of truth and goodness (see TCAI: 145–51). The new continental philosophies saw in the Enlightenment's commitment to universal reason an implicit authoritarianism – an inability to reflect upon its own presuppositions – that is potentially more insidious than the medieval authority that it seeks to overthrow. At its most graphic, a supposedly enlightened Germany could degenerate, all too readily, into the barbarism of the Nazi regime.

Habermas's philosophical and social theory had, from the first, entailed a criticism of modernity, not least in the form of contemporary capitalist (and soviet) societies. If such societies are indeed the product of the European Enlightenment, then Habermas has always been a critic of the Enlightenment (and he returns, tellingly, to the inheritance of Horkheimer and Adorno's *Dialectic of Enlightenment* in *The Theory of Communicative Action* (see § "Horkheimer and Adorno", p. 215)). Superficially, Habermas might then be expected to side with the postmodernists. However, the very notion of being beyond modernism, and thus of relinquishing wholesale the values that characterized the Enlightenment, is anathema to Habermas. The theory of communicative action stubbornly hangs on to notions such as "true" and "good" as critical tools, refusing to relinquish them to the ravages of relativism and perspectivism that at least superficially seemed to characterize the work of such heralds of postmodernism as Derrida, Foucault and Lyotard. Yet Habermas is not defending "the project of modernity" out of dogmatism or any reactionary unwillingness to engage with new intellectual developments. On the contrary, "Modernity – An Incomplete Project" announces his conviction not merely that much of the intellectual avant-garde is in error, but rather that it is in fact a form of neo-conservatism, unwittingly in league with the New Right, and serving only to inhibit the critical democratic potentials that remain in contemporary society. The problem of modernity, for Habermas, is thus focused upon the failure of the Enlightenment to understand and fulfil its own potential. The project of modernity therefore needs to be finished, not abandoned.[2]

The self-consciousness of modernity

Kant and Hegel

In the light of "Modernity – An Incomplete Project", *The Theory of Communicative Action* may be looked at anew. It may be recalled that Habermas identified three objectives. The third objective, "to make possible a conceptualisation of the social-life context that is tailored to the paradoxes of modernity" (TCA: xl), is now central. This aspiration to a critical theory of modernity already harks back to the introduction to *Theory and Practice*, and to the idea of a "theory of society conceived with a practical intention" (TP: 1). This requires an account of what Habermas calls the "social pathologies" of modern societies, which is to say, the regressive and repressive consequences of modernity and the Enlightenment project, which are encapsulated in the theory of the colonization of the lifeworld. However, the explication of the colonization can be no mere description of modern capitalism but, like psychoanalytic descriptions of the patient's neurosis, must carry with it a normative intent. The account is tested in terms of its capacity to inform political engagement, in order to free the rational potential that is inherent in human interaction. "Modernity – An Incomplete Project" suggests that, at least in part, this engagement entails debate with the postmodernists and neo-conservatives, not least in so far as they inhibit the realization of this rational potential. But, more subtly, Habermas is left with a question as to the source of his evidence for the colonization of the lifeworld.

In Chapter 5, *The Theory of Communicative Action* was treated very much like *Legitimation Crisis*, as generating a model of society that would be empirically testable. There is, however, an important difference between them. The earlier study was explicitly designed to offer an empirically testable model, and Habermas outlined at some length the theses that could be derived from it (and offered these for interrogation by his Starnberg colleagues) (see § "*Legitimation Crisis*", p. 125). *Theory* and its companion work, *The Philosophical Discourse of Modernity*, proceed differently. They do not explicitly generate testable hypotheses, and thus do not appeal so overtly to empirical evidence. They are grounded in what might be called the self-understanding of modernity: which is to say, in the manner in which sociologists and philosophers have theorized modernity since the late-eighteenth century. *The Theory of Communicative Action* works from the models, arguments and concepts of Marx, Weber, Durkheim and Parsons; *The Philosophical Discourse of Modernity* from those of Kant, Hegel, Marx and Nietzsche, as well as cultural modernists such as Baudelaire. "Modernity – An Incomplete Project", in effect, is a summary introduction to these self-understandings. The theory of the colonization of the lifeworld – with its attendant account of the evolution of system and lifeworld – may thus be seen as a diagnosis based upon the insights, blind spots and aporias of previous generations of theorists. Yet "Modernity – An Incomplete Project" makes clear that this is also the approach that Habermas takes to the critics of modernity. That is to say, the colonization of the lifeworld is not merely set up as an account in opposition to theirs, and expected to stand by its greater coherence or correspondence to social reality, but is rather presented as a diagnosis that both responds to and explains their anti-modernism (MIP: 7–8). Neo-conservatism is approached as a symptom of colonization, much as hysterical paralysis is a symptom of repressed trauma.

Habermas's analysis begins with the meaning of the term "modernity". Although the concept has been in use since the fifth century, originally it merely served to distinguish the Christian present from a pagan past (MIP: 3). In the eighteenth century, this largely chronological use of the term is transformed by a change in the Western conception of history, and specifically of the future. Within medieval Christian culture, the modern present was not yet the radically "new" age that would dawn with the second coming and, indeed, precisely in so far as the second coming was to be a radical intervention in human history, there was no sense of historical progress towards it. The Enlightenment perspective of the eighteenth century, in contrast, sees the radically new age as having already begun (with the Renaissance, Reformation and discovery of the "new world") (PDM: 5). A break is thus placed in the past, and it is one that allows history to be reinterpreted as progress into an open future (TCAI: 146). Humanity must make history, responding to historically specific problems, in a continual renewal of the break between the past and the present. Dynamic terms, such as "revolution, progress, emancipation, development, crisis, and *Zeitgeist* [spirit of the age]", have new significance in the interpretation of history (PDM: 7). Modernity is therefore not simply the present, but is rather a unique period in history (distinct in its nature and orientation from antiquity and the Middle Ages).

Yet this very uniqueness raises the question of what precisely is distinctive about this period and, more specifically, how its assumption of its very progress and superiority over the past is to be justified. The philosophical and sociological self-reflection to which Habermas appeals is therefore inherent to the very nature of modernist culture. In part, this self-reflection may be understood as an ongoing process of articulating the idea of the Enlightenment. The modern age understands itself to be distinct from all earlier periods of European history (and indeed from non-European cultures) due to its systematic appeal to reason and the discipline of scientific inquiry. We have already encountered this self-understanding in the form of the rationalization of the lifeworld. Modernity may be characterized as a cultural challenge to the traditional authority of the medieval past. Politically and morally this entails that the possession of power is rationally justified and that the legal system is given coherence, thereby challenging the traditional authority of the church and the state. In science, the authority of Aristotelianism is replaced by the empirical and rationally grounded inquiries of the likes of Galileo and Newton. The rationalization of the lifeworld is the application of modern attitudes to the taken-for-granted beliefs and competences that serve to constitute everyday life (TCAI: 340).

It is here that the problem of the justification of modernity finds its focus. The difference between the culture of modernity and the cultures of the Middle Ages and antiquity is not at issue. What is at issue is the superiority of modernity. It is precisely this point that the anti-modernists, such as Foucault and Lyotard, question. For Habermas, the problem of modernity's self-justification initially revolves about the phenomenon of the naive confidence that the Middle Ages and antiquity had in their cultures. This is to suggest that, while in terms of the Enlightenment these cultures may have been unreflective and irrational, they did give a substantive and secure shape to the lives of their members. One could, for example, identify oneself as an Athenian, recognizing and embracing the values that one held as an Athenian. The medieval peasant had a fixed and divinely ordained place in the social order. The Enlightenment offers rationality but at the cost of losing this substance and security, for it provides only the rational form of self-reflection, without necessarily offering a new substance to replace the outworn tradition. In sum, this is the now familiar criticism of the exclusive dominance of instrumental reason over social, as well as technical and economic, life; similarly, as will be seen in more detail below, it is Marx's condemnation of modernity for its alienation, or Durkheim's for its lack of guiding norms (i.e. its *anomie*). But this already hints at an important element of Habermas's criticisms of both modernity and modernity's critics. Habermas's point, very simply, is that the very self-reflection through which philosophers, social theorists and artists articulate the notion of the modern is at once a self-criticism of modernity (see PDM: 57). The modernists worry about the legitimacy of their enterprise. The concerns raised by the anti-modernists are thus seen to be inherent to the very development of modernity itself.

Habermas develops his criticisms by rehearsing the role that philosophy – and in particular German Idealism – played in defining modernity. Enlightenment philosophers, from Descartes and Bacon, through Leibniz, Locke, and Hume, can be seen to be seeking a grounding for modern science, ethics and politics, and indeed aesthetic taste. This project culminates in Kant's three "*Critiques*", where the rationality of the transcendental subject becomes the final seat of judgement for all validity claims (PDM: 18). The first, *Critique of Pure Reason*, explicates the grounds and limits to knowledge; the second, *Critique of Practical Reason*, establishes a rational ethics; and the third, *Critique of Judgement*, opens up the possibility of rationality in aesthetic judgement. For Hegel, Kant's philosophy is the authoritative self-interpretation of modernity, and yet it is precisely here that the failure of the Enlightenment may be glimpsed (and the pathologies of modernity are first hinted at). Although Kant offers a rational grounding for modernity, it ultimately lacks unity. This is not simply a matter of the substantial differences between the three "*Critiques*" (and indeed their respective appeals to faculties of understanding, reason and judgement) (PDM: 19), but also to the oppositions that remain within Kant's system: noumena against phenomena; fact against value; knowledge against faith and so on (PDM: 21). Although the diremptions (or divisions) within Kant's critical philosophy may be the diremptions of modernity itself, which is to say that Kant has produced a uniquely authoritative articulation of modernity as it is – that is, his philosophy mirrors its society in terms of its deficiencies and tensions – Hegel still criticizes Kant for failing to understand or conceptualize modernity sufficiently to recognize the significance of these deficiencies.

Kant's philosophy is ultimately ahistorical. In earlier chapters we have seen how Hegel goes beyond Kant by asking after the historical origin of the transcendental subject (§ "Hegel, labour and interaction", p. 63). Habermas reiterates this relationship in *The Philosophical Discourse of Modernity*, albeit in the context of a subtly different interpretation. Given that modernity's acute awareness of its historical nature is the source of its lack of grounding (for it is uniquely conscious of its difference from the past), it is precisely this lack of historical awareness that inhibits Kant's philosophy from providing a ground for modernity (PDM: 20). Unlike Kant, Hegel therefore treats the diremptions within the Kantian system historically, and thus as something to be overcome. The challenge of modernity's future is to restore the unity of ancient and medieval cultures, albeit without loss of Enlightened reflection. This can only be done if the diremption is seen, not as a division between the subject and some wholly alien object (as Kant suggests, for example in the relationship between the faculty of imagination and the given of the manifold of perceptions), but as a diremption within the subject itself. It is here that we again return to an image familiar from Habermas's earlier commentaries on Hegel: the criminal and the causality of fate (see § "Hegel, labour and interaction", p. 63 (TP: 159)). The criminal act is one of disrupting the ethical relationships that give substance and unity to the community. The punishment of the criminal is initially experienced as fateful (and thus arising from a wholly separate nature). It is only when the criminal recognizes their own punishment in the damage done to their victim, precisely in that the criminal recognizes that the damage in their own life is rooted in their self-imposed separation from their victim, that they become conscious of the ruptured nature of the community (PDM: 28). It is only from this perspective, which is to say from the perspective of love and mutual recognition (articulated in Hegel's early theological writings), that the Kantian diremptions can be understood not merely as historical events, but also as marks of repression and authoritarianism within modernity.

The young Hegel experiences the diremption of modernity personally through his engagement, alongside his fellow students Friedrich Hölderlin and Schelling, in the debate between Gottlieb Christian Storr's Protestant orthodoxy and Kantian Enlightenment philosophy. Protestantism, which for Hegel represented a moment of enlightenment against Roman Catholicism, promised a spirituality and morality that would inspire people and be an element of public life, which is to say that it would come from the congregation in contrast to the Catholic imposition of morality on the people. As such, it would offer genuine communal unity. In practice, Protestant orthodoxy betrays this ideal by restoring the authority of the priesthood, for it separates priestly beliefs from those of the mass of the population, and turns religion into a private belief divorced from public life (PDM: 25). Kantian morality should have been able to check this, except that it, too, failed to engage the enthusiasm of the people. Again, lacking substance, Kantian duty cannot latch on to the concrete passions and beliefs that give meaning to the lives of real people. Thus, while its grounding in universal human reason should allow it to challenge the arbitrariness of Protestant priestly rule, in practice the purely rational Kantian ethic fails to express the concrete and historical experiences of the community (PDM: 26–7). Kantian morality thereby retreats into the same private realm as Protestant orthodoxy, for it lacks any tie to the historically emergent institutions of the community. It is revealed to be the complement of Protestant orthodoxy. Both, in practice, implicitly appeal to an arbitrary authority that is, by its very nature, not rationally grounded, for it cannot be questioned or genuinely internalized by the community. In Hegel's formulation, the Kantian remains as much a slave as the "wild Mongol". Whereas the latter is dominated by an external lord, the former carries within himself or herself a law, which appears to be as alien and objective to true human sentiments as any other form of despotism (PDM: 28).

Habermas thus credits Hegel with being the first theorist to provide an adequate account of modernity. On the one hand, this claim refers to his political and economic philosophy. Hegel is the first to conceptualize the separation of "civil society" (as the sphere of commodity exchange, and the rational pursuit of private interest) from the state (as the sphere of power). In addition we may suppose that morality and religion are further marginalized into an increasingly problematic private lifeworld. This is itself a sundering of the unity of the Aristotelian conception of the polity, in which the economic unit of the household was also the basis of the political order (PDM: 37). Yet, on the other hand, Hegelian political economy serves as a frame within which his criticisms of Kant may be reinterpreted. It suggests a historical and political analysis of the Kantian diremptions. The formality of Kantian moral duties disregarded the individual moral agent's communal or historical existence. The appeal to pure reason served to shield the true source of law's authority from critical reflection. In the light of political economy, Kantian morality is revealed as an intimation of the domination of system over lifeworld (and thus of the early emergence of colonization), both in its formal rationality and in its concealed authority. Hegel is thereby the first theorist of modernity precisely in so far as he is the first to make explicit the contradictions within modernity – to begin to see its pathologies – and thus to realize modernity's self-reflection as something that is genuinely self-critical. He initiates an analysis of what Horkheimer and Adorno will call the "dialectic of enlightenment".

The neo-Hegelians

The later Hegel proposed the restoration of unity by concentrating the ethical life of the community into the state (PDM: 39). For Habermas this is indicative of his failure to recognize the potential for a theory of communicative action that was inherent in his early Jena writings. The point is again familiar from Habermas's own earlier extraction of the idea of "interaction" from the young Hegel. The later Hegel, by projecting the subjectivity of *Geist* as the sole protagonist in history, reverts to the monological philosophy of consciousness that was precisely the problem in Kantianism. Kant's transcendental subject is an individual subject writ large, with interaction between real subjects already organized into a predetermined harmony. In late Hegel, the concrete individual subjects are once more subsumed into the higher-level subjectivity of the state and *Geist* (PDM: 40). The meaning of modernity is betrayed, once again because the open and experimental consciousness of the future is distorted as the success of *Geist* is guaranteed in advance. "[E]very event of essential significance has *already* been decided" (PDM: 42). Ironically, Hegel betrays the very insight that he had originally wielded against Kant: the importance for modern consciousness of concrete historical existence, "in which the problems of an onrushing future are tangled in knots" (PDM: 53). In contrast, the Jena writings had promised a sense of community that bound subjects together through communication, and thereby allowed each subject to recognize itself in others while still retaining a sense of its own individuality (PDM: 30).

The Young Hegelians of the next generation respond to the failure of Hegelian philosophy to engage with real historical experience. Most graphically and famously this is caught in Marx's aphorism that philosophy has till now merely interpreted reality, when the point is to change it (1975c: thesis 11). Despite the fact that the Young Hegelians divide into two opposed camps (the Left Hegelians, or "party of movement", and the liberal Right Hegelians, or "party of inertia" (PDM: 58)), they share a desire to break from academic philosophy, in order to turn to a political practice that is concretely grounded, and that will expose the illusion of the false absolutes of subjective (Kantian and Hegelian) reasoning (PDM: 56). Indeed, the Right Hegelians reject intellectuals as a whole, as a new priesthood that would undermine the stability of society (PDM: 57).

The Young Hegelians are also united in their criticism of contemporary bourgeois society. However, their solutions to contemporary political problems are radically distinct. The Right Hegelians see in the ideal of bourgeois civil society the concept of society as such. In effect, the question of the legitimation of modernity is answered, at least in part, through appeal to the Hegelian concept of civil society. That is to say that market competition at once realizes individual freedom, and grounds the social order in a natural – and therefore objective – hierarchy of needs, talents and skills. Equality and democratic formation of the public will are dismissed as subjective illusions (PDM: 70). However, as it exists, the bourgeois market is riddled with imperfections, so that markets can be exploited by monopolists, and the liberty of the labourer may be undermined to the degree that they are unable to satisfy their basic needs (PDM: 294–5, n.28). The state is therefore required to check the abuses and imperfections of competition, compensating for the restlessness of bourgeois society by providing the ethical substance that it otherwise lacks (PDM: 56). Yet this Right Hegelian political project fails, for Habermas, in so far as it leads into authoritarianism and sunders the present from both past and future, thereby impoverishing the lifeworld. Its authoritarianism is manifest most graphically in the Third Reich, precisely in so far as philosophers such as Carl Schmitt find in the unmanageability of the democratic experiment of the Weimar Republic a justification for a totalitarian state (PDM: 70–71). In the post-war writings of the historian of philosophy Joachim Ritter, Habermas uncovers a more subtle working out of Right Hegelianism. Ritter conceives of modern society in terms of an economic relationship to nature. Precisely in so far as this is conceived as a purely natural relationship, and thereby consolidates the natural hierarchy that exists among social members, it serves to sunder modern society from its historical past and from the future. Perfected modern society lies at the end of history (as more recent neo-conservatives, such as Francis Fukuyama, have argued (1992)). Yet, the objective justification and legitimation of this society succumbs to the same problems as does Kantian morality. Its rational objectivity does not appeal to the hearts and sentiments of the people. In effect, Ritter has outlined a pure social system. Everyday meaning is lost, as the system comes to colonize the lifeworld. Yet, because human beings cannot live without meaning, the loss of real history and tradition must be compensated for. This Ritter proposes to do through the *Geisteswissenschaften* (the social and historical sciences) generating a museum-like tradition. What this in fact entails is that the genuinely critical potential of the *Geisteswissenschaften* is inhibited (as the preserve of destabilizing intellectuals). Only a past that has been constructed by what might now be understood as the heritage industry is allowed to count as historical knowledge (PDM: 73–4). The Right Hegelians thus capitulate to the same illusion of false absolutes as that to which they originally reacted.

The project of the Left Hegelians and, pre-eminently, that of Marx, centres about the idea of a philosophy of praxis. Marx attempts to overcome the closure of the Hegelian absolute by turning from an epistemological model – which is primarily focused on the growing self-consciousness of the *Geist* – to a model that stresses the self-realization of the subject through its own practical activity. This allows Marx to respond to the complexity of the contemporary experience of social change. On the one hand, industrial development offers clear empirical evidence of the pace of historical change. Yet, on the other hand, the nature of this change is ambiguous. The Right Hegelian concern over change is not wholly alien to Marx, again precisely in that both Right and Left Hegelians are critics of the worst of bourgeois society. While the Right Hegelians chain the dynamic of civil society through the state, Marx seeks to release industrial development as a source of a revolutionary movement that will transform and surpass bourgeois society (rather than merely consolidate its ideal). For Marx, the bourgeois state cannot be the source of ethical life, but rather functions merely to reproduce and sustain the structural inequalities and mechanisms of exploitation that characterize bourgeois civil society. As such, it is not the bourgeois state that is the source of reason, which is to say of a rational and perfected future, for the state merely consolidates the irrationalities of contemporary civil society. Marx must, then, turn to civil society as the source of a rational potential for the future. The philosophy of praxis must provide the analytic tools necessary to explicate this potential.

The key to this process of explication lies in Marx's concept of labour. Habermas sees the Marxist concept of "labour" as not merely an economic category, but also an aesthetic one. Labour is modelled on the idea of artistic production. Artists externalize their own creative powers in their art works. Through contemplation, they re-appropriate these objects, recognizing themselves in them, and thus coming to ever more mature self-understanding. The organization of industrial production in capitalism interrupts the process of re-appropriation. The product is appropriated by others, and for the purpose of realizing surplus value. As such, a benign process of objectification is transformed into a malignant process of alienation (PDM: 64). Here, for Marx, is the material ground of the illusion of the absolute that spoils Hegel's philosophy. The exploitative and irrational elements of the organization of capitalist production are concealed within the ideological structures that are entwined with alienation. Crucially the Right Hegelians buy into this illusion. For Marx, revolutionary praxis can only be made possible if this illusion is penetrated, and the producer becomes conscious of the difference between objectification and alienation. Put otherwise, the producer must see through the illusion of a natural production process and a natural hierarchy in the organization of production. Production is a cultural and historical process, and as such the product of human agency: production can be organized differently. This realization opens modernity to a radically new future, as humanity sees through the second nature of economic laws (that Right Hegelianism merely confirms as natural). Only then can the producer become aware of and realize its free agency, creating itself, in a praxis akin to that of the artist (PDM: 65).

For Habermas, Left Hegelianism is only a little more successful than its conservative opponent. Marx's conceptualization of "production" remains ambiguous, and as such leaves the problem of the realization of the good society – of ethical life – undecided. Habermas alludes, in effect, to the familiar problem of the tension between determinist and voluntarist interpretations of historical materialism. On the former account, the forces of production develop of their own accord, and determine the revolutionary moment. The growth of technology is thus an unambiguous good (for the likes of Karl Kautsky and the Second International) (PDM: 58). On the latter account, the moment of revolution can be brought about through political agency. The domination of nature that is inherent in industrial production is thus itself suspect, for it becomes entwined in the very domination of human beings (hence the work of Lukács, Bloch and the Frankfurt School)

(PDM: 66). For Habermas, the failure lies in Marx's naive assumption that the development of the forces of production can facilitate the realization of society as a transparent and meaningful lifeworld. A good society, on the model of the philosophy of praxis, is one that has done away with the meaningless second nature of the social system, so that the lifeworld – the realm of freedom – can reassert itself as the steering mechanism of society (TCAII: 340). The threat that the pace of industrialization poses to the lifeworld is countered by the self-realization of the subject of praxis (which is to say, the proletariat). Yet this begs the question of the necessity of subsystems steered by non-symbolic media in any complex society (PDM: 67). Habermas, at this point, effectively sides with the Right Hegelian moment in Weber's thought, precisely where he recognizes the inevitability of such (typically administrative) systems in any post-capitalist society (PDM: 70). Although Marx establishes the distinction between lifeworld and system – in the categories of "concrete" and "abstract" labour (TCAII: 335) and the realms of freedom and necessity (TCAII: 340) – he fails to make a distinction between the rationalization of the lifeworld – whereby the coordination of a complex modern society is necessarily handed over to systematic steering mechanisms – and the colonization of the lifeworld – whereby non-symbolic steering media invade the lifeworld, rendering everyday actions meaningless (TCAII: 341–2, 351). The Marxist conceit that the state will simply wither away under socialism, realizing the Hegelian ethical life as a pure lifeworld, is ultimately no more tenable than the Right Hegelian assumption that the state can assume the position of ethical life and invent a meaningful lifeworld from nothing.

The failure of Left Hegelianism lies in its conception of reason. Here Habermas effectively renews the criticisms of Marx that he made in *Knowledge and Human Interests*, such that the positivist moment in historical and dialectical materialism comes to dominate and exclude the hermeneutic moment. Now the point is that an exclusive focus on instrumental reason within the process of production (with only a critical dialectical reason as its alternative) proves inadequate to the task of making sense of the development of capitalism. The weakness now is not primarily that of positivism, but rather of the philosophy of the subject. The philosophy of praxis is insufficiently radical. It retains a fundamental relationship between an isolated subject and an external object, and thus uncritically reproduces a positivistic understanding of the production process as an application of instrumental reason (TCAII: 342). Only with Habermas's shift to the philosophy of communicative action can this be checked. Production becomes a communicative as well as an instrumental process (and the lifeworld is recognized as something that must be realized communicatively, and not merely let free through a monological self-understanding on the part of the producer). Ironically, both Left and Right Hegelianism then converge in a failure to realize the resources of the *Geisteswissenschaften*. Habermas's point here goes beyond that of *Knowledge and Human Interests*. There the positivistic moment suppressed the interpretative moment of the hermeneutic sciences. Now the philosophy of the subject suppresses not merely the hermeneutic search for meaning within the lifeworld, but more fundamentally a recognition of the genuinely intersubjective nature of lifeworld and system.

Nietzsche

There remains, however, one further alternative to both Left and Right Hegelianism with which Habermas must deal: to question fundamentally the Hegelian appeal to reason. This is Nietzsche's position. Habermas's interpretation of Nietzsche is at once a pivotal moment in *The Philosophical Discourse of Modernity* (not least because of the implications that it has for his interpretation of twentieth-century thinkers such as Bataille, Derrida and Foucault), and the most contested.[3] Habermas places Nietzsche as responding to the failure of the young Hegelians to provide a justification for modernism, precisely in so far as this failure entails that modernism must be equated with nihilism. A modernism that cannot legitimate itself lacks the moral foundations by which the actions of modern people may be guided. The religious culture that unified pre-modern society is now lost, as is demonstrated by the failure of the Right Hegelians to recover the moral culture through an act of remembrance (for such is the task that the Right Hegelians set for the *Geisteswissenschaften*) (PDM: 84). God is dead (Nietzsche 1979: bk 3 §116), and so everything is permitted. Nietzsche responds to this by neither capitulating to nihilism nor turning to reason to restore a moral culture; rather, he turns to art.

Hegel's contemporaries Schelling and Friedrich Schlegel had already questioned the priority of art and philosophy established by Hegel. Although, for Hegel, art and philosophy are both part of what he calls "absolute spirit", which is to say elements of human culture through which spirit (or *Geist*) achieves self-consciousness, art is very much an imperfect initial stage in the process. While art may have as its subject matter *Geist* (or, put a little more prosaically, the human understanding of the divine), the sensuous forms of stone, paint, sound and verbal imagery within which it embodies this understanding are inadequate for its full and perfect expression. Ultimately, art must fail in its goal of articulating absolute truth. At best, in the experience of beauty, we glimpse the absolute as an illusion [*Schein*] (Hegel 1975b: 111). It is only in philosophy that the truth of spirit can be grasped in terms that are appropriate to that truth – which is to say, conceptually (Hegel 1971: §§572–7). In contrast, Schelling sees in art the power to appeal to the hearts and sentiments, as it were, of the people. While concurring with the Hegelian point that philosophy emerges out of art, and more specifically out of a religious culture of mythology, Schelling argues that philosophy must also return to art, in the realization of a new mythology (through which the human subject becomes aware of itself as the creator and agent of spirit) (PDM: 89). The Romantic Schlegel takes this a radical step further. Whereas Schelling's art can offer the hope of a utopian ethical life precisely because art is grounded, philosophically, in reason (and indeed unifies theoretical and practical reason), Schlegel offers what he calls a "messianic hope" (PDM: 90). That is to say that Schlegel does not justify beauty through reason but, on the contrary, demands that art and beauty must be radically cleansed of reason. For Schlegel, the utopian future cannot be realized through reason, for it is precisely reason that irrevocably separates us from the forms of social integration that served in the past. Schlegel's new mythology is thus one that engages with a primordial chaos as at once the opposite of rational modernity, and the only possible response to the nihilism of modernity (PDM: 91).

In his first major work, *The Birth of Tragedy*, Nietzsche may be seen to take up Schlegel's thesis. Nietzsche's primordial society is that of the archaic and classical Greek city states, prior to the fourth century BCE (and crucially prior to the influence of Socrates). Focusing on the tragedies of Sophocles and Aeschylus, he argues that they achieve a unique balance between the two conflicting elements of Greek culture: the Dionysian and the Apolline. The god Dionysus is associated with intoxication and ecstasy; Apollo with order and control. Habermas emphasizes the fact that Dionysian myths present him as an absent god, wandering with satyrs and other followers of Baccus in North Africa and Asia Minor. He is thus at once outside the narrow scope of European civilization, but is also a god who is to return, and thus – like Christ – can be a focus of messianic and redemptive hope (PDM: 91). In contrast, the ever present and civilized Apollo is associated not simply with reason, but more specifically with the constructive and ordering power of the Kantian transcendental subject. The link is made via Schopenhauer, who reinterprets the Kantian noumena as an ever restless and striving will. This becomes Nietzsche's ecstatic Dionysian state. The phenomenal or Apolline world of order and stability is thus a foil, staving off the terrifying reality of the will. At the core of this phenomenal order lies the empirical subject's sense of its own individuality: the *principii individuationis*. For Nietzsche, Apolline order is therefore necessary. Without it, unmediated exposure to the Dionysian would destroy the observer, for it would strip away the very foundation of their sense of personal identity (Nietzsche 1993: §7). That way lies madness. The problem, however, is how this Apolline mediation is to be realized. The greatness of the dramas of Sophocles and Aeschylus lies precisely in the fact that they allow us a glimpse of the Dionysian, without it destroying us. The Apollonian order of the drama is disrupted by the horror of the events (Agamemnon slaying his daughter, Oedipus slaying his father, the immurement of Antigone), that ultimately cannot be reconciled or rationally accounted for. The Dionysian lies in this irreconcilable experience. It is only when the Apolline becomes so dominant that sight of the Dionysian is lost altogether that culture begins to decay. Put bluntly, Nietzsche sees the failings of modernity to be rooted in the moment at which Socratic reasoning comes to dominance. For Socrates, on Nietzsche's interpretation, all problems must have a rational solution. That which does not have a rational solution – the Dionysian – does not exist (Nietzsche 1993: §11). Socrates opens the way for not just modern philosophy, but also modern science. Reason is presented as a tool that can be used to calculate and control both the natural and the human worlds. Even drama falls under its spell, as Euripides writes rationally coherent plays, the meanings and morals of which are carefully explained to the audience (Nietzsche 1993: §§11–12). Here, in effect, is an intimation of a world of pure system, or of a pure Kantian moral order that cannot touch the hearts and sentiments of the lifeworld.

As an aside it may be noted that Nietzsche has engaged constructively with the Right Hegelians. Crucially, he has objected to the fate of the *Geisteswissenschaften* in their hands. He suggests that their approach to the past is a mere recognition that: "Things were different in all ages; it does not matter how you are" (PDM: 85, citing Nietzsche 1980: §VII). This historicism thus yields to a relativism that lacks any moral check on current practices. Right Hegelian history thereby merely serves to disguise the actual approval of pure force. Precisely in that *The Birth of Tragedy* is an exercise in the *Geisteswissenschaften*, Nietzsche seeks to restore their normative power in order to confront modern nihilism. It is precisely his failure, his capitulation to the very *Realpolitik* and perspectivism that he finds problematic in the Right Hegelians, that concerns Habermas.

In the *Birth of Tragedy*, Nietzsche responds to the problem of nihilism through what might be called an "aesthetic theodicy". This is to say that Nietzsche responds to the problem of the presence of evil – or more precisely, in Nietzsche's case, pain and suffering – in the world by presenting it as an aesthetic phenomenon. Following his account of Greek culture (and, crucially, the notion of "Greek cheerfulness", whereby they could withstand extremes of suffering contentedly), Nietzsche suggests that human life (however painful or joyous it might be) is to be understood as a drama being played out primarily for the entertainment and edification of the gods (PDM: 94–5). Art is the creation of ever new interpretations and perspectives on suffering and joy. The creativity of art thus confronts the dead hand of nihilism, and summons Dionysus back from his exile. The problem here lies in Nietzsche's understanding of modern art. When writing *Birth of Tragedy* he explicitly saw the music dramas of Richard Wagner as the modern renewal of classical tragedy, restoring a mythical culture appropriate to Germany (and as such overcoming the dominance of a facile, Euripidean, "culture of opera") (Nietzsche 1993: §19). Yet such an art is only going to avoid the problems of Right Hegelian historicism if it has some value base (PDM: 95). Without that, anything, however cruel and barbaric, can be aesthetically justified. This base is lacking in Nietzsche's vision (and, perhaps not incidentally, he breaks with Wagner precisely as the Christian elements in his work become explicit, most obviously with *Parsifal*). More precisely, on Habermas's account at least, it is not the lack of substantial moral values that is at stake, but rather that Nietzsche increasingly misrepresents art as a purely irrational Dionysian activity. Nietzsche increasingly loses sight of the rational, Apolline moment of classical tragedy, and thus, for Habermas, the rational element of modern art itself. This rational element is analysed, for example by Weber, such that art is no more exempt from the process of rationalization that characterizes modernity than any other cultural phenomenon (Weber 1958). Perhaps more significantly, it lies at the heart of Adorno's understanding of art, and not least his engagement with the music of Schoenberg (Adorno 1949, 1967). But, on another level, Habermas suggests that Nietzsche has also neglected the institutional grounding of art in the literary public sphere (as analysed in *The Structural Transformation of the Public Sphere*; see § "The literary public sphere", p. 34) (PDM: 96). Nietzsche's aesthetics may be understood as a reaction to Kant's. Kant wrote from the position of the spectator of art, and as such emphasized the disinterested pleasure that one receives from the work, and on the basis of which one judges it to be good or bad. In contrast, Nietzsche approaches art from the perspective of the artist. The artist is not the more or less passive beneficiary of a work's value, but rather the one who actively posited the work as valuable. The artist creates value (PDM: 124). Yet, for Habermas, exclusive emphasis upon this perspective reduces value (be it aesthetic or moral) to mere subjective assertion, and thus taints Nietzsche with the very emotivism and decisionism that characterized positivist theories of value. At the very least this sacrifices art's role as the preliminary training ground for moral and political discourse.

Habermas is aware that Nietzsche's analysis goes beyond the aesthetic theodicy of the *Birth of Tragedy*, but for Habermas this development only compounds the problem. It is not just in his aesthetics, but in Nietzsche's philosophy as a whole that the Apolline is increasingly marginalized. The

Dionysian comes to the fore principally in the idea of the will to power. The young Nietzsche had already argued that truth was nothing more than that which allowed humanity, a clever animal, to survive and flourish: it is a useful lie (1979: 84). Later, in *On the Genealogy of Morals*, this line of argument is pushed further. The cleverness of rational calculation is a tool that human beings use to survive, albeit at the cost of repressing their primordial animal instincts (PDM: 121). In so far as this poses a radical challenge to any correspondence theory of truth, as well as suggesting that truth claims are grounded in their practical outcomes, there is enough of pragmatism in this position for it to be both interesting and threatening to Habermas (cf. § "Pragmatism", p. 67). The doctrine of the will to power takes this further, by arguing that all judgements of truth and goodness are grounded in a struggle of individual human beings or groups of human beings to gain power over each other. The true and the good merely allow one's own kind to be dominant. Again, there is here an uncomfortable echo of, on the one hand, Habermas's own account of the cognitive interests, albeit that Nietzsche subordinates all knowledge to an interest in power, and, on the other, of ideology critique. That is to say that Nietzsche has recognized the possibility that validity claims can be contaminated by imbalances of power, so that what passes as truth is not that to which all would discursively agree; it is rather that to which a dominant group can force agreement. The difference between Nietzsche's position and that of ideology critique is simply that Nietzsche makes his critique all-consuming. All truth claims are assertions of the will to power, and there is seemingly no criterion of uncorrupted truth. The choice and judgement of truth claims therefore collapses once more into assertions of subjective taste (PDM: 123–4), and all that matters are new perspectives. Every truth claim and every moral and aesthetic valuation is reduced to one more perspective, so that still "everything is permitted".

Habermas suggests that Nietzsche does offer a criterion by which truth claims can be differentiated. Nietzsche makes a distinction between active and reactive forces, in order to establish which assertions of power deserve our esteem (PDM: 125). Thus an active "master" morality can be distinguished from a reactive "slave" morality. The former posits value, while the latter merely reacts, resentfully, to the values of the masters. In practice, this distinction entails an appeal to the superiority of the primordial. In line with the analysis in *The Birth of Tragedy*, Nietzsche always sides with the more ancient order. Sophocles and Aeschylus are to be more esteemed than Socrates and Euripides. More precisely, Socratic reason, taking as it does the form of modern science and the Enlightenment ideals of universal morality and law, is condemned as the mere victory of a perverted reactionary force over the purity of older forms (PDM: 126). Nietzsche's attempt to engage with the nihilism of modernity thus ultimately reverts to Schlegel's Romanticism. Like Schlegel, Nietzsche condones a new mythology, "in which powers influence one another and no element remains that could transcend the battle of the powers" (PDM: 125). The illegitimacy of modernity is avoided only by retreating back before the very first stirrings of the Enlightenment, and thus before Socrates' Athens.

Dialectic of enlightenment

Heidegger and Derrida

The entwining of enlightenment reason with mythology is explored in three crucial responses to the crisis of modernity, all of which have their roots in Nietzsche. These come from Heidegger and Derrida, Horkheimer and Adorno and, finally, from Foucault. Habermas's discussions of them constitute the contemporary backbone of *The Philosophical Discourse of Modernity*.

A critical stance towards Heidegger has characterized Habermas's philosophy since his first published works (see § "Introduction", p. 1). To extend this to Derrida and deconstruction is significant not least in so far as it most clearly marks Habermas's engagement with the most influential strand of continental philosophy (at least outside Germany). Yet, while Habermas's career had been characterized by a series of debates, for example with Gadamer, Luhmann and the positivists, the comments on Heidegger and Derrida in *The Philosophical Discourse of Modernity* are of a subtly different order. Previous debates were part of the process by which Habermas sought to build his theoretical position. The opponent was not to be dismissed, but to be asked to contribute to Habermas's own more encompassing project. But now Habermas speaks from a fully worked out position: that of the theory of communicative action. He may be sympathetic to the criticisms of the philosophy of subject that Heidegger and Derrida make, but ultimately he is scathingly critical of their failure to consolidate these criticisms. This failure makes possible the articulation of a superficially plausible counter-position that threatens both the theory of communicative action and the unfinished project of modernity. In summary, Heidegger opens up a return to nihilism, rendering the legitimation of modernism futile, while Derrida attacks the privileged position accorded to reason within modernity, while also attacking the speech act theory that Habermas uses in the grounding of universal pragmatics.

At the core of Heidegger's programme, at least in Habermas's reconstruction, is the process of reinstating the importance of philosophy, through a critique of the history of Western metaphysics. The young Hegelians, by attacking Hegelian idealism, began to undermine philosophy as such, so that its place would be taken increasingly by sociology, economics and political science, as well as by the natural sciences, law and even art (PDM: 131). Heidegger construes the crisis of modernism as a crisis in the metaphysical ground of philosophy (or thinking). In an argument that explicitly echoes Nietzsche's criticisms of Socrates and post-Socratic philosophy, Heidegger claims that modern philosophy has forgotten the most important of all philosophical questions: the question of the meaning of Being (Heidegger 1962: 2). This may perhaps be best understood negatively. Modern philosophy – and Habermas stresses Heidegger's focus on Descartes and the Enlightenment, although the argument is taken, by Heidegger, back to Plato and Aristotle – concerns itself exclusively with understanding and manipulating entities, or the discrete and particular objects that are the concern of an instrumental and domineering attitude to the natural and social worlds (PDM: 132–3). Pre-Socratic thinking, in contrast, asked the supposedly deeper question as to that which grounded particular entities (i.e. Being). In effect, a Kantian transcendental approach to the possibility of the existence of things is changed from an epistemological question into a purely and radically ontological one (concerned with the very nature of that which exists) (PDM: 138). Precisely in so far as philosophy characterizes Western culture as a whole, and thus its instrumentalism, the forgetting of the question of Being lies at the core of the nihilist crisis of modernity. Being thus assumes the place of Nietzsche's absent god, Dionysus (PDM: 135).

In this critical move Heidegger has begun to recognize that the failure of Enlightenment philosophy lies in its presupposition of the philosophy of consciousness. He begins to break out of the philosophy of consciousness not simply through ontology, but rather through a hermeneutic reworking of ontology. Husserl's concept of a "world" becomes central, for this is the horizon of meaning within which an individual subject comes to consciousness (PDM: 147). The world is an interpretation of the physical and natural environment within which the subject finds itself. Put otherwise, it is the "ontological preunderstanding", the conceptual framework that allows the subject to make sense of their environment and to act within it (PDM: 132, 147). At this point Heidegger's philosophy comes close to pragmatism, not least in its recognition that reflection and problem-solving are stimulated by practical challenges within a pre-interpreted environment (PDM: 148). Perhaps more significantly, Heidegger's very characterization of contemporary society turns on a criticism of the philosophy of consciousness. In forgetting the question of Being, our social relationships to others are corrupted. We relate to others merely as objects that we can manipulate and exploit. Others are to be counted on (PDM: 136). Although hinting at the need for a theory of communication, not least through an attempt to grasp the notion of mutual understanding (PDM: 137), Heidegger still fails to develop these insights, because he ultimately remains bound up within the philosophy of consciousness.

Habermas identifies Heidegger's initial failing in the weakness of his criticism of modernity. His existentialism, which would demand that individuals live authentically by taking full responsibility for their finite existences, has its purchase precisely in so far as he sees authenticity being inhibited by contemporary culture. The public realm of *"Das Man"* ["The They"] (Heidegger 1962: 167) encourages uniformity and the shifting of responsibility to an anonymous public authority. Yet, according to Habermas, this, along with the aversion to instrumental reason and technology in general (Heidegger 1996), is no more than the "prejudices of bourgeois culture critique" (PDM: 140). More importantly, it entails that the world – or, more properly, the lifeworld – is radically thrown into suspicion as something inauthentic. The lifeworld, in its "everydayness", becomes merely a threat to the existential freedom of the individual, and not the source of both socialization *and* individuation that it is in Habermas's hands (PDM: 149).

More fundamentally, by at once recognizing the hermeneutic importance of the lifeworld yet also radically condemning it, Heidegger has begun to relinquish the possibility of grounding his criticism of modernism. The problem lies in his failure adequately to analyse the lifeworld, not merely as a source of individuation and thus agency, but also as a communicative and thus linguistic structure. The work of the later Heidegger is based upon a linguistic turn that displaces the existentialism of the earlier work. If lifeworlds are corrupted, then it is because the languages that they make available to agents are not up to answering the question of the meaning of Being. Yet, although this might herald an awareness of the systematic distortion of ordinary communication, in practice Heidegger begins to institute a wholesale condemnation of everyday language, which is incapable of differentiation between distortion and legitimate consensus. He turns increasingly to poetry as a source of authentic responses to Being, but again without the discipline that accompanies, say, Adorno's aesthetics. Heidegger thereby mystifies the very question of Being, finding its articulation in the obscure and gnomic. This in turn sets up problems in the theory of meaning and truth that Heidegger offers. Within the existential framework of the earlier work, meaning could only be grasped as something that was posited (much in the style of Fichte's ego) by an individual subject. As existentialism is abandoned, Heidegger fails to abandon the philosophy of consciousness with it. The linguistic turn, ironically, does not entail any analysis of the structure of language (which may have opened the way to a theory of communication) (PDM: 163). Rather, Being itself takes on the role of agent

(PDM: 150–51). The human subject (*Dasein*) becomes the mere "shepherd" of Being (PDM: 152). Further, Heidegger's hermeneutics, combined with his failure to inquire into the structure of language, leads to a conflation of reason and understanding, which is to say that there is no space for the recognition of rational criteria of debate and assessment, other than in terms of those constitutive of particular lifeworlds (PDM: 133, 149). Heidegger is thus left with a theory of truth as a fateful or contingent "unconcealing" of the meaning of Being. That is to say that Being manifests itself in the contingent movement of history, where each moment of history, each lifeworld, is grasped as a "provincial and yet total" manifestation of truth (PDM: 154). Truth is implicitly equated with history (PDM: 155).

In summary, we have seen that Heidegger responded to the nihilistic crisis of modernity by characterizing modernity in terms of the misguided orientation of culture to the manipulation of particular entities, rather than to a concern with the ontological question of Being. However, as the question of Being becomes more mystical, the possibility of a rational grounding of a critical account of contemporary culture is lost. Although the everyday lifeworld may be inauthentic, it is equally revered as taking a perspective on the question of the meaning of Being. In practical terms, Heidegger's resultant collapse into cultural relativism leaves him with no critical resources to condemn Nazism. Indeed, the 1933 German elections were glorified by Heidegger as a unique opportunity for the German people to will its destiny (PDM: 157). More telling, perhaps, is Heidegger's inability, after 1945, to apologise for his support of the Nazis.[4]

Derrida's personal politics are antithetical to those of Heidegger, being characterized by "the anarchist wish to explode the continuum of history" (PDM: 182), in contrast to Heidegger's authoritarianism. In terms of theory, Derrida approaches the analysis of language more systematically. At the core of this is grammatology, a study orientated to "the alphabet, syllabation, reading, and writing" (PDM: 163, citing I. J. Gelb's definition of "grammatology" from Derrida (1976)). With this approach he attempts to expose and challenge the most basic assumptions of Western culture about the nature of language and meaning. Yet in this project he is explicitly a follower of Heidegger in developing a critique of Western metaphysics. Indeed, for Habermas, he is so much a follower that he ultimately re-enacts Heidegger's return to the philosophy of consciousness, so that he can no more escape relativism and nihilism than could his mentor.

Habermas introduces Derrida's work through his criticisms of Husserl's theory of meaning (from *Logical Investigations*). Crucially, Derrida recognizes that Husserl's account remains trapped within the monological philosophy of consciousness, precisely in so far as Husserl attempts to explain the meaning of signs in terms of the individual language-user's acquaintance with ideal meanings. That is to say that Husserl approaches the problem of the meaning of a sign transcendentally. Everyday meaning is made possible by the presence of an ideal meaning at the ground of any act of bestowing and any act of understanding (or intuiting) meaning (PDM: 171). Husserl approaches language as, paradigmatically, a means for knowing or stating facts. The stability of a sign's meaning or, more significantly, the possibility of repeated use of a sign such that all addressees interpret it in the same way, can only be guaranteed – at least within the framework of the philosophy of consciousness – through the object to which the sign refers being immediately available (or "present") to the language-user. This presence may be the physical object referred to by the sign, or the ideal object internalized by the language-user (PDM: 173). The same meaning is present separately to each, solipsistically isolated, speaker. Derrida objects not directly to the philosophy of consciousness, but rather to what he terms the "metaphysics of presence" that it must presuppose. If this reliance on the presence of the meaning or object of the sign can be undermined, then the philosophy of consciousness must itself be thrown into question, for it becomes unworkable without this metaphysical assumption.

The metaphysics of presence, the presupposition that meaning (and indeed truth) is guaranteed by the presence of some grounding object, can be seen in correspondence theories. The truth condition of a proposition is the actual existence of the state of affairs that it describes. In the case of Husserl, however, Derrida explicates a more subtle nuance to this metaphysics. As an aside, Husserl comments on listening to his own voice uttering the sound of a word as that which accompanies the process of thought. The sound of the word is thus present to the thinker. For Derrida, this causal remark exposes the primacy that Western metaphysics gives to sound – the phoneme – over the written sign (PDM: 176). Derrida's point is that Husserl implicitly undermines the importance of the sign as a entity that can and does exist independently of its creator, in opposition to the transitoriness of the spoken word. In contrast to Husserl's transcendentalism, Derrida's grammatology does not focus upon permanently accessible ideal meanings, nor even on the physical objects and events to which the sign refers. Rather, it focuses upon the physical, written sign itself. It is the written sign, and not a transcendental ideal, that gives the language-user access to meanings. The analysis of the process of interpreting the written sign should therefore overcome the problems of the metaphysics of presence, precisely because the written sign has an existence independent of any speaker or hearer. Derrida builds critically upon Ferdinand de Saussure's structuralist semiology, to argue that signs have meaning through their place in a conventional system of relationships to each other, and not to some present object or meaning (PDM: 179–80).

It is through the permanence of the conventional written sign that Western culture has been transmitted and preserved (PDM: 163). However, the permanence of writing is highly problematic and elusive. Western writing is phonetic, in the sense that it copies the sound of words. It is therefore rooted in phonocentricism (the primacy of sound over writing) and thus misunderstands itself in terms of the metaphysics of presence. Because of this misunderstanding, writing, and indeed Western culture, is in crisis (PDM: 163). On the one hand, for Derrida, writing has a permanence that sound lacks, in the sense that it remains in principle readable despite the absence of its author, or even the death of any audience (PDM: 166). This "absolute readability" is characterized as a promise of understanding (PDM: 177). Yet on the other hand, Derrida characterizes modernity in terms of the corruption of writing, such that the texts that do survive are typically damaged and fragmented (PDM: 165). They are not self-evidently meaningful (for how can they be, if there is nothing present to guarantee the one correct reading?). One is confronted not by a coherent and stable system of meanings, but rather by "labyrinthine mirror-effects of old texts, each of which points to another, yet older text" without any hope of ever attaining a definitive interpretation (PDM: 179). The promise of understanding is thus permanently deferred.

The absolute readability of the text cannot be grounded in presence, nor yet, if the philosophy of consciousness is unworkable, in the will of the individual subject. However, unable to escape the philosophy of consciousness, Derrida reproduces the move that Heidegger made in his "turn" from existentialism to language-orientated thinking. Now writing, rather than Being, takes on the role of subject. Absolute readability is articulated in terms of an "archewriting" [*Urschrift*]. This is "the anonymous, history-making productivity of writing" (PDM: 178), which is to say, the power of writing to create lifeworlds. Yet, like Being, the archewriting is not itself present. It can never ground a definitive reading of a text and thus, in turn, can never by the source of the legitimacy of modernity. Archewriting thus takes on the same mystical form as Being: that of the Dionysian god who is absent. The hope of understanding becomes the promise of his return (PDM: 181). Still more eloquently, Habermas compares archewriting to "a scripture that is in exile" (PDM: 181), and Derrida, like Heidegger, thereby is seen to rehearse the peculiar dialectical trajectory of the rationalism of the Enlightenment back into mysticism and myth.

Derrida's approach to language and writing has two clear consequences for Habermas. First, the status of reason is problematized. In the context of a philosophy of language, this in turn throws into question the viability of universal pragmatics and Habermas's distinction between validity claims.

Derrida's critical approach to reason can be rehearsed as follows. Habermas's allusion to archewriting as scripture provides a clue. Grammatology has served to throw into question the idea of writing as being grounded in a *logos*, which may be understood both in the sense of a Hellenic emphasis upon reason, and in the Christian sense of God's word (PDM: 164). In throwing into question the metaphysics of presence, this double grounding of writing is abandoned. For Derrida, this entails also the abandonment of any notion of truth, including truth as "unconcealment" found in Heidegger. As Habermas presents this, Heidegger still aspired to a position above the inauthenticity of the everyday lifeworld, albeit one that, due to the ultimate ineffable mystery of Being, cannot be guaranteed through a defence of its logical consistency in comparison to the inconsistencies and contradictions of the lifeworld. Derrida, still more radically, rejects this high ground, and does so by rendering the logical criterion of consistency irrelevant (PDM: 188). This is done by questioning the traditional Western opposition of reason and rhetoric. Western philosophy (not least in its manifestation in the Enlightenment) holds that reason is superior to rhetoric. At the core of Derrida's work (and thus at the core of deconstruction) lies the questioning of such hierarchical binary oppositions (just as grammatology challenged speech and writing) (PDM: 187). The political potential of such challenges cannot be denied, for they may lie at the heart of the systematic distortions in communication that interest Habermas, not least in the case of such ideologically contentious oppositions as nature and culture or male and female. However, an undermining of the binary opposition of reason and rhetoric poses unique problems for Habermas.

The primary implication of the deconstruction of reason and rhetoric is that all texts can alike be analysed in terms of their rhetoric. An example of this has already been encountered in Derrida's appeal to a casual aside in Husserl's *Logical Investigations* in order to break open the problem of phonocentricism. Again, a heightened awareness of the rhetorical play of philosophical texts is not necessarily a bad thing, especially if it increases consciousness of systematically distorted communication. However, for Habermas, the wholesale questioning of reason undermines the very notion of *systematic* distortion; indeed, for Derrida, that is the point. On the one hand, the "surpluses" of meaning exposed through analysis of rhetoric are not distortions in Habermas's sense, for they are but one more reading that can be elicited creatively from the text. On the other hand, if reason and consistency have been marginalized, there are no obvious or privileged criteria by which to judge a "system". Habermas is committed to reason precisely as a source of privileged access to truth, and as such to a position from which such critical (and political) judgements can be made. The anarchism of Derrida's position explodes the whole notion of such critical privilege, and implicitly accuses Habermas of a taking a position of dogmatic imperialism over those he would judge. In effect, Habermas's rational truth is no more justifiable than Heidegger's mystical truth.

This critical engagement can be worked through in a little more detail, if we consider the fate of philosophical texts in the hands of a literary criticism inspired by deconstruction. If, as Derrida argues, all texts are alike, then the philosophical text is indistinguishable from the literary text. This is not a matter of simply reading the philosophical text against the grain, which is to say, in spite of the intentions of its authors and traditional audience. It is rather to say that there is no essential difference between a philosophical text and a literary text (PDM: 189). Fiction is not derivative or secondary to more "serious" uses of language (PDM: 193). Rather, the creativity of fiction becomes central, as literary criticism itself adopts rhetoric not simply as an object of analysis but also as a tool of analysis (PDM: 190), and as the world-disclosing power of fiction is given primacy. All texts, including those generated in everyday practice and conversation, are understood as creating worlds (PDM: 201–4). In the terminology of universal pragmatics, all that exists is the expressive power of language (CES: 58). The cognitive and interactive modes of language are mere derivatives from this expressive mode, and the possibility of discursive redemption of the validity claims to truth, rightness and even truthfulness itself is rendered spurious, at least if discourse is understood as a peculiarly rational activity (as opposed to a further exercise in rhetorical world disclosure). Rational adjudication of positions is thus sacrificed in favour of a pluralism of different perspectives.

Habermas responds to these challenges by commenting on Derrida's exchange with John Searle over the nature of speech acts (Derrida 1977, 1982a; Searle 1977). Through an account of Austin's analysis of performative utterances, Derrida attempts to undermine the notion of normal speech, and the universal competences that language-users must possess. If Derrida is successful, then the very project of universal pragmatics is undermined. Derrida makes three critical points that may be considered in turn. First, he argues that the use of performative utterances, such as promises, in everyday life is parasitic upon their use in fiction (e.g. in dramas) and not vice versa (PDM: 195). The argument is that the enacting of a promise, for example, in real life presupposes the adoption of a conventional social role that can be repeatedly adopted in different situations. The participants in a promise are thus, for Derrida, quite literally acting. Only if such acting is comprehensible in the context of fiction, which largely abstracts from the pressures and particularities of real life, can that competence be readily transferred to any real-life situation. Habermas criticizes this argument for presupposing that social roles and theatrical roles are indistinguishable. In reply Habermas emphasizes the illocutionary force that a real life promise has that a fictional promise does not (PDM: 196). This is to say that a real promise has quite different implications for the subsequent actions of the speaker and hearer than does a fictional promise. Habermas's reply in effect summarizes his criticism of the deconstructionist's conflation of real life and fiction: what matters is not the creation of a world, as it might in fiction alone, but the ability to act in response to a world that already exists. This demands that one does not merely interpret the world, but rather solves the problem of how to go on in that world, given real constraints that are beyond one's power to change or negotiate. Habermas does not deny that this world, as a lifeworld, is constituted through a culturally mediated interpretation of the natural environment and conventions of social inter-action, but that does not render it a pure fiction. Nor does it render our actions in this world devoid of real consequences.

To this point, Habermas has done little to reinstate the importance of reason. Real consequences there may be, but our assessment of them may still depend upon the world-disclosing power of rhetoric, rather than upon rational analysis. It is Habermas's response to Derrida's other two criticisms of speech act theory that must serve to reinstate reason. Derrida's second argument concerns the problem of specifying the conditions for the illocutionary success of a speech act (PDM: 96–7). One can imagine ever more subtle changes in the context within which a promise is made that serve to make the precise implications of that promise problematic. (For example, what if the person making the promise had been hypnotised? Is this still a binding promise?) For Derrida this entails that speech acts are necessarily fluid. Again, their consequences must depend upon the world-disclosing power of language, not its cognitive or interactive powers. In reply Habermas points to the competences that ordinary language-users bring to any interac-tion, and not least the competence to draw upon commonly recognized resources in their lifeworld, in order to repair ambiguities and misunder-standings. Participants can come to an agreement about the nature of the situ-ation they are in and the conditions that determine the illocutionary force of a speech act. Crucially, this entails not simply an ability to convince one's opponent rhetorically, but also the ability to thematize problematic validity claims in rational discourse. Only the latter would entail an equally autono-mous contribution from all participants (and thus rational as opposed to a merely factual consensus). Yet, this is still to presuppose the strength of Habermas's position, and not strictly to defend the primacy of reason against Derrida's attack.

Derrida's third argument concerns the possibility of there being multiple good readings of a literary text (PDM: 198–9). August and Friedrich Schlegel, following Kant, both articulated the infinite re-interpretability of literary texts in terms of the concept of Romantic irony. However, the question here is whether this insight can be transferred unproblematically to everyday communication. Are all readings of texts "misreadings", as Derrida claims? Using this hint from the Schlegels, Habermas's response might be understood in terms of the performance of a play. *Hamlet* can be infinitely reinterpreted, and a particular performance will realize but one reading. Other performances will offer different readings, disclosing new worlds. However, in order for this one performance to be realized, the director, the actors, the designers, the lighting crew, the stagehands, and even the theatre management and ice-cream sellers must be able to coordinate their actions. Even if the actor playing Horatio is unhappy with this director's interpretation, he will still be able to be on stage at the right time, speaking his lines appropriately (at the real cost of a poor production, and possibly damage to his career). The actors will accept the legitimate authority of the director, just as the ice-cream seller accepts the authority of the manager. Habermas can thus conclude that the idea of all readings being misreadings is spurious. In situations that are consensually agreed upon by their participants, some readings will be misreadings. It is one thing to contest a director's reading of a play, and quite another to contest their authority to direct you, the contractually obligated actor. The social agent is thus not typically concerned with misreadings, but rather with questionable interpretations of the relationship of an utterance or action to the reality of a culturally constituted lifeworld. The recognition of a questionable interpretation, and the ability to discuss interpretations with others, requires that the (theatrical) actors draw upon their basic communicative competence (and not least the ability to distinguish between the four validity claims). Precisely in so far as this competence entails rational, and not just rhetorical, resources (not least in the counterfactual presupposition of the ideal speech situation), the construction of consensus cannot be a mere act of world disclosure. The very nature of language thus entails a difference between merely factual consensus and rational consensus. World disclosure can at best provide only a factual consensus. In order to live in a world that is already given – a lifeworld – agents must also draw upon their problem-solving capabilities. These include the abilities to identify real objects in the natural and social worlds, to identify binding normative relationships between actors in the social world and, crucially, to resolve disagreements definitively – at least in principle – by raising problems about these identifications at the level of rational discourse.

Habermas's relationship to Derrida can be summarized as follows. Derrida has engaged fruitfully with the crisis of modernity, so that the loss of certainty and unity that occurs with the collapse of a single legitimizing (religious) worldview is understood in terms of a fragmentation of a written textual heritage, and a problematization in its recovery and understanding. Derrida is correct in recognizing that the problem does not lie in the loss of a single grounding presence that could guarantee a correct interpretation of the heritage. However, his argument goes astray precisely where the rhetorical, world-disclosing power of language is given exclusivity. Such an argument collapses into a perspectivism that is as impotent before different political claims as is Heidegger's mysticism. If everything rests upon the rhetorical power of world disclosure, then one has progressed little, if at all, beyond the subjective decisionism that characterizes the philosophy of consciousness. Habermas therefore insists upon complementing an awareness of the world-disclosing power of language with its problem-solving cognitive and interactive powers (PDM: 207). Derrida is ultimately condemned for having an impoverished understanding of language, its intersubjective nature, and the communicative competences required by its users: an understanding that remains trapped within the presuppositions of the philosophy of consciousness.

Horkheimer and Adorno

We have seen that since Kant, European philosophy has struggled with the question of the legitimacy of modernity. Although the tensions of modern society may have been reflected in Kant's critical philosophy, it was Hegel who first brought this reflection to consciousness. The faults and tensions in Kantianism mirror the alienation that characterizes modernity. For Hegel, modernity has lost the cultural unity of the pre-modern world, and even if that old unity was naive and ultimately illusory, it still served to legitimate the practices of, for example, medieval Christendom and the classical world. Marx's materialism goes a step further by identifying class conflict as the source of alienation. Both Marx and Hegel look to a restoration of unity, albeit in a self-consciousness culture, whereby the macro-subject of society can take charge of its own destiny. Modernity has legitimacy as the rationally necessary stepping stone to a better age (PDM: 352). In contrast, the conservative Right Hegelians find the alienating complexity of modernity to be the source of its legitimacy. The issue is not to transcend bourgeois civil society, but to realize its ideal. Modernity allows the individual citizen to realize his or her true freedom, typically as an economic agent within a well-regulated society. This is echoed by the New Right thinkers of the 1970s and 1980s. Alienation is transformed into economic freedom (PDM: 353; and see TCAII: 330). The Nietzscheans side-step this approach by focusing upon the illusions of modern culture. The problem for Nietzsche lies not in the fragmentation of modern culture, but rather in its apparent unity. A culture dominated by science and the rationalism of the Enlightenment inhibits the very possibility of asking the questions that would give it legitimacy. For the Nietzsche of *The Birth of Tragedy*, at least, fragmenting modern culture opens up the possibility of glimpsing older, non-rational sources of legitimation, and placing new demands upon the individual to accept themselves as the creators, rather than mere inheritors, of values. The legitimacy of the age thereby becomes a pressing problem of human choice, but not a problem amenable to objective rational resolution. It is this course that Habermas sees Heidegger and Derrida taking, displacing the Enlightenment commitment to reason by a more or less mystical appeal to the unconcealed, the "différance" or the "trace". Yet, precisely in their abandonment of reason, Habermas sees the Nietzscheans as ultimately incapable of criticizing modernity. Their very return to the mystical leaves a rationally organized modernity untouched. Hence, Habermas's characterization of them as "young conservatives" (MIP: 14).

A critical approach to modernity requires not the wholesale rejection of Enlightenment reason, but rather a critical response that is as sensitive to the advantages of rationality as to its disadvantages. The problem with all the positions reviewed so far is that this balance is either missing – in the case of the Nietzscheans – or misplaced, with both Left Hegelians and Right Hegelians relying upon an account of rationality that is too one-dimensional to account for the complexity of modernization. Horkheimer and Adorno's notion of a "dialectic of enlightenment" may serve to open up this analysis. The dialectic of enlightenment is the reversion of enlightenment reason into pre-rational myth. More profoundly, the argument is that enlightenment and myth are inextricably entwined, with each being present in the other (PDM: 107). This entwining is manifest in modernity, in so far as the rational project of the seventeenth- and eighteenth-century Enlightenment – which understood itself as challenging, through reason and empirical evidence, the claims to knowledge and power that were grounded in tradition, superstition and myth – degenerates into a dogmatic promotion of a single form of knowledge: that of the positivistic natural sciences (PDM: 111). Modern rationality thereby stifles its own critical potential by understanding itself purely instrumentally.

Nietzsche's criticism of Socratic reason places him in much the same relationship to Horkheimer and Adorno as Kant stood to Hegel and Marx. Kant reflected modernity in thought, and Hegel and Marx translated that thought into an explicit understanding of social processes. So, for Horkheimer and Adorno, Nietzsche is one of the "black" bourgeois writers who reflect the self-destruction of contemporary rationality (PDM: 106; Horkheimer & Adorno 1972: 81ff.). The Nietzscheans rehearse the dialectic of enlightenment as an inherently philosophical process. The task remains of relating this process of thought back to its social base. Here Horkheimer and Adorno turn not just to Marx, but all importantly to Weber.

In 1947 Horkheimer published a crucial interpretation of Weber in *Eclipse of Reason*. In effect, *Eclipse of Reason* recapitulates the central thesis of *The Dialectic of Enlightenment*. For Horkheimer and Adorno, it is Weber who begins to recognize the fundamental ambiguity of the role of reason in the process of modernization, in contrast, say, to the optimism of Marx's dialectical working out of the rationalism of capitalist forces of production (TCAI: 144). It is Weber who begins to recognize what Habermas characterizes as the social pathologies of modernization. Habermas sees Horkheimer as specifically taking up two key elements of this Weberian diagnosis of modernity: loss of meaning (which is to say a loss of a unifying, typically religious, worldview); and loss of individual freedom.

The thesis of the loss of meaning is worked out, by Habermas, in terms of four points upon which Horkheimer's and Weber's accounts of modernity converge (TCAI: 350). In summary, both characterize modernity in terms of the rational criticism of mythological, religious and metaphysical worldviews; the split between the rational justification of knowledge claims in the sciences and the purely subjective justification of claims in ethics and aesthetic taste; the fragmentation of moral and aesthetic values into a "polytheism" of incommensurable meanings; the tension between the apparent irrationality of the polytheistic consequences of modernization and the rationality of the learning processes that ground the separate development of science, morality and taste. What is at stake here, however, is the exact understanding of the concept of "rationality". A consideration of each point in turn will serve to clarify the different emphases of Weber and Horkheimer and, as far as Habermas is concerned, begin to point to the weaknesses of their diagnosis of modernity.

In his introduction to the sociology of religion (published in English as the Introduction to *The Protestant Ethic and the Spirit of Capitalism*), Weber lists those areas of culture in which modern Western societies have become uniquely rational (TCAI: 157; and see Weber 1976: 13–23), including: natural science, in terms of its mathematical refinement and systematization, its grounding in controlled experimentation, and its institutionalization in the university; the method of the historical sciences; the intrinsic development of the arts (including, for example, the development of perspective in painting, and rational harmony in music), as well as the systematic application of technology to the design of musical instruments, and the publishing and distribution of the arts through the institution of periodicals, museums, theatres; the development of rational law and administration (not least in the development of the state bureaucracy); and the capitalist economy, which is characterized as much by the importance of rational accountancy methods (such as double entry book-keeping) that allow for the systematic monitoring and assessment of profit and loss, as by the institutionalization of private enterprises and the free market. Finally, for Weber, the West also develops a rational framework within which the individual can motivate and conduct their life. This emerged in the form of ascetic self-denial of the Protestant ethic, and was gradually secularized into a modern sense of professional vocation. The ascetic individual defers short-term pleasures and benefits for the sake of greater or more profound long-term rewards (see Weber 1976: 71). An initial insight to be derived from this list is that rationalization is realized at the levels of culture (science, history, art), society (the institutions of the university, the state and the market) and personality (TCAI: 158–68). Yet, despite the impressiveness of this list, the concept of "rationality" remains ambiguous. It is not clear, for example, if one can label the experimental testing of a scientific hypothesis "rational" in the same sense as one might label the inner logic of musical harmony, or the organization of a bureaucracy.

We may begin to unpack "rationality", in particular with reference to the first point of convergence between Weber and Horkheimer, in terms of the concept of "disenchantment". Modern cultures are disenchanted: literally, the magic has been taken out of them. Weber traces this process of disenchantment originally in the context of religious belief. The rationalization of symbol systems, such as religions, is understood by Weber in two respects. On the one hand, rationalization entails the establishing of an internal consistency within the religion, by clarifying and refining basic concepts, and establishing a logical consistency among its principle propositions. It is in this sense that one might also consider musical harmony or even legal systems as being rationalized. However, for Weber, in contrast to modern science, rationalization in religion and metaphysics typically has a limit, in that basic categories, such as "god" and "being", cannot themselves be subject to rational scrutiny. In the terminology that Habermas adopts from Piaget and Kohlberg, they remain conventional, and cannot achieve post-conventionality (TCAI: 214). On the other hand, rationalization entails establishing a coherence between religious belief and the modern, disenchanted, worldview. Religion is made coherent with a world that is understood primarily in terms of universal causal relationships, and the possibility of calculable instrumental manipulation of objects in the world (TCAI: 175, 213). Disenchanted (or, in theological terminology, demythologized) religions accept that prayer cannot be expected to bring about a change in the causally determinate order of the world. This crucially establishes a distinction between one's orientation to an objectified external world, and one's moral and expressive orientation to one's subjective inner life. At its most profound, this is seen in the Calvinist doctrine of predestination. The acceptance of a predetermined natural order is mapped, coherently, on to the notion of a predetermined divine order. An individual's salvation (or damnation) is thus already decided, and no actions on their part can change it. The doing of good works and even the achievement of worldly success cannot thus be seen as causal factors. One can neither work nor pray one's way into heaven. Worldly success can, however, be understood as a sign that one might already be among the saved (PE: 98ff.).

Consideration of the disenchantment of worldviews has already led to the second point of convergence. Disenchantment grounds a separation of (in Habermasian terminology) cognitive validity claims from normative and expressive claims. Weber distinguishes the cognitive from the moral and expressive in terms of formal and substantial rationality. Formal rationality embraces the assessment of the appropriateness of means for the achievement of a given end. The former entails consideration of the rationality of technique. A technical intervention in the objective world can, at its most basic, be assessed in terms of the coherence and consistency of the rules that it obeys (TCAI: 169). In effect, this echoes the requirement for internal consistency noted above for religion. Prayer may be a rational technique in this sense, if there exist strict and coherent rules for its conduct. A more demanding test of the rationality of a technique emerges once the technique is understood as being tested against an independently existing natural (or even social) world. A technique is then rational in this sense of instrumental rationality if it achieves predictable results (TCAI: 169–70). Formal rationality is consummated once there exist criteria by which the rationality of the choice of ends can be assessed (and not merely the means to those ends). Ends become something that can be assessed, for example in terms of the agent's personal welfare, rather than being merely decreed by tradition or authority (TCAI: 170). In contrast to formal rationality, substantive value rationality focuses upon the evaluative content of the ends pursued. A purely value-rational action thus proceeds solely with regard to the consistency between the actions that the agent considers to be required of them in terms of duty, vocation, piety, the pursuit of beauty and so on. This is the position of the ascetic. There is no consideration of the consequences of the action (TCAI: 171). For Weber, such rationality rests upon the subjective acceptance and assessment of the values concerned.

Horkheimer takes up this distinction between the complex of formal (or purposive) rationality and subjective value rationality, but significantly reshapes it. By understanding formal rationality simply in terms of instrumental reason, Horkheimer conflates all that Weber's discusses (both formal and value rationality) under the single label "subjective reason". Weber is taken to have demonstrated that the rationality of an action can only be assessed in terms of the efficiency of the means chosen, so that the ends ultimately remain a matter of subjective choice (however refined that choice may be in terms of logical consistency). Thus, in subjective reason, an object is considered merely in relation to an intrinsic purpose, and not in itself (Horkheimer 1992: 6). Horkheimer therefore pits "subjective reason" against "objective reason". Objective reason is understood not in terms of a simple correspondence to an object, but rather through the possibility that the object itself can meaningfully be described as rational (independently of the subjectively chosen purposes that it might serve). Horkheimer notes that "[t]he philosophical systems of objective reason implies the conviction that an all-embracing or fundamental structure of being could be discovered and a conception of human destination derived from it" (*ibid.*: 12) This is manifest, for example, in the Aristotelian notion of a good life, where the life and conduct of the individual can be assessed in terms of its place within a harmonious totality (*ibid.*: 4; TCAI: 346). What is important here is not what Habermas sees as Horkheimer's return to metaphysics with the concept of "objective reason", but rather the criticism of "subjective reason" that he is generating. He is arguing that bourgeois reason is defenceless against the extremes to which the "black writers", such as de Sade and Nietzsche, take it. Subjective reason cannot defend intuitively moral acts against the intuitive immorality of de Sade (TCAI: 347). If subjective reason is dominant in modernity, then nihilism cannot be avoided.

The third and fourth points of convergence develop this criticism. They concern the paradoxical reverse of the process of disenchantment. Rationalization gives rise to a new mythology in the form of a "polytheism". Weber writes of the "[m]any old gods" that today "arise from their graves, disenchanted and in the form of impersonal forces; they strive to gain power over our lives and resume again their eternal struggle with one another" (Weber 1946c: 149; cited in TCAI: 245). To pursue this, we turn from Weber's introduction to the sociology of religion to his "intermediate reflections" on it: the *Zwischenbetrachtung* (Weber 1946d). Here Weber outlines the implications that the concepts of formal and value rationality have for the structure of society. If value rationality entails the logically consistent elaboration of the symbol systems that cluster about certain values, then Weber proposes that each of these "value spheres" will develop according to their own inherent logic. Such value spheres will include the natural sciences, law and morality, art and religion. Science has "truth" as its guiding value, so law has "justice", morality the "good", and art "beauty" (TCAI: 176–8). Each sphere allows for the possibility of rationalization as a process of "value enhancement" (TCAI: 176). In science this develops through the elaboration of the scientific method. Law and morality are seen by Weber as developing ever more consistent and universal conceptions of justice (through stages of traditional law, the ethics of personal conviction and the ethics of responsibility, anticipating Habermas's adoption of Kohlberg) (TCAI: 177). Even in art there is a working out of basic aesthetic experiences (perhaps not simply under the value of "beauty", but also under "mimetic" and "expressive"). Weber maps this in most detail in his account of the rationalization of music, with particular reference to the way in which the Pythagorean understanding of the mathematical principles that underpin the harmonic scale are worked out and refined in Western music. Habermas gives this account a systematic presentation by reference to the three domains of the natural world, social world and the subjective world of the person, and their associated validity claims. In effect, Weber is seen to have begun to explicate the fundamental structures of the theory of communicative action (TCAI: 234–42). The process of modernization, like the emergence of capitalism, can be understood in terms of the differentiation of these distinct value spheres (or, in Habermas's terminology (TCAI: 187), cultural subsystems) (TCAI: 243–4).

It is on this basis that Weber can begin his critical diagnosis of the state of capitalism, and thus begin to identify the pathological effects of rationalization. Differentiation entails that the unity secured through religion is lost. As we have seen, on Habermas's account, an archaic culture dominated by religion will not yet have differentiated the three validity claims. Disenchantment brings about precisely that differentiation, but for Weber it does so at the cost of conflict between the different value spheres. This is not simply a question of the divergence between what counts as rational technique and method in science, art and law. It is rather the recognition that an original position in which the true, the good and the beautiful, and thus the holy, are in harmony has been lost. The values about which rational techniques develop may be incommensurable or in conflict. In "Science as a Vocation" Weber makes the following observation: since the rise of aesthetic modernism, for example in Baudelaire's *Les Fleurs du mal*, "it is a commonplace that something can be true although, and in the respect that, it is not beautiful, not sacred, and not good" (Weber 1946c: 148; cited in TCAI: 246). Values offer the perspective through which we experience a single reality. But as values multiply and diverge, that "reality" is fragmented (TCAI: 240–41). What is true for the classical poet is not true for the Romantic; what is true for the Germans may not be true for the French (see Weber 1946c: 148). Horkheimer merely reinforces this argument. As the holy finds itself no longer grounding the true, good and beautiful, but possibly in conflict with them, faith becomes increasingly private, dogmatic and potentially fanatical (TCAI: 348).

For Weber, the crisis of the loss of meaning becomes acute precisely in so far as the individual and the community must move between, and internalize, competing values (and thus continually choose between different gods within the polytheistic pantheon). In summary, the rational development of society as a whole leads to a differentiation of value spheres, and the rational development of these in turn cumulatively leads to an overarching irrationality, for the whole no longer makes sense. The nihilism of modernity is thereby confirmed. No one set of values can secure its legitimacy. For Weber, the modern individual is then thrown back upon their own resources. Polytheism is an "existential challenge" (TCAI: 247), demanding something closely akin to Heideggerian authenticity. The parallel between Weber and Heidegger becomes stronger once the second pathology, the loss of freedom, is considered, for both Heidegger and Weber are offering an image of the modern individual as being thrown against the contingency and givenness of historical existence, over which they have no power. But it is also in the exploration of modern (bourgeois) individuality that Horkheimer and Adorno begin to make their distinctive contribution to this analysis.

Weber's thesis of the loss of freedom is summarized in the image of modern society as an "iron cage" (TCAI: 248, citing Weber 1976). As capitalism develops, from the eighteenth century onwards, so the subsystems of the economy and state, within which action is governed purely by purposive rationality, become increasingly autonomous (TCAI: 244). This is to say that the ends to which these systems operate can no longer be questioned. At best, the substantive resources of value enhancement will merely further refine the subsystems in terms of such values as efficiency in social organization and productivity. The emergence of such autonomous subsystems is understood by Weber as a shift from a culture in which economic profit is pursued on an ad hoc basis, as a means to the achievement of other, subjectively chosen ends, to a culture in which profit is pursued systematically (TCAI: 223). This is explained, in large part, through the cultural development of Protestantism. The Calvinist ascetic seeks signs of salvation not in occasional good works (as might the Catholic), but rather in the conduct of their life as a whole. Thus all their actions must be organized, with increasing consistency and method (hence "Methodism"), around the ascetic values that define their religious convictions (TCAI: 223–4). Such consistency demands that all actions are rationally calculable in terms of their consequences for the system. Whereas the Protestant entrepreneur thereby infuses their economic activity with ethically charged values, they also open the way to a secularized economic (and administrative) activity that is morally neutralized. The rational consistency of the system can be divorced from any subjectively chosen and motivating moral values. Hence, from a Weberian perspective, there occurs the autonomous growth of modern bureaucracy, culminating in Adorno's image of the "totally administered society" (TCAI: 351; see TCAII: 312). At best, such bureaucracies are justified by reference to broad, utilitarian conceptions of human happiness or well being (TCAI: 352).

But if asceticism is the form that personality takes during the development of capitalism, it is not necessarily its form in mature or late capitalism. Here Weber refers to "specialists without spirit" and "sensualists without heart" (Weber 1976: 182). The former conform to modernity, accepting their place within a given subsystem. The latter pursue personal expression, exploiting the predictable resources of the system, wholly indifferent to any moral responsibility to others (TCAII: 323–4). By focusing on a subjective reason that is understood in terms of instrumentality, Horkheimer and Adorno develop this account of modern personality structures by situating self-preservation as the only coherent motivation left. The specialist and the sensualist alike are pursuing strategies that allow for their survival in modernity. This is the core of the analysis offered in "Excursus I: Odysseus or Myth and Enlightenment" in *The Dialectic of Enlightenment*.

In an ironic challenge to Nietzsche's celebration of Greek tragedy, Horkheimer and Adorno turn to Homer's *Odyssey*, finding in the figure of "cunning" Odysseus not a primal authenticity, but rather the model of bourgeois reason. The episodes of Odysseus's voyage home exemplify central Weberian themes. At its heart this is a voyage of enlightenment, as Odysseus attempts to escape the realm of myth – the polytheistic world of Poseidon – in order to secure a genuine, non-mythical home (PDM: 108). In Horkheimer's terminology, we might see home as the emphatic content of objective reason. Put into Hegelian–Marxist terminology, it is the attempt to escape one's alienation, and thus to escape one's enthralment to fetishes. Odysseus attempts this through acts of disenchantment. The gods and other mythical beings are reduced, in Odysseus's calculating mind, to predictable forces. He re-enacts the process by which archaic societies come to make fundamental distinctions between the natural and the social (PDM: 115; and see § "From archaic society to capitalism", p. 122). The very predictability of mythical figures allows Odysseus to objectify them and thus outwit them. Poseidon responds in a predictable way to the promise of offerings. If the Ethiopians are making sacrifices, Poseidon will accept them, and will thus be confined for that moment to Ethiopia, unable to touch Odysseus (Horkheimer & Adorno 1972: 50). We may, as an aside, note how the absence of a god is no longer something to be lamented, as in the case of Nietzsche's Dionysus, but rather something to be worked for and exploited. In this framework, sacrifice itself is disenchanted. It comes to be understood as a calculable exchange. Odysseus makes sacrifices no longer to pay honour to the gods, but rather to control them (*ibid.*: 49–50). Odysseus's facility in instrumental reasoning thereby guarantees his survival. The dialectical turn of this enlightened thought back into myth is revealed in the cost that Odysseus must pay for survival. If Weber's dialectic of rationalization (TCAI: 164) culminates in a loss of meaning and freedom, more radically still, Horkheimer and Adorno's dialectic of enlightenment culminates in the "atrophy of individuality" (TCAI: 354). Reason threatens to destroy the very humanity that it made possible (PDM: 110), and so makes the triumph of a return home ring hollow.

Two episodes are crucial. The Sirens lure sailors to their deaths. They drown in vain attempts to reach the Sirens' rocks. The Sirens' attraction lies not in the sensuousness of their song, but rather in the fact that they know the whole history of the person to whom they sing. They exchange this knowledge of the past for their victim's future. Whereas in an older myth, Orpheus could simply take on the Sirens in a form of musical combat and out-play them, the all too human Odysseus must outwit them. This he does by stopping the ears of his crew with wax – so that they cannot hear the Sirens – while having himself bound to the mast. He will listen, like the modern concert-goer, unable to enact what the music demands of him, and does so only because of his mastery over his crew (Horkheimer & Adorno 1972: 33–4). This elegantly simple act of cunning turns on Odysseus's ability to deny himself. There is an inflection of asceticism about it. Here, for Horkheimer and Adorno, is the key to Weberian disenchantment. Although instrumental reason is overtly used to control the external world (of nature and society), it can only be so exercised if there is a corresponding control of the inner world. The agent must subdue their own natural instincts. Agents internalize the moment of sacrifice, turning themselves into predictable (and thus controllable) objects (PDM: 109–10). Homer exposes this in the second episode. When escaping the Cyclops, Polyphemus, Odysseus is asked, "Who is there?" He replies *"Udeis"*: "Nobody". He outwits Polyphemus precisely because as an enlightened agent he can distinguish between the realm of language and the realm of reality. Words are human constructions that can have double meanings. The poor sap Polyphemus takes words at their face value. Yet, Odysseus's utterance also betrays his return to myth. He is in danger of becoming the very nobody that he merely pretends to be, and at his own risk and the risk of his crew he has to reveal his trick to Polyphemus, winning back his identity, or at least securing anew the mythical identification of his name with his self (Horkheimer & Adorno 1972: 60).

Briefly to unpack this Homeric imagery, Horkheimer and Adorno are arguing that in order to survive in contemporary society, the individual must adapt to the instrumental rationality of social systems. Because the only options left are those of self-preservation or self-destruction, and the latter is patently irrational, the individual chooses self-preservation regardless of the cost. In order to do this, the individual alienates itself, shaping itself, body and soul, to the technical apparatus of the machine or the administration (1972: 29–32). The instrumental logic of the system is internalized as the individual's super-ego. The individual disciplines itself so that it actively chooses and enjoys the only pleasures with which the system would reward it anyway. In enacting a sacrificial ritual upon itself (1972: 54), the enlightened individual has begun to inhibit the very possibility of critical (enlightened) reflection on its own instincts and desires (TCAI: 380). There can be no profound questioning of who one is, or what one's goals are. One becomes opaque to oneself. This is the largely vacuous utilitarianism according to which the importance and viability of bureaucracies are judged. The specialist and the sensualist alike serve to reproduce this system, in so far as the former is its operative, and the latter the consumer of its outputs. No desires or dreams can any longer challenge, or even fail to be accommodated by, social reality. Horkheimer thus laments over a past in which reality could be challenged by ideals, by which can be understood the critical challenge that the utopian content of objective reason would pose to a social reality shaped in accord with subjective reason (see TCAI: 381). Now reality is accepted as the ideal (TCAI: 353). The very wealth and opulence that capitalism offers to most of its members serve to blur the distinction between eutopia and dystopia. Liberal capitalism appears to be the best of all possible worlds (the reality of which the "end of history" theorists proclaim (Fukuyama 1992)).

Subjective reason has become so all embracing that the possibility of a critical stance against reality has been undermined. This radical claim is worked out in the theory of reification. As we have seen, the concept of "reification" is introduced by Lukács, in his attempt to fuse Marx's theory of commodity fetishism with Weber's rationalization thesis (see § "The theory of reification", p. 17). "Reification" is here a "prejudice" (TCAI: 355). It is a form of perception of the world that confuses the categories of objective reality, social reality and subjectivity. In broad terms, it marks a reversion to the indifference of nature and society that is characteristic of archaic culture. For Lukács this prejudice is grounded not in rationalization per se, but rather in the form that rationalization takes in capitalism: the abstractions of commodity exchange. The transformation of use value into exchange value is such that social relations among human beings (in producing and trading commodities) are perceived as social relations among the commodities themselves. Through Weber's analysis of purposive (or instrumental) rationality, this structure can be seen to have analogies in other areas of social life, and in particular in bureaucratic administration (TCAI: 356–7).

Where Lukács sees reification as a property of capitalism (and indeed one that will be transcended as the contradictions of capitalism work themselves out), Horkheimer and Adorno both generalize reification historically, and situate it more deeply in the human personality structure. Rather than reification being a result of capitalist commodity exchange, commodity exchange is presented as itself a manifestation of reification. Reification becomes the point of reference according to which human history as a whole is understood. Horkheimer and Adorno ground it in the primal act of self-preservation, and thus the use of instrumental reason to dominate nature (TCAI: 378–80; see PDM: 111). This throws the story of Odysseus into a new light. Odysseus is not by some happy chance the image of bourgeois humanity. He is rather the image of "civilized" humanity (of which bourgeois or capitalist humanity is but the most recent manifestation). Civilization requires the domination of inner nature as much as outer, and thus the dialectic of enlightenment has its full force in the recognition that at the very moment that enlightenment differentiates the categories of nature and society it also presupposes a new confusion of them.

This places Horkheimer and Adorno's relationship to Nietzsche into perspective. *The Dialectic of Enlightenment* reproduces Nietzsche's analysis of a fall from grace. While Nietzsche situates this with Socrates (and Heidegger follows suit), Horkheimer and Adorno situate it historically more deeply in the formation of the post-Neolithic personality structure. This parallel entails that Horkheimer and Adorno, as much as Nietzsche, Heidegger and Derrida, must resort to the quasi-mystical in order to articulate a consciousness that is not reified. If reification is grounded in the domination of nature, and thus the instrumental relationship between the human subject and the natural object, only a non-instrumental relationship to nature can serve as a critical standard. Adorno's concept of "mimesis" becomes, on Habermas's account, the placeholder for a primal reason, which is to say, for that which is sacrificed in the primal act of self-discipline that is required in order to form the self (TCAI: 382, 384). But if the rationality of modern society (including the cultural subsystem of science) is condemned as subjective reason, and if no more substance can be given to Horkheimer's "objective reason" than the appeal to mimesis, then Horkheimer and Adorno are left as defenceless against the collapse of modernity into myth and nihilism as are Nietzsche, Hiedegger and Derrida. At best, Adorno can self-consciously pursue the contradictions of reified "identity thinking", with hope not of escaping them, but of merely demonstrating their falsehood and violence (PDM: 186). At worst Habermas suggests that with Adorno philosophy "intentionally regresses into gesticulation" (TCAI: 385).[5]

Foucault

Before we conclude, a brief rehearsal of Habermas's response to the third of the Nietzscheans, Foucault, is required. Where Derrida's attack on speech act theory poses a direct threat to Habermas, Foucault's threat is more subtle.

This is because Foucault and Habermas appear, on the surface at least, to have much in common. Foucault's rejection of modernity and the project of the Enlightenment rests upon a diagnosis of Western culture and the social sciences that is similar to Habermas's. Both characterize modernity in terms of reification. Foucault's analyses of "biopower" (whereby the human body and its desires are disciplined and regulated through behavioural and moral regimes that have a supposed scientific justification) overlaps and complements Habermas's analyses of colonization of the lifeworld. Indeed, Foucault's formulation of a "double movement of liberation and enslavement" (to encapsulate the manner in which attempts to attain increased freedoms lead inevitably to their increased confinement and regulation) echoes Habermas's formulations of colonization and, for example, his criticisms of the workings of the welfare state (PDM: 246). More precisely, both identify a key source of colonization in the role of the *Geisteswissenschaften* (or what Foucault refers to as the "human sciences"), and in particular in the scientism and instrumentalism that characterize their positivistic approaches to the understanding and manipulation of human and social phenomena. Both thus seek to expose the value-orientations that are concealed behind the positivist's pretence of value-neutrality (PDM: 265, 269), and they both identify the root of the failure and self-deception of the human sciences in the aporias of the philosophy of consciousness (PDM: 261).

Habermas is thus appreciative of the details of Foucault's arguments or, perhaps more precisely, he is appreciative of Foucault's work as a historian documenting the abuses that occur through the application of the positivistic social sciences in the fields of medicine, psychiatry and law. His criticism of Foucault is of Foucault as a philosopher. This criticism revolves around Foucault's attempt to side-step, rather than resolve, the problems of the philosophy of consciousness. The aporia of the philosophy of consciousness is diagnosed by Foucault in terms of the anthropocentrism that lies at the heart of the human sciences. While positivism and Enlightenment thought in general present their knowledge claims as being of universal validity, for Foucault, such universal claims to "truth" and "knowledge" are nothing more than the projections of a particular and historically contingent human subjectivity, for knowledge claims are entwined with the power struggles that shape the understanding of the normal and natural at any given moment in history. Foucault thus abandons the subject altogether, and aspires to an "anti-science" that does away with the universality claimed by scientific explanation. Instead he strives to focus objectively and empirically on the historically particular, and upon events and experiences that rupture the illusory coherence of Enlightenment knowledge.

Yet, underlying this attempt to outwit Enlightenment science, there is a philosophical problem that echoes Habermas's concerns in *Knowledge and*

Human Interests. This is the problem of the relationship between empirical science and transcendental argument, which is to say, between the empirical claims made by a science (or indeed Foucauldian "anti-science") and the conditions of its possibility (see Foucault 1973: 318–22). The echo here is perhaps not that surprising. During the 1960s, Habermas and Foucault both respond to the problem of positivism in the social sciences as a problem that has its roots in Kantian epistemology. For Habermas, this leads to the theory of cognitive interests. For Foucault, it involves the development, first, of what he terms the "archaeology of knowledge" and, secondly, a "genealogical historiography" grounded in Nietzsche's theory of the will to power. It is Habermas's reconstruction and criticism of this development that we can now pursue, for it is here that the differences between Foucault and Habermas are most profound.

In *The Order of Things*, Foucault describes three epochs – the Renaissance, the classical age, and modernity – each of which entails a different regulation of discourses or, put otherwise, constitution of science (and is thus a different structure of thought or, in Foucault's terminology, a different *episteme* (Foucault 1973: 191)). In brief, knowledge as an understanding of the relationships that exist between natural objects is understood in the Renaissance in terms of the doctrine of natural signatures. Divinely given similarities between the visible properties of objects are expressive of inherent similarities and thus relationships between objects and their uses. In the classical age, this doctrine of signatures is replaced by an understanding of nature as that which can be represented by systems of conventional signs. In Spinoza's phraseology, the "order of things" can be mapped through the "order of ideas". Nature is thus understood through the taxonomic ordering of the signs that represent things (*ibid.*: 58). The system of signs is understood as a transparent medium linking the representation to what is represented. Foucault looks not merely to the overt taxonomies of natural history (such as the Linnaean system), but also to political economy and universal grammar (PDM: 258–9).

Only in the modern age, and most significantly with Kant, does the inquirer begin to reflect upon the system of representation, and thereby becomes aware of the human being not merely as that which brings together the threads of representations into a whole, but as that which constitutes the object of knowledge. The sign ceases to be a transparent medium, and is instead part of that which makes knowledge and the object of knowledge possible. In this reflection, the modern age therefore inaugurates humanity's "epistemological consciousness" of itself (PDM: 260; Foucault 1973: 309). For Foucault, this entails that modernity understands humanity as at once a finite being in the physical world, and as that which establishes the order of that world. Despite its very finitude, it is still required to perform the superhuman task of constituting and comprehending the material world. This is, in effect, what sets the agenda for the philosophy of consciousness, from Kant, through Fichte, Hegel and the German Idealists, to Husserl and Heidegger in the twentieth century. The philosophy of consciousness struggles to reconcile a double understanding of the subject, as at once infinite and finite. If knowledge claims are to be grounded as true and certain, then the finitude and contingency of the human subject must either be overcome or concealed.

On the one hand, in political terms, Foucault charts precisely this process in the constitution of madness and criminality in the eighteenth and nineteenth centuries. All that is non-rational comes to be perceived as a threat to the rational (and thus infinite and universal). The mad and criminal are not merely isolated from public life, but, in large part through a humane concern with their suffering, a cure is also sought for them. Crucially, such cures entail processes of self-reflection that mirror those definitive of the modern *episteme*. Regimes of self-reflection are encouraged, through which the insane and criminal may come to recognize and exorcize their own non-rational impulses. The rational subject is instructed to gaze, monologically, upon itself and others, in a process of objectification and analysis (PDM: 245). On the other hand, if the history of madness (and indeed the histories of punishment and sexuality) documents the struggle to repress the finite foundations of knowledge in the human sciences, then it is this struggle that is also being reflected in the philosophy of consciousness. Kant attempts to ground the finite being's knowledge in the universality and rationality of the transcendental ego. Hegel offers a process of developing self-consciousness, where *Geist* restores its infinite nature by recognizing itself in the alienated, and finite, objects of the material world. This is echoed in Lukács's proletariat as the subject–object of history, and even in Freud's goal of displacing the id with the ego (PDM: 263). Crucially, if, as Foucault argues, such aspirations are doomed to failure, then the attempt to overcome the finitude and contingency of the human subject is in fact merely the concealment of that finitude.

From this rehearsal of Foucault's arguments, Habermas may be seen to be reading archaeology fundamentally as a response to Kant, and crucially to the status of transcendental analysis. First, Foucault has situated Kant at a particular moment in history. The Kantian *a priori* is thus robbed of its appearance of universality, for it is revealed as the projection of a specific historical manifestation of subjectivity, as opposed to subjectivity as such. But, crucially, Foucault cannot make the same move that Hegel (and indeed Lukács) made in responding to Kant. Still within the philosophy of consciousness, Hegel could identify the Kantian transcendental subject as one moment (one form of consciousness) in a progress towards self-consciousness of a macro-subject. But if there is no such thing as subjectivity as such – and thus no macro-subject any more than there is a given human nature – then the *epistemes* can be related only in terms of their difference from one another. If there are no overarching notions of reason, truth or even knowledge – for all are constituted within an *episteme* – by which any particular *episteme* can be judged, then there is no sense of historical progress, or the gradual unfolding of knowledge. The seventeenth and early-nineteenth centuries mark radical ruptures, and not, as they might from a Hegelian perspective, moments in the development of European culture.

Yet, on the other hand, Foucault remains deeply indebted to Kant. The notion of the *episteme* as that which is constitutional of knowledge is Kantian, albeit that the universality of the Kantian synthetic *a priori* has been abandoned. In addition, Foucault is aware that there is no ground for knowledge claims outside the *episteme*. He is critical of his own early work on madness, precisely because he there sought the authentic voice of madness, the truth of madness prior to its constitution by science (PDM: 240). This is no pre-discursive truth or knowledge. In Kantian terms, such knowledge claims would correspond to the nonsensical metaphysical aspiration to grasp the noumena. Yet, if Foucauldian archaeology is Kantian, it is still Kantianism without the subject. Following structuralism, Foucault conceives of the synthetic role of the transcendental subject being taken over, in the *episteme*, by an anonymous, rule-guided ordering of elements (PDM: 256).

For Habermas, the core problem with Foucauldian archaeology lies in its inability to ground itself as critique. While Foucault's intention is seemingly to expose the contradictions and deceptions of modern science, the relativism that is implicit in archaeology, such that each *episteme* is merely different from, rather than better or worse than the others, begs the question of why one should work to break down this current *episteme*, for any subsequent *episteme* would be as incommensurable with modernity as are classicism and the Renaissance, and thus in so sense better or worse. By abandoning the philosophy of the subject, one is left with no transcendent criteria by which the truth or justice of a postmodern *episteme* could be judged. Foucault himself responds to this problem in his shift to genealogy. This is to suggest that a concern with constitutive rules (and thus with *episteme*) alone is insufficient. Analysis must also embrace the application and implication of those rules in practice (PDM: 268). Rules cannot regulate themselves, so the structuralist conception of an anonymous ordering of elements is insufficient as an explanation of the movement or change of *epistemes*. Foucault here turns to the phenomenon of power, initially in the earlier writings in terms of a somewhat ad hoc concern with institutional and social practices, before more rigorously focusing on the role that power plays in struggles over knowledge, and thus in the constitution of an *episteme*.

Foucault's genealogy is derived from a reading of Nietzsche. Foucault's inspiration is not merely *On the Genealogy of Morals* and *The Will to Power*, but also "On the Use and Abuse of History for Life", the second of Nietzsche's *Untimely Mediations*. The intentions of the archaeology are thus reinforced, as genealogy continues to challenge orthodox, Enlightenment approaches to the writing of history. Crucially, there is a rejection of hermeneutic approaches that present the task of the historian as an inter-pretative engagement with texts or documents from their position in the present. Foucault seeks rather to expose the illusion of the privileged position of the present by demonstrating its contingency. Again, he aspires to objectivity by analysing the constitution of a given moment in history, while himself side-stepping that constitution. Now it is power that takes on the dual role of a transcendental and yet empirical condition for the possibility of knowledge (PDM: 256). The hermeneutic concern with the meaning of a document (and with the author as its origin) is thus displaced by treating documents as monuments to power struggles. Precisely in so far as they embody knowledge claims, documents become, as it were, points at which power has crystallized. Human and social groups are controlled, as Nietzsche suggests in his analysis of master and slave moralities, by constructing edifices of knowledge claims that will constrain the behaviour in terms of certain conceptions of the normal, natural and good. The gaze of the genealogist is thus cynical, precisely in so far as the shifts and appar-ent developments in knowledge formations, which are identified with a stoic acceptance by the archaeologist, are explained in terms of expressions of a fundamental will to power (PDM: 248–53). At its most profound, this analysis pursues power relationships into the interactions of groups, face-to-face confrontations, and struggles over the constitution and regulation of the body. It recognizes the manner in which the constitution of normal-ity is at once a process of boundary creation that excludes and subjugates groups that, through this process, becomes heterogeneous. The genealogist's focus on power is thus a focus on the sensual and the contingent, and above all it stands in opposition to any universalization of knowledge claims (as themselves no more that the attempt to exercise power over others).

Superficially, the genealogy appears more conducive to a well-grounded critique of modernity than does archaeology, precisely in so far as it allows for the characterization of modernity not merely as a form of knowledge, but rather as an exercise of power. Yet, for Habermas, this is only a superficial appearance. Ultimately, the problems of grounding remain, for Foucault must justify the status of the knowledge claims made within gene-alogy. On one level, there is the danger that power itself becomes a univer-sal phenomenon, that substitutes for the role of the subject in the philosophy of consciousness. In effect, Foucault thereby responds to the problems of

Kantianism by turning, unwittingly, to Schopenhauer. Schopenhauer identifies Kant's noumena as the will. That which is itself not constituted – the noumena – and which as such should fall outside language and discursive articulation, is thereby illicitly made available for discussion. In establishing the will to power as the transcendental condition of knowledge, Foucault is in danger of violating his own self-criticism concerning the attempt to establish the authentic, pre-constituted truth of madness.

Further, if the cynical gaze of the genealogist is turned on genealogy, can it be revealed as anything other than itself a play in a power struggle? Foucault may be seen to answer this, and to answer it affirmatively, precisely in so far as he grounds his challenges to orthodox history and social science in exposing the position of the marginalized: the insane, the criminal and people of diverse sexualities. Genealogy appeals to modes of knowledge that have been disqualified by orthodox science, and as such to knowledge claims that articulate the experience of subjugated groups (PDM: 279–80). Yet, for Habermas, this merely takes for granted the injustice of subjugation, rather than striving to articulate a just alternative. It is merely assumed that the inversion of existing power relations, giving voice to those currently subjugated, will be an act of justice. Yet, again, without an overarching theory of justice that transcends particular historical epochs or distributions of power, the liberation of those who are currently subjugated can be articulated merely as a change in power relations, and not as a gain in justice. (Why is it any more just to marginalize the experiences of white middle-class men, than it is to marginalize those of black working-class women?) Again, the question posed by the archaeology returns: what should motivate one to bring about change if one can only achieve difference and not improvement?

Habermas ultimately criticizes Foucault for being unable to avoid relativism. Just as the archaeology merely side-stepped the problems of the philosophy of consciousness by abandoning the subject, so the genealogy side-steps the problems of justifying critique and political involvement by inverting what for Habermas is the proper relationship of knowledge and power. For Habermas, power is legitimated through knowledge, which is to say, through the well-informed redemption of validity claims. By making knowledge a product of power, Foucault removes the possibility of legitimation (PDM: 274). Foucault thereby renders himself insensitive to what Habermas acknowledges as substantial developments in justice and accountability in modern constitutional democracies, as well as developments in the social sciences away from positivism and scientism (PDM: 288–91). In sum, Foucault fails to take seriously the "double movement of liberation and enslavement", focusing merely upon the inevitability of enslavement.

Foucault is thereby condemned as a relativist, but not because he cannot take an objective stance that transcends the movements of history (for

Habermas suggests that any such attempt is doomed to failure, and Foucault's own analyses are as embedded in the present as are those of any other historian (PDM: 277)). Rather, he fails to engage with the inevitable fact that inquiry proceeds from a given moment in history. In contrast to Foucault, hermeneuticians recognize that they write from a specific historical present, but use the past in a critical engagement with that present. Foucault's own attempt at such an engagement is short-circuited, precisely because he is unable to reflect upon his own constitution as an historian (PDM: 279–82). This in turn highlights the subtlety of Habermas's own position. Crucially, the reconstruction of the ideal communication community as a counterfactual presupposition of all communicative interaction does not provide a substantive point that transcends history, but rather a procedural framework through which substantial struggles within and between lifeworlds can seek legitimacy.

One last observation can serve to highlight the divergence between Foucault and Habermas. In *The Order of Things*, Foucault looks to economics and linguistics as core examples of the human sciences. As such, he recognizes, along with the Habermas of *Knowledge and Human Interests*, the centrality of labour and language to human existence (see PDM: 264). Yet, precisely because Foucault lacks Habermas's grounding in both pragmatism and hermeneutics, he becomes trapped within a structuralist paradigm. This at once inhibits any explanation of how discourses or *epistemes* might hook on to and receive feedback from the material world, and of the role that interaction plays in overcoming the philosophy of consciousness. Foucault thus cuts himself off from Habermas's two strategies for managing the tension between the empirical and the transcendental. He can appeal neither to the quasi-transcendental status of labour and language in a theory of knowledge-constitutive interests (see PDM: 272), nor to the interrelationship of language and intersubjectivity, and thus the theory of communicative action, through which Habermas finally extracts himself from the problems of the philosophy of consciousness.[6]

The tasks of a critical theory of society

Responding to Weber

Habermas's review of modern philosophy and social theory seems to confirm the ineluctable failure of all attempts to derive critical resources out of modernism. One either overtly justifies modernism, in all its inequality and repression, in the style of the Right Hegelians, or covertly justifies modernism, by sacrificing the rational resources that Habermas sees as necessary to stabilize criticism. Habermas responds, of course, by arguing that all the positions considered above remain trapped within the philosophy of consciousness. The nature of this entrapment may be explored by returning to Weber.

Weber's sociology is grounded in a theory of action. Weber recognizes the need to distinguish between mere physical behaviour and meaningful action. The collision of two cyclists is mere behaviour, for neither cyclist intended the collision. The apologies or accusations after the collision are action. They are meaningful, because the actors intend to bring about some event in the world: they intend to realize some goal. Weber's analysis of action may thus be seen to rest upon the idea of individual intention, and thus, as Habermas notes, upon a theory of consciousness, not upon a theory of meaning (TCAI: 279). Meaning depends upon the way in which an individual actor interprets a situation, and that interpretation in turn depends upon the goals that the actor intends to realize. The theory of action is thus, from the first, bound to the primacy of purposiveness (and thus to purposive rationality), and is couched within the monological framework of the philosophy of consciousness. In the *The Dialectic of Enlightenment*, Horkheimer and Adorno only consolidate this way of thinking, reducing all action to the instrumental preservation of a solipsistic self.

The implications of the philosophy of consciousness reach further. It was noted above that Marx treats society as being analogous to an individual subject. Superficially, Weber's overt methodological individualism (i.e. his approach to social problems "from below", in terms of the actions of the individuals who make up the social whole) would seem to avoid this problem. Weber approaches society from the perspective of the lifeworld, and thus from the interpretations that individuals make of society. However, because of the inadequacy of the grounding theories of meaning and action, he can only approach the functions of the macro-structures of society in the same terms as he approaches individual action. Social subsystems – the value spheres – are thus handled in terms of a model of purposive rationality that is tacitly assumed to be wholly analogous to the purposiveness of individual actors. The subsystem is thereby treated as an individual subject. Its activities, and the activities of organizations such as bureaucracies and enterprises, are understood as "purposive-rational action writ large" (TCAII: 306).

Habermas's point is that Weber has begun to recognize the two levels of society – of system and lifeworld – albeit only imprecisely. In contrast to Marx's naive optimism with reference to the lifeworld, which assumes that administrative systems will wither away as the macro-subject of society takes command of its own destiny, Weber recognizes the indispensability of systematic organization in complex societies. Weber can describe bureaucratic organizations as "objectified intelligence" or "animate machines"

(Weber 1968: 1402). Yet in this metaphor, the all important concept of purposive-rational action begins to be broken up. A human agent can legitimately be said to work (where "work" is a manifestation of purposive-rational action). Machines, however, "function" (TCAII: 307). The difference is crucial, for it is the difference between the human and the system, and thus the difference between a concept of reason that can be applied to meaningful human action, and a distinct concept (functionalist reason) that can be applied to systems (be these systems actual machines, or the "animated machines" of social systems). This is the difference between the communicative rationality through which the lifeworld is organized, and functional rationality of a system. Weber's recognition of this difference remains imprecise, because the philosophy of consciousness inhibits him from adequately theorizing the intersubjective relationships through which individual agents reproduce the larger social whole. He is thus ultimately unable to make full use of his recognition of the differentiation of value spheres, precisely because he cannot distinguish between differentiation within the lifeworld, and the differentiation between the lifeworld and subsystems. Horkheimer and Adorno again compound this failing, crucially failing to recognise the significance of the differentiation of value spheres (TCAII: 333). By treating all existent social action purely in terms of instrumental reason, they reduce the individual human being to a system that more or less exactly mirrors the larger social systems that they serve. They avoid a decline into a Luhmannesque systems theory, only in so far as they recognize a remaining trace of resistance in the instincts and drives repressed by the system. They recognize that a totally administered society is an "extreme horror", and not, as Luhmann thinks, a "trivial presupposition" (TCAII: 312). However, because such drives are the victims of "reason", as we have seen, they can only be redeemed through the non-rational category of "mimesis" (see TCAI: 354).

A similar impasse afflicts Weber. Habermas comments on the ambiguities and prevarications in his work. In particular, this focuses on the question of whether or not Occidental rationalism has universal significance and validity (TCAI: 178–9). Given that Weber is working against the intellectual background of Dilthey's historicism, which is to say that contemporary approaches to the writing of history strongly repudiated the idea of searching for universal laws of social change, he is inhibited from exploring the possibilities that the theory of rationalization has for an evolutionary account of social change (TCAI: 153–4). He thus tends to lapse into a "culturalist" (or perspectivist) position, whereby Occidental rationalism might have universal significance as a methodology within the *Geisteswissenschaften*, opening up uniquely valuable insights into Western and other cultures, but without thereby saying anything about the value or rationality of those other cultures (TCAI: 179–80). Weber stops short of making judgements about the rationality of social practices in any universalist sense. Thus a "thing is never irrational in itself, but only from a particular rational point of view" (Weber 1976: 194).

This ambivalence can be untangled. Although Weber is well aware of the complexity of the concepts of "rationality" that he deploys, his overt emphasis on purposive-rational action conceals a number of crucial distinctions. Purposive rationality entails that an action is judged in terms of its success in controlling the physical or social worlds. This objective can be universalized, in so far as any culture can be judged in terms of its control over its environment and its social organization (TCAI: 182). Weber is correct in refusing to reduce the overall assessment of a culture to such technical control. However, he fails to see that his own concept of "disenchantment" opens up alternative criteria for judgement. Disenchantment cannot simply be equated with purposive rationality for, more profoundly, it entails the "decentring" of worldviews (in Piaget's sense) (TCAI: 72, 236). Disenchantment involves critical reflection, whereby the subject can distance itself from its immediate involvement with the principle or value under consideration. It is manifest most clearly in the differentiation of value spheres, and the articulation of their inner logics. It is thus what Habermas understands as the rationalization of the lifeworld. Again, Weber's understanding of his own achievement is muddled. The characterization of modern polytheism rests upon the assumption that the incommensurability of the substantive values that lies at the heart of the different value spheres also entails an incommensurability of their formal logics. Rationality is thereby assumed to be fragmented, and the possibility of universal judgement undermined.

Habermas responds by clarify a series of underlying confusions. First, the largely ad hoc list of value spheres that Weber offers can be systematically regrouped. The theory of communicative action thus suggests that any substantial sphere is a manifestation of one of three types: cognitive, normative and expressive (TCAI: 183). Whereas the substance of a particular value sphere may be incommensurable with any other, the processes of disenchantment to which this substance is subjected may be open to judgement according to universal criteria (TCAI: 249). Secondly, this places purposive rationality in perspective. Within the lifeworld, it is the rationality of cognition, and of cognition alone. This still leaves the possibility of reason being fragmented in terms of the three validity claims. But it is precisely Weber's failure to develop a procedural account of rationality that would encompass normative claims, in particular, that inhibits his scope for working through this problem (TCAII: 304). Weber fails to recognize that he has already, in the concepts of "cultural rationality" and "value enhancement", begun to articulate the procedures by which moral and aesthetic values are rationalized, and that crucially (contra the reduction brought about by Horkheimer and Adorno) they are not simply asserted subjectively.

Habermas has thus sought to distinguish both reason at the level of system from reason at the level of the lifeworld and, in the latter, reason in relation to the three principle validity claims. With this apparatus in place, Weber's diagnosis of the pathologies of modernity can be reassessed. Habermas accepts that modernity is characterized by crises in meaning and freedom, but does not accept Weber's explanation of these in terms of the loss of any substantive grounding to purposive rationality. Rather, he approaches this in terms of the relationship of the subsystems of the state and the economy to their environment, a lifeworld composed of a private sphere (constituted from private households) and a public sphere (of communicative networks that support cultural institutions, the press and the mass media). As we have seen (§ "System", p. 175), the state is organized through the medium of power, and the economy through that of money, while the institutions of the lifeworld are organized through communicative action. However, the exchanges between system and lifeworld (such that the economy exchanges labour for goods, and the state exchanges political decisions for mass loyalty) entail that these exchange-relations play a dominant part in defining social roles in the lifeworld. Agents come to see themselves as employees and consumers, clients and citizens (TCAII: 319). What Weber perceived as a threat to individual freedom thereby lies in the dependency of the employee and the client upon their respective subsystems (TCAII: 323).

This dependency is compounded through the loss of meaning. In exchanges with the subsystems, the meaningful and concrete activities and resources of the lifeworld must be treated abstractly. This is to say, particular activities must be reinterpreted in such a way that they are universally comparable and interchangeable. The paradigms of this process remain the transformation of concrete labour into the abstract commodity of labour power, and of use value into exchange value. We have noted above how even the most elementary market exchange encourages a stripping away of all concrete communication, so that the interaction is purely governed in terms of the buyer and seller's separate orientation to price (§ "System", p. 175). But this opens up the possibility that the non-symbolically interpreted goals of the subsystems can begin to intrude into the lifeworld. Relationships and activities within the lifeworld can be interpreted and structured in terms of the non-symbolic media of money and power, rather than the communicative meanings about which cognitive, normative and expressive activities should cluster (TCAII: 322). Weber's "specialist without spirit" is thus the employee whose life is motivated by the pursuit of crudely characterized utilitarian pleasures and successes, and conducted in terms of the functional rationality demanded by the subsystems. The "sensualist without heart" pursues similarly crudely articulated hedonistic goals, but now without the constraint of rationality at all (TCAII: 325). Habermas's point is that such pathological distortions do not occur because of the loss of a unifying religious worldview, nor even because of the increasing complexity of society, but rather because, in the process of the colonization of the lifeworld itself, instrumental rationality (as functionalist reason), has expanded from its appropriate realm of system organization into the lifeworld, and has thereby begun to erode the communicative competences of the members of that lifeworld.

Weber's ambiguity over the universal significance of Occidental rationalization can ultimately be resolved if one is able to recognize that the pathological manifestations of colonization arise from the selective exploitation of the resources that rationalization offers. That is to say that in having conceded ground to historicism, Weber is unable to conceptualize disenchantment as a rationalization of the lifeworld, and thus as an evolutionary learning mechanism (TCAII: 312). For Habermas, as we have seen, only in the rational reconstruction of this learning mechanism can one find the resources necessary to stabilize a rational criticism of modernity. Such criticism would allow for the renewal of effective political action by grounding it in an identification of the conditions under which rationalization degenerates into colonization.

Responding to the first generation Frankfurt School

The final section of *The Theory of Communicative Action* (VIII.3) is entitled "The Tasks of a Critical Theory of Society". Habermas summarizes these tasks in terms of the need to construct a framework within which "interdisciplinary research on the selective pattern of capitalist modernisation" (TCAII: 397) can take place. A critical theory of society must avoid the collapse into conservativism that has afflicted the Young Hegelians and Nietzscheans alike. This it can do only if critical theory can recover the "normative content of modernity" (PDM: 336ff.). The first stage of this recovery entails reformulating Weber's dialectic of rationalization and Horkheimer and Adorno's dialectic of enlightenment in terms of the system–lifeworld model of society. From what we have reviewed above, in this chapter and in Chapter 5, this dialectic may be summarized so: the rationalization of the lifeworld stimulates the growing complexity of social organization; in order to dissipate the risks of organization through the construction and maintenance of mutual understanding, at key points of complexity an evolving society can utilize its learning capacity in order to transfer certain tasks of social organization to the care of non-symbolic steering media; this "mediatization" of the lifeworld (TCAII: 186) (where "mediatization" refers to the process of increasingly organizing social interaction through the steering media of power and money) opens the possibility of a gradual uncoupling of system and lifeworld, such that the subsystems (in particular of the state and the economy) develop according to their own logic; the colonization of the lifeworld occurs as the functional requirements of the autonomous subsystems of welfare-state mass democracies begin to intrude into the lifeworld itself. Colonization thereby marks the moment at which the dialectic of rationalization turns back upon itself, in so far as the very process that the rationalization of the lifeworld has made possible begins to deform the lifeworld, creating pathologies at the level of cultural reproduction, social integration and socialization (PDM: 355). In a Weberian account, colonization would be irreversible. The recovery of the normative content of modernity entails demonstrating that it is not irreversible.

This process of recovery can be explicated by looking more closely at the problem of colonization itself. Habermas begins with the pathologies of modernity, and treats these initially as problems of the lifeworld. Centrally these are problems of the loss of meaning at the level of cultural reproduction (accompanied by a withdrawal of legitimation at the level of society, and a crisis of orientation for the person); anomie at the level of society (with a parallel unsettling of collective identity in culture and personal experiences of alienation); and psychopathologies at the level of the person (accompanied by the cultural rupture of tradition, and the withdrawal of motivation to participate in society) (TCAII: 143). Such pathologies are initially seen as failures of social reproduction, and are part of the everyday experience of social actors. However, the source of such pathologies lies not in the lifeworld as such, but rather in the relationship between lifeworld and system. Here we also begin to see how Habermas's analysis in *The Theory of Communicative Action* differs from that in *Legitimation Crisis*. In so far as the latter had not fully articulated the place of the lifeworld, crises were primarily seen as system crises. Society as a whole managed crises by shifting the burden of the crises between systems. In *The Theory of Communicative Action* the system crises manifest themselves in a disruption of the lifeworld. This, of course, raises the question of the nature of those crises.

Within Western welfare-state mass democracies the subsystems of the economy and the state have a high degree of autonomy, but also a dependence upon the resources of the lifeworld and a mutual interdependence (TCAII: 384–5). As noted above, the inputs to the economy from the lifeworld are labour power and consumer demand; the outputs are income, and goods and services. The inputs into the state are tax revenue and mass loyalty; the outputs are organizational achievements and political decisions (TCAII: 320). In addition, the state requires from the economy material resources, and the economy requires from the state long-term social stability.

While the subsystems may be expected to suffer intermittent periods of disequilibrium, due to insufficient inputs or outputs (and characterized, for example, in the notion of the business cycle), such disequilibria become crises only if the subsystems are unable to meet minimal performance expectations. Long-term failures in material production or social organization will be manifest in the lifeworld in terms of overt conflict and resistance to the economy and the state (TCAII: 385).

Habermas suggests that crisis becomes the endemic condition of welfarestate mass democracies, largely due to the tensions that exist in the realization of the goals of a welfare state. The welfare state is expected to achieve a just distribution of resources, but within the framework of a market economy (NC: 58–9). This at once requires large-scale intervention in both the lifeworld and the economy. The latter at once puts high demands upon the economy in terms of the material resources required and, through increased regulation and intervention, threatens the autonomy of the economy. The potential cost of this is a disruption of the material reproduction of the society. The welfare state similarly places high demands in terms of taxation on the citizen, and can justify taxation only with the delivery of a just social order. The failure or compromise of this provision leads to a crisis in legitimacy, and a withdrawal of the citizens' motivational commitment to the state. This primarily concerns the lifeworld at the level of society, giving rise to anomie (whereby the normative grounding of the state dissipates). Such a crisis can be staved off, however, only if the subsystems can exploit the resources that the lifeworld makes available at the level of culture and personality. Culture can provide interpretative resources to respond creatively to the legitimation crisis. The ideological struggles over the fate of capitalism may be taken as a case in point. As Habermas notes, crises can be interpreted either in terms of a weak state allowing too much licence to the economy (thereby serving to legitimate expanded state administration), or of a strong state fettering enterprise and disrupting the natural equilibrium of the market (and hence New Right condemnation of "big government"). Capitalist ideologies oscillate between these poles (PDM: 356). The personality domain can similarly offer resources, in the form of a strengthening of personal identity that can secure continued social interaction. Here, presumably, educational and other policies to promote responsible citizenship strive to shift the burden of social organization away from the state.

Precisely because these exchanges between the subsystems and the lifeworld are conducted in the non-symbolic media of money and power, the excessive exploitation of lifeworld resources leads to what Horkheimer and Adorno analysed as reification. The non-symbolic media of money and power displace meaningful communication within the lifeworld, crucially at the point of the private household. As Foucault recognizes, administrative intervention infuses subtly and variously into the constitution of private life and selfhood. At the level of culture this leads to the loss of meaning recognized by Weber, and at the level of personality the psychopathological inability to develop normal social competency.

Although not denying the real implications of colonization, Habermas insists that social pathologies are not as all-encompassing as Horkheimer and Adorno believe. He suggests that the contemporary family is no longer the passive dupe of reification. Rather, it has developed genuinely meaningful forms of communication that avoid the systematic distortion of communication typical of colonization. Crucially, this occurs as the family, through the continuing rationalization of the lifeworld, becomes less patriarchal and hierarchical. As evidence of this, Habermas cites the decline in significance of the Oedipal complex. The child no longer confronts a strong authoritarian father figure, and so no longer faces the same problem of internalizing the authority of the system. While this may now lead to greater adolescent insecurity and irritability, it also opens up new resources for the exploration of personal identity and the development of oppositional youth cultures (TCAII: 387–8).

Similarly, Habermas rejects Adorno's radical questioning of mass culture (in the notion of the "culture industry" (Horkheimer & Adorno 1972: 120ff.)). Early Frankfurt School accounts of the mass media would suggest that they should be understood as non-symbolic media. Indeed, at his most radical, Adorno argues that the culture industry, particularly in the form of advertising, serves to bring the consumer's judgements of utility (and thus of use value) under the control of the economy, thereby eliminating subjective (and meaningful) choice. In reply, Habermas distinguished between two types of media that relieve the burden of establishing mutual understanding. One contains the non-symbolic media of power and money; the other contains "generalised forms of communication" (TCAII: 390). Such forms are sufficiently abstract to be divorced from any particular context. However, they continue to require the communicative competences of the lifeworld in order to be interpreted. Thus, modern mass media may be highly concentrated, communicating a highly structured and selective message, and this allows them to remain as significant tools of social control. However, precisely because the reception of these messages requires the hermeneutic skills of the lifeworld, they can be debated, challenged and subverted. In part, this encourages the media to internalize certain controls (such as ethical standards of good reporting), and open themselves up to feedback from the receiver of the message (TCAII: 390–91).

Habermas's concluding contention is that the rationalization of the lifeworld remains a vital force in contemporary society. The post-conventional development of the modern personality does not merely facilitate the continuing questioning of structures and patterns of behaviour within the lifeworld (hence, for example, the scrutiny given to the family since the Second World War), but also allows for active responses to colonization. Such responses will, however, take diverse and shifting forms. Habermas cites examples of the "new politics", which is concerned with human rights, quality of life, individual realization and participation (in contrast to the "old politics" of labour against capital), the peace movement, pressure groups centring upon such issues as health and ageing, the women's movement and the green movement (TCAII: 392–4). If the critical theorist is to play a role in this, then it is not as Derrida's rhetorician, but rather as the mediator between the public and specialist expert groups, renewing the potential within the public sphere. It is to this role that we turn in Chapter 7.

CHAPTER 7

Law and democracy

Introduction

The political changes of the late 1980s and 1990s were even more dramatic than the ideological and cultural shifts of the preceding decades (BFN: 491–2, 514). For a European, the fall of the Berlin Wall is the mid-point of this period. This extraordinary event was the fulcrum upon which turned the exposure of the economic and political bankruptcy of the old Soviet Union, the subsequent reunification of Germany and the reshaping of Central Europe (as, on the one hand, countries such as Poland, that were independent but effectively occupied reasserted their autonomy and, on the other hand, states such as Lithuania, the Ukraine and Uzbekistan emerged from their absorption in the USSR). This change was complemented by the less dramatic but no less significant expansion and strengthening of the European Union in the West (culminating in its incorporation of various countries from the old Soviet bloc in 2004). An important consequence of these events, repeatedly noted by Habermas, is an increase in economic and political migration from the impoverished margins of global and European society to its affluent centres (see BFN: Appendix II; IO: Ch. 8). From a global perspective, this was also the period that saw a series of challenges to the status and legitimacy of the United Nations. At the core of this was the crisis of Iraq, and the two Gulf Wars (of 1991 and 2003). But to this list may be added the necessity of UN intervention in Serbia and Somalia, and the civil war in Rwanda. Finally, the first decade of the new century was marked by "9/11" and the supposed "war against terror" (PTT: 25ff.; FHN: 101ff.). The latest stage of Habermas's intellectual trajectory occurs as much in response to this political and historical context as it does through the momentum developed in working out the problems and implications of the theory of communicative action.

Habermas has commented on current political issues throughout his career (intermittently published as collections of "minor" political writings, or *Kleine Politische Schriften*). With the completion of *The Theory of Communicative Action*, these writings took on, at least for an English-speaking audience, an importance that they had not had since the 1960s. They marked a new merging of Habermas's political commentary with his social and political theory. Collections such as *The New Conservativism* (originally published between 1985 and 1987), *A Berlin Republic* (1995), and *The Postnational Constellation* (1998) engage with European and in particular German politics, not least through the possibility of its historical understanding (PC: 1–57), while also developing the themes of his major theoretical essay of this period, *Between Facts and Norms* (1993). This contribution "to a discourse theory of law and democracy" applies the social theory and philosophy worked out in *The Theory of Communicative Action* in a largely normative account of the modern legal system, with particular reference to the need for its legitimation in a democratic public sphere. By focusing on the nature of constitutional government, *Between Facts and Norms*, along with a collection of complementary essays, *The Inclusion of the Other*, addresses not merely the legitimacy of the modern nation state but also that of transnational organizations such as the European Union and the United Nations. As such it offers a powerful and presentient framework for the analysis of the crises of contemporary global society. The initial objective of this final chapter will be to outline the basic argument of *Between Facts and Norms*, to highlight its links back to Habermas's earlier work, and to underline its contemporary relevance. Despite the length and complexity of the book, this can be done relatively briefly (not least thanks to the summary commentaries that Habermas himself has already provided). The chapter will conclude with a summary of Habermas's understanding of the role of the philosopher in contemporary society.

Law and democracy

First thoughts

Habermas has shown a strong interest in law throughout his career. This is unsurprising given the role that law plays, as the core policy instrument of state administrations, in the organization and integration of complex societies. Hence in the 1960s, apart from philosophical reflections on the doctrine of natural law published in *Theory and Practice* (TP: 88–141), *The Structural Transformation of the Public Sphere* discusses the development of European constitutions from a basis in private law – which protects the formal freedom of individual citizens – to the public law of the welfare state, guaranteeing the citizen access to certain substantial resources (see § "Social welfare mass democracies", p. 44). *Legitimation Crisis* and *The Theory of Communicative Action* begin to engage with systems theory approaches to law. I shall briefly rehearse their arguments.

Both *Legitimation Crisis* and *The Theory of Communicative Action* approach the question of law from the perspective of Weberian sociology, and in particular from that of Weber's rationalization thesis. For Weber, law is a paradigmatic case of the process of rationalization (Weber 1976: 14). However, for Habermas, Weber's analysis of law is symptomatic of the inherent tensions in Weber's theoretical framework. In *Legitimation Crisis* Habermas accepts that the law, like other spheres of expert culture, has an inherent logic that guides its development (LC: 88). The development of law is seen to be entwined with the development of morality. This is crucial, for it makes explicit the fact that the rationalization of law is a process of legitimation. That is to say that law develops in attempts to justify it as a legitimate institution. It is ultimately not sufficient for law merely to be backed by physical force. To some degree it must be accepted and internalized by those to whom it is addressed. It is precisely this process of legitimation that concerns Habermas in both *Legitimation Crisis* and *The Theory of Communicative Action*. Thus, in the former, he notes that in the transition from pre-conventional to conventional societies, the legal culture begins to be differentiated from moral culture, as the traditional, taken-for-granted normative framework of particular communities, tribal groupings or families begins to be subject to rational reflection (LC: 86). This serves to identify the crucial function of law in social integration. As societies grow more complex, communicative competences that had been developed within the intimacy of the family or small tribal group become inadequate for organizing fleeting and complex interactions with strangers. Law provides a medium for the regulation of such interaction (and thus, according to the model of the rationalization of the lifeworld, complex problems of social organization are deferred to non-symbolic steering media – or "relief mechanisms" – in order to prevent the overburdening of lifeworld competences (see TCAII: 181; and § "Lifeworld and system", p. 165)). In the early modern period, this gives rise to the initiation of a process of "juridification", which is to say the process by which modern law becomes both more extensive in its scope and is more intensively organized in terms of its fine detail (TCAII: 357).

In *Legitimation Crisis* this process of rationalization is outlined in terms of the development of three traditions of jurisprudence (of modern natural law, utilitarianism and Kantian formal morality), which seek to ground the elements of law in broader, unifying principles (LC: 88–9). What is important in this account is less its brief details (which are in any case surpassed by the account in *The Theory of Communicative Action*), but rather the nature of the tensions that continually disrupt this process. In the separation of law from morality, Habermas indicates that a stress emerges between the particular scope of law (for a legal system governs the behaviour of people only within the particular society to which it is addressed), and the universal aspiration of morality. Put otherwise (in the terminology that became familiar in *The Structural Transformation of the Public Sphere*), law is concerned with the citizen, and morality with the human being as such, "*l'homme*". The three traditions of jurisprudence all fail for they are unable to work through this tension. The aspiration to universality is expressed only through a concern with the purely formal questions of the consistency of the legal system. As such they are unable to ground law in the concrete motivations of the citizen (LC: 88–9). For Habermas, this tension can only be resolved in a "universal political morality", such that legal principles are grounded in the same, universal processes of justification, which ideally serve to redeem all the normative validity claims (LC: 88). It is precisely at this point that *Legitimation Crisis* begins to explore the possibility of discourse (or "communicative") ethics (LC: 89).

Yet, in *Legitimation Crisis*, the recourse to discourse ethics is interrupted by a further significant reflection on the problem of the legitimation of the law. The key role that Weber plays as a theorist of legitimacy is brought to the fore. This foregrounding allows Habermas to outline schematically two contemporary approaches to legal legitimacy, precisely in that they can be traced back to the inherent contradictions in Weber's own approach. One side, articulated in Luhmann's systems theory, is rooted in the Weberian concern with purposive rationality (LC: 98–9). The alternative is rooted in value rationality (LC: 99–100).

In brief, Luhmann is primarily concerned with positive law (i.e. law that is understood as a conventional product of human invention) as a social subsystem that serves the function of social integration. Assuming that citizens relate to each other strategically (TCAI: 260), at least within the social realms that need to be regulated by law, law is treated as a medium for the organization of other subsystems (TCAII: 365). What matters, then, is not the substance of the law, but rather its consistency. Law is legitimate in so far as it is the source of responsible decisions, made according to definite rules, which ensure the resolution of conflicts and the maintenance of the social order (LC: 98). The problem with such an approach, for Habermas, is that it is concerned with what he calls "legality", and not legitimacy proper. It need only be interested in the formal consistency of the law, for that alone is sufficient to secure the integration of strategic agents. It is indifferent to the particular content of law (LC: 100). The legal system of a dictatorship may be as consistent (and functionally effective) as that of a democracy, and a legal system based upon apartheid as formally consistent as one grounded in the recognition of universal human rights. For Luhmann, one cannot go beyond the social fact of the law to these deeper questions as to the normative rightness of the political and economic systems that the law serves to organize and integrate. For Habermas, Luhmann is thus unable to say anything significant about the use of law as an instrument of oppression (TCAI: 265).

An alternative, which looks to value rationality, would superficially seem to fill the gap left by the formalism of systems theory. Here the legitimacy of the law would rest not simply upon its consistency, but rather upon substantive grounding values. All those who are subject to the law could then acknowledge it as a substantial expression of their understanding of justice (LC: 99). In this framework, the difference between, say, equal human rights and apartheid matters. However, this appeal to value rationality also fails, for it leaves the source of values underdetermined. More precisely, it reduces law to the expression of the values of a particular community. While the difference between equal human rights and apartheid may be noted, it is unclear how the latter's claim to be an expression of justice can be disputed. There is no guarantee that the grounding values of a legal system have any firm claim to universality. Further, in the tacit assumption of a culturally homogeneous community, it can offer no explanation of how legal systems are to work in modern pluralist societies, or in the face of Weber's "polytheism" of values (LC: 100). If both systems theory and value rationality thereby lead to decisionism, with values being ultimately rendered purely subjective, then *Legitimation Crisis* must turn, of course, to an analysis of the discursive redemption of normative validity claims in order to resolve this problem.

The Theory of Communicative Action takes further the analysis of the tension between purposive rationality and value rationality in law. The more subtle account of the relationship between system and lifeworld that characterizes the later work allows for an articulation of the place that law serves in the colonization of the lifeworld. In this light, the distinction between the two forms of Weberian reason ceases to be that between mere frameworks within which legal systems might be legitimated, as they become rather expressions, respectively, of system and lifeworld perspectives. In this context, a more substantial account of juridification traces the development of modern law through four "global waves" (TCAII: 358): the absolutist bourgeois state; the constitutional bourgeois state; the democratic constitutional state; and the democratic welfare state.

In its initial stage, modern law serves primarily to protect the bourgeois citizen from the lifeworld that has been shaped by a feudal past. As such, the contemporary lifeworld is left to the organizational capacities of the market, while the legal system does little more than defend individual liberty. It is only in the second stage, with the formulation of a constitution, that law comes to be justified in terms of a "rule of law" (and thus an explicit constitution), and thus in terms of some claim to universal moral grounding. It acquires greater consistency and complexity, and serves to protect the individual citizen and his[1] lifeworld against intrusions from the state (and its administrative systems). With the last two stages the relationship of system and lifeworld becomes more ambiguous. The expansion of the franchise allows more citizens to be involved in the authorship and formal acceptance of law. The legitimation of the law therefore shifts from being a purely rational task, and comes increasingly to rely upon the free discursive involvement of all those subject to the law. But, Habermas cautions, already this systematically organized extension of the franchise begins actively to constitute (and thus restrict) the forms that this collective process of legal authorship and legitimation (what Habermas calls "collective will formation") can take (TCAII: 361). Finally, with the welfare state, colonization of the lifeworld occurs, paradoxically, as attempts to guarantee freedom and in particular to protect the citizen's lifeworld from infringement by the economic system (by granting citizens substantial welfare rights, rather than just negative rights to liberty), take freedom away (TCAII: 362).

Habermas's argument can be interpreted as follows. If law is understood as the medium for organizing a system, as Luhmann claims, then it is, by its very non-symbolic nature, meaningless from the perspective of the lifeworld. Here Habermas acknowledges the accuracy of Luhmann's account. As a medium, all that matters is law's internal consistency. While the law is serving to regulate strategic action within systems (such as the economy and the political administration) this is not a problem. Indeed, in the first two waves of juridification, it serves to keep those systems in check, and allow the lifeworld to flourish. However, Habermas complements Luhmann's account of law as a medium with an account of law as an "institution" (TCAII: 365). As an institution, law is concerned with substantial normative issues (and Habermas offers examples from criminal law, such as murder, rape and abortion). Such law does not merely regulate strategic action; it rather constitutes communicative action. The democratic welfare state becomes implicated in the colonization of the lifeworld, precisely in so far as welfare law comes to be constructed as a systems medium, and not as an institution. As a medium, it overtly regulates the lifeworld activities (such as childcare, health and education) that are the object of concern of a welfare state. The normative questions that would be explicit, if the law were understood institutionally, are suppressed. The constitutive role of the law thereby goes unnoticed and unchallenged. This results in a constitutive process that increasingly shapes the lifeworld of the recipients of welfare to the (meaningless) imperatives of the economic and administrative systems (TCAII: 367).

This may be briefly illustrated, improvising a little on one of Habermas's own examples, through reference to the modern educational system. Increasingly, in order to ensure that pupils receive an education of an appropriate quality and that all pupils have equal access to that education, the educational system at all levels is subject to increased monitoring by the state. This laudable intention is subverted, however, because the legalization and administration of the educational environment, in accord with law as a medium, leads to the impoverishment of that environment. The communicative interaction that should lie at the core of the education as lifeworld – and, indeed, as one of the processes by which the meaningful or symbolic content of the lifeworld is reproduced – is gradually replaced by strategic action. Teachers no longer relate communicatively to pupils, but rather treat pupils strategically, as a means to the fulfilment of criteria of success set by the system (and which in their quantitative simplicity are hopelessly inadequate as attempts to grasp the qualitative richness of the educational experience). Similarly, pupils increasingly see themselves in a role akin to that of "client", and thus as entitled to exploit the teacher instrumentally as a means to the realisation of educational success. Education is thereby reduced to an instrumental experience, and not an intrinsically valuable and meaningful process of socialization and self-discovery (see TCAII: 371).

To summarize this section, we have seen that Habermas's consideration of law as part of his wider social theory has entailed a linking of legal norms to moral norms. The problems of legitimizing law are ultimately revealed to be problems in diagnosing or concealing the colonization of the lifeworld, where Luhmann's systems theory serves to conceal colonization precisely because it attempts to render the normative questions of the lifeworld meaningless. Although Habermas continues to be concerned with the development and legitimacy of constitutional law, *Between Facts and Norms* marks a distancing from the theory of juridification, at least in its link to colonization (BR: 154). Indeed, Habermas can be seen to be returning to the problems of democracy in the form that they were left in the conclusions to (and further reflections on) *The Structural Transformation of the Public Sphere*. There, Habermas reflected upon the possibility of a "bulwark" between systems and lifeworld that would inhibit the encroachment of the system (FR: 444). A similar "siege" model is offered in "Popular Sovereignty as Procedure" (BFN: 463–90; Habermas 1996b), a paper contemporary to the "Further Reflections" (on *The Structural Transformation of the Public Sphere*). Yet, as we shall see, *Between Facts and Norms* goes further, fundamentally rethinking the relationship of law to morality, and thus the process of legitimizing law, in order to offer a more optimistic "sluice" model (BFN:

345–8). This model allows for the existence of democratic and constitutional procedures that make possible public influence on the centres of political and economic power (BR: 134), and do so in the context of the unavoidable – and indeed desirable – pluralism of contemporary societies.

Law and morality

Habermas's philosophy of law may be seen to begin with questions about the form and function of modern law. The very title of Habermas's study (in German, *Faktizität und Geltung*) gives the clue to his understanding of law: law stands between facticity [*Faktizität*] and validity [*Geltung*] (BFN: xi). On the one hand, law has a coercive power that makes it a fact of our social lives. The criminal can look upon the law strategically, in terms of the negative consequences of being caught. The more law-abiding can approach law in terms of the possibility of predicting the "average compliance" of others to that law, thereby making their behaviour predictable. On the other hand, the law is also something that should be respected, and as such one approaches it "performatively" (BFN: 448). Most citizens do not abide by the law simply out of fear of punishment; rather, they abide by the law because they accept that it is right. This is, in effect, to reiterate the distinction between instrumental rationality (or legality) and value rationality (or legitimacy), and again to stress that neither alone is adequate as an account of law.

But Habermas is now setting up a position that can go further than the mere reduction of legal norms to moral norms (and thus the subservience of legality to legitimacy) that characterized *Legitimation Crisis* and *The Theory of Communicative Action*. He stresses the role that both the facticity and the validity of law play in social integration. On the one hand, as facticity, law holds together a society that at worst can be characterized in terms of conflicts over interests or values – law is "what is left of the crumbling cement of society" (RJ: 329) – and at best in terms of contacts between strangers. The legality of law holds, and law will be enforced, regardless of one's particular value commitments or attitudes to fellow citizens. On the other hand, a legitimate law suggests a post-conventional moral consciousness, which accepts norms on the grounds of good reasons (RJ: 330). Together, legality and legitimacy generate "morally obligatory relationships of mutual respect … among strangers" (BFN: 460). The task at hand is to articulate exactly what are to count as the "good reasons" that give rise to legitimacy, and to show that they are at once more and less than is entailed in moral reasoning.

The problem of the legitimacy of law lay at the heart of the process of juridification. The main strands of this process may now be considered in a new light. Specifically, Habermas approaches two schools of jurisprudence: legal positivism and natural law theory. The first is broadly familiar to us from our consideration of Luhmann. By stressing the conventional nature of law, the legal positivist looks only to legality: the consistency of the legal system. In contrast, the natural law tradition attempts to ground law in a non-conventional morality. An example of this, at the stage of the constitutional bourgeois state, would be Locke's use of the fiction of a state of nature. In brief, Locke uses the thought experiment of imagining a condition (the state of nature) before the development of government (and thus before the conventions of positive law), in order to ask what freedoms people in that condition would have. To this he answers that "[m]an ... hath by nature a power ... to preserve his property – that is, his life, liberty, and estate – against the injuries and attempts of other men" (Locke 1980: Ch. 7, §87). Thus, precisely in so far as law serves to protect these liberties – liberties that exist prior to law – law is legitimate. In Habermas's earlier reflections on law, although he could not be described as a natural law theorist, he did share with them a commitment to a hierarchy that subordinated law to prior moral principles. This he now challenges.

Law and morality can be distinguished in terms of three characteristics: autonomy, scope and reasoning (IO: 256–8). Modern law, from the absolutist bourgeois constitution onwards, has at its core the notion of negative rights. In order to protect the freedoms of citizens, law is constructed in terms of a series of prohibitions. Everything is allowed that is not explicitly prohibited. The citizen is thereby understood primarily as a holder of certain rights (such as the Lockean rights to liberty, life and property) that guarantee their private autonomy. In contrast, morality (and in particular Kantian morality) makes the position of rights dependent upon the prior exercise of duties. You have rights, only because I have a prior duty to respect you as a person (RJ: 331). What matters is the obligation of the moral agent to act in accord with their duty, and thereby exercise their moral autonomy. The reason for this difference lies in both the source and scope of law and morality; it is the difference between the citizen and *l'homme*. Legal rights are ultimately bestowed by the state. The citizen is thus constituted as a citizen of a particular state, and their rights are determined accordingly. The rights are ideally functional to their activities as a citizen. In contrast, the aspiration of morality is universal not merely in the sense that a moral system speaks to all human beings, but also in the sense that it encompasses the whole of their life; as Habermas puts it, it encompasses the "integrity of fully individuated persons" (BFN: 452).

Thus, turning to the second characteristic, law may be seen to be both narrower and broader in scope than morality. It is narrower, for it is concerned only with the agent's behaviour as citizen. Much that may be deemed immoral (e.g. adultery in Western culture) is left untouched by legislation, precisely because such behaviour is not seen to impact upon the body politic. However, it is broader in scope, for it regulates and coordinates the public behaviour of citizens in order to realize political goals, and in order to enact political policy. Thus, again, much that is legal is not moral. (Morally it does not matter which side of the road we drive on; however, once the decision for left or right is made, the rest of traffic regulation must, as Luhmann and the positivists stress, be consistent with it.) This leads to the final characteristic, for a difference in scope entails that the forms of reasoning that moral and legal discourse take will necessarily also be different. While moral reasons will be important in the discussion and justification of certain laws (e.g. whether or not the hunting of animals should be outlawed), it is not the only form of reason to which appeal should be made, for empirical, prudential and pragmatic matters, as well as a concern with the consistency of the law and willingness to compromise, must all be taken into account (RJ: 332–3; and see JA: 1–17). Hence the putative immorality of hunting may be set against the impact that a ban will have on the rural economy, the possibility of widespread civil disobedience, and even the governing party's chances for re-election (see BFN: 452). Habermas can then conclude that law is neither reducible to morality (as natural rights theorists argue) nor separable from it (as positivists argue), but rather that morality and law stand in a complementary relationship (BFN: 453).

This argument has important implications not merely for the philosophy of law, but also for Habermas's own discourse ethics. It may be recalled (from § "Discourse ethics", p. 157) that Habermas articulated discourse ethics in terms of two principles, the principle of discourse ethics (D) and the principle of universalization (U):

(D) Only those norms can claim to be valid that meet (or could meet) with the approval of all affected in their capacity *as participants in a practical discourse*;
(U) *All* affected can accept the consequences and the side effects its *general* observance can be anticipated to have for the satisfaction of *everyone's* interests (and these consequences are preferred to those of known alternative possibilities for regulation).

(MCCA: 65 & 66, original emphasis)

Habermas observes that U cannot apply to law, precisely because the jurisdiction of a law is restricted to a given state. Thus U is restricted to morality whereas D can be set at a greater level of abstraction, so that it can underpin both law and morality. Habermas justifies this greater abstraction by identifying an ambiguity in two terms within D. "Norms" (or "action norms" in the version given in *Between Facts and Norms* (BFN: 107)) can refer to moral or legal norms, whereas "practical discourses" (now "rational discourses") can encompass all forms of legal deliberations. This entails that, as against the "universal political morality" to which *Legitimation Crisis* appealed, *Between Facts and Norms* need only seek to ground law in D: bluntly separating the "universal" and the "moral" from the "political". This entails that the project of *Between Facts and Norms* is to specify how D is to be understood in the context of law.

Human rights and popular sovereignty

A discourse theory approach to law, and specifically to the question of the legitimacy of law, requires that the formulation and deliberation of law is grounded in the democratic participation of citizens. It is self-evident that only some form of democracy will fulfil the conditions of D, not least in so far as D may be understood as the counterfactual presupposition grounding democratic political action. In order to articulate this understanding of democracy, Habermas situates discourse theory as a response to the two dominant traditions of political philosophy in the West: liberalism and civic republicanism.

Liberalism may be characterized in terms of its stress on a constitution and human rights as means of protecting the private autonomy of citizens. As has been seen above, in the characterization of the bourgeois constitutional state, negative rights serve to protect the citizen from the intervention by the sovereign in their private affairs. By grounding rights in a rationally justified constitutional device (such as the natural law theory, or the Lockean derivation of rights from a state of nature), no one can be seen to be above the law. On this conception the state can only play the role of an administration, serving a society that it primarily understands in terms of markets and the exchanges and conflicts of individual economic agents. The political process is thus understood as one within which individual agents struggle to gain access to that state administration in order to shape it to their particular interests. The success of the government can then be assessed simply in terms of the aggregate of expressions of approval (akin to a market, driven by the aggregate preferences of individual consumers) (IO: 239–44).

In contrast, the older civic humanist or republican model – which has its roots in Aristotle's *Politics*, and finds articulation in Machiavelli's *The Discourses* in the fifteenth century and Harrington's *Oceana* in the seventeenth century, has echoes in Hegel's *The Philosophy of Right*, and today finds a new form in the communitarianism of the likes of Michael Walzer and Michael Sandel – looks first to the good of the society, and not of the individual member of that society. Negative rights are replaced by civic virtues that characterize what the good citizen can do for their community. Rights are primarily understood as rights to participate in the community, and indeed to constitute that community, not least by determining its collective goals and self-understanding. Public autonomy, in the sense of the active participation of all in the running of the political community, therefore replaces private autonomy as the central focus of the political process. Politics must therefore be understood as a process of collective will-formation, characterized by reasoned dialogue, and not the simple expression of subjective preferences through voting (IO: 239–44). Society is seen primarily to be a forum, not a marketplace (Elster 1986).

Superficially, Habermas looks like a republican, not least in his advocacy of dialogue as against the plebiscites that characterize the contemporary party political system. His precise relationship to republicanism must therefore be traced with some care. We may begin by recognizing the stark contrast between the two traditions in terms of their respective emphases on human rights and on popular sovereignty. Liberalism presents the popular sovereignty that is at the heart of republicanism as a threat (IO: 258) – and here Mill's fears over the "tyranny of the majority" are highly representative, with the assumption that a mass, infused with prejudice or superstition, could potentially demand laws that infringe the liberties of minorities or individuals (Mill 1869: 4). (The collapse of the Weimar Republic, and the resultant promulgation of anti-Semitic law and practice under the Nazis, remains a historical reminder of the kernel of truth in such a fear.) Inalienable human rights check any legislator from promoting such discriminatory laws. The rule of law must therefore take priority over the republican pursuit of political aims.

However, Habermas suggests that this solution to the problem of popular sovereignty is incoherent. The sovereign may be interpreted as the author of positive law, or as the enactor of natural law. The first interpretation falls into contradiction, for the creativity of the sovereign is being paternalistically restricted, so that positive law cannot in fact be pure positive law (but must rather be the mere articulation of natural law). The second interpretation is incoherent, for it is unclear why a sovereign who simply enacts natural law should wish, or even be able, to enact laws that violate human rights. The liberal fear would then be superfluous (BFN: 454; IO: 259).

The solution to this tension between human rights and popular sovereignty is implicit in the third wave of juridification, and not least in its articulation by Kant. With the expansion of the franchise, a republican theme creeps into the issue of the legitimation of law. Legitimacy rests upon the involvement of the people as the authors of the law. In Kant's moral philosophy, more explicitly, this can be seen in the requirement that the only moral laws that agents ought to obey – and therefore the only moral laws that have, as it were, legitimacy – are those rules that agents are able to will, rationally, for themselves. In the context of law, this allows one to recognize that the liberal conception of popular sovereignty is confused. The sovereign does not stand over and against the people; it is the people. As such, the only legitimate laws are those laws of which the people is both author and addressee (BFN: 454).

This will not, however, settle liberal doubts, not least concerning the tyranny of the majority. Here Habermas's distance from republicanism becomes explicit. He condemns much republican thought as being simply too idealistic. It remains within the philosophy of consciousness, implicitly conceiving political society as a subject writ large (IO: 248), and thereby takes for granted a largely homogeneous population, who are all virtuous enough to devote themselves to public welfare (IO: 244). Put bluntly, in matters of politics, the Kantian model of a moral agent is not wholly appropriate. In part this is because of the difference between moral and legal discourse, but also because of different conceptions of autonomy. Kantian moral autonomy is, as Habermas puts it, "all of one piece" (RJ: 331). Republicanism reproduces this unity, in so far as it seemingly offers the citizen no life outside politics. The liberal concern with private autonomy is completely overridden. Republicanism may therefore be judged to be insufficiently sensitive to the practicalities of politics, both at the level of involvement that contemporary politics may demand and, equally significantly, in its scope for understanding pluralistic societies. Crucially, pluralism suggests that the people retreat from the politics of the state not just into their individual concerns, but also into the life of communities and cultural groups that do not map in any simple or conflict-free way onto the structure of the state. In the language of Rawls (1985), with which Habermas has much sympathy, republicanism reduces the "political" to the "metaphysical" – which is to say, the political organization of the state is conceived only in terms of the ideological or religious doctrines that give the community its sense of identity (see IO: Chs 2 & 3).

Habermas must therefore correct the naiveties of republicanism by looking for a way in which conditions conducive to rational discourse can be institutionalized, in terms of a liberal rule of law. "Rational discourse" here must be understood as political and not moral discourse. This is to say that it must be accepted that prudence and pragmatism, compromises and strategic actions, and indeed the whole context of power will remain in play during such discourse (IO: 245). Put differently, republicanism emphasizes something that liberalism ignores, which is to say the place of solidarity in social integration. However, unless political philosophy can also recognize the parts played by money and power, and thus the dependence of modern societies on system integration, it will remain impractical (IO: 249).

The problem faced by Habermas is that of articulating a set of civil rights that go beyond the liberal protection of private autonomy, but without committing everyone to the impractical panoply of republican virtues. At the core of his analysis lies the idea of citizens being both authors and subjects of the law. The crucial question to be answered concerns the rights that citizens should mutually accord to one another (BFN: 458). An initial step, and one that is *prima facie* unproblematic precisely in that it self-evidently derives from D, is to place communicative rights at the centre of any constitution. Citizens should have "equal opportunities for the public use of communicative liberties" (BFN: 458). Although seemingly unproblematic in itself, this marginalizes the traditional liberal rights (liberty, life and the enjoyment of property), and indeed welfare rights (such as rights to education, health, and pensions). Without these rights, the private autonomy of the individual once more seems to be vulnerable. Yet, it is not clear how such rights could be grounded in D. Habermas responds to this by looking again at the problem of the mutual granting of rights, in effect in order to examine its preconditions.

The mutual granting of rights cannot be done by human subjects as such. Precisely in so far as rights are legal entities, concerning the organization and regulation of the public good, their granting and withholding only makes sense in terms of the interaction of subjects as citizens: as legal subjects. This is to say, that rights refer to the relationship of subjects in their public capacity, and therefore presuppose a division between their public and private autonomy. As Habermas expresses this, law is the only available language through which such legal subjects can communicate with each other (BFN: 455). Put otherwise, even as the non-symbolic steering medium of the systems theorists, law still interacts with the lifeworld. As a language, it shapes or encodes the way in which issues in the lifeworld are understood and handled as issues between citizens – not human subjects per se – in the political–legal realm. From this, Habermas can conclude that the legal code must be in place, defining the nature of the citizen as rights-holder (regardless of the particular rights attributed to them), prior to the enactment or legitimation of any particular law. A constitution is the precondition of citizenship. Without it, there are only human subjects per se, and the problem of the excessive and idealistic demands of republicanism re-emerge. Precisely in so far as classical human (and welfare) rights constitute the citizen, not least in so far as they guarantee the separation of public and private autonomy, they must be part of that legal code.

However, if the legal code is to be justified in terms of its legitimacy, and not merely its legality – which is to say, if the legal code is not to be imposed on the sovereign law-maker, as the flawed liberal model suggests – then the republican model of legitimation must be invoked. The rule of law itself acquires legitimacy only from its free and rational acceptance by citizens. This is to say that the rule of law is legitimated only through the exercise of public autonomy. This entails that the activity of citizenship, the exercise of public autonomy, must be the precondition of any legitimate constitution (and thus of the protection of private autonomy). In summary, human rights (and private autonomy) and popular sovereignty (public autonomy) are each the precondition of the other's existence (RJ: 332).

Habermas can conclude this discussion by identifying five categories of rights that follow from D (BFN: 122–3). The first category is made up of the traditional liberal rights (and thus "the right to the greatest possible measure of equal individual liberties"). The second includes rights of membership (which thereby secure the citizen's place as a member of a particular legal community – "a voluntary association of consociates under law"). The third includes rights of due-process (which guarantee legal remedies to which those who feel that their rights have been infringed can resort). Together these three categories define the legal person and guarantee private autonomy. The rights of political participation follow (and ensure the legitimacy, rather than mere legality, of the system). Finally, social-welfare rights are included, for the preceding four categories of rights cannot be properly exercised without the satisfaction of certain basic material needs.

The public use of reason

Some of the institutional details entailed by the discourse theory of law may now be rehearsed. It is important to consider the process through which the communicative rights of citizens come to affect political decision-making. The model offered in *The Theory of Communicative Action* stressed, as was noted above, the resistance of the political system to the influence of the lifeworld. Habermas now modifies this model, in part by focusing on what is required of the lifeworld and its public sphere in a democratic society, but also by introducing the concepts of "communicative power" and "administrative power", as a framework within which the impact of public opinion on law and policy formulation may be analysed.

Communicative rights must be understood as genuinely collective rights. That is to say that in exercising their communicative rights, citizens do not act exclusively in order to promote their personal goals (as the liberal paradigm of the market suggests), but rather in order to focus on collective goals (BFN: 461). Communicative rights are thus exercised as a genuinely public use of reason. In order to arrive at reasonable assessments and regulations of their status as private people, citizens must be willing to participate in an evaluation of their own needs that recognizes their public relevance and interpretation (RJ: 334). Yet such a public attitude on the part of citizens crucially depends upon their lifeworlds and, it may be added, the widespread development of a post-conventional moral consciousness (BR: 145). This immediately exposes the ultimate fragility of communicative democracy (BFN: 462). A commitment to the collective good cannot be administratively manufactured. Habermas now seems to be less troubled by this weakness than he was in writing either *Legitimation Crisis* or *The Theory of Communicative Action*. Rather, he stresses the role that a "democratic *Sittlichkeit*" (or "ethical life") plays in nurturing the legal system (BFN: 461) or, more precisely argues that democracy presupposes the rationalized lifeworld of a decentred society (IO: 251–2). Such a society is characterized by the differentiation of the formal political structures of the state from an active political culture, within which the problems of society as a whole can be identified and interpreted.

In part, this model returns to the concerns of *The Structural Transformation of the Public Sphere*. Habermas argues that the "sovereign" of a genuinely democratic society must be understood not concretely as the people (let alone an individual ruler), for such concreteness would entail a reversion to the naive homogeneity of a republican model of society. A society in which a people is sovereign is potentially closed and intolerant, with the people's ideology dominating politics, to the potential exclusion of private autonomy. The sovereign must therefore be conceived structurally, as the more or less informal institutions of the public sphere, which allow for the public use of reason in the formulation of public opinion. If such institutions are sufficiently sensitive and inclusive of all cultural worldviews, they serve as channels or "sluices" (IO: 250) through which citizens' interests, values and identities can be drawn upon, in order to provide reasons and arguments for the identification of social problems. This process of will-formation gives rise to "influence", or "communicative power". Given that only the state can rule, the law of a constitutional state thus acts as the medium for transforming communicative power into administrative power (BFN: 169). The communicative power of elected and deliberating bodies in the public sphere is transformed through legislative programmes and court judgments into administrative power (BFN: 333).

The relationship between communicative and administrative power – with the mediating role of law – must be understood as a two-way process. The issue at stake is not merely the possibility of communicative action influencing the formulation of law, but also the role that formulated and enacted law plays in the public self-understanding of the citizen. Law is, by its very nature, something about which there will be dissensus. Laws and court judgements throw into relief competing interpretations of interests and needs. But by being focused on the law, the socially disruptive effect of dissensus and conflict becomes socially integrative, precisely in so far as that dissensus is realized as a reflective, discursive and thus public exercise of reason (BFN: 462). Again, the mutual presupposition of private and public autonomy is at play, as law at once constitutes the citizen (and thus the scope of their private autonomy), and is legitimated or challenged by the exercise of public autonomy (for example, in testing whether the legal scope given to private autonomy is sufficient or fair). A mere exercise of private autonomy could amount to little more than a short-sighted refusal to accept the validity of the law (e.g. by breaking it anyway, or by refusing to recognize the court that stands in judgment over the individual dissenter). Although eminently critical of the law as it stands, such a position neglects the facticity of law. Pure public autonomy, conversely, would subsume the individual into their legal definition, leaving the individual in the position of passively accepting whatever legal judgments are made upon them (and as such accepting the fact of the law at the expense of questioning its normativity).

An illustration can serve to conclude this section. The history of feminist challenges to the law is instructive in exposing the shortfalls of traditional legal paradigms (BFN: 409–27; IO: 262–4)). Under a liberal paradigm, with its emphasis upon private autonomy secured through formal equality of civil rights, the feminist seeks justice by ensuring that rights are gender blind. Women will secure formal equality of opportunity in the pursuit of income, status and life chances, typically in so far as these resources are distributed via the market. The failure of liberal feminism highlights the failure of the liberal paradigm as such. Liberalism secures only formal equality. Such equality is undermined by the substantive inequalities of the market. Class and gender inequalities continue to be significant, not least in so far as they are drawn into the interpretation of the law. The feminist response to liberalism and the mere provision of equal rights may be understood, in the context of the present discussion, as part of the continuing process of interpreting and negotiating the way in which the law articulates its citizens' needs. As Habermas frames this, it is a problem of establishing the public context within which legislators and judges are able to "know what it in each case means to treat like cases alike" (RJ: 334). Liberalism is exposed as inadequate, for in ignoring substantial inequality, it treats substantially different cases as if they were alike.

The welfare-state paradigm would seek to remedy the weaknesses of liberalism by intervening in private life, and offering compensation for the inequalities that occur through the distribution of income, wealth and other material resources. It is in this context that, for example, childcare and divorce law are extended. The failure of welfarism has already been identified in terms of the colonization of the lifeworld. A paternalistic welfare state, in order legally to regulate private activity, creates stereotypes of dependency, which enforce its "clients" into a compliance that fails to address their real needs. The stereotype entails that, once again, unlike cases are being treated as if they were alike. However, whereas in *The Theory of Communicative Action* Habermas remains pessimistic in the face of colonization, now he cites radical feminism as an example of the continuing resistance that welfarism (and by implication colonization) will face. Crucially, radical feminism breaks from the dichotomy of the liberal and welfare-state paradigms. Both presuppose a model of human beings as economic producers, and thus focus upon the best way to realize private autonomy. The place of public autonomy, and thus the relationship of public and private autonomy that is central to Habermas's "proceduralist paradigm", is ignored. Radical feminism brings forth the problem of the interpretation of gender and gender-roles as a matter for public debate (IO: 263). Only through the exercise of public autonomy can citizens identify what differences between feminine and masculine experiences are actually relevant to understanding the nature of liberty, and thus to distinguishing like and unlike cases. Again, only such public debate can create a "democratic *Sittlichkeit*" within which legislation and judgment can occur fairly.[2]

Cosmopolitanism

Of the range of issues that arise out of Habermas's proceduralist paradigm, one is especially close to a concern that runs throughout Habermas's work: the tension between the particular and the universal. That morality aspires to a universality while a legal system overtly addresses only the citizens of a particular nation is a core premise of Habermas's separation of morality and law. This may be articulated in terms of the distinction between human rights and civil (or positive) rights. While the latter depend upon the authority of a particular state for their legitimacy and enforcement, the former – as, for example, with the United Nations Declaration of Human Rights – seemingly apply to all human beings, regardless of their nationality (BFN: 456; IO: 189ff.). Indeed, Habermas is prepared to assert that, while the West must still learn about the blind-spots in its own law and morality through dialogue with other cultures, "the normative substance of those rights which emerged in the West will withstand the usual accusation that it is merely a reflection of Western traditions" (RJ*: 452). These rights can be used to check the practices of particular states. Yet, Habermas recognizes that the defence and respect of human rights remains problematic in the context of a world structured in terms of autonomous nation states. This can be seen not only in the potential repression of citizens within their own state, but also through states' policies towards economic migrants and political asylum seekers (e.g. IO: 204–36).

More subtly, precisely in so far as proceduralism entails the rejection of the pure conventionality of positive law (and thus, for example, Luhmann's suppression of normative questions), it suggests that there are formal, or more precisely procedural, aspects of law that will be common to all legitimate legal systems, regardless of their substantive content. It may therefore be suggested that, while *Legitimation Crisis*'s aspiration to a universal political morality has been abandoned, there remains a universalist impetus within proceduralism. This raises the question of exactly what the relationship between legitimate procedural law and the cultures and traditions of particular nations might be. Put more bluntly, one may ask whether it makes sense to talk of a universal legal procedure without specifying a universal normative content.

This tension can be explored by considering Habermas's reflections on the nature of the nation. As a form of social organization, the nation state emerges as the administrative infrastructure of modern law (in the context of the emergence of capitalism). It is, in effect, bound up with juridification, from the first wave onwards. The nation state may be understood as the embodiment of citizenship and the jurisdiction of a particular legal system. Yet, for Habermas, its foundation and self-understanding, not least in the notion of "nationalism", is more subtle and problematic. The concept of "nation" is superficially ambiguous in terms of its relationship to the notions of "ethnos" or "demos". That is to say, there is an ambiguity according to the degree to which a nation understands itself through reference to an ethnic homogeneity, or as a primarily political entity, united through a democratic constitution. Habermas's thesis is that typically nations are formed politically. The nation represents sovereignty, and as such, in the early modern period, is an assertion of the sovereignty of the people against the power of (feudal) monarchy (BFN: 494; IO: 133). Hence, in the process of juridification, the initial liberal (or constitutional bourgeois) wave develops the rule of law as a check on monarchical power. Habermas also cites the historically crucial events of the French Revolution and American Declaration of Independence. One might also add the English Civil War and "Glorious Revolution" of 1688, and even, as a proto-event, the signing of the Magna Carta. However, this political self-understanding is retrospectively disrupted through the imposition of a narrative of ethnic homogeneity upon the history of the nation. While such narratives and myths may, especially in the nineteenth century, have served an important function in motivating people to political struggle, they remain myths. For Habermas, citizenship is conceptually tied to "demos", not "ethnos" (BFN: 495).

"Ethnos" becomes increasingly problematic in the context of modern politics. Indeed, it is entwined with the more problematic elements of republicanism, noted above. Certain forms of republicanism, and Habermas engages in particular with the "constitutional theory" of Carl Schmitt (IO: 134ff.), see ethnic homogeneity as a prerequisite to coherent notions of citizenship and political autonomy. Thus, Schmitt presents a common ethnic origin as the substantial grounding of the equality of citizens (IO: 135). This does not merely lead to problems of relativism, in so far as the rule of law is inseparable from the particular ideological, religious or metaphysical culture of the nation; it also generates both an intolerance to those who are identified as being heterogeneous to the national ethnicity and, in so far as the ethnic group is part of a large political entity, to demands for secession (as the only conceivable solution to the problem of political organization) (IO: 143).

The procedural paradigm of law replaces the substantial unity of the ethnos with the exercise of public autonomy. In effect, this is once more to challenge republicanism as a manifestation of the philosophy of consciousness, through an intersubjective understanding of social organization. In terms of the relationship between cultures within a pluralist society, and in particular the relationship of the dominant culture to minority cultures, a "model of inclusion sensitive to difference" is required (IO: 143–6). That is to say that the republican emphasis on ethnos cannot simply be dismissed. Not least, as Habermas's appeals to Mead's pragmatism show, the successful socialization of the individual (not least as the subject of liberal private autonomy), and thus the formation of a personal identity, presupposes an initial cultural context (even if the socialized adult is later to reject that particular cultural identity) (BFN: 498; IO: 145). There is a strong sense in which an individual may understand themselves as a Catalan rather than a Spaniard, or primarily Welsh rather than British. A dominant culture must thus be sensitive to that reality. A mere majority politics that, on a crude liberal model, subsumes the minority voice in the great weight of votes of the majority, will do nothing to bring about political unity. However, the position and identity of the minority cannot be stereotyped. That is to say, a dominant culture risks prescribing the nature and aspirations of a minority culture, and thus enforcing its compliance to a limited identity, much in the way that welfarism risks constituting its clients.

The unity of demos, as opposed to ethnos, may therefore be understood as the risky historical struggle of a nation to understand what public autonomy, and thus democracy, means. It is the process through which what was referred to above as "democratic *Sittlichkeit*" is formed and renewed. As Habermas presents this, the rule of law will only contribute to democracy if it exists for a people who are "accustomed to political freedom and settled in the 'we' perspective of active self-determination" (BFN: 499). It is therefore suggested that, in this process of self-discovery, the dominant culture will ideally become increasingly abstract, and as such it may become the language through which diverse groups and individuals can express their self-understanding and interpret their needs, articulating the difference between alike and non-alike cases to each other as citizens.

In what is perhaps his most significant development of this idea, Habermas borrows a notion from the (broadly republican or communitarian) philosopher Charles Taylor: that of "strong evaluation" (Taylor 1985). In expressing our needs and interests, Taylor argues, we might simply assert our subjectively held preferences as if they were culinary tastes, incapable of further articulation. For example, "I like sweet coffee". One cannot convince someone, at least through reasoned argument, that they should like bitter coffee. They just do not. This "weak" evaluation is fine for one's preference in beverages, but is problematic if it is extended to one's moral and political judgements (invoking, not least, the decisionism of which Habermas accused positivism). "I like fox hunting" or "I like a minimalist state" cannot stand without further reasonable defence. In Taylor's terminology, political and moral preferences demand "strong evaluation". One must be able to articulate reasons in defence of one's judgements and, for Taylor, in particular reasons that are grounded in a critical understanding of what it is to be human. Again, for Habermas this entails drawing upon the values and aspirations of the community or communities from which you draw your sense of personal identity. Drawing on these ideas, Habermas can argue that the defence and articulation of law depends, not merely upon the pragmatic, empirical and moral reasons that have been noted above, but also upon strong evaluations (IO: 144). This is to suggest that, within the proceduralism of public autonomy, a constitution will be interpreted in the light of different cultures and traditions (BFN: 500): different understandings of what it is to be human. If the constitutional framework of the law provides the language through which citizens speak to each other as citizens, then strong evaluations grounded in particular cultures provide the idioms and dialectics of that language.

Habermas summarizes this position as "constitutional patriotism" (BFN: 500), which, with liberal political culture committed to a constitution, can be the common denominator for a people who, despite their cultural differences, understand themselves as united through the continuing exercise of public autonomy: and thus as demos, not ethnos. The implication that may be drawn from this is that a nation that genuinely allows for the exercise of public autonomy, and thus a nation that is striving to put in place the seemingly universal procedures that underpin a legitimate legal system, will be on a historical path to realizing certain universal human rights as part (but never the whole) of its law. In effect, the history of a legal system may then be understood in pragmatist terms, as a series of responses to felt problems. A just society is one that is sensitive enough both to recognize problems and to test their putative solutions – and this it does, above all, through the exercise of public autonomy. The potentially monolithic implications of a "universal political morality" are thereby replaced by an image of continuing dialogue, which thrives on cultural and individual diversity (and Habermas's comments on the "painful task of narrowing distances between different cultures" serve to highlight this (RJ*: 450)).

Yet, if the weakness of nations in respecting and enforcing human rights is to be taken seriously, then the importance of cosmopolitanism in Habermas's thinking must be recognized. Political constitutionalism must eventually become a transnational phenomenon, such that the constitutions of organizations such as the United Nations and the European Union come to play a central role in the lives of all citizens. On one level, this is a demand that the United Nations is strengthened: given the power to enforce its resolutions (BFN: 456), in particular in "peace-keeping, human-rights politics and protection against global ecological, technological and criminal risks" (RJ*: 451). On another level, Habermas can defend the European Union (BFN: 500–507), and indeed aspirations to a federal Europe, despite the fact that at present Europe seems to have no cultural identity (parallel to, say, the cultural identity that a Spaniard or a Pole has in the context of their nation) that could form the lifeworld of a European parliament. Habermas sees this as an illusory problem, because it is again premised upon the confusion of ethnos and demos. If Habermas's suggested history of the nation state is correct, and a sense of national identity emerges out of the process of law-making and constitutional agreement, then the very existence of a European parliament will be a catalyst to the formation of a European culture (IO: 158–61).[3]

Philosophy as stand-in and interpreter

Throughout his career, Habermas has sought to develop philosophical and social theory as the basis upon which to take a measured critical stance against contemporary capitalist society. Put bluntly, the task of a critical theory is to pose the questions that capitalism finds unpalatable. Quite early in his career he suggested that no post-Hegelian philosophy can be neutral with respect to the dominant capitalist ideology. As the process of self-reflection and rationalization leaves nothing unexamined, and thus as the naively accepted starting assumptions of "first philosophy" are eroded, so too is philosophy's grounding in the religious and other substantive values of the lifeworld. Crucially such values can no longer simply be assumed. Habermas's criticism of positivism further demonstrated that the retreat into science, and the supposed value-freedom of scientific research, offers no solution to this problem. Positivism, precisely in its studied suppression of values, sides with capitalism. In so far as the value base of a philosophy is subject to critical examination, so too is the social order with which those values are entwined (PP: 12, 14). Here, centrally, was the challenge of the Young Hegelians – either to justify or to criticize the bourgeois civil order – that was explored in detail in *The Philosophical Discourse of Modernity*. Yet it is also the "young conservativism" of the postmodernists and poststructuralists (MIP: 8). To pose the wrong questions against capitalism, or to pose questions that are thought through with insufficient rigour, however well-intentioned their author may be, serves implicitly to support capitalism, at the very least by inhibiting whatever critical resources are still available. The formulation of a well-informed critical stance against capitalism is thus what lies at the heart of the useful catchphrase with which Habermas summarized his project in the "Introduction" to *Theory and Practice*. Habermasian critical theory is "social theory with practical intention" (TP: 1).

Habermas offered this catchphrase just as his own understanding of what critical theory entailed shifted from the psychoanalytic model of *Knowledge and Human Interests* to the theory of communicative action. Crucially, in either model, a critical stance presupposes the ability to justify one's position. In part it was the problem of articulating a coherent justification in terms of the model of psychoanalytic intervention that led to the development of universal (or formal) pragmatics. The fragility and uncertainty of the moment of the psychoanalytic cure makes the processes of diagnosis and treatment themselves radically uncertain and a process of reciprocal treatment, not least in the model provided by the later Freud, as he abandons the conceit of a "cured" and neurosis-free analyst, and the psychoanalytic dialogue becomes increasing a dialogue of the ill.

Universal pragmatics offered Habermas a way out of such a radical rejection of foundations, albeit one that raised for his critics the spectre of a return to first philosophy. Communicative competence comes to be seen as the transcendental condition of the possibility of human social existence (and in his most recent writings, Habermas has come to re-examine and reassert the quasi-transcendental nature of his work (TJ: 17–22)). As such, it grounds not merely a social theory – by providing the basic conceptual resources through which the reproduction of society may be understood – but also a theory of justification. That is to say that, as we have seen, universal pragmatics makes explicit the procedures necessary to justify both empirically grounded scientific explanation and moral and political judgements. A critical theory informed by universal pragmatics is thus able to justify its descriptions of society and its normative assessment of the justice of that society.

A theme that has run throughout Habermas's work, and one that arises necessarily from the rejection of first philosophy and the need for continued self-reflection in critical theory, is the rejection of any sort of reductionism. This theme first appears in Habermas's attacks on scientism, and is nicely summarized in his criticism of the followers of Wilfrid Sellars, who take seriously Sellars's suggestion that the language-games of our everyday life should be substituted by supposedly objective descriptions of mental processes (FHN: 106). Just as everyday language cannot be reduced to positivistic descriptions of mental processes or physical behaviours, so the lifeworld cannot be reduced to systems (or indeed vice versa), values to facts, or the participant perspective of competent lay agents to the observer perspective of scientific expertise. Precisely because such a claim to irreducibility demands that both poles of the dichotomy must be kept in play, it serves, on the one hand, as a critical tool against scienticism (even in its most sophisticated versions, such as Luhmann's systems theory). On the other, it is a critical tool against those who would eliminate the disciplined position of scientific inquiry altogether. Philosophy cannot abandon its grounding in reason and logic in order to pursue rhetoric and poetry. Here, then, is the source of much of Habermas's criticism of the neo-conservativism inherent in postmodernist and poststructuralist thought (and indeed, in hermeneutics' claim to universality). A critical theory requires the disciplines of science and philosophy, articulating epistemological as well as normative justifications, as much as it requires a sensitivity to the nuances of everyday thought and practice.

The reliance upon a strong theory of universal pragmatics seems to leave Habermas open to criticism, and this, in effect, is to reframe the doubts about whether universal pragmatics is a "first philosophy". Precisely, it is to ask whether the framework of universal pragmatics does not, despite Habermas's best intentions, leave him insensitive to the diversity of the lifeworld. From the perspective of the postmodernist, it is to ask whether Habermas has not succumbed to the evils of the Enlightenment, in so far as universal pragmatics marks a point beyond which critical self-reflection cannot go. Habermas himself suggests, following Adorno, that this is the core problem that philosophy has faced since Hegel. For Adorno it is the contradiction between a self-reflective philosophy that necessarily must forbid itself the absolute (and thus the dogmatism that led to the abuses of Nazism and Soviet communism), and the need to continue appealing to what Adorno calls "the emphatic conception of truth" (PP: 1). To claim access to universal truths invites hubris, a "raving madness" that can no longer recognize, apart from anything else, the privileged social position of the philosopher himself or herself (PP: 5, 8); yet to abandon the concept of truth in favour of cultural relativism or rhetoric leaves one powerless before injustice.

In Habermas's case, the use of developmental theories (ontogenesis and phylogenesis) compounds the problem. On one level the theories of social evolution and individual cognitive and moral development offer frameworks within which the weaknesses of societies and individuals may be judged. However, they also seem to be exclusionary. At the level of society, Habermas is prepared to say that some social formations are less developed than others. Although he studiously avoids the patronizing attitudes of early-twentieth-century cultural anthropology (which could dismiss the achievements of supposedly "primitive" cultures), it is still not wholly clear how an equal multicultural dialogue can be established on such a footing. Perhaps more pointedly, at the level of the individual, it is not clear how Habermas's formulations of discourse ethics – to the effect that all those with an interest in a decision should be allowed to participate – can be squared with the limited or non-existent communicative capacities of many of those who have such an interest.

The field of bioethics offers countless examples of the need to decide on behalf of the unborn child, the comatose and those with severe learning difficulties or mental illnesses. Indeed, Habermas's own recent comments on genetic engineering seem to indicate the limits of discourse ethics. If the subject of genetic engineering is the unborn – indeed, not yet conceived – human being, then it necessarily cannot be involved in the very practical discourse that will determine its existence or the nature of that existence. Habermas then turns back to the resources of the lifeworld, and in particular religious imagery. A human being that determines, through genetic engineering, the "natural essence" of another human being has disrupted the equality of all human beings that is expressed in the theological notion of the human being as God's creature: that which has been created by God (FHN: 115). On one level such an argument serves to highlight the danger of reductionism. Discourse ethics offers a formal or procedural account of ethical decision-making. In no case is this formal framework adequate to decide (let alone predetermine) the solution to a moral dilemma. The formalism of the decision-making procedure is necessarily complemented by the substantive resources that real participants bring to that procedure from the lifeworld. Yet, on another level, in the case of genetic engineering, it appears as if those substantive resources have overwhelmed the discursive procedure. The critical power of discourse ethics has been surrendered to the contingency of the lifeworld, with the possibility that a radically secular society might no longer have the ethical resources necessary to provide the sort of resistance to genetic engineering that Habermas desires.

To some degree, these concerns can be explored by considering Habermas's reflections on the role of philosophy. Habermas has commented on the continuing relevance of philosophy throughout his career (see PP: 1–19, TJ: 277–92). His description of philosophy as "stand-in and interpreter" seems to bear a continuing relevance (MCCA: 1–20), and it is with these two notions that we can conclude.

To suggest that philosophy should be a stand-in (or placeholder), is to recognize the role that philosophical ideas have played in the development of the human and social sciences. Philosophy, Habermas suggests, is the placeholder for "[e]mpirical theories with strong universalistic claims" (MCCA: 15). What he means by this becomes clearer, first from his classical examples – the work of Freud, Marx, Mead, Durkheim, Weber, Piaget and Chomsky – and, secondly, from examples from his own research – the relationship of the philosophy of science to the history of science, of speech act theory to formal pragmatics, and of philosophical theories of informal argumentation to empirical approaches to natural argumentation (MCCA: 16). Philosophical ideas, such as those of Freud (and the theory of repression), Weber (and the grand projection of modernization as rationalization) or Chomsky (and the Kantian notion of a deep grammar) are each inserted into empirical research programmes "like a detonator" (MCCA: 15). Here is, perhaps most obviously, *Legitimation Crisis*'s complex implications for research, but also *The Theory of Communicative Action* and its bold conception of the fundamental nature of social organization and, more profoundly still, its conception of the tragically flawed nature of that organization.

In this role, philosophy is not merely seeding ideas that are to be reaped by the empirical researcher. Habermas's long engagement with pragmatism plays a crucial role here, and the relevance of this can be seen in the theory of communicative action.[4] The framework of universal pragmatics that grounds the theory cannot ultimately be demonstrated through purely philosophical resources. Habermas is not in the position of Kant, Schelling or Hegel, who could articulate the justification of their theories from within their philosophical systems. Even if universal pragmatics may be inspired by a philosophical vision, and not least an idea of what it means to be human, ultimately it is put forward as a complex of hypotheses. As such, it is refutable through empirical research. In effect, Habermas may be seen to place an enormous weight on the notion of fallibilism. One avoids dogmatism (and indeed, first philosophy itself) by being profoundly aware that one may be wrong, and one articulates this in part through the Peircean "hypothesis of reality". One has faith that an external, resisting world (be it that of physical nature or of human society) will check the bad theory. However, without falling back into Adorno's quietism and the paralysing fear that any action may have tragic consequences, one may still reflect upon the risk that is inherent in any practical application of a fallible theory. Natural and social scientific theory invite grand experiments in living, from the extremes of Soviet communist and National Socialist social organization and the Keynesian welfare state, through to the development and distribution of genetically modified foodstuffs, atomic power and high-rise housing schemes. The implications of any such programme cannot wholly be foreseen. The risk of practice is thus grounded in the long-term viability of the theory that grounds the action. Fallibilism and the ineradicablity of risk entail that such experiments in living can only be conducted justly within the context of democratic openness. From the position of discourse ethics, this is the call for critical reflection upon and discussion of the distribution of the burden of risk, and the legitimacy of the power of those who determine both the risk and its distribution, through the involvement of all who may be affected. But this, once more, merely serves to stress the danger of any discourse that cannot be fully inclusive.

In an early review of Ernst Bloch's *The Principle of Hope*, Habermas makes the following observation on the classification of scientific and philosophical inquiry (PP: 75). He initially proposes two forms of inquiry: utopian and speculative. Utopian thought recognizes the necessity of transforming the present, which is to say, of engaging practically with existing social conditions because they are unjust and because they can be changed. It does this by taking seriously the expressions of suffering and desire for a better life that are offered by the inarticulate, excluded and repressed, much in the style of Freudian dream interpretation. It is informed in this engagement by the social, natural and hermeneutic sciences. Science determines the objectivity of needs claims and the practicality of realizing them. Utopianism is thus tested in practice, and recognizes itself as fallible. In contrast, speculative thought holds that the philosophical project is immune from empirical scientific refutation. The "absolute" is worked out in thought, and reference to a real and uncertain world that is unfolding historically is unnecessary. This is the position of Lukács, as well as of idealist philosophers such as Hegel. Despite the sketchiness of such an outline, "utopian thought" seems to sum up Habermas's own aspirations, most precisely in *Knowledge and Human Interests*.

Yet, against these two models, Habermas finds in Bloch a third. Bloch provides a "utopian variation on the usual speculation". The speculative thinker has a faith in the truth or, in this context, more accurately the redemptive power of their theory. Bloch checks this faith by a radical uncertainty in what Habermas terms the "guarantee of salvation". At its most fundamental it is the recognition that should utopia be realized, then it would be "otherwise" than was expected (PP: 76). Historical existence is radically unpredictable, surprising and frequently disappointing. Indeed, the realization of utopian plans is invariably accompanied by a "melancholy of fulfilment" as the reality fails to meet one's expectations (PP: 74). On another level, Habermas himself echoes this idea of the loss of a guarantee of salvation in "the myth of the atheistic God" (TP: 218–19; and see § "Crisis and critique", p. 20). Speculation, be it Hegel's or Lukács's, assumes that the absolute has always already been achieved. God guarantees from the first his (hers or its) own redemption. Bloch's utopianism abandons any such guarantee, and it is perhaps precisely here that we find Habermas's own philosophy.

Ultimately, Habermas's philosophy retains a utopian moment that entails that it is not merely a stand-in for empirical research. It is rather a place-holder for the utopian realization of the satisfaction of the objective needs that it has sought to identify. Indeed, it is precisely here that Habermas seemed to recognize, at least in this early essay, the project of the Enlightenment. He notes that the renunciation of a utopian moment in philosophy – and thus of a notion of radically uncertain historical progress – even with respect of a recognition of the "melancholy of fulfilment", is a manifestation of the "counterenlightenment" (PP: 76; and see PP: 64). The continual, uncertain and high-risk struggle for redemption – the struggle to realize utopia – is necessary and must therefore be taken seriously. To abandon philosophy for scientism (on the one hand) or rhetoric, literature and perspectivism (on the other), is to relinquish philosophy's place as stand-in, and with it the struggle. Yet, to lose sight of the great risk of failure under which the struggle is pursued is to relapse into a dogmatism, to confuse an aspiration with its realization, and thus to confuse philosophy for that for which it is standing-in, and this just as effectively inhibits the very possibility of redemption.

These reflections, of course, still have not resolved the problem of those who are unable to engage in communication. At best they offer a further dimension to the notions of uncertainty and risk. A lead has been given however, in so far as Bloch's approach to utopia, as just noted, has something in common with Freud's dream interpretation. A dream may be seen as an attempt to articulate that for which the subject does not have adequate expressive competence. The notion of philosophy as "interpreter" may therefore be taken up, in order to explore this further. Habermas's principle intention in describing philosophy as an "interpreter" is to situate it in the gap that exists between expert cultures and the lifeworld. The philosopher, be it of science, morality and law, or even art, becomes the mediator between increasingly autonomous experts and a lay public that is at once disenfranchised from expert debate and yet deeply affected by the consequences of that debate. The philosopher, precisely because he or she refuses to accept Sellars's suggestion of a reduction of the lifeworld to the objectifying descriptions of the expert observer, retains a familiarity with both worlds. As such, the philosopher is uniquely equipped for the role of "public intellectual", exploiting the resources of the public sphere in order to challenge the colonization of the lifeworld.

In a recent essay, "Faith and Knowledge" (2003d), Habermas gives this idea a further twist. He remarks that, after 9/11 and in the light of the challenges of a multicultural and multifaith world, the "mode for nondestructive secularisation is translation" (FHN: 114). The reference to secularization is important, for it returns us, explicitly, to the question of social progress and thus the framework of social evolution. While secularization is an element of the Weberian process of rationalization, the rise of religious fundamentalism and the mere continuation of religious observance and spiritual belief in modern secular societies seem to check any confidence in the inevitability, let alone the worth, of the process of modernization. Yet, again, this is merely another side of the irreducibility of the lifeworld to the system. It is in this context that philosophy as interpreter takes on a new depth. If translation is the paradigm form of interpretation, as Gadamer has argued, then in the context of critical theory what matters is a process of translation that is informed not merely by Gadamer's hermeneutics, but also by a scientific awareness of colonization and, crucially, by an awareness of forms of systematically distorted communication that have their models in psychoanalysis.

"Faith and Knowledge" explores the space between religion and science, and thus is exemplary of the approach of philosophy as "interpreter". Yet, although Habermas sees himself involved in a process of enlightenment, his objective is not to dissolve religious belief, and thus not to reduce religious belief to social or psychological facts, and so to explain it away.[4] Interpretation takes religious belief seriously – again much as Bloch takes utopian longings seriously and Freud takes dreams seriously – in order to engage in a process of demythologization. This process finds in such beliefs at once expressions of real suffering and alienation, the resources to think through pressing social and moral problems, and ultimately a critical check on the hubris of the secularized scientist. The rich resources of the lifeworld – be they in the form of religious beliefs or secular sets of values and perspectives – can no more be taken at face value than can the manifest content of dreams. Yet, interpreted with sufficient sensitivity, those resources offer possibly the only source of a voice for those who cannot communicate otherwise (including the only approximation available for the voice of those not yet born). This is to suggest, perhaps, that beneath the optimistic surface of Habermas's philosophy, manifest not least in the confidence that *Between Facts and Norms* displays in the workings of the public sphere, there lies a radical uncertainty, and again the myth of the atheistic God. Fallibilism and the utopian "melancholy of fulfilment" undercut all claims to finality. Ultimately, Habermas's philosophy may never escape the problem of the inclusion of the radically other, the disenfranchised and inarticulate, for that would mean escaping the problems of Freudian dialogue, and in particular the problems of a mutually therapeutic dialogue of the ill. Ironically, the very strength of Habermasian philosophy lies in its being not an escape from, but a celebration of that dialogue.

Notes

Chapter 1: The Marxist heritage

1. For background on the Frankfurt School, and Habermas's relationship to it, see Jay (1973), McCarthy (1978), Held (1980), Benhabib (1986) and Wiggershaus (1994).
2. This example will be referred back to frequently in the following discussions.
3. For further discussion of Habermas and positivism, see Keat (1981), Holub (1991: 20–48) and Hesse (1982).

Chapter 2: The public sphere

1. The *Habilitationsshaft* is the postgraduate qualification for a university lecturer.
2. The parallels to the situation in Europe and America forty years on, with increasing concern over low voter turnouts as well as widespread protests at intergovernmental summits, again by those feeling themselves to be excluded from the formal institutions of government, are worth noting.
3. For further discussion of Habermas's account of the public sphere, see Holub (1991: 1–19), Cahoun (1992) and Crossley *et al.* (2004).

Chapter 3: The idea of critical theory

1. For discussions of Habermas's theory of cognitive interests, see Ahlers (1970), Huch (1970), Wellmer (1970), Dallmayr (1972a, 1972b), Giddens (1982), Ottman (1982), Honneth (1991) and Powers (1993).
2. For discussions of Habermas's relationship to pragmatism, see Aboulafia *et al.* (2001), Arens (1994) and Koczanowicz (1999).
3. References to Peirce's collected works are traditionally in the form N.MMM, where N refers to the volume number, and MMM to the paragraph.
4. For a general philosophical discussion of this topic, see Chambers (1999).
5. For a discussion of Habermas and Wittgenstein, see Pleasants (1999).
6. For further discussion of Habermas and hermeneutics, see Thompson (1981), Holub (1991: 49–77), How (1995), Roberts (1995), Teigas (1995), Hahn (2000: 463–500) and Harrington (2001).
7. For further discussion of Habermas and psychoanalysis, see Keat (1981).

Chapter 4: Legitimation crisis

1. For discussions of *Knowledge and Human Interests*, see Ahlers (1970), Huch (1970), Wellmer (1970), Dallmayr (1972a, 1972b), Giddens (1982), Ottman (1982), Honneth (1991) and Powers (1993).
2. For discussions of Habermas's response to systems theory, see Habermas & Luhmann (1975), Holub (1991: 106–32) and Roberts (1995).
3. For discussions of Habermas's interpretation of historical materialism and history, see Schmid (1982), Rockmore (1989), McCarthy (2001) and Owen (2002).
4. This is only an outline of an argument, and presupposes a more adequate account of social role theory. It is, however, empirically questionable in the light of recent discoveries of evidence of Neanderthal burials and even art work.
5. For discussions of Habermas's contribution to the sociology of art and to aesthetics, see Roblin (1990) and Duvenage (2003).
6. For discussion of *Legitimation Crisis*, see Held (1982).

Chapter 5: The theory of communicative action

1. Habermas's later position shifts from a concern with mutual recognition of intention to mutual acceptance of the verifiability of the claims raised in the speech act (see TCAI: 295–305).
2. For discussions of universal pragmatics, see Thompson (1982), Cooke (1994), Nussbaum (1998), Zinkin (1998) and Swindal (1999).
3. It may be noted that Habermas used the notion of a private language, despite accepting Wittgenstein's criticisms. This apparent anomaly can be explained, for Wittgenstein's criticism focuses on the unreliability of conscious memory. These memories need confirming and stabilizing by a community. In contrast, Freud presupposes the accuracy of the unconscious memory. In part, the very fallibility of conscious memory is explained in terms of neurosis and the repression of memories into the ominously reliable structure of the unconscious.
4. For discussion of discourse ethics, see Benhabib & Dallmayr (1990), Rehg (1994), Kitchen (1997), Finlayson (1998) and Hahn (2000: 173–256).
5. For reference, Rawls's (1972: 302) principles of justice are:
    (i) Each person is to have an equal right to the most extensive total system of equal basic liberties compatible with a similar system of liberty for all.
    (ii) Social and economic inequalities are to be arranged so that they are both:
    (a) to the greatest benefit of the least advantaged, consistent with the just savings principle, and
    (b) attached to offices and positions open to all under conditions of fair equality of opportunity.
6. For discussions of Habermas and Lyotard, see Holub (1991: 133–61), Raffel (1992), Fairfield (1994) and Foster (1999).
7. For discussions of *The Theory of Communicative Action*, see Ingram (1987), White (1987), Brand (1990), Honneth & Joas (1991), Hahn (2000: 1–172) and Heath (2001).

Chapter 6: Modernity

1. For a rehearsal of a defense of the philosophy of consciousness, from Dieter Henrich, see Freundlieb (2003).
2. For discussions of Habermas and modernity, see Bernstein (1985), White (1987),

Honneth (1995), Passerin d'Entrèves & Benhabib (1996), Fleming (1997) and Trey (1998).
3. For discussions of Habermas's interpretation of Nietzsche, see Babich (2004).
4. For a discussion of Habermas and Heidegger, see Kompridis (1998).
5. For discussions of Habermas's response to Adorno and Horkheimer, see Geuss (1981), Alway (1995), Morris (2001) and Cook (2004).
6. For discussions of Habermas's response to Foucault, see Kelly (1994), Best (1995), Healy (1997) and Ashenden & Owen (1999).

Chapter 7: Law and democracy

1. "His", for at this stage the law remains patriarchal, with, for example, the English law of coverture subjecting the married women to the rule of her husband, just as the husband is subject to the monarch.
2. For feminist responses to Habermas's work in political theory and as a whole, see Meehan (1995) and Fleming (1997).
3. For discussions of Habermas's philosophy of law and later political philosophy, see Matustik (1993), Bernstein (1995), Chambers (1996), Deflem (1996), Cooke (1997), Rosenfeld & Arato (1998), Hahn (2000: 257–422), Marsh (2001), Schomberg & Baynes (2002) and Eriksen (2003).
4. For discussions of Habermas and religion and theology, see Siebert (1985), Browning & Fiorenza (1992), Campbell (1999), Habermas (2002) and Garrigan (2004).

Bibliography

Dates of original publication, where significant, are in brackets after the date of the cited edition.

Works by Jürgen Habermas

1954. "Die Dialektic der Rationalisierung: Vom Pauperismus in Produktion und Kunsum", *Merker* 8, 701–24.

1961, with L. von Friedeburg, C. Oehler & F. Weltz. *Student und Politik: Eine Soziologische Untersuchung zum politischen Bewußtsein Frankfurter Studenten*. Neuwied: Hermann Luchterhand.

1970a. "On Systematically Distorted Communication", *Inquiry* 13, 205–18.

1970b. "Towards a Theory of Communicative Competence", *Inquiry* 13, 360–75.

1970c. "Summation and Response", *Continuum* 8(1), 123–33.

1971a [1968]. *Knowledge and Human Interests*, J. J. Shapiro (trans.). Boston, MA: Beacon Press.

1971b [1968–69]. *Toward a Rational Society: Student Protest, Science and Politics*, J. J. Shapiro (trans.). London: Heinemann.

1974a. "On Social Identity", *Telos* 19, 91–103.

1974b. "The Public Sphere: An Encyclopaedia Article", *New German Critique* 3, 49–55.

1975. "The Place of Philosophy in Marxism", *Insurgent Sociologist* 5, 41–8.

1975, with N. Luhmann. *Theorie der Gesellschaft oder Sozialtechnologie: was leistet die Systemforschung?* Frankfurt: Suhrkamp.

1976a [1971]. *Theory and Practice*, J. Viertel Boston (trans.). Boston, MA: Beacon Press.

1976b [1973]. *Legitimation Crisis*, T. McCarthy (trans.). London: Heinemann.

1976c [1969]. "The Analytical Theory of Science and Dialectics". In *The Positivist Dispute in German Sociology*, T. W. Adorno *et al.*, 131–62. London: Heinemann.

1976d [1969]. "A Positivistically Bisected Rationalism". In *The Positivist Dispute in German Sociology*, T. W. Adorno *et al.*, 198–225. London: Heinemann.

1976e. "Some Distinctions in Universal Pragmatics", *Theory and Society* 1(3), 155–67.

1977f [1968]. "Between Philosophy and Science: Marxism as Critique". See Habermas (1976a), 195–252.

1977g [1963]. "Dogmatism, Reason and Decision: On Theory and Praxis in our Scientific Civilization". See Habermas (1976a), 253–82.

1979a [1976]. *Communication and the Evolution of Society*, T. McCarthy (trans.). Boston, MA: Beacon Press.

1979b. "History and Evolution", *Telos* 38, 5–44.

1980 [1970]. "The Hermeneutic Claim to Universality". In *Contemporary Hermeneutics: Hermeneutics as Method, Philosophy and Critique*, J. Bleicher, 181–211. London: Routledge & Kegan Paul.

1981a. *Kleine Politische Schriften 1–4*, Frankfurt: Suhrkamp.

1981b. *Philosophisch–Politische Profile*. Frankfurt: Suhrkamp.

1982. "A Reply to my Critics". See Thompson & Held (eds) (1982), 219–83.

1983a. *Philosophical–Political Profiles*, F. G. Lawrence (trans.). London: Heinemann.

1983b [1980]. "Modernity – An Incomplete Project". In *Postmodern Culture*, H. Foster (ed.), 3–15. London: Pluto Press.

1984a [1981]. *The Theory of Communicative Action, vol. 1: Reason and the Rationalisation of Society*, T. McCarthy (trans.). Cambridge: Polity.

1984b. *Vorstudien und Ergänzungen zur Theorie des Kommunikativen Handelns*, Frankfurt: Suhrkamp.

1987 [1981]. *The Theory of Communicative Action, vol. 2: Lifeworld and System: A Critique of Functionalist Reason*, T. McCarthy (trans.). Cambridge: Polity.

1988a [1985]. *The Philosophical Discourse of Modernity: Twelve Lectures*, F. G. Lawrence (trans.). Cambridge, MA: MIT Press.

1988b [1967]. *On the Logic of the Social Sciences*, S. Weber Nicholsen & J. A. Stark (eds). Cambridge: Polity.

1989a [1962]. *The Structural Transformation of the Public Sphere: An Inquiry into a Category of Bourgeois Society*, T. Burger & F. Lawrence (trans.). Cambridge: Polity.

1989b [1985]. *The New Conservatism: Cultural Criticism and the Historians' Debate*, Shierry Weber Nicholsen (trans.). Cambridge, MA: MIT Press.

1990 [1983]. *Moral Consciousness and Communicative Action*, C. Lenhardt & S. Weber Nicholsen (trans.). Cambridge, MA: MIT Press.

1992a. *Autonomy and Solidarity: Interviews with Jürgen Habermas*, P. Dews (ed.). London: Verso.

1992b [1988]. *Postmetaphysical Thinking: Philosophical Essays*, W. M. Hohengarten (trans.). Cambridge, MA: MIT Press.

1992c. "Further Reflections on the Public Sphere", T. Burger (trans.). In *Habermas and the Public Sphere*, C. Cahoun (ed.), 421–61. Cambridge, MA: MIT Press.

1993a. *Justification and Application: Remarks on Discourse Ethics*, C. Cronin (trans.). Cambridge: Polity.

1993b. "A Reply". In *Communicative Action: Essays on Jürgen Habermas's* The Theory of Communicative Action, A. Honneth & H. Joas (eds). Cambridge: Polity.

1994 [1990]. *The Past as Future*, M. Pensk (trans.). Cambridge: Polity.

1996a [1993]. *Between Facts and Norms: Contributions to a Discourse Theory of Law and Democracy*, W. Rehg (trans.). Cambridge: Polity.

1996b [1988]. "Popular Sovereignty as Procedure". See Habermas (1996a), 463–90.

1997 [1995]. *A Berlin Republic: Writings on Germany*, S. Rendall (trans.). Lincoln, NE: University of Nebraska Press.

1998a [1996]. *The Inclusion of the Other: Studies in Political Theory*, C. Cronin & P. de Greiff (eds). Cambridge, MA: MIT Press.

1998b. "Law and Morality". In *The Tanner Lectures on Human Values*, vol. VIII, S. M. McMurrin (ed.), 217–79. Salt Lake City, UT: University of Utah Press.

1999a. *On the Pragmatics of Communication*, M. Cooke (ed.). Cambridge: Polity.

1999b. "Introduction", *Ratio Juris* 12(4), 329–35.

1999c. "A Short Reply", *Ratio Juris* 12(4), 445–53.

2001a [1997]. *The Liberating Power of Symbols: Philosophical Essays*, P. Dews (trans.). Cambridge: Polity.

2001b [1989]. *The Postnational Constellation: Political Essays,* M. Pensky (trans.). Cambridge, MA: MIT Press.

2001c. *On the Pragmatics of Social Interaction: Preliminary Studies in the Theory of Communicative Action*, B. Fultner (trans.). Cambridge: Polity.

2001d. "Constitutional Democracy: A Paradoxical Union of Contradictory Principles?", *Political Theory* 29(6), 766–81.

2002. *Religion and Rationality,* E. Mendieta (ed.). Cambridge: Polity.

2003a [1999]. *Truth and Justification*, B. Fultner (trans.). Cambridge, MA: MIT Press.

2003b [2001]. *The Future of Human Nature*, H. Beister (trans.). Cambridge: Polity.

2003c. "On Law and Disagreement. Some Comments of 'Interpretative Pluralism'", *Ratio Juris* 16(2), 187–94.

2003d [2001]. "Faith and Knowledge". See Habermas (2003b), 101–15.

2005. *Time of Transitions*. Cambridge: Polity.

Other works cited

Aboulafia, M., M. Bookman & C. Kemp (eds) 2001. *Habermas and Pragmatism*. London: Routledge.

Adorno, T. W. 1949. *Philosophie der neuen Musik*. Tübingen: Mohr.

Adorno, T. W. 1967 [1955]. *Prisms*, S. Weber & S. Weber (trans.). London: Spearman.

Adorno, T. W. 1973 [1966]. *Negative Dialectics*, E. B. Ashton (trans.). London: Routledge & Kegan Paul.

Adorno, T. W. 1974 [1951]. *Minima Moralia: Reflections on a Damaged Life*, E. F. N. Jephcott (trans.). London: Verso.

Adorno, T. W. 1984 [1970]. *Aesthetic Theory*, C. Lenhardt (trans.). London: Routledge & Kegan Paul.

Adorno, T. W., E. Frenkel-Brunswik, D. J. Levinson & R. Nevitt Stanford 1950. *The Authoritarian Personality*. New York: Harper.

Adorno, T. W., H. Albert, R. Dahrendorf *et al.* 1976 [1969]. *The Positivist Dispute in German Sociology*, G. Adey & D. Frisby (trans.). London: Heinemann.

Ahler, R. 1970. "Is Technology Intrinsically Repressive?", *Continuum* 8(1), 111–22.

Alford, C. F. 1985. *Science and the Revenge of Nature: Marcuse and Habermas*. Gainesville, FL: University Presses of Florida.

Alway, J. 1995. *Critical Theory and Political Possibilities: Conceptions of Emancipatory Politics in the Works of Horkheimer, Adorno, Marcuse, and Habermas*. Westport, CT: Greenwood Press.

Apel, K.-O. 1980 [1972/73]. *Towards a Transformation of Philosophy*, G. Adey & D. Frisby (trans.). London: Routledge & Kegan Paul.

Apel, K.-O. 1981. *Charles S. Peirce: From Pragmatism to Pragmaticism*, J. M. Krois (trans.). Amherst, MA: University of Massachusetts Press.

Apel, K.-O. 1998. "Openly Strategic Uses of Language: A Transcendental-Pragmatic Perspective (A second attempt to think with Habermas against Habermas)". In *Habermas: A Critical Reader*, P. Dews (ed.), 272–90. Oxford: Blackwell.

Arens, E. 1994. *The Logic of Pragmatic Thinking: From Peirce to Habermas*. Atlantic Highlands, NJ: Humanities Press.

Ashenden, S. & D. Owen (eds) 1999. *Foucault contra Habermas*. London: Sage.

Austin, J. L. 1975 [1960]. *How to Do Things with Words*, J. O. Urmson & M. Sbisà (eds). Oxford: Clarendon Press.

Babich, B. E. (ed.) 2004. *Habermas, Nietzsche, and Critical Theory*. Amherst, MA: Humanity Books.

Baxter, H. 1987. "System and Life-World in Habermas's *Theory of Communicative Action*", *Theory and Society* 16(1), 39–86.

Benhabib, S. 1986. *Critique, Norm, and Utopia: A Study of the Foundations of Critical Theory*. New York: Columbia University Press.

Benhabib, S. & F. Dallmayr (eds) 1990. *The Communicative Ethics Controversy*. Cambridge, MA: MIT Press.

Benjamin, W. 1970 [1936]. "The Work of Art in the Age of Mechanical Reproduction". In his *Illuminations*, H. Arendt (ed.). London: Fontana.

Bentham, J. 1843. *The Commonplace Book*. In his *Works*, vol. 10, J. Bowring (ed.). Edinburgh: William Tait.

Bernstein, R. J. (ed.) 1985. *Habermas and Modernity*. Cambridge: Polity.

Bernstein, J. M. 1995. *Recovering Ethical Life: Jürgen Habermas and the Future of Critical Theory*. London: Routledge.

Best, S. 1995. *The Politics of Historical Vision: Marx, Foucault, Habermas*. New York: Guilford Press.

Borradori, G. 2003. *Philosophy in a Time of Terror: Dialogues with Jürgen Habermas and Jacques Derrida*. Chicago, IL: University of Chicago Press.

Bowring, F. 1996. "A Lifeworld without a Subject: Habermas and the Pathologies of Modernity", *Telos* 106, 77–104.

Brand, A. 1990. *The Force of Reason: An Introduction to Habermas' Theory of Communicative Action*. Sydney: Allen & Unwin.

Browning, D. S. & F. S. Fiorenza (eds) 1992. *Habermas, Modernity, and Public Theology*. New York: Crossroad.

Cahoun, C. (ed.) 1992. *Habermas and the Public Sphere*. Cambridge, MA: MIT Press.

Campbell, M. M. 1999. *Critical Theory and Liberation Theology: A Comparison of the Initial Work of Jürgen Habermas and Gustavo Gutierrez*. New York: Peter Lang.

Caygill, H. 1995. *A Kant Dictionary*. Oxford: Blackwell.

Chambers, A. F. 1999. *What is This Thing Called Science?*, 3rd edn. Buckingham: Open University Press.

Chambers, S. 1996. *Reasonable Democracy: Jürgen Habermas and the Politics of Discourse*. Ithaca, NY: Cornell University Press.

Cook, D. 2004. *Adorno, Habermas and the Search for a Rational Society*. London: Routledge.

Cooke, M. 1994. *Language and Reason: A Study of Habermas's Pragmatics*. Cambridge, MA: MIT Press.

Cooke, M. 1997. "Authenticity and Autonomy: Taylor, Habermas, and the Politics of Recognition", *Political Theory* 25(2), 258–88.

Crossley, N. & J. M. Roberts (eds) 2004. *After Habermas: New Perspectives on the Public Sphere*. Oxford: Blackwell.

Dallmayr, F. 1972a. "Reason and Emancipation: Notes on Habermas", *Man and World* 5, 79–109.

Dallmayr, F. 1972b. "Critical Theory Criticized: Habermas's *Knowledge and Human Interests* and its Aftermath", *Philosophy of the Social Sciences* 2, 211–29.

Deflem, M. (ed.) 1996. *Habermas, Modernity and Law*. London: Sage.

Derrida, J. 1976 [1967]. *Of Grammatology*, G. C. Spivak (trans.). Baltimore, MD: Johns Hopkins University Press.

Derrida, J. 1977. "Limited, Inc.", *Glyph* 2, 162–254.

Derrida, J. 1982a [1972]. "Signature Event Context". In his *Margins of Philosophy*, A. Bass (trans.), 307–30. Brighton: Harvester.

Derrida, J. 1982b. "Différance". In his *Margins of Philosophy*, A. Bass (trans.), 1–28. Brighton: Harvester.

Dews, P. (ed.) 1998. *Habermas: A Critical Reader*. Oxford: Blackwell.

Durkheim, E. 1984 [1902]. *The Division of Labour in Society*, W. D. Halls (trans.). Basingstoke: Macmillan.

Duvenage, P. 2003. *Habermas and Aesthetics: Limits of Communicative Action*. Cambridge: Polity.

Edgar, A. 1995. "Discourse Ethics and Paternalism". In *The Social Power of Ideas*, Y. Hudson & W. Creighton Peden (eds). Lampeter: Edwin Mellen Press.

Elster, J. 1986. "The Market and the Forum: Three Varieties of Political Theory". In *Foundations of Social Choice Theory*, J. Elster & A. Hylland (eds), 128–42. Cambridge: Cambridge University Press.

Eriksen, E. O. 2003. *Understanding Habermas: Communicative Action and Deliberative Democracy*. London: Continuum.

Fairfield, P. 1994. "Habermas, Lyotard and Political Discourse", *Reason Papers* 19, 58–80.

Finlayson, J. G. 1998. "Does Hegel's Critique of Kant's Moral Theory Apply to Discourse Ethics?". See Dews (1998), 29–52.

Finlayson, J. G. 2005. *Habermas: A Very Short Introduction*. Oxford: Oxford University Press.

Fleming, M. 1997. *Emancipation and Illusion: Rationality and Gender in Habermas's Theory of Modernity*. University Park, PA: Pennsylvania State University Press.

Flyvbjerg, B. 1998. "Habermas and Foucault: Thinkers for Civil Society?", *The British Journal of Sociology* 49(2), 210–33.

Foster, R. S. 1999. "Strategies of Justice: The Project of Philosophy in Lyotard and Habermas", *Philosophy and Social Criticism* 25(2), 87–113.

Foucault, M. 1970 [1966]. *The Order of Things: An Archaeology of the Human Sciences*. London: Tavistock.

Foucault, M. 1971 [1961]. *Madness and Civilization: A History of Insanity in the Age of Reason*. London: Tavistock.

Foucault, M. 1973 [1969]. *The Archaeology of Knowledge*, A. M. Sheridan Smith (trans.). London: Tavistock.

Foucault, M. 1976 [1963]. *The Birth of the Clinic*. London: Tavistock.

Foucault, M. 1977 [1975]. *Discipline and Punish: The Birth of the Prison*. Harmondsworth: Penguin.

Foucault, M. 1981 [1976]. *The History of Sexuality, vol. 1: An Introduction*. Harmondsworth: Penguin.

Foucault, M. 1986. "Nietzsche, Genealogy, History". In *The Foucault Reader*, P. Rabinow (ed.), 76–100. Harmondsworth: Penguin.

Freud, S. 1962 [1910/1926]. *Two Short Accounts of Psycho-Analysis*. Harmondsworth: Penguin.

Freud, S. 1976 [1900]. *The Interpretation of Dreams*, J. Strachey (trans.). Harmondsworth: Penguin.

Freud, S. 1985. *Civilization, Society and Religion: Group Psychology, Civilization and Its Discontents and other Works*, J. Strachey (trans.). Harmondsworth: Penguin.

Freundlieb, D. 2003. *Dieter Henrich and Contemporary Philosophy: The Return to Subjectivity*. Aldershot: Ashgate.

Fukuyama, F. 1992. *The End of History and the Last Man*. London: Hamish Hamilton.

Garfinkel, H. 1967. *Studies in Ethnomethodology*. Englewood Cliffs, NJ: Prentice-Hall.

Garrigan, S. 2004. *Beyond Ritual: Sacramental Theology after Habermas*. Aldershot: Ashgate.

Geuss, R. 1981. *The Idea of a Critical Theory: Habermas and the Frankfurt School*. Cambridge: Cambridge University Press.

Giddens, A. 1982. "Labour and Interaction". See Thompson & Held (eds) (1982), 149–61.

Hahn, L. E. (ed.) 2000. *Perspectives on Habermas*. Chicago, IL: Open Court.

Hanks, J. C. 2002. *Refiguring Critical Theory: Jürgen Habermas and the Possibilities of Political Change*. Lanham, MD: University Press of America.

Harrington, A. 2001. *Hermeneutic Dialogue and Social Science: A Critique of Gadamer and Habermas*. London: Routledge.

Healy, P. 1997. "Between Habermas and Foucault: On the Limits and Possibilities of Critical and Emancipatory Reason", *South African Journal of Philosophy* 16(4), 140–49.

Heath, J. 2001. *Communicative Action and Rational Choice*. Cambridge, MA: MIT Press.

Hegel, G. W. F. 1931 [1807]. *The Phenomenology of Mind*, J. B. Bailley (trans.). London: Allen & Unwin.

Hegel, G. W. F. 1942 [1821]. *The Philosophy of Right*, T. M. Knox (trans.). Oxford: Clarendon Press.

Hegel, G. W. F. 1948. *Early Theological Writings*, T. M. Knox (trans.). Chicago, IL: University of Chicago Press.

Hegel, G. W. F. 1970 [1817]. *Philosophy of Nature*, A. V. Miller (trans.). Oxford: Clarendon Press.

Hegel, G. W. F. 1971 [1817]. *Philosophy of Mind*, W. Wallace & A. V. Miller (trans.). Oxford: Clarendon Press.

Hegel, G. W. F. 1975a [1817]. *Hegel's Logic*, W. Wallace (trans.). Oxford: Clarendon Press.

Hegel, G. W. F. 1975b [1835]. *Hegel's Aesthetics*, 2 vols, T. M. Knox (trans.). Oxford: Clarendon Press.

Hegel, G. W. F. 1986. *The Jena System, 1804–5: Logic and Metaphysics*, J. W. Burbidge & G. di Giovanni (eds). Montreal: McGill-Queen's University Press.

Heidegger, M. 1962 [1927]. *Being and Time*, J. Macquarrie & E. Robinson (trans.). Oxford: Blackwell.

Heidegger, M. 1996 [1953]. "The Question Concerning Technology". In his *Basic Writings: Martin Heidegger*, D. Farrell Krell (ed.). London: Routledge.

Held, D. 1980. *Introduction to Critical Theory: Horkheimer to Habermas*. London: Hutchinson.

Held, D. 1982. "Crisis Tendencies, Legitimation and the State". See Thompson & Held (eds) (1982), 181–95.

Hesse, M. 1982. "Science and Objectivity". See Thompson & Held (eds) (1982).

Holub, R. C. 1991. *Jürgen Habermas: Critic in the Public Sphere*. London: Routledge.

Honneth, A. 1991. *The Critique of Power: Reflective Stages in a Critical Social Theory*, K. Bayes (trans.). Cambridge, MA: MIT Press.

Honneth, A. 1995. "The Other of Justice: Habermas and the Ethical Challenge of Postmodernism". In *The Cambridge Companion to Habermas*, S. K. White (ed.). Cambridge: Cambridge University Press.

Honneth, A. & H. Joas (eds) 1991. *Communicative Action: Essays on Jürgen Habermas's* The Theory of Communicative Action. Cambridge, MA: MIT Press.

Horkheimer, M. 1972. *Critical Theory: Selected Essays*, M. J. O'Connell (trans.). New York: Herder & Herder.

Horkheimer, M. 1992 [1947]. *Eclipse of Reason*. New York: Continuum.

Horkheimer, M. & T. W. Adorno 1972 [1944]. *The Dialectic of Enlightenment*, J. Cumming (trans.). New York: Seabury Press.

How, A. 1995. *The Habermas–Gadamer Debate and the Nature of the Social: Back to Bedrock*. Aldershot: Avebury.

Huch, K. J. 1970. "Interest in Emancipation", *Continuum* 8(1), 27–39.

Hume, D. 1996 [1757]. "Of the Standard of Taste". In his *Selected Essays*, S. Copley & A. Edgar (eds), 133–54. Oxford: Oxford University Press.

Ingram, D. 1987. *Habermas and the Dialectic of Reason*. New Haven, CT: Yale University Press.

Jay, M. 1973. *The Dialectical Imagination: A History of the Frankfurt School and the Institute of Social Research, 1923–1950*. London: Heinemann.

Jay, M. 1984. *Marxism and Totality: The Adventures of a Concept from Lukács to Habermas*. Berkeley, CA: University of California Press.

Kant, I. 1933 [1781/1787]. *Critique of Pure Reason*, N. Kemp-Smith (trans.). Basingstoke: Macmillan.

Kant, I. 1952 [1790]. *Critique of Judgement*, J. C. Meredith (trans.). Oxford: Clarendon Press.

Kant, I. 1983a [1784]. "An Answer to the Question: What is Enlightenment?". In his *Perpetual Peace and Other Essays*, T. Humphrey (trans.), 41–8. Indianapolis, IN: Hackett.

Kant, I. 1983b [1784]. "Idea for a Universal History with a Cosmopolitan Intent". In his *Perpetual Peace and Other Essays*, T. Humphrey (trans.), 29–40. Indianapolis, IN: Hackett.

Kant, I. 1983c [1985]. *Grounding for the Metaphysics of Morals*. In his *Ethical Philosophy*, W. A. Wick (ed.), J. W. Ellington (trans.), 1–69. Indianapolis, IN: Hackett.

Keat, R. 1981. *The Politics of Social Theory: Habermas, Freud and the Critique of Positivism*. Oxford: Blackwell.

Kelly, M. (ed.) 1994. *Critique and Power: Recasting the Foucault/Habermas Debate*. Cambridge, MA: MIT Press.

Kitchen, G. 1997. "Habermas's Moral Cognitivism", *Proceedings of the Aristotelian Society* 97, 317–24.

Koczanowicz, L. 1999. "The Choice of Tradition and the Tradition of Choice: Habermas' and Rorty's Interpretation of Pragmatism", *Philosophy and Social Criticism* 25(1), 55–70.

Kompridis, N. 1988. "Heidegger's Challenge and the Future of Critical Theory". In *Habermas: A Critical Reader*, P. Dews (ed.), 118–50. Oxford: Blackwell.

Kortian, G. 1980. *Metacritique: The Philosophical Argument of Jürgen Habermas*. Cambridge: Cambridge University Press.

Lévi-Strauss, C. 1969 [1949]. *The Elementary Structures of Kinship*, J. H. Bell, J. R. von Sturmer & R. Needham (trans.). Boston: Beacon Press.

Li, Kit-Man 1999. *Western Civilization and Its Problems: A Dialogue between Weber, Elias and Habermas*. Aldershot: Ashgate.

Locke, J. 1980 [1690]. *Second Treatise of Government*, C. B. Macpherson (ed.). Indianapolis, IN: Hackett.

Lukács, G. 1971 [1923/1968]. *History and Class Consciousness: Studies in Marxist Dialectics*, R. Livingstone (trans.). London: Merlin.

Luhmann, N. 1982. *The Differentiation of Society*, S. Holmes & C. Larmore (trans.). New York: Columbia University Press.

Luhmann, N. 1987. "Modern Systems Theory and the Theory of Society". In *Modern German Sociology*, V. Meja, D. Misgeld & N. Stehr (eds), 173–86. New York: Columbia University Press.

Luhmann, N. 1995. *Social Systems*. Stanford, CA: Stanford University Press.

Lyotard, J.-F. 1984 [1979]. *The Postmodern Condition: A Report on Knowledge*, G. Bennington and B. Massumi (trans.). Minneapolis, MN: University of Minnesota Press.

Lyotard, J.-F. 1985 [1979]. *Just Gaming*, W. Godzich & B. Massumi (trans.). Minneapolis, MN: University of Minnesota Press.

Marsh, J. L. 2001. *Unjust Legality: A Critique of Habermas's Philosophy of Law*. Lanham, MD: Rowman & Littlefield.

Marx, K. 1975a [1859]. "Preface to *A Contribution to the Critique of Political Economy*". In his *Early Writings*, L. Colletti (intro.), R. Livingstone & G. Benton (trans.), 424–8. Harmondsworth: Penguin.

Marx, K. 1975b [1859]. "Introduction to *A Contribution to the Critique of Hegel's Philosophy of Right*". In his *Early Writings*, L. Colletti (intro.), R. Livingstone & G. Benton (trans.), 243–57. Harmondsworth: Penguin.

Marx, K. 1975c [1845]. "Theses on Feuerbach". In his *Early Writings*, L. Colletti (intro.), R. Livingstone & G. Benton (trans.), 421–3. Harmondsworth: Penguin.

Marx, K. 1976 [1867]. *Capital: A Critique of Political Economy*, vol. 1, B. Fowkes (trans.). Harmondsworth: Penguin.

Marx, K. & F. Engels 1973 [1847]. "The Manifesto of the Communist Party". In his *The Revolutions of 1848*, D. Fernbach (ed.), 62–98. Harmondsworth: Penguin.

Matustík, M. J. 1993. *Postnational Identity: Critical Theory and Existential Philosophy in Habermas, Kierkegaard, and Havel*. New York: Guilford Press.

Matustík, M. J. 2001. *Jürgen Habermas: A Philosophical-Political Profile*. Lanham, MD: Rowman & Littlefield.

Mauss, M. 1966 [1925]. *The Gift: Forms and Functions of Exchange in Archaic Societies*. London: Routledge & Kegan Paul.

McCarthy, G. E. 2001. *Objectivity and the Silence of Reason: Weber, Habermas, and the Methodological Disputes in German Sociology*. New Brunswick, NJ: Transaction.

McCarthy, T. 1978. *The Critical Theory of Jürgen Habermas*. London: Hutchinson.

McCarthy, T. 1982. "Rationality and Relativism: Habermas's 'Overcoming' of Hermeneutics". See Thompson & Held (eds) (1982), 57–78.

Meehan, J. (ed.) 1995. *Feminists Read Habermas: Gendering the Subject of Discourse*. London: Routledge.

Mill, J. S. 1869. *On Liberty*, 4th edn. London: Longman, Roberts & Green.

Morris, M. 2001. *Rethinking the Communicative Turn: Adorno, Habermas, and the Problem of Communicative Freedom*. Albany, NY: SUNY Press.

Mulhall, S. & A. Swift 1992. *Liberals and Communitarians*. Oxford: Blackwell.

Negt, O. & A. Kluge 1993 [1972]. *Public Sphere and Experience: Toward an Analysis of the Bourgeois and Proletarian Public Sphere*, P. Labanyi, J. O. Daniel & A. Oksiloff (trans.). Minneapolis, MN: University of Minnesota Press.

Nietzsche, F. 1974 [1882]. *The Gay Science: With a Prelude in Rhymes and an Appendix of Songs*, W. Kaufmann (ed.). New York: Vintage.

Nietzsche, F. 1979 [1873]. "On Truth and Lies in a Nonmoral Sense". In his *Philosophy and Truth: Selections from Nietzsche's Notebooks of the Early 1870s*, D. Breazeale (ed.) Brighton: Harvester.

Nietzsche, F. 1980 [1874]. *On the Advantage and Disadvantage of History for Life*, P. Preuss (trans.). Indianapolis, IN: Hackett.

Nietzsche, F. 1993 [1872]. *The Birth of Tragedy: Out of the Spirit of Music*, S. Whiteside (trans.). Harmondsworth: Penguin.

Nussbaum, C. 1998. "Habermas on Speech Acts: A Naturalistic Critique", *Philosophy Today* 42(2), 126–45.

Offe, C. 1984. *Contradictions of the Welfare State*, J. Keane (ed.). London: Hutchinson.

Offe, C. 1985. *Disorganized Capitalism: Contemporary Transformations of Work and Politics*, J. Keane (ed.). Cambridge: Polity.

Offe, C. 1987. "Towards a Theory of Late Capitalism". In *Modern German Sociology*, V. Meja, D. Misgeld & N. Stehr (eds), 324–39. New York: Columbia University Press.

Offe, C. 1992. "Bindings, Shackles, Brakes: On Self-Limitation Strategies". In *Cultural-Political Interventions in the Unifinished Project of the Enlightenment*, A. Honneth, T. McCarthy, C. Offe, A. Wellmer (eds), 63–94. Cambridge, MA: MIT Press.

Ottmann, H. 1982. "Cognitive Interests and Self-Reflection". See Thompson & Held (eds) (1982), 79–97.

Outhwaite, W. 1994. *Habermas: A Critical Introduction*. Cambridge: Polity.

Outhwaite, W. (ed.) 1996. *The Habermas Reader*. Cambridge: Polity Press.

Owen, D. S. 2002. *Between Reason and History: Habermas and the Idea of Progress*. Albany, NY: SUNY Press.

Passerin d'Entrèves, M. & S. Benhabib (eds) 1996. *Habermas and the Unfinished Project of Modernity: Critical Essays on* The Philosophical Discourse of Modernity. Cambridge: Polity.

Peirce, C. S. 1960. *Collected Papers of Charles Sanders Peirce* (8 volumes), C. Hartshorne & P. Weiss (eds). Cambridge, MA: Harvard University Press.

Pleasants, N. 1999. *Wittgenstein and the Idea of a Critical Social Theory: A Critique of Giddens, Habermas and Bhaskar*. London: Routledge.

Powers, M. 1993. "Habermas and Transcendental Arguments: A Reappraisal", *Philosophy of the Social Sciences* **23**(1), 26–49.

Pusey, M. 1987. *Jürgen Habermas*. Chichester: Ellis Horwood.

Raffel, S. 1992. *Habermas, Lyotard and the Concept of Justice*. Basingstoke: Macmillan.

Rasmussen, D. M. 1990. *Reading Habermas*. Oxford: Blackwell.

Rasmussen, D. & J. Swindal (eds) 2002. *Jürgen Habermas*. London: Sage.

Rawls, J. 1972. *A Theory of Justice*. Oxford: Clarendon Press.

Rawls, J. 1985. "Justice as Fairness: Political not Metaphysical", *Philosophy and Public Affairs* **14**(3), 223–51.

Rehg, W. 1994. *Insight and Solidarity: a Study in the Discourse Ethics of Jürgen Habermas*. Berkeley, CA: University of California Press.

Ricoeur, P. 1970. *Freud and Philosophy: An Essay on Interpretation*, D. Savage (trans.). New Haven, CT: Yale University Press.

Roberts, D. (ed.) 1995. *Reconstructing Theory: Gadamer, Habermas, Luhmann*. Melbourne: Melbourne University Press.

Roblin, R. (ed.) 1990. *The Aesthetics of the Critical Theorists: Studies on Benjamin, Adorno, Marcuse, and Habermas*. Lampeter: Edwin Mellen Press.

Rockmore, T. 1989. *Habermas on Historical Materialism*. Bloomington, IN: Indiana University Press.

Roderick, R. 1986. *Habermas and the Foundations of Critical Theory*. Basingstoke: Macmillan.

Rose, G. 1978. *The Melancholy Science: An Introduction to the Thought of Theodor W. Adorno*. Basingstoke: Macmillan.

Rosenfeld, M. & A. Arato (eds) 1998. *Habermas on Law and Democracy: Critical Exchanges*. Berkeley, CA: University of California Press.

Ryle, G. 1963 [1949]. *The Concept of Mind*. Harmondsworth: Penguin.

Searle, J. 1977. "Reiterating the Differences: A Reply to Derrida", *Glyph* 1, 198–208.

Siebert, R. J. 1985. *The Critical Theory of Religion: the Frankfurt School: from Universal Pragmatic to Political Theology*. Berlin: Mouton.

Schomberg, R. von & K. Baynes (eds) 2002. *Discourse and Democracy: Essays on Habermas's* Between Facts and Norms. Albany, NY: SUNY Press.

Schmid, M. 1982. "Habermas's Theory of Social Evolution". See Thompson & Held (eds) (1982), 162–80.

Swindal, J. 1999. *Reflection Revisited: Jürgen Habermas's Discursive Theory of Truth*. New York: Fordham University Press.

Taylor, C. 1985. "What is Human Agency?". In his *Human Agency and Language: Philosophical Papers vol. 1*. Cambridge: Cambridge University Press.

Teigas, D. 1995. *Knowledge and Hermeneutic Understanding: A Study of the Habermas-Gadamer Debate*. Cranbury, NJ: Associated University Presses.

Thompson, J. B. 1981. *Critical Hermeneutics: A Study in the Thought of Paul Ricoeur and Jürgen Habermas*. Cambridge: Cambridge University Press.

Thompson, J. B. 1982. "Universal Pragmatics". See Thompson & Held (1982), 116–33.

Thompson, J. B. & D. Held (eds) 1982. *Habermas: Critical Debates*. London and Basingstoke: Macmillan.

Trey, G. 1998. *Solidarity and Difference: The Politics of Enlightenment in the Aftermath of Modernity*. Albany, NY: SUNY Press.

Villa, D. R. 1992. "Postmodernism and the Public Sphere", *The American Political Science Review* **86**(3), 712–21.

Weber, M. 1946a. *From Max Weber: Essays in Sociology*, H. H. Gerth & C. W. Mills (eds). London: Routledge & Kegan Paul.

Weber, M. 1946b [1921]. "Bureaucracy". See Weber (1946a), 196–244.

Weber, M. 1946c [1919]. "Science as a Vocation". See Weber (1946a), 129–56.

Weber, M. 1946d [1915]. "Religious Rejections of the World and their Directions".

See Weber (1946a), 323–59.

Weber, M. 1958 [1921]. *The Rational and Social Foundations of Music*, D. Martindale, J. Riedel & G. Neuwirth (trans.). Carbondale, IL: Southern Illinios University Press.

Weber, M. 1968 [1921]. *Economy and Society*, G. Roth & C. Wittich (eds). New York: Bedminster Press.

Weber, M. 1976 [1904–5]. *The Protestant Ethic and the Spirit of Capitalism*, T. Parsons (trans.). London: Allen & Unwin.

Wellmer, A. 1970. "Empirico-Analytical and Critical Social Science". *Continuum* 8(1), 12–26.

White, S. K. 1987. *The Recent Work of Jürgen Habermas: Reason, Justice and Modernity*. Cambridge: Cambridge University Press.

White, S. K. (ed.) 1995. *Cambridge Companion to Habermas*. Cambridge: Cambridge University Press.

Wiggershaus, R. 1994. *The Frankfurt School: Its History, Theories and Political Significance*. Cambridge: Polity.

Wittgenstein, L. 1958. *Philosophical Investigations*, G. E. M. Anscombe (trans.). Oxford: Blackwell.

Zinkin, M. 1998. "Habermas on Intelligibility", *Southern Journal of Philosophy* 36(3), 453–72.

Index

287